史 Essays on the Sources
for Chinese History

Dedicated to

Charles Patrick FitzGerald

by the

Department of Far Eastern History

Australian National University

Essays on the
Sources for
Chinese History

Editors:

Donald D. Leslie
Colin Mackerras
Wang Gungwu

UNIVERSITY OF SOUTH CAROLINA PRESS
Columbia, South Carolina

Published 1973 in the Commonwealth of Australia by the Australian National University Press, Canberra, A.C.T.

Published 1975 in the United States of America by the University of South Carolina Press, Columbia, S.C.

Library of Congress Cataloging in Publication Data

Main entry under title:

Essays on the sources for Chinese history.

  "Dedicated to Charles Patrick Fitzgerald by the Dept. of Far Eastern History, Australian National University, Canberra."
  Includes bibliographies.
  1. China—History—Sources—Addresses, essays, lectures. 2. FitzGerald, Charles Patrick, 1902–
I. FitzGerald, Charles Patrick, 1902–
II. Leslie, Donald, 1922–   ed. III. Mackerras, Colin, ed. IV. Wang Gungwu, ed.
V. Australian National University, Canberra. Dept. of Far Eastern History. VI. Title.
DS734.7.E83 1975   951   74–10508
ISBN 0–87249–329–6

Preface

This book is dedicated to Emeritus Professor C.P. FitzGerald who was the Head of the Department of Far Eastern History, Research School of Pacific Studies of the Australian National University from 1954 until his retirement in 1968. When it was first thought of, Dr Lo Hui-min and Dr Donald Leslie suggested that instead of the usual *Festschrift* a unified work be attempted. This idea was adopted by the Acting Head of the Department at the time, Dr Wang Ling, and other members of the Department, and the present work is the result.

The first stage of organising and inviting contributions was undertaken by Dr Leslie. After he left the Department in 1970, Dr Mackerras and myself took over the final stages of editing. All three editors received valuable support from other members of the Department, Dr Igor de Rachewiltz, Dr Stephen FitzGerald, Dr Noel Barnard, and Dr Andrew Fraser. Help and advice was also obtained from Professor Jan de Jong, Dr Ken Gardiner, and Dr Rafe de Crespigny. All the contributors have been connected with Professor FitzGerald in one way or another over the past twenty years or more, either as students, colleagues, or friends. On behalf of my fellow editors, I would like to thank all of them, and in particular those from overseas, for their kind and generous help.

The volume is designed to revolve around a particular theme, but we do not claim that it is in any sense comprehensive. Some topics have also been treated in existing reference works and are only briefly considered here; others are not as well known and have been included in the hope that they will stimulate further interest. In general, however, the papers show how a particular kind of source can help towards an understanding of Chinese history in general (especially those dealing with traditional China); or where to look for sources on a particular aspect of the history of China. It has not been possible to be rigid about the approach of different authors or to standardise the length of the chapters. The differences mainly reflect the range and variety of the sources considered, as well as the origins and backgrounds of Professor FitzGerald's many admirers around the world: China, Japan, Europe, America, Southeast Asia and, not least, those of us in Australia.

Each chapter is accompanied by a bibliography, except the last one where the nature of the subject makes it unnecessary. These lists are not exhaustive but are intended merely as guides. Bibliographic details of books cited are mentioned in the footnotes only when the work in question is not included in the bibliography of the relevant chapter.

Standard systems of romanisation have been followed throughout: e.g. the Wade-Giles for Chinese, the Library of Congress for Russian. In general we have not thought it necessary to translate the titles of books and articles in Chinese and Japanese. All characters can be found in the comprehensive index at the end. Only when the context makes it absolutely essential have characters been written in the main body of the book.

It gives me great pleasure to thank Dr Leslie and Dr Mackerras for the tremendous amount of work they have done to make this volume possible. I should also like to take this opportunity to express our gratitude to Professor O.H.K. Spate, the Director of the Research School of Pacific Studies, who has shown interest in the work and arranged a subsidy which made its publication possible.

Department of Far Eastern History   Wang Gungwu
Australian National University
Canberra, 1971

Contents

Contents

Contributors

Professor DERK BODDE is now Professor of Chinese at the University of Pennsylvania. His main publications include *China's First Unifier* (Leiden, 1938), *Tolstoy and China* (Princeton, N.J., 1950), *Peking Diary* (New York, 1950), and *Law in Imperial China* (Cambridge, Mass., 1967, with Clarence Morris).

Dr BILL BRUGGER is a Lecturer in politics at the Flinders University of South Australia. He lived in Peking from 1964 to 1966 and has written several articles on contemporary China.

Professor JEAN CHESNEAUX is Professor of Contemporary Far Eastern History at the Sorbonne, and was a Visiting Fellow in the Department of Far Eastern History, Australian National University, in 1970. He is the author of numerous works on China and Vietnam, especially *Le mouvement ouvrier chinois de 1919 à 1927* (Paris, 1962) and *Contribution à l'histoire de la nation vietnamienne* (Paris, 1955).

Dr RAFE de CRESPIGNY was Secretary-General of the 28th International Congress of Orientalists held in Canberra in 1971 and is at present a Senior Lecturer in the Department of Chinese, Australian National University. He has written several books and articles on second and third century and present-day China, especially *The Last of the Han* (Canberra, 1969).

Dr JOSEF FASS is a Research Fellow in the Oriental Institute of the Czechoslovak Academy of Sciences. He is the author of several articles on Sun Yat-sen and the 1911 Revolution and of a book called *Sunjatsen* (Prague, 1966).

Dr STEPHEN FITZGERALD is Australian Ambassador to the People's Republic of China. He has written several articles on Chinese policy towards the Overseas Chinese and is the author of *China and the Overseas Chinese; A Study of Peking's Changing Policy 1949-1970* (Cambridge, 1972).

Professor JOSEPH FLETCHER is Professor of Chinese and Central Asian History at Harvard University. He has contributed four chapters for the *Cambridge History of China* and the *Cambridge History of Inner Asia* and is the author of a forthcoming monograph entitled *The* Erdeni-yin erike *as a Source for the Reconciliation of the Khalkha Mongols, 1684-1688.*

Professor FUJIEDA AKIRA is at present Professor at the Jimbun kagaku kenkyūjo. He has worked extensively on the Tun-huang manuscripts and on local government during the Period of Division. His main publications include *Kyokyōkan*, 2 vols. (Kyoto, 1955-8), co-editor with Murata Jirō, and *Moji no bunkashi* (Tokyo, 1971), awarded the 1972 Prix Stanislas Julien.

Dr K.H.J. GARDINER is at present a Senior Lecturer in Chinese culture and history in the Department of Asian Civilizations at the Australian National University, Canberra. His publications include *The Early History of Korea* (Canberra, 1969) and numerous articles on the history and culture of Korea and north-eastern China.

Professor CHÜN-TU HSÜEH is Professor of Government and Politics at the University of Maryland. He is the author of numerous articles and books on twentieth century China. These include *Huang Hsing and the Chinese Revolution* (Stanford, 1961; 1968), *The Chinese Communist Movement, An Annotated Bibliography* (Stanford, 1960-2), and *Revolutionary Leaders of Modern China* (New York, 1971). A French edition of *Revolutionary Leaders of Modern China* is scheduled to be published by Editions Calmann-Levy of Paris in 1973.

C. KIRILOFF is Principal Lecturer in Languages at the College of Advanced Education, Canberra. He has written several articles on early Sino-Russion relations, and on Chinese language.

Dr JOSEF KOLMAŠ is Head of the Department of Eastern Asia, Oriental Institute of the Czechoslovak Academy of Sciences, Prague. He has written several books and articles on Tibetan history. These include *Tibet and Imperial China* (Canberra, 1967) and *A Genealogy of the Kings of Derge* (Prague, 1968).

Dr D.D. LESLIE has been a Fellow in the Department of Far Eastern History, Australian National University and Associate Professor in the Department of Philosophy, University of Tel Aviv. Since 1972 he has been Senior Lecturer in History at the Canberra College of Advanced Education. He has compiled a bibliography on local gazetteers (with J. Davidson) and written widely on the Jews of K'ai-feng, especially in *The Survival of the Chinese Jews; the Jewish Community of Kaifeng* (Leiden, 1972).

Professor LI CHI is Professor of Archaeology at Taiwan University and Director of the Institute of History and Philology, Academia Sinica,

Taiwan. He is one of the founders of modern Chinese archaeology and has written numerous books and articles on the subject. His books include *The Formation of the Chinese People* (Cambridge, Mass., 1928).

Professor LIU TS'UN-YAN is a Fellow of the Australian Academy of the Humanities and Head of the Department of Chinese, Australian National University. He has written numerous books and articles on Taoism and Chinese literature, especially *Chinese Popular Fiction in Two London Libraries* (Hong Kong, 1967) and *Buddhist and Taoist Influences on Chinese Novels* (Wiesbaden, 1962).

Dr LO HUI-MIN is a Senior Fellow in the Department of Far Eastern History at the Australian National University. He is working on the Morrison Papers and his publications include *Foreign Office Confidential Papers Relating to China* (Paris, 1969).

Dr MICHAEL LOEWE has been a Lecturer in Classical Chinese at the University of Cambridge since 1963. He has written widely on Han China, especially in *Records of Han Administration*, 2 vols. (Cambridge, 1967) and *Everyday Life in Early Imperial China* (London, 1968).

Dr COLIN MACKERRAS is a Research Fellow in the Department of Far Eastern History, Australian National University. His main publications are *The Uighur Empire According to the T'ang Dynastic Histories* (Canberra, 1972) and *The Rise of the Peking Opera (1770-1870)* (Oxford, 1972).

Professor MATSUMARU MICHIO was a Research Officer in the Department of Far Eastern History, Australian National University, from 1966 to 1970, when he became Associate Professor at the Research Institute of Oriental Culture, University of Tokyo. He has written numerous monographs and articles on oracle bones, including *Kōkotsu monji* (Tokyo, 1959).

Dr PNG POH-SENG is a Senior Lecturer in the Department of History, University of Singapore. He has written several articles on twentieth century China and Japan and on the Chinese in Southeast Asia.

Professor TIMOTEUS POKORA is Head of the Department of Eastern Asia, Oriental Institute of the Czechoslovak Academy of Sciences, Prague. He has written a book on Ch'in shih huang-ti and has done a partial translation of Wang Ch'ung's *Lun-heng* and a complete one of Huan T'an's *Hsin-lun*.

Dr PAUL A. RULE has made a detailed study of the Jesuits in Manchu China. He is a Lecturer in the Department of History of the University of Melbourne.

Professor OTTO van der SPRENKEL was Associate Professor in the Department of Asian Civilizations, Australian National University for many years until his retirement at the end of 1971. He has written extensively on Chinese history and contemporary China, especially on the Ming civil service. He is at present working on the monumental 'Selective Annotated Bibliography of Chinese History, Thought and Institutions', which will be published shortly.

Professor WANG GUNGWU is a Fellow of the Australian Academy of the Humanities and Head of the Department of Far Eastern History, Australian National University. His principal publications include *A Short History of the Nanyang Chinese* (Singapore, 1959) and *The Structure of Power in North China during the Five Dynasties* (Kuala Lumpur, 1963).

史 A Personal Tribute to C. P. FitzGerald

WANG LING

Men and women attracted to each other at first sight do not necessarily become lasting lovers and people who make friends easily do not always make life-long friends. Patrick FitzGerald is one of those people who are not easy to talk to at first meeting, but the longer one knows him, the closer one feels to him, and the more convinced one is that he is a selfless person worthy of the trust of friendship.

There is an ancient Chinese story about a man who lived by the sea-shore and loved sea-gulls. At first they flew away when he came near them. Gradually they got used to one another and played together. Whenever he arrived the birds flocked to him in hundreds, some settling on his shoulders, others flapping their wings over his head and playfully pecking his hair. One day his father asked him to capture some sea-gulls and bring them home, but when he went back to the beach they realised he had betrayed their friendship and flew away and would not return. We sea-gulls, however, treat Patrick as one of us and know that our friendship with him will never end through any betrayal of his.

Perhaps spontaneity is the best word to describe not only his personal relationships but also his role as head of department. Somehow, little by little, he built up or, more suitably, let grow a department of considerable size, embracing a diversity of subjects from tortoise-shell records of the second millennium B.C. to Morrison's railway tickets of our own century, and a variety of nationalities from Hyperboreans beyond the north wind to Australians under the sky of the Southern Cross. Everyone co-operates and everything proceeds spontaneously under the influence of his example rather than by discipline and authority. In the words of Lao-tzu, a Chinese philosopher of the sixth century B.C.

> The best ruler, people do not know he exists,
> The next best, they love and praise,
> The next, they fear,
> The next, they revile,
> But of the best ruler, when his task is accomplished and his work done,
> the people all remark 'We have done it ourselves'.

史 Charles Patrick FitzGerald
A Selected Bibliography

LO HUI-MIN

From the publication of his first book in 1933, Professor C. P. FitzGerald (b. 1902) has been a most prolific writer. The output to date amounts to some 380 items. The following list represents some of the better known and more accessible of his works. It is divided into two categories: books, and pamphlets, articles, and chapters. Items are arranged chronologically within each category. Translations into foreign languages and editions revised under a new title are listed separately. Dates within parentheses signify a reprint or translation.

Books

1933   *Son of Heaven, A Biography of Li Shih-min, Founder of the T'ang Dynasty*, Cambridge, 1933; reprinted (pirated) Taipei, 1970. 232 pp.

1935   *China, A Short Cultural History*, London, 1935; reprinted 1942; 2nd ed., 1950; reprinted 1954 and 1958; 3rd ed., 1961; first paperback ed., London, 1965; also 2nd ed., New York, 1954; 3rd ed., New York, 1961; reprinted 1965, 1967. 624 pp.

(1935) *Li Che-min, Unificateur de la Chine, 600 à 649*, translated and with preface by G. Lepage, Paris, 1935; a translation of *Son of Heaven*. 247 pp.

1941   *The Tower of Five Glories, A Study of the Min Chia of Ta Li, Yunnan*, London, 1941. 280 pp.

1948   *Introducing China*, co-author George Yeh, London, 1948. 116 pp.

1952   *Flood Tide in China*, London, 1952. 286 pp.

1952   *Revolution in China*, London, 1952. 290 pp.

1955   *The Empress Wu*, Melbourne, 1955; reprinted 1958 (with additional epilogue). 252; 263 pp.

(1961) *Chung-kuo wen-hua chien-shih*, translated by Jen-huan, 2 vols., Taipei, 1961; a translation of *China, A Short Cultural History*. 562 pp.

1961   *Finding out about Imperial China*, Exploring the East Series, London, 1961. 143 pp.

3

(1964)   *The Birth of Communist China*, revised paperback ed. of *Revolution in China*, Harmondsworth, 1964; reprinted New York, 1967. 288 pp.

1964   *The Chinese View of their Place in the World*, London, 1964; reprinted twice 1965; reprinted with postscript 1966 and 1967; paperback with addendum, Oxford, 1969 and 1970. 82 pp.

1965   *Barbarian Beds, The Origin of the Chair in China*, Canberra, 1965. 85 pp.

1965   *The Third China, The Chinese Communities in South-East Asia*, Melbourne, 1965; reprinted 1966. 109 pp.

1966   *A Concise History of East Asia*, Melbourne and New York, 1966. 310; 306 pp.

(1968)   *Des Manchous à Mao Tse-Tong, Les révolutions chinoises du XXᵉ siècle, Les grandes vagues révolutionnaires*, translated by Henri-Louis Méhu, Paris, 1968; translation of *The Birth of Communist China* and *Flood Tide in China*. 315 pp.

1969   *The Horizon History of China*, New York, 1969. 415 pp.

(1969)   *Storia dell' Estremo Oriente dagli antichi imperia alle nazioni d'oggi*, translated by Ettore Capriolo, Milan, 1969; translation of *A Concise History of East Asia*. 453 pp.

1971   *Communism Takes China*, Library of XX Century Series, London, 1971. 127 pp.

1972   *China: a World So Changed*, co-author Myra Roper, Melbourne, 1972. 243 pp.

1972   *The Southern Expansion of The Chinese People 'Southern Fields and Southern Ocean'*, Canberra, 1972. 230; xxi pp.

Pamphlets, Articles, and Chapters

1932   'A New Estimate of the Chinese Population under the T'ang Dynasty', *The China Journal* XVI, 1 (January 1932), pp. 5-14, 62-72.

1936   'Further Historical Evidence for the Growth of the Chinese Population', *The Sociological Review* XXVIII, 3 (July 1936), pp. 267-73.

1950   'The Chinese Revolution: New Democracy and Imperial Traditions', *Chatham House Review, World Today* VI, 6 (June 1950), pp. 237-48.

1950   *Korea: the Background*, Current Affairs No. 116 (30 September 1950). 18 pp.

1951   'The Chinese Revolution and the West', *Pacific Affairs* XXIV, 1 (March 1951), pp. 3-17.

1951   *The Revolutionary Tradition in China*, George Ernest Morrison Lecture in Ethnology No. 13 [delivered in Canberra on 19 March 1951], Sydney, 1951. 22 pp.

1951   'The Chinese Novel as a Subversive Force', *Meanjin* X, 3 (Spring 1951), pp. 259-66.

1951   'Peace or War with China', *Pacific Affairs* XXIV, 4 (December 1951), pp. 339-51.

1952   'The Revolutionary Tradition in China', *Historical Studies, Australia and New Zealand* V, 18 (May 1952), pp. 93-105.

1953   'China's Foreign Policy', *Current Affairs Bulletin* XI, 12 (March 1953), pp. 179-92 (unsigned).

1954   'China, Korea and Indo-China', in Gordon Greenwood, ed., *Australian Policies Towards Asia* (Melbourne, 1954), pp. 200-42.

1955   *The Character of Far Eastern History, An Inaugural Lecture Delivered at Canberra on 9 May 1955*, Canberra, 1955. 23 pp.

1955   'East Asia after Bandung', *Far Eastern Survey* XXIV, 8 (August 1955), pp. 113-19.

1955   'South-East Asia after Bandung', *The Australian Quarterly* XXVII, 3 (September 1955), pp. 9-17.

1956   *Report to the Council of the Australian National University on the Visit to China of the Australian Cultural Delegation*, co-author P.H. Partridge, Canberra, 1956. 34 pp.

1956   'Continuity in Chinese History', *Historical Studies, Australia and New Zealand* VII, 26 (May 1956), pp. 136-48.

1956   'The Renaissance Movement in China', *Meanjin* IX, 2 (Winter 1956), pp. 98-108.

1956   'Persuasion and Propaganda in China', *The Australian Quarterly* XXVIII, 3 (September 1956), pp. 32-9.

1956   'China in 1956', *Australian Journal of Politics and History* II, 1 (November 1956), pp. 19-36.

1956   'On Revisiting China', *Current Affairs Bulletin* XIX, 2 (November 1956), pp. 19-27.

1956   'The Restoration of the Chinese Empire under the Sui and T'ang Dynasties', *Australian Outlook* X, 4 (December 1956), pp. 13-25.

1957   'Australia and Asia', in Gordon Greenwood and Norman Harper, eds., *Australia in World Affairs 1950-1955* (Melbourne, 1957), pp. 200-42.

1960   'Asian Studies in Australia', *Vestes* III, 3 (September 1960), pp. 57-60.

1962   'China', in F.H. Hinsley, ed., *The New Cambridge Modern History*, Vol. XI, *Material Progress and World-Wide Problems 1870-1898* (Cambridge, 1962), pp. 437-63.

1962   'Oriental Studies in the National University', *Hemisphere* VI, 2 (February 1962), pp. 13-15.

1962   'Overseas Chinese in South East Asia', *Australian Journal of Politics and History* VIII, 1 (May 1962), pp. 65-77.

1963   'The Chinese View of Foreign Relations', *The World Today* XIX, 1 (January 1963), pp. 9-17.

1963   'The Boxer Rebellion', *New Left Review* 19 (March-April 1963), pp. 79-83.

1963   'A Fresh Look at the Chinese Revolution', *Pacific Affairs* XXXVI, 1 (Spring 1963), pp. 47-53.

1963   'Chinese Expansion in Central Asia', *Hemisphere* VII, 4 (April 1963), pp. 17-19; *The Royal Central Asian Journal* I, 3-4 (July-October 1963), pp. 290-4.

1963   'The Dispute between China and the Soviet Union', *The Australian Quarterly* XXXV, 4 (December 1963), pp. 7-16.

1964   'The Sino-Soviet Balance Sheet in the Underdeveloped Areas, The Changing Cold War', *The Annals of the American Academy of Political and Social Science* 351 (January 1964), pp. 40-9.

1964   'The Historical and Philosophical Background of Communist China', *The Political Quarterly* XXXV, 3 (July-September 1964), pp. 247-59.

1964   'The Historical Background of Chinese Military Traditions', *The Journal of the Oriental Society of Australia* II, 2 (June 1964), pp. 29-48.

1965   'The Chinese Middle Ages in Communist Historiography', *The China Quarterly* 23 (July-September 1965), pp. 106-21.

1966   'Chinese Foreign Policy', in Ruth Adams, ed., *Contemporary China* (New York, 1966), pp. 7-25.

1966   'The Origin of the Chinese Revolution', *Current History* V, 301 (September 1966), pp. 129-33.

1966   'Religions in China', 'Pan-Asianism', and 'The Australian Attitude Towards Asia', in Guy Wint, ed., *Asia, a Handbook* (Harmondsworth, 1966), pp. 389-94, 409-17, and 576-86.

1967   'Historical Perspective', in *The China Giant: Perspective on Communist China* (Glenview, Ill., 1967), pp. 40-6.

1967   'Present Trends in China', *Journal of the Royal Central Asian Society* LIV, 1 (February 1967), pp. 24-32.

1967   'Religion and China's Cultural Revolution', *Pacific Affairs* XI, 1-2 (Spring and Summer 1967), pp. 124-9.

1967   'Tension on the Sino-Soviet Border', *Foreign Affairs* XLV, 4 (July 1967), pp. 683-93.

1968   'Introduction' to *Quotations from President Liu Shao-ch'i* (Melbourne, 1968), pp. 17-22.

1968   'Reflections on the Cultural Revolution in China', *Pacific Affairs* XLI, 1 (Spring 1968), pp. 51-9.

1968   'Pacific Signposts: 4, China and Australia; a Continuing Relationship', *Meanjin* XXVII, 4 (1968), pp. 389-98.

1968   *Europe and China: An Historical Comparison* [lecture delivered to the Australian Humanities Research Council at its 13th Annual General Meeting at Canberra, 5 November 1968], Sydney, 1969. 14 pp.

1968   *China in the 21st Century*, Sir John Morris Memorial Lecture, Hobart, 1968. 14 pp.

1969   'Introduction' to *Quotations from Chou En-lai* (Melbourne, 1969), pp. i-vii.

1969   'China: A Threat in Southeast Asia?', in A. Taylor, ed., *Peace, Power and Politics in Asia* (Wellington, 1969), pp. 64-77.

1969-70 'The 1911 Revolution', in A.J.P. Taylor, ed., *History of the 20th Century* (London, 1969-70), pp. 300-5.

1969-70 'The Long March', in A.J.P. Taylor, ed., *History of the 20th Century*, pp. 1,351-9.

1969-70 'China; Communist Victory', in A.J.P. Taylor, ed., *History of the 20th Century*, pp. 2,082-91.

1969-70 'China; the Authoritarian Tradition', in A.J.P. Taylor, ed., *History of the 20th Century*, pp. 227-30.

1970   'Developments or Changes in China's Foreign Policy', *World Review* IX, 2 (July 1970), pp. 3-13.

1970   'Chinese Manuscripts', *Manuscripts* XXII, 2 (Spring 1970), pp. 79-87.

1970   'China', in Roger Scott, ed., *The Politics of New States* (London, 1970), pp. 68-76.

1970   'China and Asia', in Max Teichmann, ed., *Power and Policies* (Melbourne, 1970), pp. 53-64.

1970   'Sino-Soviet Relations since 1950', in Max Teichmann, ed., *Power and Policies*, pp. 65-76.

1971   *Changing Directions of Chinese Foreign Policy*, Roy Milne Lecture, Hobart, Melbourne, 1971, 26 pp.

1971   'Die chinesisch-sowjetischen Beziehungen und die Bedeutung des Grenzenkonflikts', *Europa Archiv* 26 (1971), pp. 43-54.

1971   'Chinese Reactions Towards Tendencies to Condominium', in Carsten Holbraad, ed., *Super Powers and World Order* (Canberra, 1971), pp. 74-89.

1971   'Symposium on Chinese Foreign Policy. Contribution', *Problems of Communism* XX (1971), pp. 21-4.

1971   'Historical Background and the Chinese Revolution', in J.A. Johnston and Maslyn Williams, eds., *The New China* (Sydney, Melbourne, Wellington, Auckland, 1971), pp. 11-19.

1971   'Art and Culture', in J.A. Johnston and Maslyn Williams, eds., *The New China*, pp. 34-41.

1971   'Asia Awakened', in Alan Bullock, ed., *The Twentieth Century* (London, 1971), pp. 161-70.

1971   'What has Happened to China?'. *Current Affairs Bulletin* XLVIII, 3 (August 1971), pp. 83-95.

史　1: Archaeological Studies in China

LI CHI

The archaeological awakening of modern China is usually dated from the year 1920 when J.G. Andersson sent his collector Liu Chang-shan to the northern part of Honan where Liu discovered the first prehistoric village at Yang-shao in the Mien-ch'ih district south of the Yellow River. The site was subsequently studied and excavated by Andersson under the auspices of the Geological Survey in Peking; the results of this digging were first communicated in a scheduled meeting of the Geological Society of China and later published in the Society's bulletin of 1923.

For a number of years following this first discovery, the Geological Survey in Peking played an important role in the advancement of prehistoric researches in north China, especially in the promotion of field work. Most of the collections gathered by the field archaeologists were sent to the Survey's headquarters in Peking and scientific reports were published mainly in three periodicals: *Bulletin of the Geological Society of China* (1922-); *Memoir of the Geological Survey* (1920-);[1] *Palaeontologia Sinica* series D and new series D (1923-). The last of these is especially important because it includes not only the reports concerning neolithic culture, especially of the painted pottery group, but also almost all the important studies on Sinanthropus from the earliest writings of Davidson Black to the last monograph of Franz Weidenreich.[2]

Archaeology as a branch of academic research won its first government support in 1928 when the Institute of History and Philology of Academia Sinica organised an archaeological section as one of the three research units in its official programs. The Archaeological Section of the Institute started its field work in the autumn of 1928 at An-yang. From the very beginning, the excavation became world famous because of its important discoveries. Among these, the oracle bone inscriptions, which proved to be

[1] Some of the most important contributions to this periodical are: J.G. Andersson, 'Preliminary Report on Archaeological Research in Kansu' (with a note on the physical characteristics of the prehistoric Kansu race by Davidson Black), series A, no. 5 (June 1925); C.C. Yang, 'Fossil Man and Summary of Cenozoic Geology in China', series B, no. 5 (1933); and W.C. P'ei, 'Choukoutien Excavation', series B, no. 7 (1934).

[2] For a list of the main contributions in this periodical see the bibliography at the end of this chapter.

the earliest known scripts in the whole of eastern Asia and the Pacific region, attracted particular attention from classical scholars and aroused international interest among historians. This excavation was continued for nine successive years during which fifteen expeditions were organised. In the course of the excavation, the field archaeologists located, in addition to the capital of the Shang dynasty of the Yin period, a cemetery site where the royal tombs were found. Although, as is true with the remains of other ancient cultures, both the buried capital and the tombs had been plundered more than once after they were abandoned, the field workers nevertheless recovered abundant structural remains and many hidden treasures. The field reports and the detailed studies of the artifacts discovered have been reported in a number of journals published by the Institute. The most important of these publications are: *Report of the Anyang Excavation*, 1 (1929), 2 (1930), 3 (1931), 4 (1933); *Bulletin of the Institute of History and Philology* (1928-   ); *Archaeologia Sinica*;[3] *T'ien-yeh k'ao-ku pao-kao* (no. 1); *Chung-kuo k'ao-ku hsüeh-pao* (nos. 2-4); Monographs of the Institute. No. 4 of *Chung-kuo k'ao-ku hsüeh-pao*, compiled and edited by the Institute, was printed under the Communist government without changing the contents, although the title page was mutilated.

The collections of the An-yang excavation include the following important items: inscribed turtle shells and shoulder blades; stone and jade artifacts; bronzes consisting of ceremonial vessels, weapons and tools, and chariot fittings; ceramics; animal bones; human skeletons; architectural remains. All these materials suffered a certain amount of damage and loss during World War II. On the whole, however, the most important part of this collection, through the combined efforts of government organisations and the devotion of many workers, has been saved and is well preserved; it is now available for scientific studies in the Institute at Nan-kang, Taipei, where a visitor still finds in the archaeological building a number of white-haired workers who participated in the early digging. Their studies have been continued all these years and are published by the Institute from time to time in monographs as well as in shorter articles in the various bulletins of the Institute of History and Philology.

The Communist régime was established in mainland China in 1949. It lost no time in continuing archaeological excavations under the direction of its Institute of Archaeology of the Academia Sinica. Although this was reorganised by the Communists on the basis of a different ideology, the name of the institution, originally created by the government of the Republic

[3] No. 1 of this periodical is a paper entitled *Ch'eng-tzu-yai* by Li Chi and others (1934), which has been translated into English as a book by Kenneth Starr (New Haven, 1956). No. 2 deals with Hsiao-t'un and contains contributions by Shih Chang-ju (on the site, its discovery and excavations, and architectural remains); Tung Tso-pin, Ch'ü Wan-li, and Chang Ping-chüan (on inscriptions); and Li Chi (on artifacts such as pottery). No. 3 deals with Hou-chia chuang and contains papers by Kao Ch'ü-hsün.

of China, was retained. The archaeological activities were also carried out by various other organisations. Field workers trained in the former decades were mainly responsible for the amazing achievements. They worked on the old sites and discovered many new ones. During the industrial and economic reconstruction of the régime, thousands of ancient sites and burials were uncovered.

In continuing the important work of the early period, excavations were first resumed in 1949 at Chou-k'ou tien. In 1956 and 1957, remains of Gigantopithecus were found in Kwangsi Chuang Autonomous Region, dating as early as the Lower Pleistocene Period. Paleolithic findings as old as or even older than Peking Man were excavated in the district of Jui-ch'eng of Shansi and also in the Lan-t'ien district of Shensi. The latter yielded a nearly complete pithecanthropus lower jaw and some molar teeth. Other paleolithic sites of a later age have been turned up in Szechwan, Hupeh, Kwangsi, Kwangtung, Yunnan, and Inner Mongolia.

Since 1949 thousands of neolithic sites have been discovered scattered all over mainland China. Studies have centred on the social characteristics and cultural contents as well as on the sequence of these cultures. The physical traits and the biological environment of their inhabitants have also been studied. At An-yang, work was resumed at the royal cemetery in 1950 and excavations added greatly to the amount of new materials. Many other Yin-Shang sites were found not only in Honan, but also in Hopeh, Shantung, Anhwei, Shansi, and Shensi. Investigations and diggings have also been undertaken to trace a number of the ancient capitals of China from the Western Chou to the Liao dynasty; in fact, all over mainland China in this period, historical dwelling sites and burials of every dynasty have been excavated.

To report on these discoveries, important monographs have been compiled by the Institute of Archaeology and published by the Science and Wen-wu Press of Peking. Other archaeological institutes and museums, as well as individual authors, have also produced valuable books.[4] Among the many periodicals which contain field reports, essays, book reviews and archaeological news, the most important are: *Vertebrata Palasiatica Institute of Vertebrate Palaeontology and Palaeoanthropology*, Academia Sinica, Peking, 1957- ; *Acta Palaeontologia Sinica*, The Paleontological Society of China, Peking; *K'ao-ku t'ung-hsün*, bimonthly, Peking, 1955-8 (title changed to *K'ao-ku* after 1958); *K'ao-ku*, monthly, Peking, 1959- ; *K'ao-ku hsüeh-pao*, Peking; *Wen-wu ts'an-k'ao tzu-liao*, monthly, Peking, 1950-9; *Wen-wu*, monthly, Peking, 1959- .

As mentioned, modern Chinese archaeology owes its start to the introduction of Western methodology. Many Western and Japanese scholars

---

[4] Some of the monographs written on the mainland since 1949 are listed in the bibliography.

11

have made contributions in Chinese archaeological field work as well as studies and researches in this period. We have mentioned briefly the work of J.G. Andersson and also made reference to the works of the geologists and palaeontologists connected with the Chinese Geological Survey. The contributions of Pierre Teilhard de Chardin, Davidson Black, and Franz Weidenreich are world famous. Sir Mark Aurel Stein, Professor Paul Pelliot, and a number of other European scholars did much work in Kansu and Sinkiang in the pre-Republican period, followed later by Andersson, who earned his reputation as a prehistorical archaeologist by his field work in Kansu. From 1927 to 1934, Folke Bergman of the Sino-Swedish Expedition located a series of prehistoric sites along the route from Kalgan of Inner Mongolia westward to the region of Lopnor. In the Red Basin and along the Yangtze Valley, stone implements and pottery remains were collected by J.H. Edgar, D.S. Dye, N.C. Nelson, and others. In Manchuria and Mongolia, Japanese scholars found and identified many neolithic and neolithic-like cultures. Chinese bronzes have for many decades been widely studied in the West. The reports of this field work and investigation appear in monographs and many learned journals published in Japan and Europe. They are undoubtedly better known to the English-speaking public than those in Chinese.

Finally, a few words should be said about the archaeological source materials of the Taiwan area. The Department of Archaeology and Anthropology of the National Taiwan University has been engaged for nearly twenty years in the training of archaeologists and in field investigation. At present, archaeology as an academic discipline is gradually winning recognition by the general public. Some of the field work carried out in the last twenty years has been extremely fruitful and of great importance, not only for the prehistoric study of this island, but also for the whole area of the southern Pacific. Most of the results are published in the *Bulletin of the Department of Archaeology and Anthropology* of the National Taiwan University, which has been published semi-annually since May 1953.

BIBLIOGRAPHY

Some of the papers in series D and new series D of *Palaeontologia Sinica* are:
Series D (*Ancient Man in China*)
Vol. 1. *Neolithic Man in China I*
Andersson, J.G., 'The Cave-deposit at Sha Kuo T'un in Fengtien', fasc. 1 (1923).
Arne, T.J., 'Painted Stone Age Pottery from the Province of Honan, China', fasc. 2 (1924).
Black, Davidson, 'Human Skeletal Remains from the Sha Kuo T'un Cave Deposit in Comparison with those from Yang Shao Tsun and with Recent North China Skeletal Material', fasc. 3 (1925).

Vol. 6. *Neolithic Man in China II*
Black, Davidson, 'A Study of Kansu and Honan Aeneolithic Skulls and of Specimens from Later Prehistoric Sites in Comparison with North China and Other Crania, Part 1, On Measurements and Identification', fasc. 1 (1928).

Vol. 7. *Lower Quaternary Man in China*
Black, Davidson, 'On a Lower Molar Hominid Tooth from the Chou Kou Tien Deposit', fasc. 1 (1927).

——, 'On an Adolescent Skull of Sinanthropus Pekinensis in Comparison with Other Hominid Skulls', fasc. 2 (1931).

'Observations on the Form and Proportions of Endocranial Casts of Sinanthropus Pekinensis and the Great Apes: A Comparative Study of Brain Size', fasc. 4 (1936).

'The Mandibles of Sinanthropus Pekinensis, A Comparative Study', fasc. 4 (1936).

New Series D
'The Dentition of Sinanthropus Pekinensis, A Comparative Odontography of the Hominids', no. 1 (1937).

Weidenreich, Franz, 'The Ramification of the Middle Meningeal Artery in Fossil Hominids and its Bearing upon Phylogenetic Problems', no. 3 (1938).

——, 'The Extremity Bones of Sinanthropus Pekinensis', no. 5 (1941).

P'ei Wen-chung, 'The Upper Cave Industry of Choukoutien', no. 9 (1939).

Weidenreich, Franz, 'The Skull of Sinanthropus Pekinensis, A Comparative Study on a Primitive Hominid Skull', no. 10 (Chungking, 1943).

Monographs
Important monographs published on the mainland since 1949 include the following. Publications listed by title are collective works.

Ch'ang-sha fa-chüeh pao-kao, Peking, 1957.

Cheng-chou Erh-li kang, Peking, 1959.

Chia Lan-p'o, *Chung-kuo yüan-jen*, 5th ed., Shanghai, 1954.

——, *Ho-t'ao jen*, revised ed., Shanghai, 1955.

——, *K'o-ho, Shan-hsi hsi-nan pu chiu shih-ch'i shih-tai ch'u-ch'i wen-hua i-chih*, Peking, 1962.

——, *Pei-ching jen ti ku-chü*, Peking, 1958.

——, *Shan-ting tung-jen*, 2nd ed., Shanghai, 1951.

Chiang Pao-keng and others, *I-nan ku hua-hsiang shih-mu fa-chüeh pao-kao*, Peking, 1956.

Chiang-su Hsü-chou Han hua-hsiang shih, Peking, 1959.

Feng Han-chi, *Ch'ien-Shu Wang Chien mu fa-chüeh pao-kao*, Peking, 1964.

Hsi-an Pan-p'o, Peking, 1963.

Hsia Nai, *Collected Archaeological Papers*, Peking, 1961.

Hu Hou-hsüan, *Yin-hsü fa-chüeh*, Shanghai, 1955.

Huang Wen-pi, *T'a-li-mu-p'en-ti k'ao-ku chi*, Peking, 1958.

——, *T'u-lu-fan k'ao-ku chi*, Peking, 1958.

Hui-hsien fa-chüeh pao-kao, Peking, 1956.

Kuang-chou Hsi-ts'un ku-yao i-chih, Peking, 1958.

Kuo Pao-chün, *Shan-piao chen yü Liu-li ko*, Peking, 1959.

Lo-yang Chung-chou lu (Hsi-kung tuan), Peking, 1959.

Lo-yang shao-kou Han-mu, Peking, 1959.

Miao-ti kou yü San-li ch'iao, Peking, 1959.

Nan T'ang erh-ling fa-chüeh pao-kao, Peking, 1957.

P'ei Wen-chung, *Tzu-yang jen*, Peking, 1957.

——, *Yen-pei wen-wu k'an-ch'a t'uan pao-kao*, Peking, 1951.

San-men hsia ts'ao-yün i-chi, Peking, 1959.

Shan-hsi T'ung-ch'uan Yao-chou yao, Peking, 1965.

Shang-ts'un ling Kuo-kuo mu-ti, Peking, 1959.

Shou-hsien Ts'ai-hou mu ch'u-t'u i-wu, Peking, 1956.

Su Pai, *Pai-sha Sung-mu*, Peking, 1957.

T'ang Ch'ang-an Ta-ming kung, Peking, 1959.

Tseng Chao-chü and others, *Nan-ching fu-chin k'ao-ku pao-kao*, Nanking, 1952.

Wang-tu erh-hao Han-mu, Peking, 1959.

Wu Wen-liang, *Ch'üan-chou tsung-chiao shih-k'e*, Peking, 1957.

Yin Huan-chang, *Hua-tung hsin shih-ch'i shih-tai i-chih*, Shanghai, 1955.

Yün-nan Chin-ning Shih-chai shan ku-mu ch'ün fa-chüeh pao-kao, Peking, 1959.

史 11: Oracle Bones

MATSUMARU MICHIO[1]

In 1899 there was a flood in the Yüan River which flows near the small village of Hsiao-t'un located in the north-west of An-yang County of Honan Province. The flood caused some layers of earth to crumble, revealing tortoise carapaces and animal bones with inscriptions in ancient Chinese characters. This was the discovery of the so-called 'oracle bone inscriptions' which have attracted the scholarly attention of the world because of the epoch-making role they have played in the reconstruction of China's ancient history.

At the outset, there were a number of difficulties in deciphering the inscriptions and in assessing their nature as historical documents. However, vigorous research carried out by many scholars and large-scale scientific excavations during the 1920s and 1930s have thrown light on many important aspects of the inscriptions. For example, we now know that the oracle bones are the product of the Yin or Shang family, the very existence of which, in spite of references in early Chinese historical documents, had been doubted. This Yin or Shang dynasty existed from about the fourteenth to the eleventh century B.C., and the inscriptions are records of the divinations carried out in the Yin royal palace. They range from the nineteenth king of Yin, P'an-keng, to the last king, Ti-hsin, embracing the reigns of eleven out of the thirty known Yin kings, and covering a period of more than 200 years. The object of the divination, as recorded in the inscriptions, may be described as seeking divine guidance on whether or not the royal court should observe certain sacrifices and rites, or engage in wars, or whether the king should act in one way or another.

There are a number of reasons for the special importance of these inscriptions. First, we now have a primary and contemporary source for the study of Yin China. This is important, since, although various accounts of the Yin are included in the Chinese Classics, we did not possess, before the turn of this century, any historical material of the Yin period itself from which its history could be studied scientifically. Thus, we are now able to draw a clearer line between what is probably half-legend and what may be

[1] I wish to express my sincere thanks to Mr Kenichi Takashima of the University of Arizona and Dr Kenneth Gardiner of the Australian National University for help in the translation of this paper.

15

regarded as historical fact. As to the historicity of the Yin dynasty, the opinions of the so-called *i-ku p'ai* (what might be called the school of sceptics, that is of those who doubt the classical antiquities of China) have been found to be completely groundless. Furthermore, the progress made in the study of the inscriptions, concurrently supported by the archaeological evidence from Hsiao-t'un, has clarified various cultural elements of the Yin dynasty. The most important contribution to the study of the inscriptions is that of those scholars, prominently headed by Wang Kuo-wei, who succeeded in reconstructing the genealogy of the Yin Royal House for almost the entire dynasty. This success became the basis for another success, namely Tung Tso-pin's attempt to divide the oracle bone inscriptions into five periods. Ch'en Meng-chia and others have attempted an even more detailed periodisation than Tung's. Owing to the nature of the inscriptions, i.e. the fact that they are records of divination, we must naturally expect a certain limitation in the historical information they provide. Nevertheless, we have been able to clarify such problems as the social and economic structure of Yin China, the configuration of the sacrifices and rites, the calendar, the kinship structure, and the material culture in general.

Another reason for the importance of the inscriptions springs from the fact that, being the oldest extant Chinese documents, they constitute the oldest body of Chinese script available in large quantity. The study of the Chinese script, owing to its special nature, has been popular among Chinese men of letters and has occupied a cardinal place in Chinese philology since early times. On the one hand, the long tradition of this scholarship has made relatively fast progress in deciphering the inscriptions possible. On the other hand, it has brought about a drastic change in the traditional approach to Chinese philological studies. We may say that the oracle bone inscriptions as historical material have not fully been digested from the standpoint of the study of Chinese script. Such an approach still awaits further effort. In conjunction, studies in ancient Chinese language should be made, i.e. from the standpoint of grammar, but these have not yet produced much in the way of satisfactory results.

The foregoing is intended as a cursory introduction to the purpose of this chapter: to supply briefly some bibliographical information to those who are interested in utilising the inscriptions as research material. Customarily, they have been reproduced by the traditional Chinese method of rubbing and have been published as such, but sometimes they have also been reproduced as photographs and as lithographs. Since the inscriptions are thinly engraved by a sharp chisel-like object, rubbings are the best way to reproduce the originals.

The earliest collection of rubbings was published in 1903 by Liu O, the discoverer of the bones (52).[2] This is a monumental publication in the sense

[2] These numbers refer to those in parentheses at the end of each item in the bibliography.

of being the very first of its kind on oracle bone inscriptions; however, it is not so clearly reproduced because of the lithographic printing. Stimulated by Liu's discovery, Lo Chen-yü has endeavoured to collect the inscriptions and has published them in several volumes (53-8), using a collotype plate, which reproduces them exquisitely, and with their rich content, his collections still have a tremendous value. Lo's ablest disciple, Wang Kuo-wei, helped compile one work (7), containing his own interpretations and with annotations on every inscription in it. This was the first of its kind and became the model for many other works.

In the same year that Wang Kuo-wei's book appeared, another (61) was published in Shanghai by the Rev. James M. Menzies. He was quick to recognise the value of the inscriptions and was the first Westerner actively to engage in collecting them. After this publication, he still continued to collect inscriptions from bones, and his collection finally included about 8,000 pieces, most of them still unpublished and stored in the Royal Ontario Museum in Toronto. After Menzies, a few more collections of the inscriptions were published by Westerners (2, 3, 4, 62). With the exception of the last of these, however, the inscriptions were reproduced by hand-writing (lithograph), and they are therefore not very legible. In addition, it is regrettable to note that these collections contained a not inconsiderable proportion of forgeries. We may hope for publication of rubbings of these pieces. There are many more unpublished inscriptions on bones scattered in various universities and museums in Europe and America, and we would hope that these too will be published.

In contrast to the situation of the inscriptions on bones held in Europe and America, most of those in China and Japan are published. In China, in addition to those inscriptions collected by Lo Chen-yü and Wang Kuo-wei, good collections with detailed interpretations and annotations appeared one after the other, for instance, those of Shang Ch'eng-tso (63, 64), Jung Keng (40), Kuo Mo-jo (45, 46), Sun Hai-po (66, 67), Li Tan-ch'iu (alias Li Ya-nung, 49, 50, 51), Kuo Jo-yü (43, 44), etc. As by far the most outstanding figure in this field, we should single out Hu Hou-hsüan who collected and published inscriptions of oracle bones scattered in China (19-28). We must note here that the various conditions under which the inscriptions were collected are not clear; this is detrimental to their archaeological and palaeographical value. However, with the exception of what is referred to as Liu T'i-chih's (Shan Chai's) old collection of 28,000 pieces we may say that, thanks to Hu Hou-hsüan's effort, not too many inscriptions remain unpublished.

Of the bones that were brought to Japan, the Japanese scholar, Hayashi Taisuke, published one (17). A few other collections were issued by Chinese scholars in Japan in early years of inscription studies (11, 12, 37, 45). In recent years, beginning with Kaizuka Shigeki's monumental annotated work (41), those of Aoki Tsuguya (1), Matsumaru Michio (59), and Itō Michiharu (34, 35) have introduced various inscriptions to Japan. There are still, however, some which remain unpublished.

All the publications mentioned so far are of the so-called 'stolen pieces'. That is, they are the pieces which came into the hands of collectors, private or public, through antique-shop owners who had bought them from farmers who lived around Hsiao-t'un Village. We are certain that these pieces came from Hsiao-t'un, but we do not know the conditions under which they were found—the exact spots where they were discovered, or which pieces were found together. It goes without saying that this decreases the value of such pieces as research materials.

The scientific excavation of the so-called 'wastes of Yin' (Yin-hsü) was begun in 1928 by the Academia Sinica and continued until 1935, totalling altogether fifteen seasons. From the first excavation to the ninth and from the thirteenth to the fifteenth, a great harvest of bones was found, particularly in the thirteenth excavation when more than 18,000 pieces came out of one pit. Only a small number of these were at first briefly reported (74) and their complete publication did not see the light of day until after World War II. Tung Tso-pin then published his monumental works (72, 1 vol. and 73, 3 vols.); in the former he documents the bones collected from the first to the ninth excavations, and in the latter, those collected from the thirteenth to the fifteenth. These volumes are extremely valuable research material, but were unfortunately not published satisfactorily. Firstly, they were published initially without interpretations or annotations. Later, Ch'ü Wan-li published the *Hsiao-t'un, ti-erh pen, Yin-hsü wen-tzu chia-pien k'ao-shih, t'u-pan* (1961), which is an interpretation with annotations of the first work. No book to accompany the second has yet been published, although a very small number of mimeographed copies of tentative interpretations were produced in 1959 by Akatsuka Kiyoshi, Katō Michitada, and Matsumaru Michio. Secondly, since the bones were moved from one place to another, many were broken into smaller pieces and were then published without having been pieced together. Chang Ping-ch'üan remedied this deficiency and has thus far published five volumes (84) by piecing together the inscriptions discussed in Tung Tso-pin's second work. Chang's work is not yet complete. Thirdly, the exact pits in which the bones were found are not accurately recorded. Later Shih Chang-ju in his *Hsiao-t'un, ti-i pen, Yin-hsü chien-chu i-ts'un* (1959), pp. 320-3, clarified the issue for most of them, although not yet for all. In spite of these drawbacks in Tung's works, the bones were excavated under the auspices of the Academia Sinica and the quality of the works is generally good, unparalleled by others. Some of the outstanding bones are the complete large tortoise carapaces. In general, the volumes are the most important source for research materials on the oracle bone inscriptions.

18

I append a list of published catalogues of oracle bone inscriptions, complete, as far as I am aware, although I have not included works that duplicate material.

BIBLIOGRAPHY [3]

Catalogues of Oracle Bone Inscriptions

Aoki Tsuguya, 'Shodō hakubutsukan zō kōkotsu monji', *Kōkotsugaku* VI-X (1958-64), L. 350. (1)

Chalfant, F.H. and Britton, R.S., *The Couling-Chalfant Collection of Inscribed Oracle Bones*, Shanghai, 1935, L. 1680. (2)

——, *The Hopkins Collections of Inscribed Oracle Bones*, New York, 1939, L. 484. (3)

——, *Seven Collections of Inscribed Oracle Bones*, New York, 1938, L. 527. (4)

Ch'en Meng-chia, *Yin-hsü pu-tz'u tsung-shu*, *t'u-pan*, Peking, 1956. R., P., L. 49. (5)

Ch'en Pang-huai, *Chia-ku wen ling-shih*, Tientsin, 1959, R. 160. (6)

Chi Fo-t'o, *Chien-shou t'ang so-ts'ang Yin-hsü wen-tzu*, Shanghai, 1917, R. 655. With interpretations by Wang Kuo-wei. (7)

Chin Hsiang-heng, 'Chia-na-ta To-lun-to ta-hsüeh An-ta-li po-wu kuan so-ts'ang i-p'ien niu chia-ku k'e-tz'u k'ao-shih', *Chung-kuo wen-tzu* XXXVIII (1971), R., P., & L. 1. (8)

——, 'Kuo-li Chung-yang t'u-shu kuan so-ts'ang chia-ku wen-tzu', *Chung-kuo wen-tzu* XIX, XX (1966), L. 648. (9)

Chin Tsu-t'ung, 'I-chai so-ts'ang chia-ku wen-tzu', in *Yin-hsü pu-tz'u chiang-hua*, n.p., 1935, R. 24. (10)

——, *Kuei-pu*, Shanghai, 1948, R. 125. (11)

——, *Yin-ch'i i-chu*, Shanghai, 1939, R. 1459. (12)

Chou Fa-kao and Chang Ping-ch'üan, 'Tung-yin lu ts'ang chia-ku wen-tzu', *Bulletin of the Institute of History and Philology, Academia Sinica* XXXVII (1967), R. 660. (13)

Ch'ü Wan-li, *Hsiao-t'un, ti-erh pen, Yin-hsü wen-tzu chia-pien k'ao-shih, t'u-pan*, Taipei, 1961, R. 10. (14)

Creel, H.G., *The Birth of China*, Plate, London, 1936, P. 7. (15)

Hamada Kōsaku, ed., *Kyōto teikoku daigaku chinretsukan kōko zuroku*, Kyoto, 1922, P. 5. (16)

Hayashi Taisuke, *Kikō jūkotsu monji*, 1921, R. 1032. (17)

Hosaka Saburō, 'Keio Gijuku toshokan zō kōkotsu monji', *Shigaku* XX, 1(1941), R. 18. (18)

Hu Hou-hsüan, 'Amoy University Collection of Oracle Bones', in *Chia-ku hsüeh Shang-shih lun-ts'ung ch'u-chi*, Ch'eng-tu, 1944, L. 29. (19)

——, *Chan-hou Ching-Tsin hsin-huo chia-ku chi*, Shanghai, 1954, R. 5642. (20)

---

[3] R rubbing, P photograph, L lithograph.

Hu Hou-hsüan, *Chan-hou nan-pei so-chien chia-ku lu*, Peking and Shanghai, 1951, L. 3776. (21)

——, *Chan-hou Ning-Hu hsin-huo chia-ku chi*, Peking, 1951, L. 1145. (22)

——, 'Chan-hou Yin-hsü ch'u-t'u ti hsin ta-kuei ch'i-pan', *Shang-hai chung-yang jih-pao wen-wu chou-k'an* XXII-XXXI (1946), R?7, unacquainted—see *Kōkotsugaku* IX (1961), p. 182. (23)

——, *Chia-ku hsü-ts'un*, Shanghai, 1955, R. or L. 3773. (24)

——, 'Chia-ku liu-lu' in *Chia-ku hsüeh Shang-shih lun-ts'ung san-chi*, Ch'eng-tu, 1945, R. & L. 670. (25)

——, 'Shuang-chien-i so-ts'ang chia-ku wen-tzu', in *Chia-ku hsüeh Shang-shih lun-ts'ung ssu-chi*, Ch'eng-tu, 1946, R. & L. 254. (26)

——, 'Sung-chai so-ts'ang chia-ku wen-tzu', in *Chia-ku hsüeh Shang-shih lun-ts'ung ssu-chi*, Ch'eng-tu, 1946, R. & L. 13. (27)

——, 'Yüan-chia tsao-hsiang shih so-ts'ang chia-ku wen-tzu', in *Chia-ku hsüeh Shang-shih lun-ts'ung ssu-chi*, Ch'eng-tu, 1946, R. & L. 270. (28)

Huang Chün, *Yeh-chung p'ien-yü ch'u-chi*, Peiping, 1935, R. 245. (29)

——, *Yeh-chung p'ien-yü erh-chi*, Peiping, 1937, R. 93. (30)

——, *Yeh-chung p'ien-yü san-chi*, Peiping, 1939, R. 214. (31)

'I-chiu-wu-pa—i-chiu-wu-chiu nien Yin-hsü fa-chüeh chien-pao', *K'ao-ku* (1961-2), L. 1. (32)

'I-chiu-wu-wu nien ch'iu Hsiao-t'un Yin-hsü ti fa-chüeh, ch'a-t'u', *K'ao-ku hsüeh-pao* III (1958), R. 1. (33)

Itō Michiharu, 'Ko-Ogawa Chikanosuke-shi zō kōkotsu monji', *Tōhōgakuhō* (Kyoto) XXXVII (1966), R., P., & L. 7. (34)

——, 'Fujii-Yūrinkan shozō kōkotsu monji', *Tōhōgakuhō* (Kyoto) XLII (1971), R. & P. 16. (35)

Jao Tsung-i, 'Hai-wai chia-ku lu-i', *Journal of Oriental Studies* IV, 1-2 (1957-8), R. & P. 101. (36)

——, 'Jih-pen so-chien chia-ku lu (1)', *Journal of Oriental Studies* III, 1 (1956), P. 56. (37)

——, *Ou Mei Ya so-chien chia-ku lu-ts'un*, Singapore, 1970, R. or P. 200. (38)

——, *Pa-li so-chien chia-ku lu*, Hong Kong, 1956, L. 26. (39)

Jung Keng and Ch'ü Jun-min, *Yin-ch'i pu-tz'u*, Peiping, 1933, R. 871. (40)

Kaizuka Shigeki, *Kyōto daigaku Jimbun kagaku kenkyūjo zō kōkotsu monji*, plate volumes, 1959, R. 3246; text volume 1960, R. 10. (41)

Kuan Pai-i, *Yin-hsü wen-tzu ts'un-chen*, Series 1-8, 1931-5, R. 800, Series 5-8, unacquainted. (42)

Kuo Jo-yü, *Yin-ch'i shih-to*, Shanghai, 1951, R. 560. (43)

——, *Yin-ch'i shih-to ti-erh pien*, Shanghai, Peking, 1953, R. 493. (44)

Kuo Mo-jo, 'Jih-pen so-ts'ang chia-ku tse-yu', in *Pu-tz'u t'ung-tsuan*, Appendix II, Tokyo, 1933, P. 87. (45)

——, *Yin-ch'i ts'ui-pien*, Tokyo, 1937, R. 1595. (46)

Kuo Pao-chün, 'I-chiu-wu-ling nien ch'un Yin-hsü fa-chüeh pao-kao, t'u-pan', *K'ao-ku hsüeh-pao* V (1951), R. 1. (47)

Kyōto daigaku bungakubu chinretsukan kōkogaku shiryō 3, Kyoto, 1963, P. 31. (48)

Li Tan-ch'iu, *T'ieh-yün ts'ang-kuei ling-shih*, Shanghai, 1939, R. 93. (49)

——, *Yin-ch'i chih-i*, Peking, 1941, R. 118. (50)

Li Ya-nung, *Yin-ch'i chih-i hsü-pien*, Peking, 1950, R. 343. (51)

Liu O, *T'ieh-yün ts'ang-kuei*, n.p., 1903, R. 1058. (52)

Lo Chen-yü, *T'ieh-yün ts'ang-kuei chih yü*, n.p., 1915, R. 40. (53)

——, *Yin-hsü ku ch'i-wu t'u-lu*, n.p., 1916, P. 4. (54)

——, *Yin-hsü shu-ch'i (ch'ien-pien)*, n.p., 1912, R. 2229. (55)

——, *Yin-hsü shu-ch'i ching-hua*, n.p., 1914, P. 68. (56)

——, *Yin-hsü shu-ch'i hou-pien*, n.p., 1916, R. 1104. (57)

——, *Yin-hsü shu-ch'i hsü-pien*, n.p., 1933, R. 2016. (58)

Matsumaru Michio, 'Nihon sanken kōkotsu monji shūi', *Kōkotsugaku* VII-X (1959-64), L. 446. (59)

Meiji daigaku kōkogaku chinretsukan annai, Tokyo, 1962, P. 9. (60)

Menzies, J.M., *Oracle Records of the Waste of Yin*, Shanghai, 1917, L. 2369. (61)

——, *The Paul D. Bergen Collection of Chinese Oracle Bone Characters*, Shanghai, 1935, R. & L. 72. (62)

Shang Ch'eng-tso, *Fu-shih so-ts'ang chia-ku wen-tzu*, Nanking, 1933, R. 37. (63)

——, *Yin-ch'i i-ts'un*, Nanking, 1933, R. 1000. (64)

She Yü-sen, *T'ieh-yün ts'ang-kuei shih-i*, n.p., 1925, R. 240. (65)

Sun Hai-po, *Ch'eng-chai Yin-hsü wen-tzu*, Peking, 1940, R. 500. (66)

——, *Chia-ku wen-lu*, Honan, 1937, R. 930. (67)

T'ang Lan, *T'ien-jang ko chia-ku wen-ts'un*, Peking, 1939, R. & L. 108. (68)

Tseng I-kung, *Chia-ku chui-ho pien*, plates, n.p., 1950, R. 72. (69)

Tung Tso-pin, 'Ch'ao-pen Wu-i pu-tz'u shih-i pan', *Ta-lu tsa-chih* IX, 2 (1954), L. 11. (70)

——, 'Han-ch'eng ta-hsüeh so-ts'ang ta chia-ku k'e-tz'u k'ao-shih', *Bulletin of the Institute of History and Philology, Academia Sinica* XXVIII (1957), R. & P. 1. (71)

——, *Hsiao-t'un, ti-erh pen, Yin-hsü wen-tzu chia-pien*, Nanking, 1948, R. 3942. (72)

——, *Hsiao-t'un, ti-erh pen, Yin-hsü wen-tzu i-pien*, part 1, n.p., 1948; part 2, n.p., 1949; part 3, Taipei, 1953, R. 9105. (73)

——, *Hsin-huo pu-tz'u hsieh-pen*, Peking, 1928; also published in *An-yang fa-chüeh pao-kao*, Vol. 1, 1929, L. 381. (74)

—— (with Chin Hsiang-heng), 'Pen-hsi so-ts'ang chia-ku wen-tzu (T'ai-wan ta-hsüeh so-ts'ang chia-ku chih erh)', *Bulletin of the Department of Archaeology and Anthropology, National Taiwan University* XVII-XVIII (1961), R. 7. (75)

——, 'T'ai-wan ta-hsüeh so-ts'ang chia-ku wen-tzu', *Bulletin of the Department of Archaeology and Anthropology, National Taiwan University* I (1953), R. 5. (76)

Tung Tso-pin, *Yin-hsü wen-tzu wai-pien,* Taipei, 1956. R. & L. 464. (77)

Umehara Sueji, *Kanan Anyō ihō,* Kyoto, 1940, P. 144. (78)

Wang Hsiang, *Fu-shih Yin-ch'i cheng-wen,* Tientsin, 1925, R. 1125. (79)

White, W.C., *Bone Culture of Ancient China,* plate, Toronto, 1945, L. 27. (80)

Yao Hsiao-sui, 'Chi-lin ta-hsüeh so-ts'ang chia-ku hsüan-shih', *Chi-lin ta-hsüeh she-hui k'o-hsüeh hsüeh-pao* (1963-4), unseen. (81)

Yen I-p'ing, 'Mei-kuo Na-erh-sen i-shu kuan ts'ang chia-ku pu-tz'u k'ao-shih', *Chung-kuo wen-tzu* 22-5, 29 (1966-8), L. 12. (82)

Yü Hsing-wu, *Shuang-chien-i ku ch'i-wu t'u-lu,* Peking, 1940, R. & P. 4. (83)

Catalogues of Pieced Materials

Chang Ping-ch'üan, *Hsiao-t'un, ti-erh pen, Yin-hsü wen-tzu ping-pien,* part 1, i, Taipei, 1957; part 1, ii, Taipei, 1959; part 2, i, Taipei, 1962; part 2, ii, Taipei, 1965; part 3, i, Taipei, 1967, R. 512. (84)

Ch'ü Wan-li, *Hsiao-t'un, ti-erh pen, Yin-hsü wen-tzu chia-pien k'ao-shih,* Taipei, 1961, R. 211. (85)

Kuo Jo-yü, Tseng I-kung, and Li Hsüeh-ch'in, *Yin-hsü wen-tzu chui-ho,* Peking, 1955, R. 482. (86)

Tseng I-kung, *Chia-ku chui-ho pien,* n.p., 1950, L. 396. (87)

——, *Chia-ku chui-ts'un,* n.p., 1939, R. 75. (88)

史 III: Pre-Han Literature

TIMOTEUS POKORA

A great deal has been written on pre-Han literature, taken in a very broad sense—hundreds of studies have been devoted to analyses of spurious works and chapters. But when we approach this vast collection of writings from the point of view of what it has to say about Chinese history, we are by no means on secure ground. The spirit of criticism prevailing in Ch'ing scholarship and the sinological research of the last decades has done away with many legendary and suspect elements in pre-Han sources, but even now we do not have much reliable information. For example, there is no thorough comparative study of the three so-called commentaries to the *Ch'un-ch'iu*: *Tso-chuan*, *Kung-yang chuan*, and *Ku-liang chuan*; and almost nothing of importance has been published on the ideas which shaped Chinese historiography in its origins.

It is true that much attention has been paid to the reliability or spurious-ness of ancient texts, but the results are by no means of a final nature, and, in not a few cases, they conflict with one another. There was surely somewhat too much speculation and too much of an iconoclastic attitude in the 1920s, and it is only thanks to more exact methods (study of grammatical features, etc.) that more reliable results have been achieved. Still missing is a general study summing up not only the factual findings on relevant ancient texts but also the more general conclusions on the ideas which were instrumental in the endeavour to produce history, even if the relevant information did not exist and had to be created *ad maiorem historiae gloriam*. In other words, we have to know why and how the dry historical texts came to be mixed with elements of fiction, and how the legends were historicised.

Historical Writings

There are roughly two kinds of ancient written sources bearing on Chinese history: firstly, those written more or less as records of facts to be accepted by contemporary and later generations, and secondly, sources like the songs of the *Shih-ching* or the ideas of the philosophers, which pursue basically non-historical aims, even though what they mention by the way may be relevant for later historians. It is hardly necessary to stress that the boundary between the two categories of writings may not always be clear.

There are cases where this principle may be applied without hesitation. We might adduce as an example the chronicle *Ch'un-ch'iu*, contrasting it with the *Shih-ching*, but there are also quite a few examples where an interest is manifested in both history and stories, as in the *Tso-chuan* and *Chan-kuo ts'e*. It is typical of the Chinese attitude to history—and to historians—that a non-historical purpose on the part of a compiler of an ancient historical source has generally been supposed to exist. One example suffices: the endless discussions on the hidden meaning of the *Ch'un-ch'iu*.

We find the concept of purpose already there in the most ancient Chinese historians, who were dignitaries of the court, and, as such, had to note down everything of importance for the state: ceremonies, sacrifices, heavenly phenomena, and also facts of secular importance like the conferring of a fief, the arrival of foreign missions, and, of course, the speeches and declarations of the ruler. In fact, the *Shang-shu*, later known as *Shu-ching*, records more the words than the facts or deeds. It is highly purposeful, for some of its utterances may be characterised as propaganda speeches justifying the Chou conquest of the Shang.

Nevertheless, this collection of ordinances and admonitions, the title of which is translated as *The Book of Documents*, is at the same time a collection of documents. Since documents belong to history, another translation has been proposed and applied more recently—*The Book of History*. A great deal has been written on the reliability of the present text of *The Book of History*, with the result that among its fifty-eight chapters only twenty-eight are now accepted as textually reliable. The entire text of the book has been translated by J. Legge in volume 3 of his *Chinese Classics*, while B. Karlgren has translated and reinterpreted the 'unforged' chapters only.[1] A part of the spurious chapters pretending to belong to the recovered text *Ku-wen Shang-shu*, allegedly belonging originally to K'ung An-kuo, was submitted to the throne only in A.D. 317-23. It has been shown, especially by the Ch'ing scholars and P. Pelliot, that those pseudo-K'ung chapters have very little relation (perhaps even none at all) to the original text.

It is also supposed that the original text of the *Shang-shu* was concerned more with the Chou period (when it was written), while the chapters on the most ancient history (or mythology) are of a somewhat later origin. This does not necessarily mean that the text was forged, but that the whole text of *The Book of History* had been put together, enlarged and edited over a long period. This fact also illustrates the well-known principle that on the most ancient history later Chinese sources give more information (not necessarily reliable) than earlier ones.

The Book of History evidently represents an unsystematic collection of documents of variable value, in which no attempt was originally made to

[1] 'The Book of Documents', *Bulletin of the Museum of Far Eastern Antiquities* XXII (1950), pp. 1-81.

attain completeness or provide a chronology. It was 'brought into order' only during the Han (and even later), as one of the classics, and therefore its value for the present-day historian is more in the ideas it proposes than in the facts it records.

Parts of *The Book of History* were known to Confucius, and quotations from it appear several times in the *Lun-yü*. The same may be said of another historical source, the *Ch'un-ch'iu*, the form of which is in fact totally contrary to that of *The Book of History*. The *Ch'un-ch'iu* records, strictly chronologically, the history of the state of Lu for the period between 722 and 481 B.C., i.e. for 242 years. In fact, this kind of history consists of extremely brief statements on matters relating to the court and to the country. There is not a single word of direct speech, no attempt to link affairs together or even to interpret them. The entries are dated by the years of reign of the respective dukes of Lu, and, for shorter periods, by seasons and months.

There are no textual problems concerning the *Ch'un-ch'iu*, but the book nevertheless enjoyed the most intensive attention by generations of Chinese scholars—in indirect proportion to the readability of the dry account. One of the most influential pseudo-explanations of the conspicuous absence of a 'higher' sense of history in the work was the attribution of its authorship to Confucius. This, in its turn, resulted in the generally accepted theory that the text created or adapted by him includes his secret message to following generations: by a careful selection of terms Confucius had expressed his personal evaluation of the recorded facts.

While there is no way to disprove the traditional theory of its connection with (and even authorship by) Confucius, it seems much more reasonable to understand the *Ch'un-ch'iu* as nothing more than a mere chronicle. It has been shown by G.A. Kennedy that omissions and other defects of the text may be explained quite simply by 'natural causes' without recourse to any far-fetched theory.[2] The *Ch'un-ch'iu* is thus important to the historian of China for its chronology and the relatively high reliability of the simple facts it records.

The events of the Spring and Autumn period are recorded in three other books—the *Kung-yang chuan*, the *Ku-liang chuan*, and the *Tso-chuan*—all of which were therefore held for a long time to be commentaries on the *Ch'un-ch'iu*. To avoid any misunderstanding, it is better not to translate the word *chuan* as 'commentary' but as 'tradition'.

It is still necessary, however, to differentiate between the *Kung-yang chuan* and the *Ku-liang chuan* on the one hand, and the *Tso-chuan* on the other. Whereas the first two books coincide exactly with the period covered by the *Ch'un-ch'iu*, the *Tso-chuan* has entries until the year 468 when Duke Ai of Lu died. The laconic style of the *Ch'un-ch'iu* was undoubtedly one of the reasons

---

[2] 'Interpretation of the Ch'un-ch'iu', p. 48.

why whole books were written to explain it. The first was evidently the *Kung-yang chuan*, written entirely in the form of questions and answers, and possibly based on original oral transmission. The *Ku-liang chuan* was inspired by the *Kung-yang chuan*, but it is much more 'orthodox' since it is written as a straightforward exposition of the terminology of the *Ch'un-ch'iu*.

Neither the *Kung-yang* nor the *Ku-liang* tries to offer new historical facts. The former book's ideas were more influential. They fitted the pattern of Han Confucianism, as developed by Tung Chung-shu and others, and in this way played a great though not yet clearly defined role in the development of Chinese historiography, already begun with Ssu-ma Ch'ien.[3]

The last of the three *chuan* is the *Tso-chuan*, which is the largest, most important and most discussed source for the history of the Spring and Autumn period. It is also of key importance for ancient historiography. It includes numerous prophecies of events which 'really' happened (but, it should be noted, some of the *Tso-chuan* prophecies had not materialised) at the predicted time. At the same time, the *Tso-chuan* displays a disrespect towards the alleged authority of some supernatural forces. It was one of the latest books accepted into the Confucian canon (only in the first century A.D.). Accusations were, in fact, brought forward that the *Tso-chuan* was forged by Wang Mang's scholars in order to enhance his ideological claims.

It is probable that the *Tso-chuan* was originally independent of the *Ch'un-ch'iu*, since it contains much information unrelated to the events mentioned in the original chronicle. The present division of the *Tso-chuan* under the years of the *Ch'un-ch'iu* probably derives from a later date, for the *Tso-chuan* often describes events taking place over longer periods and its information differs from that in the *Ch'un-ch'iu*. Although the principal aim of the *Tso-chuan* is to illustrate moral lessons, it is definitely a real and rich historical source, the reports of which may be corroborated not only by other written sources but also by archaeological data.[4]

There has been much speculation on the authorship of the *Tso-chuan* but it is generally accepted that the bulk of the book was written in the fourth century B.C., although some ideas and the final touches were added to the text only at the beginning of the Han. The *Tso-chuan* may be compared with the *Kung-yang chuan* and the *Ku-liang chuan* since it also includes a small commentary to the *Ch'un-ch'iu*. Nevertheless, and this is important, it represents an independent historical source. The *Kung-yang* and *Ku-liang* may have been compiled in their final forms in the first century of Han rule.

A very long period of time is covered by another book in the form of a chronicle, the *Chu-shu chi-nien*, which records events from the Yellow Emperor until 299 B.C. This book was found, together with several other texts (sixteen

[3] V.A. Rubin, 'Kak Syma Tsian' izobrazhal period Ch'un'ts'iu', pp. 76-86.
[4] R. Felber, 'Neue Möglichkeiten und Kriterien für die Bestimmung der Authentizität des Zuo-Zhuan', p. 91.

works in seventy-five chapters) in 281 A.D. in a royal tomb of *c.* 300 B.C. The *Chu-shu chi-nien* is important for ancient history. Its main portion was a chronicle of the state of Wei, but a chronological account of the state of Chin and another one on the whole empire had been added. The undoubtedly genuine text had been in existence for at least nine centuries, after which it was lost. It was some time during the Ming that a *rifacimento* was compiled by some unknown editor (and later translated by J. Legge, see his introduction to volume 3 of *The Chinese Classics*, Hong Kong, 1960). The Ming text is unreliable (although it has been used as a historical source as late as 1956),[5] and may be used only when corroborated by fragments found in pre-Sung encyclopaedias or in other similar books.

The original *Chu-shu chi-nien* was partially reconstructed by Wang Kuo-wei in his *Ku-pen Chu-shu chi-nien chi-chiao* in 1917, and in 1956 was enlarged by Fan Hsiang-yung in *Ku-pen Chu-shu chi-nien chi-chiao ting-pu*. This reconstruction represents but a small part of the original text, and does not present an all-round picture of the respective periods. Relatively useful information may be gathered from the *Chu-shu chi-nien* concerning the activities of the northern 'barbarians', since both the Chin and Wei States were exposed to their raids.

Another book (or books?) bearing on history was found in 281 A.D. in Chi. It is the *I Chou-shu*, also entitled *Chi-chung Chou-shu*. The present text of ten chapters only is sometimes suspected of being unreliable, but no detailed study has yet been made on the credibility or importance of these surviving sections.

The last work on the Spring and Autumn period is *Kuo-yü*, which is very much akin to the *Tso-chuan* and has traditionally been attributed to the same author, Tso Ch'iu-ming. Both books were probably written about the same time. Their authors might have belonged to the same school, but the slight differences in style show that they were not written by the same man. There is not much new in the *Kuo-yü* which cannot be found in the *Tso-chuan*, but some information and insight may be gained by comparing the two books.

If we now turn to sources concerning the centuries following the Spring and Autumn period, known generally as the time of the Warring States, the first book that calls for mention is the *Chan-kuo ts'e*. It is a rather peculiar work, of which no unanimous evaluation has yet emerged among specialists. The *Chan-kuo ts'e* belongs in some respects to the same genre as the *Tso-chuan*, since it records numerous facts of political history as well as short or quite long speeches, and because it also intentionally presents 'unreal' information. The difference between the two books lies in the fact that whereas the

---

[5] A. Dębnicki, *The 'Chu-shu-chi-nien' as a Source to the Social History of Ancient China* (Warsaw, 1956), p. 44. For a critical review see J. Průšek in *Rocznik orientalistyczny* XX, 2 (1958), pp. 131-46.

authors of the *Tso-chuan* were able to predict, thanks to their keen observation, the unknown author (or authors) of the *Chan-kuo ts'e* preferred to
realise his intention by clever persuasion. In other words, the basic approach
of the author of the *Chan-kuo ts'e* is not to record facts for their own sake but
for some actual political aim.

It has never been doubted that the *Chan-kuo ts'e* includes both facts and
ideology. Since the ancient Chinese conception of historiography did not
reject the coexistence of reality and fiction in one work, the *Chan-kuo ts'e* was
accepted under the Han without hesitation as a source of history. Because
such a mixture of *Dichtung und Wahrheit* is unacceptable to a modern historian,
the whole work was relegated to the category of fiction. However, it has
been shown very convincingly by K.V. Vasil'ev that much information
given *en passant* in what might perhaps be called informatory parts of the
Chan-kuo ts'e can be corroborated from other sources. Unconfirmed information of this peculiar kind may thus also be used with due caution.

On the other hand, Vasil'ev is perfectly aware that the text of the *Chan-kuo
ts'e* includes many anachronisms and far-fetched statements, which are
more persuasive and propagandistic in character than factual. These cannot
be accepted as basic material for a political history of the time. In his
opinion, it may not be difficult to distinguish between those two kinds of
materials in the *Chan-kuo ts'e*: the utterings in numerous speeches which
are relevant only for the history of political ideas but only indirectly for
history proper are generally presented in an artistic (or artificial) form, and
their concrete purpose may be discovered.[6] Moreover, besides the information on political history, the *Chan-kuo ts'e* also provides on different occasions
but without any immediate purpose very useful data on social and economic
history.

Though the *Chan-kuo ts'e* and the *Kuo-yü* differ in the periods they cover,
both of them are 'all-China' histories, since they are divided into chapters
according to the then existing important states. From the accounts of the
mutual contacts between the 'powers', information on the small states can
also be gleaned. The data of the *Kuo-yü* bear mostly on political history.

All the above-mentioned works were written as records of history, and
we have to accept them as such, even though the approaches of the authors
may have been different from that of a contemporary historian. Before we
pass to a description of books written for another purpose but bearing also
on history in one way or another it will be necessary to mention a book which
stands somewhere between those not always strictly distinguishable categories.

The *Chou-kuan*, known also as *Chou-li*, gives such a careful description of
the nature and organisation of Chou officialdom that some scholars have
rejected the formerly held view that it was compiled by the Duke of Chou,

[6] *Plany srazhaiushchikhsia tsarstv.*

one of the traditional cultural heroes. This alleged authorship is evidently not supported by facts, though that does not mean that the data of the *Chou-kuan* are totally unreliable. As with the *Tso-chuan*, Wang Mang has been suspected, among others, of having forged the text, but B. Karlgren has shown convincingly that such charges cannot be proved.[7] The problem was studied anew by S. Broman, who used a different method but came to the same conclusion. Basing his work on the comparable data given *en passant* in the so-called free texts (in contradistinction to the systematising 'bound' texts concentrating on particular topics), Broman was able to show that the information in the *Chou-li* depicts a government system which actually prevailed in the middle and late feudal Chou in the various states and had its roots in late Yin and early Chou.[8] A similar conclusion was proposed independently and simultaneously by S. Kuchera, relying mostly upon bibliographical information in different ancient books.[9]

Non-historical Writings

Among the literary sources relevant for ancient history the foremost is the *Shih-ching*, the composition of which took about 500 years from the beginning of the Chou until Confucius. Irrespective of whether the texts of the *Shih-ching* represent real folklore or had been written by court poets, they show many aspects of common life as well as religious and political ideas. Various methods have been used to fix the dates of the respective parts of the *Shih-ching*, and most recently W.A.C.H. Dobson has shown by linguistic analysis that the *Chou-sung* represents the oldest stage of the *Shih-ching* and the *Ta-ya* and *Hsiao-ya* the intermediate stages, while the *Kuo-feng* belong to the latest stratum.[10] From the contemporary historian's point of view this conclusion is relevant for the interpretation of the data given in those parts.

Because of the poetical form, the relevant information is sometimes sketchy and ambiguous. One example suffices to illustrate the difficulties confronting the historian of socio-economic problems: contradictory explanations have been given of the eight characters 雨我公田遂及我私, translated by J. Legge as follows: 'May it rain first on our public fields, and then come to our private ones!'[11] The ostentatious unselfishness of the primitive rural community (or of whom?) can hardly be accepted at face value.

Information on political events and important personalities may often be found in the works of philosophers. For the pre-Han period those texts

[7] 'The Early history of the Chou Li and the Tso Chuan Texts', *Bulletin of the Museum of Far Eastern Antiquities* III (1931), pp. 1-59.
[8] 'Studies on the Chou Li', pp. 1-89.
[9] 'K voprosu o datirovke i dostovernosti "Chzhou-li"', pp. 111-20.
[10] 'The Origin and Development of Prosody in Early Chinese Poetry', pp. 249-50.
[11] *Shih-ching*, vol. 2, book 6, ode 8, verse 3, translated in Legge, *The Chinese Classics*, vol. 6, p. 381.

were not written down by their reputed authors but recorded by their students and adherents. The Confucian *Lun-yü* is, of course, indispensable for any study of the history of Lu and of other states during the sixth/fifth centuries, although, as might be expected, the book does not deal in much detail with affairs unfavourable to Confucius. There are still many other problems concerning the use of the *Lun-yü* as a source for history. First, as for all the classics, the *Lun-yü* had been interpreted for centuries according to Chu Hsi's exegesis which was accepted, among others, by J. Legge. Even the critical approach of the Ch'ing and later scholars towards Sung learning was unable to penetrate further than to the explanations of the text prevailing in the Han. Secondly, the pre-Han text of the *Lun-yü* evidently differed in many places from the present one, but we have no way of reconstructing it. Of the twenty chapters, only seven (3-9) are believed to be reliable and authentic; the first ten chapters are earlier than those that follow. Chapters 16, 17, 18, and 20 especially are very late and cannot be interpreted in the same way as those of the first half of the book.[12]

A similar Confucian source, the *Meng-tzu* in seven double chapters, belongs to the same category as the *Lun-yü*, though the present text of the *Meng-tzu* seems to be more reliable and relatively free from interpolations. On the other hand, Mencius's account is much more systematised and may sometimes reflect more the author's ideas than the real conditions of his time. It is in *Meng-tzu* that we find the later very influential story of the well fields (*ching-t'ien*).[13] The text attributed to Mencius is also important for political history, since he reinterpreted Confucianism to correspond with the growing role of the common people. Mencius was the first Chinese thinker to acknowledge the people's right to oppose and even to overthrow a tyrannical ruler.[14]

Another trend of thought found in pre-Han literature was Taoism, which was more interested in all-human affairs than in fixing the dates of political and similar events. The extreme case is the *Tao-te ching*, which does not give any personal or place name or any date. It may perhaps not even be the work of one author but a collection of Taoist utterances.

The same characteristic of authorship might apply also to *Chuang-tzu*, generally attributed to one Chuang Chou. Everyone agrees that the first seven chapters (*Nei-p'ien*) are genuine, while the others are mostly of a secondary nature, taking up again some themes mentioned already in the *Nei-p'ien* and even in the *Tao-te ching*. The 'outer' (*Wai-p'ien*) and 'miscellaneous' (*Tsa-p'ien*) parts are clearly of a later date and may represent the

---

[12] For a recent study see Leslie, 'Notes on the Analects: Appendixed by a Select Bibliography for the Analects', pp. 1-63.
[13] Book 3, part 1, chap. 3, paragraphs 13, 18, 19, translated in Legge, *The Chinese Classics*, vol. 2, pp. 243-5.
[14] Ibid., 'Prolegomena', p. 44.

ideas of the *Lao-tzu* (i.e. *Tao-te ching*) wing of Taoist thought. In these respects they contrast with the seven 'inner' chapters. *Chuang-tzu* was very seldom quoted during the Han, and in the 1930s this fact, together with some other assumptions, was used as an argument that the text was compiled as late as the third century A.D., not, as tradition has it, in the fourth/third century B.C. This opinion is no longer accepted. On the other hand, it has been proved by A.C. Graham, by means of linguistic and text-critical arguments, that the present text of another Taoist work *Lieh-tzu* is evidently a fake produced by an unknown author not long after 285 A.D.[15] Graham also stated that the seventh chapter of the *Lieh-tzu*, presenting the ideas of Yang Chu, is contradictory to the other chapters, although not necessarily of an earlier date.[16]

A major source is *Mo-tzu*, attributed to Mo Ti (*c.* 479-390 B.C.), and one of the earliest Chan-kuo texts. The present text of seventy-one chapters has a complicated history, and many lacunae have yet to be filled. It is not possible to say much with any certainty about the authorship of different chapters (or groups of chapters), only that the book was written by several groups of Mo Ti's direct and later disciples.

The small book *Sun-tzu ping-fa* had a lasting influence on Chinese and Far Eastern military thought, and is more than a mere handbook of military drill and tactics. According to two scholars,[17] the author of the book was not the reputed Sun Wu of the sixth century B.C., but in all probability Sun Pin of the fourth century B.C., the text having been written between 350 and 320 B.C. As shown by the recent translator, S.B. Griffith, the later date is given by the introduction of cavalry and of trousers into China, not mentioned by *Sun-tzu*.[18] Although the text is corrupt in several places, modern commentators have been able to improve it.

There is a very long text consisting of eighty-six chapters, the *Kuan-tzu*, which has unfortunately been very little used as a source for history, partly because the translation of some chapters has not been satisfactory. Ch'ing scholars long since concluded that *Kuan-tzu* had nothing to do with the personality of the Ch'i statesman Kuan Chung (died 645 B.C.). Thanks to the excellent study and translation of twelve chapters of the *Kuan-tzu* by W.A. Rickett in 1965,[19] we can now state that the compilation of the *Kuan-tzu* was probably begun by the scholars of the Chi-hsia Academy founded *c.* 302 B.C. in Ch'i State, that most of the chapters belong to the third century, while some may be still earlier, and others were added in the second or even first century B.C. Thus the book was mostly written before the Han

[15] 'The Date and Composition of Liehtzyy', p. 197.
[16] 'The Dialogue between Yang Ju and Chintzyy', p. 293.
[17] Průšek, 'Quelques remarques sur l'Art de la Guerre de Sun-tsï', pp. 426-7 and Sinitsyn, 'Ob avtorstve i datirovke traktata "Sun'-tszy"', pp. 98, 103.
[18] *Sun Tzu, The Art of War*, p. 11.
[19] *Kuan-tzu, A Repository of Early Chinese Thought*, pp. 12-13.

period, even though some of its ideas are of a later date. Of course, the present text is corrupt in many places and it may be used only with proper caution until the textual problems are solved and reliable translations published. Rickett has shown convincingly that, contrary to current opinion, the *Kuan-tzu* is an important repository of early Chinese thought, although by its diversity it is also relevant for almost all aspects of social and economic life.

Among the books which influenced history through the ideas of Legalism, put into practice finally in the Ch'in State and dynasty, a foremost place is held by the *Shang-chün shu* which, if its title is to be believed, was written by Wei Yang, the Lord of Shang, known more frequently as Shang Yang. Nevertheless, the general opinion among modern scholars is that the book was written not later than the first half of the third century B.C. by Shang Yang's disciples. There is now a new translation of all the twenty-six chapters by L.S. Perelomov who has also studied the history of the text in a long introduction. His conclusions are that there may have been an older stratum written by Shang Yang himself, characterised, *inter alia*, by ready-made formulae and stable constructions; that chapters 2 and 19 are the oldest strata of the text containing the rough drafts of royal edicts drawn up by Shang Yang; that most of the text is of later origin.[20]

The *Han Fei-tzu* also does not belong entirely to its reputed author Han Fei (died 233 B.C.), the last of the pre-Han philosophers. It is generally accepted that not much has been added to it by Han Fei's various followers or by the Taoists with differing concepts; but there is no agreement as to which chapters belong to which group.

Of great importance from the point of view of the history of philosophy are the thirty-two chapters of *Hsün-tzu*, the author of which, also called Hsün-tzu, contributed to both Confucianism and Legalism. Chapters 17, 21, 22, 23, and 25 belong to the core of Hsün-tzu's ideas, while the last six are believed to have been written by his disciples. There is again no agreement among contemporary scholars on the reliability of many chapters, but there seems to be a consensus that all the text is of pre-Han origin. H.H. Dubs translated twenty-three chapters of the *Hsün-tzu* into English,[21] but there is now a full and reliable German translation by H. Köster.[22]

Lü-shih ch'un-ch'iu is a long book in twenty-six parts completed in 240 B.C. by scholars of various schools invited by the Ch'in chancellor Lü Pu-wei. As an exception to the general rule, there are, surprisingly, no problems of authorship or textual faking, and, since the book has already been fully translated into German by R. Wilhelm,[23] one wonders why its rich and

---

[20] See Perelomov, *Kniga pravitelia oblasti Shang* (*Shang Tsziun'-shu*), pp. 13-42.

[21] *The Works of Hsüntzu* (London, 1928).

[22] *Hsün-tzu ins deutsche übertragen.*

[23] *Frühling und Herbst des Lü Bu We.*

many-sided material is not used more. The book was a mine of information for Han period scholars and thus shaped their point of view to some degree.

The last work is again a book on history proper which was written in the Han period but is of relevance for the last few years of the Ch'in dynasty, as shown by Iu. L. Kroll in 1961.[24] It is Lu Chia's *Ch'u-Han ch'un-ch'iu* of which only fragments are still extant. Despite its title, the book has not been written in annalistic form, and the period treated in it extends from August 209 B.C. until, at least, 180 B.C.

Conclusion

These notes have covered only a part of the pre-Han literature. Two kinds have been given special treatment: those pertaining directly to history and those giving only some occasional information on it in another context. Of course, almost any book pertains to history in some way and it is not easy to find a final criterion to distinguish those which do not.

We did not take into account the undoubtedly ancient text of the fourth century B.C. *Mu t'ien-tzu chuan*[25] or the *Shan-hai ching*, both with fantastic geography, and representing a certain transition from history mixed with fiction (like the *Chan-kuo ts'e*) towards a more literary approach (beginning of the *hsiao-shuo* genre).

Later on, during the Han, there appeared collections of stories and anecdotes relating pre-Han events (like *Hsin-hsü, Shuo-yüan*, etc.), but they evidently belong to a genre which has yet to be studied systematically. Although all such stories had some relation to historical reality, their evaluation as historical sources will present serious difficulties.

BIBLIOGRAPHICAL NOTES

It is both impossible and unnecessary to give a full bibliography concerning pre-Han literature. As a rule, the only works quoted are those which are quite recent and may not easily be found in existing bibliographies. The great majority are mentioned in the above footnotes.

An excellent evaluation of pre-Ch'in sources is that by H.G. Creel, *The Origins of Statecraft in China*, vol. 1 (Chicago, 1970), Appendix A: 'The Sources', pp. 444-86. A general account of sources relating to the five centuries between 722 and 222 B.C. has been given by Cho-yun Hsu, 'Authenticity and Dating of Pre-Ch'in Texts', in his book *Ancient China in Transition, an Analysis of Social Mobility, 722-222 B.C.* (Stanford, 1965), pp. 183-92; his small but valuable study should be consulted by the interested reader. Several books by B. Watson are also useful. They include *Records*

[24] '"Vesna i osen' kniazhestv Chu i Han" Lu Tszia', pp. 133-44.
[25] See Riftin, 'Zhizneopisanie syna nebes Mu kak literaturnyi pamiatnik', pp. 350-7.

of the Grand Historian of China, 2 vols. (New York, 1961), and *Early Chinese Literature* (New York, 1958, 1962). The following are also important:

Broman, S., 'Studies on the Chou Li', *Bulletin of the Museum of Far Eastern Antiquities* XXXIII (1961), pp. 1-89.

Creel, H.G., *What is Taoism? And Other Studies in Chinese Cultural History*, Chicago, 1970.

Crump, J.I., Jr., *Intrigues. Studies of the Chan-kuo Ts'e*, Ann Arbor, 1964.

——, *Chan-Kuo Ts'e*, Oxford, 1970.

Dobson, W.A.C.H., 'The Origin and Development of Prosody in Early Chinese Poetry', *T'oung Pao* LIV (1968), pp. 231-50.

——, 'Authenticating and Dating Archaic Chinese Texts', *T'oung Pao* LIII (1967), pp. 233-42.

Felber, R., 'Neue Möglichkeiten und Kriterien für die Bestimmung der Authentizität des Zuo-Zhuan', *Archiv orientální* XXXIV (1966), pp. 80-91.

Graham, A.C., 'The Date and Composition of Liehtzyy', *Asia Major* VIII (1961), pp. 138-98.

——, 'The Dialogue between Yang Ju and Chyntzyy', *Bulletin of the School of Oriental and African Studies* XXII (1959), pp. 291-9.

Griffith, S.B., *Sun Tzu, The Art of War*, Oxford, 1963.

Kennedy, G.A., 'Interpretation of the Ch'un-ch'iu', *Journal of the American Oriental Society* LXII (1942), pp. 40-8.

Köster, H., *Hsün-tzu ins deutsche übertragen*, Kaldenkirchen, 1967.

Kroll, Iu. L., '"Vesna i osen' kniazhestv Chu i Han" Lu Tszia' ['Lu Chia's "Springs and Autumns of the Dukedoms of Ch'u and Han"'], *Narody Azii i Afriki* IV (1961), pp. 133-44.

Kuchera, S.K., 'K voprosu o datirovke i dostovernosti "Chzhou-li"' ['The Date and Authenticity of the Chou-li'], *Vestnik drevnej istorii* 3 (1961), pp. 111-20.

Leslie, D., 'Notes on the Analects: Appendixed by a Select Bibliography for the Analects', *T'oung Pao* XLIX (1961), pp. 1-63.

Perelomov, L.S., *Kniga pravitelia oblasti Shang (Shang Tsziun'-shu)* [*The Book of Lord Shang*], Pamiatniki pis'mennosti Vostoka XX, Moscow, 1968.

Průšek, J., 'Quelques remarques sur l'Art de la Guerre de Sun-tsï', *Archiv orientální* XIX (1951), pp. 409-27; reprinted in his book *Chinese History and Literature* (Prague, 1970), pp. 49-67 under the new title 'L'Art de la Guerre de Sun-tzŭ'.

——, 'The Authenticity of the Chu-shu-chi-nien', *Chinese History and Literature*, pp. 35-48.

Rickett, W.A., *Kuan-tzu, A Repository of Early Chinese Thought*, Hong Kong, 1965.

Riftin, B.L., 'Zhizneopisanie syna nebes Mu kak literaturnyi pamiatnik'

['The Biography of Mu T'ien-tzu as a literary classic'], *Istoriko-filologi-cheskie issledovaniia*, Moscow, 1967, pp. 350-7.

Rubin, V.A., 'Kak Syma Tsian' izobrazhal period Ch'un'ts'iu' ['How Ssu-ma Ch'ien Depicted the Ch'un-ch'iu period'], *Narody Azii i Afriki* II (1966), pp. 76-86.

Sinitsyn, E.P., 'Ob avtorstve i datirovke traktata "Sun'-tszy"' ['On the Authorship and Date of *Sun-tzu*'], *Narody Azii i Afriki* IV (1964), pp. 97-103.

Vasil'ev, K.V., *Plany srazhaiushchikhsia tsarstv* [*Intrigues of the Warring States*], Moscow, 1968.

Wilhelm, R., *Frühling und Herbst des Lü Bu We*, Jena, 1928; latest edition Düsseldorf, 1971, introduction by W. Bauer, pp. v-xxiii.

史 IV: Wooden Documents

MICHAEL LOEWE

Students of early Chinese history have been accustomed, *faute de mieux*, to rely on compilations such as the standard histories or the collections of writings attributed to leading men of the age as their most primary material. The transmission of these compilations over the centuries has sometimes been subject to considerable hazard, and scholars are frequently faced with the difficulty or impossibility of tracing the authenticity or textual history of a work from the time of writing until publication in printed form during the Sung period. For this and other reasons considerable importance is attached to the meagre volume of the surviving source material that is known to be contemporary with the events concerned; and while the subject matter of such material is of a type that would not necessarily interest historians of areas or periods that are illustrated by more copious documents, the recently discovered records of Chinese administration of the early empires will attract the attention of students, if only because of their unique contribution to our knowledge of the period.

Until perhaps the fourth century A.D., official records were in all probability made normally on wood, a substance that is cheaper, and fortunately more durable, than silk. The surviving material, usually in the form of narrow strips or fragments of such strips, may be classified as follows:[1]

1 For the pre-Han period: strips or fragments have been found at several tombs that are associated both in time and in place with the pre-imperial kingdom of Ch'u. These total 152 pieces found near Ch'ang-sha; 28 + 80 pieces at Hsin-yang (modern Honan province); and 24 + 13 pieces at Wang-shan (modern Hupeh province).[2]

2 For the Han period:

(a) During his expeditions to Central Asia, Sir Aurel Stein found 705 + 166 pieces at various sites near Tun-huang, and the dates that appear on some of these inscriptions fall between 98 B.C. and 137 A.D.; more recently (1944) a further 42 pieces were found at two of the sites.[3]

---

[1] For full details see Loewe, *Records of Han Administration*, vol. 1, pp. 6ff.

[2] See *Wen-wu ts'an-k'ao tzu-liao* 3 (1954); 12 (1954); 9 (1957) and *Wen-wu* 5 (1966).

[3] See the entries in the bibliography under Chavannes, Maspero, and Hsia Nai.

(b) 71 pieces have been found at Lopnor, bearing dates between 49 and 8 B.C.[4]

(c) The Sino-Swedish expedition that was led by Folke Bergman between 1927 and 1934 found a total of approximately 10,000 strips and fragments at 21 sites that were parts of the line of fortifications leading to Chü-yen lake (Edsen-gol). The dates mentioned in the inscriptions fall between 102 B.C. and 98 A.D.[5]

(d) Some 500 pieces were found in tombs of the Eastern Han period at Mo-tsui-tzu, Kansu province, in 1959.[6]

(e) Single pieces of inscribed wood are also known to have been found in Han settlements at Ch'ang-sha and in Korea.[7]

3 For the post-Han period: some 500 pieces that may be dated in the third and fourth centuries A.D. have been found at Tun-huang and at sites in north-west China: some of those sites lay beyond those areas where officials of a Chinese imperial government were established regularly.

It will be seen that the richest cache of finds is that of the ten thousand pieces found at Chü-yen. However, due allowance must be made for differences between the sites where the pieces were found (e.g. a distance of over 200 kilometres separates two of the four major sites of Chü-yen from each other; and the quantitative distribution of pieces at the various sites was very uneven). Most of the pieces found at Tun-huang are kept in the British Museum, and the finds of Chü-yen have recently been sent from Washington to the care of Academia Sinica, Taipei. The remainder of the material is presumably in China, but it is not known whether it is available for inspection. Facsimiles, transcriptions, and annotations have been published for the great majority of the wooden strips and fragments.[8]

The wooden material includes some examples of documents which were written in their entirety on single strips or boards; two rolls each made up of a number of strips with the strings that bound them together still preserved in their original positions; and strips or fragments of strips that formed members of multi-strip documents. Of these categories, the third accounts for the great bulk of the material.

Documents written entirely on single pieces include labels and other descriptive captions used in the transmission of official mail along the lines of official posts; passports, which entitled civilians to travel through the

---

[4] See bibliography under Huang Wen-pi.
[5] Loewe, *Records*.
[6] See *Wu-wei Han-chien*, and Loewe, 'The Wooden and Bamboo Strips Found at Mo-chü-tzu', pp. 13-26.
[7] See Loewe, *Records*, vol. 1, p. 130, note 32.
[8] For bibliographical details, see ibid., pp. 5-8 and notes 16-33 (pp. 128ff). In addition versions of some of the post-Han finds were published by Chavannes in Stein, *Ancient Khotan* (Oxford, 1907), vol. 1, pp. 537ff.

officially controlled check points; labels attached to equipment as a means of identification or as a mark of ownership; military despatches which were circulated to command posts at speed; and a few very small blocks of wood that have been identified as amulets. In addition, there are some specimens of documents of the type that were regularly written on a number of strips and that will be described below.

The two examples of multi-strip rolls whose strings still survive are of invaluable use in reconstructing the form of the majority of the documents which now exist in a fragmentary state only. The shorter of the two, which consists of three strips, is a report written in 42 B.C. concerning facilities for mourning, needed by an officer on the occasion of his father's death;[9] the second example, which has no less than 77 strips, is an inventory of stores and equipment held by a small military unit during the period 93-5 A.D.[10]

Some of the multi-strip documents were compiled on a single occasion as a report for immediate submission to a higher authority; some are in the form of ledgers, in which daily or periodic entries succeed one another in the course of transacting official business (e.g. the issue of supplies on a daily basis from a depot). There are reasons to believe that some documents may have been made out in duplicate; and some were apparently drafted in tabular form. There are also examples of documents which were made out in two or more stages, and carry the handwriting of two or more participants to the transaction (e.g. reports on the issue of clothing, bearing the name of the serviceman, a list of items issued, and a mark of receipt).

A small proportion of the inscriptions were made as matters of private communication between a serviceman and his fellow, and no general statement can be made regarding their contents or nature. This type includes inventories of funerary objects and texts of an astrological nature; in addition, the text of a decree that was reverently placed over a man's coffin may be mentioned in this context.[11]

A further category of fragments derives from literary texts or exercises in calligraphy. The most spectacular and complete example of literary texts is the series of copies of some chapters of the *I-li*, found at Mo-tsui-tzu, and amounting to over 450 very long strips. Other pieces, which carry parts of the *Chi-chiu p'ien* and the *Ts'ang-chieh p'ien*, were presumably written either as part of a teacher's instruction in calligraphy or as a pupil's exercises therein; and a few strips inscribed with the terms of the sexagenary cycle probably derive from the same origin.[12]

The official documents were compiled in the course of administration by

---

[9] Chü-yen document 57.1; see Loewe, *Records*, vol. 1, pp. 11, 83 and plate 3 (nos. 1, 2).
[10] Chü-yen documents 128.2; see Loewe, *Records*, vol. 1, p. 11; p. 130, note 36; vol. 2, p. 360 and plates 46, 47.
[11] That is, the group of ten strips found in grave no. 18, Mo-tsui-tzu (see note 6 above).
[12] See Loewe, *Records*, vol. 2, pp. 418-19.

civil and military officials who served in the Han or later provincial offices of government. The area where the strips were found was not subject to the same degree of official supervision as were the commanderies of the interior; some of the institutions of government were practised only in those remote areas where officials had perforce to take cognisance of and deal with members of a non-Chinese population; and the sites of Tun-huang and Chü-yen derive from the establishment of garrison forces on a permanent basis, which occurred only in the north. For these reasons, although it is likely that the documents of which we possess fragments were compiled in the form and style that was common to all administrative records, their content may represent aspects of the work of officials that were not necessarily of general application.

There are a very few references on the Han strips to senior officials of the central government such as the Chancellor (*ch'eng-hsiang*) or the Imperial Counsellor (*yü-shih ta-fu*).[13] The highest authorities to be mentioned are usually the governor (*t'ai-shou*) and commandant (*tu-wei*) of the commanderies (*chün*) in which the Chinese forces or officials were operating. The great majority of the inscriptions were written by officials serving under the jurisdiction of the commandants, i.e. the officers who were in command of the companies, platoons, or sections of the garrison. The following subjects or types of report have been identified in the surviving archive:

1 The handling and transmission of official mail. Reports include descriptive notes of the contents of correspondence, records of despatch and delivery according to a scheduled service.

2 Lists of officers or servicemen, made out as nominal rolls of units and their officers, as service-records of officials, or, possibly, to note the issue of equipment and stores to individuals.

3 Records of the issue of weapons and equipment to units, clothing to servicemen, and food supplies (grain and salt) to servicemen and their families, together with accounts of the receipt of grain from supplying depots.

4 Financial administration, including notes of the disbursement of official funds to individuals as stipends or for specified purchases; the receipt of funds; outstanding sums due for payment as officials' stipends; and possibly the collection of taxes.

5 Control of travellers; either of civilians passing in and out of the barriers (*kuan*) where their documents and the goods that they carried were subject to inspection, or of officers who were given access through the military lines so as to proceed on official or approved business.

6 The daily activities of servicemen, such as construction, lumber work, fodder collection, and the maintenance of patrols.

[13] For example Chü-yen documents 10.33; 10.30; 10.32, etc., and 254.10. See Loewe, *Records*, vols. 1, p. 66 and 2, p. 229.

7 Registers of equipment held in units and of officially owned cattle.

8 Inspectors' reports on the condition and efficiency of the units of the garrison.

9 Reports of incidents (e.g. the observation of enemy activity, records of observed routine signals received from posts along the line, accounts of skirmishes).

10 Copies of imperial decrees or other documents, issued either as a notification of a current order or as a cumulative list of earlier decrees for purposes of consultation.

11 Calendars.

The standard histories that are concerned with the Han period frequently include passages from the documents on which they were based; but it is by no means always possible to determine whether such passages have been edited by the compiler, presented in summarised form, or mutilated in the course of transmission; and in view of the long textual history that has intervened, the form of the original documents cannot necessarily be reconstructed from the extant editions of those works.[14] In addition to throwing light on the original form of officials' reports, orders distributed by the government, and the routine reports of administration, the wooden material can occasionally be related to events or texts that are cited in the standard histories. Thus, there are a very few fragments of the texts of decrees that are given in the *Han-shu* for the dates 142 and 128 B.C.[15]

In general the standard histories and other sources are concerned with the accomplishments or discussions of the senior members of the administration, while the works of junior officials, together with their place in society and their relations with other members of the population, were not deemed suitable for inclusion in those august compilations. In this respect the wooden archives constitute a source of information that is unique until considerably later periods of Chinese history. Thanks to the strips of Tun-huang and Chü-yen it is possible to reconstruct some of the procedure for framing and despatching official documents and the system of postal delivery; we learn about military organisation as practised in the field, with its complement of officers and its arrangements to assign conscripts to garrison or agricultural duties; and we may infer something of the conditions of living at the frontier posts. Above all, the strips give an insight into the professional quality of the Han armed forces, with their meticulous attention to the maintenance of records, to keeping specified schedules in the daily routine of the service, to ensuring that weapons and equipment were in a satisfactory state and to the discipline of officers and men during active service.

[14] At least two stone inscriptions help with this problem; see ibid., vol. 2, p. 236, note 2.
[15] See ibid., pp. 228-9.

There are two principal difficulties in the interpretation of this material, its fragmentary condition and its assumption of technical knowledge on the part of the reader. While the assembly of pieces as parts of single multi-strip documents may be attempted for a small number of the strips and fragments, the majority must be treated as single elements of documents whose size cannot be estimated. It is necessary to determine the form of the original document and to infer the purpose for which it was compiled. Individual pieces must be compared not only with those that have an identical lay-out and use identical formulae, but also with those whose content is similar but whose mode of expression is different. At the same time it is necessary to set the inscriptions in an institutional context that is not completely described in the other source material and that must be ascertained from the pieces themselves; and there is no other source available for seeking details of the daily working of the service (e.g. the type and distribution of weapons, the criteria used for distributing grain) which were matters of common knowledge to those who wrote and read the official reports that are under scrutiny.

BIBLIOGRAPHY

Chavannes, E., *Les documents chinois découverts par Aurel Stein dans les sables du Turkestan Oriental*, Oxford, 1913.

Chü-yen Han-chien chia-pien, Peking, 1959.

Conrady, A., *Die chinesischen Handschriften—und sonstigen Kleinfunde Sven Hedins in Lou-lan*, Stockholm, 1920.

Hsia Nai, 'Hsin-huo chih Tun-huang Han-chien', *Bulletin of the Institute of History and Philology* XIX (1948), pp. 235-65.

Huang Wen-pi, *Lo-pu-nao-erh k'ao-ku chi*, Peiping, 1948.

Lao Kan, 'Chü-yen Han-chien k'ao-cheng', *Bulletin of the Institute of History and Philology* XXX, 1 (1959), pp. 311-491.

——, *Chü-yen Han-chien t'u-pan chih pu*, Taipei, 1957.

Loewe, Michael, 'Some Notes on Han-time Documents from Tun-huang', *T'oung Pao* L, 1-3 (1963), pp. 150-89.

——, 'Some Military Despatches of the Han Period', *T'oung Pao* LI, 4-5 (1964), pp. 335-54.

——, 'The Wooden and Bamboo Strips Found at Mo-chü-tzu (Kansu)', *Journal of the Royal Asiatic Society* 1-2 (1965), pp. 13-26.

——, *Records of Han Administration*, 2 vols., Cambridge, 1967.

Maspero, H., *Les documents chinois de la troisième expédition de Sir Aurel Stein en Asie Centrale*, London, 1953 (posthumous).

Sommarström, B., *Archaeological Researches in the Edsen-Gol Region Inner Mongolia*, 2 vols., Stockholm, 1956-8.

Wu-wei Han-chien, Peking, 1964.

史　v: Standard Histories, Han to Sui

K. H. J. GARDINER

The phrase 'official' or 'dynastic' histories—more correctly, 'standard' histories (*cheng-shih*)—refers to the *Shih-chi* and twenty-four other works, which in general followed its plan of construction and, perhaps more significant, were all eventually accepted as presenting the orthodox and received account of the successive periods into which Chinese history was divided. Although the works with which we are here concerned had all gained recognition in their present form by the middle of the eleventh century, it should be noted that many of them did not originate as officially commissioned books. Thus Pan Ku (32-92) began his *Han-shu* as a private venture, intending simply to fulfil his father Pan Piao's plans for a continuation of the *Shih-chi*, while Ch'en Shou's *San-kuo chih*, written at the end of the third century, did not receive official recognition until the completion of P'ei Sung-chih's commentary to the work in 429. Even where a history was actually commissioned by a reigning dynasty, it might happen, as with the *Hou-Han shu*, that political disturbances prevented the work's being brought to a satisfactory conclusion, so that by the time Fan Yeh (398-445) came to write what was to be regarded as the standard account of the Later Han period (in the fifth century, some 200 years after the Later Han dynasty had passed away), twenty or more different histories of the dynasty had already appeared,[1] many or most of which must have made use, directly or indirectly, of the original 'official' records of the Later Han compiled by Pan Ku and his successors. Even where a work was actually completed, and received recognition as the standard account of a period, it sometimes lost that status under later régimes. Thus Ts'ui Hung's *Shih-liu kuo ch'un-ch'iu*, apparently accepted as the standard account of the period *c.* 300-439 under the T'o-pa Wei dynasty,[2] lost this status under the reconstituted Sui-T'ang empire, when the various northern dynasties of the fourth century were dismissed as rebel régimes. As a result the book itself disappeared (at least by the Yüan period).

As to the actual category *cheng-shih* or standard histories, this is first found

[1] For a list, see Bielenstein, 'The Restoration of the Han Dynasty', pp. 11-13.
[2] See G. Schreiber, 'The History of the Former Yen Dynasty', *Monumenta Serica* XIV (1949-55), p. 381. Schreiber is citing Ch'üan Tsu-wang.

42

in the bibliographical chapters of the *Sui-shu* and the two *T'ang-shu*. These works, however, classify as standard histories not merely the books which were later grouped together under that heading, but also other books which played an important part in their formation, such as the *Tung-kuan Han-chi* and the *Wei-lüeh*. Indeed, when these bibliographies were written, not all of the works to which the title standard history was later restricted had assumed their modern form, the treatises from Ssu-ma Piao's *Hsü Han-shu* not receiving official recognition as part of the *Hou-Han shu* until 1022.[3] The Southern Sung encyclopaedia *Yü-hai*, written by Wang Ying-lin in the thirteenth century, describes the collation and printing of the standard histories by imperial decree in the first half of the eleventh century, mentioning in this connection only the fifteen works here discussed together with the (*Chiu*) *T'ang-shu*.[4] However, in another section specifically dealing with standard histories,[5] the *Yü-hai* lumps together with these fifteen, works such as the *Tung-kuan Han-chi* and Hua Ch'iao's *Han hou-shu*. The eleventh century printing may perhaps be taken as the first official indication of a special status accorded to the group of books which form the subject of this essay. By that time these fifteen histories, whether they originated as private ventures or as officially commissioned works, and whether they were written by individuals or by boards of historians, had come to be accepted as providing collectively the 'standard' account of pre-T'ang history. From the T'ang dynasty onwards, the writing of histories of this type was systematised and a History Office was instituted, so that those works produced as successors to the first fifteen histories were written under somewhat different conditions and require separate consideration.

On the first of the standard histories, the *Shih-chi* by Ssu-ma Ch'ien, there is no need for further comment here, since the work was written as a 'universal history' and is thus appropriately discussed elsewhere. Its successor, the *Han-shu*, compiled during the second half of the first and the first half of the second century, was the first standard history to limit its scope to a single dynasty (although even here the 'Table of Ancient and Modern Worthies' (*Ku-chin jen-piao*) included by Pan Ku surveys outstanding figures from the most remote periods down to the fall of Ch'in, i.e. ending before the Han dynasty itself begins). Later historiographers argued that, in selecting the rise and fall of a single dynasty as the proper chronological limits to his work, Pan Ku was arbitrarily dividing a continuum, and that his example, followed by most later compilers of standard histories, was in this respect unfortunate. It is certainly true that the limitations imposed by a dynastic framework often involved a historian in distortions—for example, he would tend to see the confused period in which his dynasty came into being exclu-

[3] See Bielenstein, 'The Restoration', p. 17.
[4] *Yü-hai*, Che-chiang shu-chü recut blockprint of 1883, 43.16a-17a.
[5] Ibid. 46.11a-53a.

sively from the point of view of the dynastic founder. However, it is also probable that by concentrating upon a chronologically narrower perspective, Pan Ku and his imitators were able to present a selection of information of greater variety and depth than would otherwise have been feasible.

Pan Ku was also responsible for other important innovations. Whereas Ssu-ma Ch'ien had arranged his work in five sections, Pan Ku omitted the section 'Hereditary Houses' (*Shih-chia*)—the fourth of Ssu-ma Ch'ien's five—in the belief that a hereditary nobility did not require separate treatment in a period of unified empire. On the other hand, in the treatises (Ssu-ma Ch'ien's *shu*, which became known as *chih* under Pan Ku and his successors), Pan Ku introduced important new sections: one on administrative geography (*Ti-li chih*), and one on bibliography (*I-wen chih*), virtually a catalogue of books in the imperial library.

Pan Ku was also commissioned by Emperor Ming (57-75) to write a history of the reign of the founder of the Later Han, and at subsequent periods in the dynasty, other emperors entrusted various scholars with the task of continuing this compilation. The decades of civil war and political disruption which supervened in China at the end of the second and the beginning of the third centuries prevented this work, known as the *Tung-kuan Han-chi*, from being recast as an acceptable standard history, and it was treated as source material by a number of historians who wrote histories of the Later Han during the third and fourth centuries. In fact, the next book to gain recognition as a standard history similar to the *Shih-chi* and the *Han-shu* was Ch'en Shou's *San-kuo chih*, a history of the 'Three Kingdoms Period' from the fall of Han to 265.

Ch'en Shou (233-97), a minor courtier of the kingdom of Shu who later received a similar post at the court of Chin, collected historical records of the states of Wei, Shu, and Wu, after the conquest of the latter by Chin in 280, and wrote his book in sixty-five chapters, thirty dealing with Wei (*c.* 190-265), fifteen with Shu (*c.* 190-264), and twenty with Wu (*c.* 190-280). Unlike the author of any other standard history, Ch'en Shou makes no attempt to arrange his chapters into annals and biographies; although those concerning rulers are written in an annalistic form, they are not termed 'annals', and in essence the book might be said to consist of sixty-five chapters of biographies.[6] Although without treatises or tables, the *San-kuo chih* does contain, in the last chapter of its account of Wei, a 'biography' of the various northern or north-eastern tribes which had dealings with the Wei state. Similar chapters on the surrounding peoples are to be found amongst the

[6] I retain the term 'biography' as perhaps the most familiar translation of *lieh-chuan*. Burton Watson, *Ssu-ma Ch'ien, Grand Historian of China* (New York, 1958), pp. 120-34, in the course of a lengthy discussion of the evolution of the term, suggests the translation 'memoir'. See also D.C. Twitchett, 'Chinese Biographical Writing' in *Historians of China and Japan* (Oxford, 1961), pp. 95-114, where *lieh-chuan* is translated 'biography'.

biographies in the *Shih-chi* and the *Han-shu*. Curiously enough, the *San-kuo chih* has no separate accounts of the tribes bordering on Shu in the west, or Wu in the south. One noteworthy feature of the *San-kuo chih* is that it makes no distinction between rulers who styled themselves emperors and their ancestors (such as Ts'ao Ts'ao) who held political power without assuming any titles during their lifetimes; both receive the same annalistic treatment.

The value of Ch'en Shou's book was enormously enhanced by the commentary appended to it by the scholar P'ei Sung-chih (372-451) in the early fifth century. Searching through a multitude of other sources concerned with the Three Kingdoms period, P'ei Sung-chih quotes a wide variety of parallel or variant versions of stories recorded in the *San-kuo chih* itself; frequently these quotations are from works which have now disappeared and for which his commentary is the only source extant.

At about the time that P'ei Sung-chih was composing his commentary, another scholar, Fan Yeh, set out to write yet one more history of the Later Han period, dividing his work into annals and biographies, and utilising various histories which had been written during the preceding 300 years. His work was eventually accepted as the standard history of Later Han. However, since it was without tables or treatises, the sixth-century commentator, Liu Chao, feeling that the book was incomplete, took eight treatises from a history of the Later Han written in the third century, the *Hsü Han-shu* of Ssu-ma Piao (240-306), and added them to Fan Yeh's *Hou-Han shu*. It was not, however, until 1022 that an edition of the *Hou-Han shu* was published by imperial decree including the chapters which Liu Chao had added from Ssu-ma Piao (the rest of whose history had long since disappeared);[7] from this time onwards, the *Hsü Han-shu* treatises were generally printed together with Fan Yeh's work. Even with this supplement, however, the *Hou-Han shu*, like several of the subsequent standard histories, still lacks a separate tables section.

The Chin dynasty restored unity to a divided China by conquering Wu in 280, but as a result of internal dissensions and barbarian pressure, was forced to take refuge south of the Yangtze early in the fourth century. Its historical records, like those of the Later Han, go back to writings commissioned under the dynasty itself, the history of the immediate ancestors of the first Chin emperor being undertaken by the famous poet and critic, Lu Chi (261-303). But Lu perished in the Chin civil wars, and the official annals, taken up again later in the fourth century by Wang Yin and his father, never reached the stage of an acceptable standard history. Some twenty survey histories of the Chin dynasty are known to have been composed by the sixth century; some, such as the *Chin-shu* of Ts'ang Jung-hsü (415-88) in 110 chapters, using the 'annals and biographies' technique of Ssu-ma

---

[7] See H. Bielenstein, 'The Restoration', p. 18.

Ch'ien, others, such as the *Chin-chi* of P'ei Sung-chih of which only a single phrase remains, written as chronicles. There were also other works concerned with Chin history, such as census records or books dealing with particular series of events; an example being Lu Lin's *Chin pa-wang ku-shih,*[8] which survived into the T'ang dynasty.

Influenced by a number of *literati* who declared that none of the extant works on Chin history was written in a sufficiently elegant or elevated style to rank with the *Han-shu* and the *San-kuo chih*, Emperor T'ai-tsung commissioned a new history of the Chin to be prepared by a board of twenty or more historians under his own presidency.[9] The *Chin-shu* thus produced became the standard history while the earlier works disappeared; it is noteworthy as the first of the Chinese histories which was written by a committee. In its general arrangement, the T'ang *Chin-shu* resembles the pattern established by the *Shih-chi* and the *Han-shu*; there are no tables, however, and the book contains a special section of biographies, termed *Tsai-chi*, thirty chapters describing the lives of the barbarian rulers who governed all or part of north China during the fourth and early fifth centuries. Most of these barbarian states at one time had histories of their own, compiled either by private individuals or by official historians; although some of these histories, such as Fan Heng's *Yen-shu*, were still extant in the eleventh century, when they were consulted by Ssu-ma Kuang in the course of writing the *Tzu-chih t'ung-chien*, they all eventually disappeared, being replaced as a definitive record by the *Tsai-chi* of the *Chin-shu* (which, however, seem mainly to have been written from the point of view of the southern court, which was naturally generally hostile towards the northern régimes). Early in the sixth century, Ts'ui Hung, a courtier of the Wei dynasty, in north China, had used the various histories of the fourth-century barbarian states to compile a work called the *Shih-liu kuo ch'un-ch'iu*, which was officially presented to the throne by his son in 528-9. However, at this time the Northern Wei dynasty was on the point of collapse, and the official status of the work lapsed under succeeding dynasties. At least by the early eleventh century, Ts'ui Hung's work had disappeared, although under the Ming a forgery purporting to be this one-time 'standard history' began to circulate.

It is noteworthy that, in its account of the Chin imperial family, the T'ang *Chin-shu* treats the three immediate ancestors of the first Chin emperor

[8] Lu Lin was apparently a (younger?) contemporary of Lu Chi; he is mentioned in a single line of the *Chin-shu* (Po-na ed.) 44.5b as one of those who accompanied the emperor on the disastrous retreat from Yeh in 304. In addition to this book, *Chin pa-wang ku-shih* in ten chapters, he is also credited with a work in four chapters, *Ssu-wang ch'i-shih*. Both works are listed in the bibliographies of the Sui and two T'ang histories, although with varying numbers of chapters.

[9] Emperor T'ai-tsung would appear to have contributed to the *Chin-shu* at least the 'appraisals' appended to the lives of Ssu-ma I (*Chin-shu* 1), Emperor Wu (*Chin-shu* 3), Lu Chi (*Chin-shu* 54), and the calligrapher, Wang Hsi-chih (*Chin-shu* 80).

as legitimate rulers, giving them the title of emperor and recording their lives amongst the annals. This practice, which resembles the *San-kuo chih*'s treatment of such figures as Ts'ao Ts'ao, already noted, probably goes back to Lu Chi's original account of the Chin ancestors.[10] It was followed in an even more exaggerated form by the sixth-century *Wei-shu*, the dynastic history of the T'o-pa Wei, the barbarian dynasty which united north China under its rule in the fifth century. Writing under the Northern Ch'i, one of the two rival successor states to the T'o-pa Wei, the court official Wei Shou inserted an introductory chapter in which no less than twenty-seven of the ancestors of T'o-pa Kuei, the first member of the family actually to style himself 'emperor', were decorated posthumously with the imperial title and received annalistic treatment,[11] most of these men having lived as nomad chieftains somewhere in the northern steppes.

Wei Shou's history presents little else in the way of innovation, consisting of the by now standard three parts: annals, biographies, and treatises (in that order). However, although the *Wei-shu* resembles other histories written in the period of Northern and Southern dynasties in containing no bibliographical treatise, it does include a special treatise dealing with the state of Buddhism and Taoism under the T'o-pa Wei, a feature which was unfortunately not incorporated into subsequent histories, although several of these, such as the *Chin-shu* and the *Pei-Ch'i shu*, contain the biographies of individual Buddhist monks.[12]

Wei Shou worked with a team of historians in compiling the *Wei-shu*, but it was his influence which dominated and shaped the book. Bitter opposition followed the history's presentation to the throne in 554 from men who felt that their relatives had been slandered in a narrative which continued down to 550. After the reunification of China by the Sui in 589, exception was also taken to Wei Shou's treatment of the southern dynasties which had ruled in opposition to the T'o-pa Wei. Wei Shou had scornfully relegated these southern rulers to the chapters dealing with neighbouring barbarians at the end of the biographies, where they appeared under their personal names with the opprobrious epithet *tao-i*, 'island barbarians'. These and other objections to the *Wei-shu* led to the composition of other histories of the T'o-pa Wei, such as Wei Tan's *Hou Wei-shu*, written under the Sui dynasty; they may also have been partly responsible for the imperfect state

[10] See Chiang Liang-fu, *Lu P'ing-yüan nien-p'u* (Shanghai, 1957), pp. 56-7.

[11] The accounts of the Sixteen States in the *Chin-shu* and in the *Tzu-chih t'ung-chien* make it clear that the posthumous ennobling of ancestors of a ruling family as emperors had also been standard practice under the barbarian régimes which preceded the T'o-pa in northern China.

[12] Although persecuted under the third T'o-pa emperor, Buddhism later assumed such a significant position under this dynasty as virtually to constitute an established religion. For a summary, see K. Ch'en, *Buddhism in China: A Historical Survey* (Princeton, 1964), pp. 145-83 and Bibliography, pp. 518-20.

in which the *Wei-shu* has been transmitted: of its twelve chapters of annals, two, including the final chapter, are missing, as are twenty of the ninety-two biographies and two of the chapters of treatises.[13] On the other hand, those histories which were intended to replace Wei Shou's work have almost entirely disappeared, except insofar as they have been utilised under the Northern Sung to fill in the gaps in the *Wei-shu*.

Other standard histories written during the period of Northern and Southern dynasties were the *Sung-shu* of Shen Yüeh (441-513) and the *Nan-Ch'i shu* of Hsiao Tzu-hsien (489-537), both histories of the southern courts. Shen Yüeh's *Sung-shu* is one of the few early examples of a standard history commissioned by the relevant dynasty's immediate successor. The Southern Ch'i emperor ordered its compilation in 487 and the work was completed and presented to the throne in the following year. It was based upon various incomplete histories of the Sung period undertaken during that dynasty itself. The haste with which it was compiled led to various mistakes and omissions for which the work was subsequently criticised. Similar criticisms were also levelled at the *Nan-Ch'i shu*, originally known simply as the *Ch'i-shu*, since Hsiao Tzu-hsien was himself, like the first emperor of Liang under whom he wrote, a member of the Ch'i ruling house, and could therefore scarcely have been expected to write with impartiality. Both these histories were written in the three part form, and comprise annals, treatises, and biographies.

Standard histories for the remaining Northern and Southern dynasties were compiled during the first decades of T'ang rule: they are the *Liang-shu* by Yao Ch'a (533-606) and his son Yao Ssu-lien (d. 637); the *Ch'en-shu* by Yao Ssu-lien; and, dealing with Northern dynasties, the *Pei-Ch'i shu*, by Li Te-lin (530-90), who had formerly served as a compiler of history under Northern Ch'i, and his son, Li Po-yao (565-648); the *Chou-shu*, by a board of historians headed by Ling-hu Te-fen (583-666). None of these works contains either treatises or tables, and, owing to the objections which had already been raised to the *Wei-shu*, *Sung-shu* and *Nan-Ch'i shu*, the decision was eventually taken to rewrite the history of the period of Northern and Southern dynasties in two survey histories. Both of these were compiled by committee, a practice which, with the establishment of a History Office during the T'ang, came to be standard. In both cases Li Yen-shou headed the board of historians, and the overall scheme of the two histories which emerged presumably represents his ideas. Unfortunately, it can scarcely be said that these works, the *Nan-shih* or *Southern History*, and the *Pei-shih* or *Northern History*, represent much of an advance over the works which they were intended to replace. The slighter of the two, the *Southern History*, covers

---

[13] Echoes of the generally hostile attitude towards Wei Shou are to be found in the *Shih-t'ung*, written by Liu Chih-chi in the eighth century. See P'u Ch'i-lung, *Shih-t'ung t'ung-shih*, Kuo-hsüeh chi-pen ts'ung-shu 399 (Taipei, 1969), 'Wai-pien' 3, pp. 42-3.

the period from the accession of the Liu Sung dynasty in 420 up to the conquest of Ch'en by Sui in 589, while the *Northern History* takes in the period from T'o-pa Kuei's assumption of the imperial title in 386 to the fall of the Sui dynasty in 618. Both works consist principally of summarised and reworded versions of information to be found in the separate histories of the dynasties concerned, with very little added. In neither work are there any treatises, nor has the opportunity been taken to bring out continuities rather than discontinuities in the periods surveyed. Thus in the *Pei-shih*, after five chapters of Wei annals, in which the ancestors of the Ch'i ruling house are treated as usurping ministers, there follow the annals of Ch'i, in which these same men are treated as the legitimate emperors. In this and various other ways, the two works remain recastings of earlier sources rather than works in their own right, and show no such sense of a general scheme of history as pervades a work like the *Shih-chi*.

Standing slightly apart from the other histories compiled at the beginning of T'ang is the *Sui-shu*, compiled by Wei Cheng (580-643), Yen Shih-ku (581-645), K'ung Ying-ta (d. 648), Ling-hu Te-fen, Li Yen-shou, and others. This work was commissioned in 629, and the annals and biographies, fifty-five chapters in all, were ready by 636. In the following years, most of the historians engaged upon the *Sui-shu* became involved with the writing of earlier drafts for the *Nan-shih* and *Pei-shih*, and the ten treatises, in thirty chapters, were not completed until 656. These treatises are of particular interest in that they survey the period of Northern and Southern dynasties, and thus materially supplement the nine previous 'standard' histories. They include lengthy discussions of laws and administrative geography, and a rather imperfect bibliography. The *Sui-shu* is traditionally ranked as the thirteenth standard history (the *Nan-shih* and *Pei-shih* being ranked as fourteenth and fifteenth respectively) and is the last history to be considered here. Like the *Pei-shih*, it carries the history of China down to the establishment of the T'ang dynasty in 618.

In spite of the weakness of some of the later works in this series, the first fifteen standard histories form a body of documentation for the early history of China that is impressive both in quantity and quality, and one to which no other culture can offer a parallel. For the later periods—even to some extent for the T'ang dynasty—they can be supplemented by relatively abundant literary sources—poems, letters and essays, etc.; but for the dynasties before T'ang, where literary remains of this nature are much less plentiful, and such important later sources of information as local histories virtually unknown, the standard histories form an invaluable guide to China's past. The treatises dealing with administrative geography in works such as the *Han-shu*, *Hou-Han shu*, *Chin-shu*, and *Sui-shu* provide some idea of the broad movements of Chinese population, while the bibliographical treatises indicate the works that may have been accessible to the writers of a given period. In the field of religion, there is no summary of the social role of any of the major cults in the Roman Empire which could compare with Wei Shou's chapter on Buddhism and Taoism.

The standard histories have their shortcomings, many of which are probably inseparable from the form in which they are written. Because they are in general dynastic histories, they distort history by forcing it into a dynastic framework. Moreover, since the writer of each subsequent history is generally conscious of most of his predecessors, there is an ever increasing tendency towards historical cliché, towards recasting the lives of the subjects of biographies to fit more and more closely into the standard pattern of filial son, devoted wife, just or unjust official, etc. Nevertheless, with all their faults, the standard histories before T'ang provide an unrivalled source of information; it is hard to imagine the shape which Chinese history would assume were it not for them.

BIBLIOGRAPHICAL NOTES

A useful synopsis of the titles, dates, authors, and commentaries of the standard histories can be found in Yang Lien-sheng, *Topics in Chinese History*, Harvard-Yenching Institute Studies, no. IV (Cambridge, Mass., 1950), pp. 32-8. For the texts of those standard histories written before or during the Sung period, the Po-na edition is generally considered standard—for details see below under the individual histories. Other noteworthy editions are the Erh-shih-wu shih published by K'ai-ming shu-tien (Shanghai, 1935), and the Wu-chou t'ung-wen shu-chü lithographic reprint (Shanghai, 1903) of the Ch'ien-lung 'Palace' edition of 1739, the last-mentioned being the one used by the Harvard-Yenching Index Series.

As for the individual histories, the *Han-shu*, of which the Po-na edition goes back to the 1034-8 printing, can scarcely be studied without the annotated edition produced by the Ch'ing commentator, Wang Hsien-ch'ien, *Han-shu pu-chu* (Ch'ang-sha, 1900 and reprints). An index to both the text and notes in this edition is no. 36 in the Harvard-Yenching Index Series, *Han-shu chi pu-chu tsung-ho yin-te* (Peiping, 1940). The best discussion of the background and composition of the *Han-shu* in English is A.F.P. Hulsewé's 'Notes on the Historiography of the Han Period' in W.G. Beasley and E.G. Pulleyblank, eds., *Historians of China and Japan* (London, 1961), pp. 31-43. Considerable portions of the *Han-shu*—specifically the first twelve chapters, constituting the Imperial Annals, and the three-part biography of Wang Mang (Chapter 99)—have been translated into English by H.H. Dubs as *History of the Former Han Dynasty. A Critical Translation with Annotations*, 3 vols. (Baltimore, vol. 1, 1938; vol. 2, 1944; vol. 3, 1955), which includes a text of the translated passages.

Fan Yeh's *Hou-Han shu*, of which the Po-na edition including Ssu-ma

Piao's treatises goes back to the Sung printing of 1131-62, is most conveniently studied through the annotated *Hou-Han shu chi-chieh* (Ch'ang-sha, 1915) and reprints. Although passing under the name of Wang Hsien-ch'ien, the *Chi-chieh* was largely compiled by disciples of the great Ch'ing commentator, and is rather inferior to his annotated *Han-shu*. The Harvard-Yenching index, *Hou-Han shu chi chu-shih tsung-ho yin-te* (Peiping, 1949) covers both text and notes to the *Hou-Han shu*. A rather more complete index to the *Hou-Han shu* is the Japanese *Go-Kan jo goi shūsei*, published by the Institute for Humanistic Studies, Kyōto University, 3 vols. (Kyōto, 1960-2). Individual chapters of the *Hou-Han shu* have been translated into Western languages, but there is no very extensive translation of this history. The complicated history of its composition, however, has been fully dealt with by H. Bielenstein in 'The Restoration of the Han Dynasty; with Prolegomena on the Historiography of the Hou Han shu', *Bulletin of the Museum of Far Eastern Antiquities XXVI* (1954), pp. 9-81.

For the *San-kuo chih* together with the commentary of P'ei Sung-chih, Lu Pi's *San-kuo chih chi-chieh* (Peking, 1957; Shanghai, 1962), now supersedes all other annotated editions. Unfortunately, the only index to the *San-kuo chih* is the *San-kuo chih chi P'ei-chu tsung-ho yin-te* in the Harvard-Yenching Index Series 33 (Peiping, 1938). The historiography of this work is fully discussed in Rafe de Crespigny, *The Records of the Three Kingdoms*, Occasional Papers 9, Centre of Oriental Studies (Canberra, 1970). A complete bibliography of translations from *San-kuo chih* and subsequent 'standard' histories up to the *Hsin Wu-tai shih* is H.H. Frankel's *Catalogue of Translations from the Chinese Dynastic Histories for the Period 220-960*, Chinese Dynastic Histories Translations Supplement no. 1 (Berkeley and Los Angeles, 1957). There is unfortunately no single catalogue of translations made since the date of Frankel's list.

The *Chin-shu* and subsequent histories lack most of the research aids which facilitate the study of the earlier works in this series. For the *Chin-shu* there is the *Chin-shu chiao-chu* compiled by Liu Ch'eng-kan and Wu Shih-chien in 1927, but compared with the commentaries of Wang Hsien-ch'ien and Lu Pi this is a rather slipshod piece of work, and for the remaining histories up to and including the *Sui-shu* there is not even this. Nor is there any adequate discussion of the historiography of the *Chin-shu* in English, although Yang Lien-sheng's 'Notes on the Economic History of the Chin Dynasty', *Harvard Journal of Asiatic Studies* IX (1946) provides a few indications, and a translation of the relevant treatise from the *Chin-shu*. The fragmentary lost histories of the Later Han and Chin periods are collected in *Huang-shih i-shu k'ao* by Huang Shih (n.p., 1934), and in the Ts'ung-shu chi-ch'eng collection (Shanghai, 1935-7). For the *Wei-shu* there is a translation of the treatise dealing with Buddhism and Taoism: L. Hurvitz, *Wei Shou on Buddhism and Taoism* (Kyōto, 1957). For the *Sui-shu* there are translations by E. Balazs, *Le Traité Economique du 'Souei-chou'*, Études sur la société et l'économie de la Chine médiévale I (Leiden, 1953), and *Le Traité Juridique du 'Souei-chou'*, no. II in the same series (Leiden, 1953).

An invaluable aid to the study of the standard histories is the collection of studies published as *Erh-shih-wu shih pu-pien* by the K'ai-ming shu-tien (Shanghai, 1936-7) and reprinted by the Chung-hua shu-chü in 1957. These include attempts to compose bibliographies for some of the histories that lack them, lists of provincial and central government officials, genealogies, etc. Another useful work is the *Erh-shih-wu shih jen-ming so-yin*, an index of people whose names occur in the standard histories arranged by the four-corner system, originally published by K'ai-ming shu-tien, and republished by Chung-hua shu-chü in 1956.

Finally two of the many modern Chinese works dealing with historiography may be recommended as convenient introductions to the subject: Chang Shun-hui's *Chung-kuo li-shih yao-chi chieh-shao* (Wuhan, 1956) and Chin Yü-fu's *Chung-kuo shih-hsüeh shih* (Shanghai, 1962).

史　VI: Some Comments on the Later Standard Histories

WANG GUNGWU

Nine standard histories cover the period 618-1644, that is, the 1,026 years from the founding of the T'ang to the fall of the Ming dynasty.[1] They are:

Standard Histories	Period Covered	No. of *Chüan*	Period of Compilation
Chiu T'ang-shu	618-906	200	940-5
Hsin T'ang-shu	618-906	225	1032?-1060
Chiu Wu-tai shih	907-59	150	973-4
Hsin Wu-tai shih	907-59	74	(1054?-71?)
Sung-shih	960-1278	496	1343-5
Liao-shih	916-1125	116	1343-4
Chin-shih	1115-1234	135	1343-4
Yüan-shih	1206-1368	210	1369-70
Ming-shih	1368-1644	332	1678-1739

The first four cover the T'ang dynasty and the Five Dynasties, with the *Hsin T'ang-shu* replacing the *Chiu T'ang-shu* and the *Hsin Wu-tai shih* replacing the *Chiu Wu-tai shih* as standard histories during the period from the eleventh to the eighteenth century. There are other overlaps of period. The *Chin-shih* overlaps completely with the *Sung-shih* while the *Liao-shih* overlaps partly with the two *Wu-tai shih* and partly with the *Sung-shih*. Although the various dynasties ruled over different parts of China during the periods of overlap, the fact that there was more than one dynasty claiming legitimacy raised difficulties for official historiography. It was certainly the main reason for the delay of over sixty years in compiling the three histories of the Sung, Liao, and Chin dynasties.

All nine works employ the composite *chi-chuan* (annals-biographies) form used in the fifteen earlier standard histories compiled for the periods before the T'ang. They were, however, compiled from fuller materials

[1] For the general works on Chinese traditional historiography, see the works listed after the essay by K.H.J. Gardiner in this volume. Most of them include information relevant to these later standard histories.

which were collected and edited by bureaucrats in the History Office, an institution established in the early years of the T'ang. Eight of the nine were brought together in their final forms by teams of historians ordered by imperial edict. Only the *Hsin Wu-tai shih* by Ou-yang Hsiu was privately done and even this was mainly a revision of a work compiled in the History Office.

The principles and methods of official historiography have been explained by traditional historians from time to time, and recently in English by Yang Lien-sheng.[2] The key feature is that there were several stages of collecting and sifting. Beginning with *ch'i-chü chu* (diaries of activity and repose) and *shih-cheng chi* (records of current government), these were compiled into *jih-li* (daily records) and eventually, at the end of each reign, into *shih-lu* (veritable records). From time to time, some emperors ordered the preparation of *kuo-shih* (national histories), *hui-yao* or *hui-tien* (collected statutes), and similar collections. Some of these final collections, together with standard histories compiled from the above materials by the succeeding dynasty, were then published. The primary documents and the preliminary compilations remained secret in the imperial archives.

Most of the preliminary works were probably compiled with great care. Certainly the veritable records of the first emperors of the T'ang, Sung, and Ming dynasties were subject to vigorous scrutiny, and many others were supervised by distinguished historian-officials. But the impression remains that most of the History Office compilations were routine and even perfunctory, including some of the final standard histories themselves. Of the eight officially compiled histories, six were done in great haste (five within two years and one in five years). The two exceptions were the revision work of the *Hsin T'ang-shu* and the hotly debated and elaborately constructed *Ming-shih*. It is important to note that both were edited during periods when history-writing was taken seriously by a large number of scholars and officials, the former during the eleventh century and the latter during the seventeenth and eighteenth centuries. It is no mere coincidence that the six compiled in haste were long and repetitious, while the *Hsin T'ang-shu* and the *Ming-shih* were compact and concise and the private work, the *Hsin Wu-tai shih*, even more so.

Nevertheless, whether long or concise, all the standard histories have been regarded as unsatisfactory at different times and for various reasons. Both the *Chiu T'ang-shu* and the *Chiu Wu-tai shih* were found wanting 100 years after compilation, and both were replaced for 600 years by what were thought to have been improved versions. There were also several attempts

[2] Yang Lien-sheng, 'The Organisation of Chinese Official Historiography; Principles and Methods of the Standard Histories from the T'ang through the Ming Dynasty', in W.G. Beasley and E.G. Pulleyblank, eds., *Historians of China and Japan*, pp. 44-59. The present essay should be read as supplementary notes to Professor Yang's authoritative article.

by individual historians to follow Ou-yang Hsiu and produce revised versions of the *Sung-shih* and the *Yüan-shih* (no attempt was made to revise the *Liao-shih* and the *Chin-shih* because Chinese historians during the Ming denied the legitimacy of the Liao and Chin dynasties and subsumed them under the Sung). The most notable were the *Sung-shih hsin-pien* by K'o Wei-ch'i, the *Sung-shih chih* by Wang Shu, and the *Hsin Yüan-shih* by K'o Shao-min.[3] The first two, completed during the Ming, were openly antiforeign and were rejected by the scholars of the Manchu Ch'ing dynasty. The third was revised over a period of thirty years and was completed in 1920. It was adopted by a warlord-controlled régime in Peking as a standard history (the twenty-fifth) in 1921, but this decision has not been widely accepted. Efforts to revise the *Ming-shih* were minor, partly because it was one of the most carefully compiled of the standard histories and partly because dissatisfaction was centred on its treatment of Sino-Manchu relations and it was impolitic to press this point during the Ch'ing.

Traditional criticism of these later standard histories was largely concerned with perfecting each of them so that it could be comprehensive and accurate, and thereby worthy of being a standard history alongside the great work of Ssu-ma Ch'ien and Pan Ku and able to provide a continuous series of invaluable histories for the period 618-1644. In fact, none of the nine could really have been as important as most of the earlier fifteen. Many more varieties of documents and collected writings were preserved from the T'ang dynasty on, and increasingly more from the Sung on, after the development of printing, the growth of educational institutions and the preservation of bigger and better libraries. The later nine could merely serve either as basic introductions to the periods covered or as some of the key reference collections for later historians. The following comments concentrate on the historiographical similarities and differences in these later standard histories which deserve noting.

Firstly, comparing the *Chiu T'ang-shu* and the *Hsin T'ang-shu*, we ask how far the latter was an improvement on the former. The three great eighteenth century historical critics, Wang Ming-sheng, Ch'ien Ta-hsin, and Chao I, have already pointed to the valuable details found in the *Chiu T'ang-shu* but omitted by the editors of the revised version. Their contemporaries agreed with them and the Ch'ing court was persuaded to re-admit the original version as one of the standard histories. This view has been confirmed by recent research on the T'ang,[4] and reflects the recognition that T'ang historiography was at a transitional stage between the Northern and Southern dynasties period, when standard histories were vital documents, and the Sung-Yüan-Ming period when standard histories constituted merely one

---

[3] Chin Yü-fu, *Chung-kuo shih-hsüeh shih* (Chungking, 1944), pp. 132-53.
[4] Most notably the writings of Ts'en Chung-mien, R. des Rotours, E.G. Pulleyblank, and D.C. Twitchett.

of many types of source, so that both T'ang standard histories were seen as necessary.

The *Hsin T'ang-shu* editors claimed to have used fewer words to describe more details of T'ang history. Repetition was carefully avoided. The verbose officialese used in the earlier version was pruned and a fresh and lively style was introduced to make events and institutions easier to understand. In this way, it did become a better introduction to the T'ang, but, because of the tampering with the original wording, was also a less reliable set of documents.

Wang Ming-sheng drew attention to another failure to improve on the *Chiu T'ang-shu*.[5] This was in the historians' 'comments' at the end of each *chuan*, the *lun* and *tsan* which often reveal the historians' awareness of their profession. The *Chiu T'ang-shu* comments are more concrete, and, although facts are repeated in the argument, they are specific to the person or persons discussed. In the *Hsin T'ang-shu*, however, the comments are general, ideological, and sometimes irrelevant. The following examples make this clear.

On Kao-tsu, the first T'ang emperor, the *Chiu T'ang-shu* emphasises how he seized the opportunity to inherit the empire and how his errors endangered his new régime, and ends with praise for his son and successor who saved the empire. The *Hsin T'ang-shu*, on the other hand, contains a longish and platitudinous essay on the mysteries of the Mandate of Heaven as applied to earlier founders of dynasties, and only briefly remarks on Kao-tsu's unexceptional virtues and his son's abilities as a basis for a long-lived and successful empire. The *Chiu T'ang-shu* mentions one of Kao-tsu's major mistakes of judgment concerning the two men P'ei Chi and Liu Wen-ching, how he promoted one and executed the other. This is followed in the later *chuan* on the two men by specific comment on why the historian thought P'ei Chi was wrong and Liu Wen-ching did not deserve his fate. The *Hsin T'ang-shu* does not mention Kao-tsu's errors and, in the short comment on P'ei and Liu, points to general principles why P'ei came off better for a while and Liu came to grief so early.[6]

Similarly, on T'ai-tsung, the second emperor, the *Chiu T'ang-shu* mixes general historical analogies with specific attention to his actual successes with his generals and ministers. Although not all the comparisons are flattering to T'ai-tsung, the overall effect is favourable. The comment in *Hsin T'ang-shu* follows on the earlier one on Kao-tsu by further remarks on the founders of great dynasties and fulsome praise for T'ai-tsung as a most exceptional ruler. The comment ends with some general criticism in a high moral tone and betrays ideological bias in its doubtful reference to T'ai-tsung's support for Buddhism.[7] The later comments on Empress Wu Tse-

---

[5] Wang Ming-sheng, *Shih-ch'i shih shang-ch'üeh*, vol. 3, p. 726.
[6] *Chiu T'ang-shu* 1.10a-b; 57.11a-b; *Hsin T'ang-shu* 1.11a-b; 88.9a-b.
[7] *Chiu T'ang-shu* 3.12a-b; *Hsin T'ang-shu* 2.12a-b.

t'ien are even more significantly different. The *Chiu T'ang-shu* roundly condemns the Empress and gives specific reasons for this, but does end with a few examples of her ability and political skill. The *Hsin T'ang-shu* produces an essay on political morality and historical judgment and tries to confirm the meaningfulness of the concept of retribution even though someone evil like Empress Wu was not punished.[8]

Three other pairs of comments on emperors are worth noting. The *Chiu T'ang-shu* has long and detailed comments on the failures of Hsüan-tsung and the well-meaning second-last emperor, Chao-tsung, and simply quotes the great Han Yü's original comment on Shun-tsung in the veritable records Han Yü compiled for the seven-month reign in 805. The *Hsin T'ang-shu*, however, is surprisingly brief on Hsüan-tsung, remarking on the role of women in national disasters, and no less brief on Chao-tsung, commenting on his misfortune. As for Shun-tsung, there is merely a short reference to Han Yü's comment.[9] By being specific, the *Chiu T'ang-shu* continues throughout to make historical judgments. By adopting a high moral tone, the *Hsin T'ang-shu* editors found it difficult to be as direct and relevant about most of the rulers.

On the other hand, the *Hsin T'ang-shu* is less pretentious than the *Chiu T'ang-shu* in the biographies section and the comments are not as markedly different from those in the *Chiu T'ang-shu*. In the prefaces (*hsü*) to the monographs (*chih*) and the group biographies (for example, eunuchs, rebels, loyal officials, Confucians, etc.), where both sets of editors exercised historical judgments on institutions, actual policy decisions, and human types, the differences between them are again not so remarkable. On the whole, the prefaces begin with general ideological principles and then turn to historical surveys. Moreover, the *Chiu T'ang-shu* is a little more specific in its references to people, while the *Hsin T'ang-shu* is superior in literary style and in its more vivid use of classical allusions and analogies. The excellence of the *Hsin T'ang-shu* prefaces comes out clearly in the sections on rites and music, on the calendar, on the five elements, and on bibliographies, and the preface to the new section on the army is not only well written but also original, the first of its kind. In short, a close look at both the works is necessary. They bring out the differences between the historical thinking of the mid-tenth century and that of a century later, and they also reveal the different insights two separate groups of official historians had about the same events.

A similar comparison can also be made of the *Chiu Wu-tai shih* and the *Hsin Wu-tai shih*. The compilers of the first were younger contemporaries of those of *Chiu T'ang-shu* and still had the same ideas about historiography. They preserved more of the original documents and chronicled details from the surviving veritable records as their predecessors had done. The author

[8] *Chiu T'ang-shu* 6.9a-b; *Hsin T'ang-shu* 4.16a-b.
[9] *Chiu T'ang-shu* 9.15b-16b; 14.4a-b; 20B.18a-19a; *Hsin T'ang-shu* 5.18a; 7.17a; 10.11b.

of the *Hsin Wu-tai shih*, Ou-yang Hsiu, was one of the chief editors of the *Hsin T'ang-shu* and probably the person most responsible for the high moral tone and the re-styling of documents in the *Hsin T'ang-shu*.[10] Therefore, it is not surprising that, although his *Hsin Wu-tai shih* is less than half the length of the *Chiu Wu-tai shih* and his comments are also proportionately fewer, they are never perfunctory. On the contrary, they are consistently superior in literary quality and far more confident in strong moral and historical judgments, as were all the writings of the eleventh century.

The *Chiu Wu-tai shih* is a better record of events and developments in north China, the *Hsin Wu-tai shih* contains more details about the various kingdoms in west, central, and south China and is a more balanced work. Neither, however, does justice to the social, political, and economic changes which were taking place during the period 907-59. This is a weakness in the *chi-chuan* form of the standard histories, and periods of division come off very poorly, as can be seen in the many efforts to present the history of an earlier period of division, that from the third to the sixth centuries. Never before and never again was the *chi-chuan* form strained as much as for the Five Dynasties and Ten Kingdoms period. Both the standard histories are unsatisfactory and, to a greater extent than with any others, much of the two has to be read in conjunction with the relevant chapters of the *Tzu-chih t'ung-chien*.[11] Nevertheless, it is a pity that the *Chiu Wu-tai shih* was replaced as a standard history in the eleventh century (the original edition was then lost and our present edition was reconstructed during the eighteenth century from various encyclopaedias, especially from the *Yung-lo ta-tien*). It has the better collection of documents, although it is a poor introduction to the subject. For the better general picture of the period, the reader must still turn to the *Hsin Wu-tai shih*.

The next four standard histories were compiled during the fourteenth century, almost 300 years after the revision of the T'ang and Wu-tai histories: 747 *chüan* in just over two years 1343-5 and another 210 *chüan* twenty-five years later. Although these are the official dates of compilation, much of the work on the *Liao-shih*, based on the Liao veritable records, had been done by 1148 (twenty-three years after the fall of Liao). This was later revised during the years 1189-1207. Work on the *Chin-shih*, also based mainly on the Chin veritable records, had begun in 1261 (twenty-seven years after the fall of Chin), but was held up while the Mongols were conquering the Southern Sung. In 1279, following the fall of Sung, the Yüan Emperor

[10] There were two main compilers of the *Hsin T'ang-shu*. Ou-yang Hsiu, who was responsible for the basic annals and the monographs, wrote the more ideological comments and prefaces, while Sung Ch'i, who prepared the biographies, was more conventional and closer to the bureaucratic traditions of the History Office.

[11] Wang Gungwu, 'The *Chiu Wu-tai shih* and History-writing during the Five Dynasties', *Asia Major* VI, 1 (1957), pp. 1-22; also *The Structure of Power in North China during the Five Dynasties* (Kuala Lumpur, 1963), pp. 216-20.

Kubilai Khan ordered the compilation of the *Sung-shih* as well. All three histories were then further delayed because of serious disagreements about legitimacy and the three were not finally completed until another sixty-five years later. The *Yüan-shih*, in contrast, was ready two years after the fall of Yüan.

Since the basic work on *Liao-shih* and *Chin-shih* had started much earlier, it can be argued that we are dealing essentially with works of the twelfth (*Liao-shih*), mid-thirteenth (*Chin-shih*), late-thirteenth (*Sung-shih*) and late-fourteenth (*Yüan-shih*) centuries. Certainly the main record of events and the main documents were put together at different times, but as the primary compilations had been done in the History Offices of the four dynasties (Liao, Chin, Sung, and Yüan), it is not surprising that the contents of the four standard histories are of the same kind. There are minor variations in style, selection of materials, presentation, emphasis, and bias towards different groups of non-Chinese. Only the comments (*lun-tsan*) and prefaces (*hsü*) were probably written about the same time, that is, in the fourteenth century. In short, only these were very likely to have reflected the representative views of the period.

I have drawn attention elsewhere to the significant lack of comments in the *Yüan-shih*.[12] The Sung, Liao, and Chin histories have fairly full comments and all four have prefaces to the monographs and group biographies. Some brief comparisons are worth making, and the rest of this essay will make two kinds. The first comparison is between some of the comments on emperors in the *Sung-shih*, *Liao-shih*, and *Chin-shih*. The second comparison brings in our last standard history, the *Ming-shih*, which is a much later work (nearly 400 years later) and much more carefully done. I propose to make some brief comparisons of some of its prefaces with those of the *Sung-shih* and *Yüan-shih*.

First, the Sung, Liao, and Chin 'comments'. On their respective founders (each called T'ai-tsu) Chao K'uang-yin, Apaochi, and Akuta, the comments differ significantly.[13] The *Sung-shih* relates Chao K'uang-yin to the classical sage-emperors and accepts that he was mediocre and wanting. He is then compared with lesser military usurpers and his unexpected success in laying the foundations of a 300-year dynasty comparable to the great Han and T'ang dynasties is briefly described. It is hinted gently that this must have been because Chao had the Mandate of Heaven. The *Liao-shih* comment dwells on Apaochi's ancestors and the different stages the Khitan tribes went through to achieve civilisation, and portrays Apaochi as the conqueror who built upon the inheritance of several generations. As for the *Chin-shih*, the emphasis is on Akuta's fine leadership qualities and his father's ambitions. His eventual success is mainly attributed to his rejecting the Liao system of government and adopting that of the Sung.

[12] Wang Gungwu, 'Early Ming Relations with Southeast Asia: a Background Essay', in John K. Fairbank, ed., *The Chinese World Order* (Cambridge, Mass., 1968), pp. 44–6.
[13] *Sung-shih* 3.14a–b; *Liao-shih* 2.8a–b; *Chin-shih* 2.22b–23a.

The comments on the second emperors (Chao K'uang-i, Yeh-lü Te-kuang, and Wu-ch'i-mai) confirm the above bias.[14] All three are fully praised for their achievements, and only Chao K'uang-i's faults are listed. Yet it is clear who comes from the long line of the sage-rulers. Chao's qualities of 'compassion and frugality' are emphasised, Mencius is quoted to suggest that Chao was a true Son of Heaven, and he is considered a 'ruler of excellence'. Yeh-lü Te-kuang is described as having 'majesty and virtue', but the comparison with the lords of the Warring States clearly denies him legitimacy. As for Wu-ch'i-mai, he was wise and modest, and most properly preserved his elder brother's ruling line.

Other comments on the three ruling houses are also revealing. Let me use as a final example the comments on the last emperors of each line, the three Sung child-emperors (1275-8), Yeh-lü Yen-hsi (1101-25), and Wan-yen Shou-hsü (1224-34).[15] The *Sung-shih* comment has much to say about the Mandate of Heaven and emphasises the operation of 'humaneness', 'rites and righteousness', 'grace and kindness', while noting how these qualities can lead to weakness. It concludes by briefly noting that the transmission of the Mandate to the Mongol Yüan was legitimate. The *Liao-shih* comment avoids the question by giving a historical survey which contrasts the 'majesty and authority' of the founding emperors and the errors and failings of Yeh-lü Yen-hsi himself. *Chin-shih* also passes over the question of the Mandate by referring to the ups and downs of the dynasty's 'strength' and 'majesty', its sole example of 'government by humaneness', and the inevitable decline and fall after 1209. The reference to Yüan's growing power and virtue implies Heavenly Approval, but this falls short of the Mandate. Yüan historians between 1279 and 1345 met with great difficulties over the question of legitimacy, and although the decision to produce all three standard histories suggests that they regarded all three dynasties as legitimate, the comments by the historians concerned clearly showed where their bias lay.

The second set of comparisons concerns the prefaces in the *Sung-shih*, *Yüan-shih*, and *Ming-shih*. It has often been pointed out that, structurally, these three standard histories are almost identical. The first two were proportionately longer than the *Ming-shih*, the *Sung-shih* having the largest number of monograph chapters (nearly one third of the work; only just over one fourth in *Liao-shih* and well under one fourth in *Ming-shih*), and the *Yüan-shih* omitting some monographs and group biographies (notably, the section on bibliographies and the biographies of literary men). But the important difference stems from the fact that the *Sung-shih* and *Yüan-shih* were compiled nearly 400 years before the *Ming-shih* and standards of historiography had changed. This is fairly apparent when reading the three

[14] *Sung-shih* 5.25b-26b; *Liao-shih* 4.16a-b; *Chin-shih* 3.17b.
[15] *Sung-shih* 47.22a-b and 29a; *Liao-shih* 30.7b-8a; *Chin-shih* 18.12a.

histories side by side, but comes out most clearly when the historians self-consciously introduce their views in the prefaces.

The *Sung-shih* and *Yüan-shih* prefaces on geography, for example, summarise the data on the size of the two empires but make no comment, while the *Ming-shih* preface is concise and carefully makes the point about size and strategic locations being inadequate if rulers and ministers are perverse and not virtuous.[16] Similarly the prefaces on rites and music in *Sung-shih* are long historical surveys and those in *Yüan-shih* distinguish between what was Chinese and what was Mongol, but only the *Ming-shih* preface comments on the irrelevance of minute details of rites which are not really used with understanding.[17]

The differences are even more marked in the prefaces on astronomy, five elements, and finance. In their prefaces on astronomy, both the *Sung-shih* and *Yüan-shih* stress the traditional views about heavenly signs warning rulers on unseasonable changes, give long historical accounts about what had been recorded in the past, and summarise the main developments in the Sung and Yüan dynasties respectively. The *Ming-shih* notes that the sky, the stars, and the planets do not change. It remarks that the changes in techniques and equipment and the superior astronomers which each age produces are specially worth recording, and goes on to praise the contributions of Matteo Ricci.[18]

The prefaces on the five elements are also revealing. The *Sung-shih* and *Yüan-shih* prefaces show complete faith in the five elements theory that natural phenomena determine social harmony. They both mention earlier historians and their efforts at recording unnatural events; only the *Yüan-shih* preface throws doubt on the work of these earlier historians. Both prefaces summarise the developments during the respective dynasties and note the abuses and errors. The *Sung-shih* preface notes that the Southern Sung concentrated on evil omens only; it goes on to generalise about the interpretation of unnatural phenomena and warns of the element of human error, not only errors of interpretation, but also moral turpitude as a stimulus for evil and astrologers turning good to evil by their own lack of virtue. The *Yüan-shih* preface is less emphatic; it describes the four conditions any government may find itself in and arranges them in the following order of preference: the best is for there to be no unnatural changes and to have no need for self-examination and correction, the next is to understand the changes and make the necessary corrections, the third is to perceive change without understanding and to scrutinise and correct actions pointlessly, and the last, the worst, is to see changes and disasters followed by defeat and destruction and yet not know that correction and reform are needed.

[16] *Sung-shih* 85.1a-4b; *Yüan-shih* 58.1a-2b; *Ming-shih* 40.1a-3a.
[17] *Sung-shih* 98.1a-4b; *Yüan-shih* 67.1a-2b; *Ming-shih* 47.1a-2b.
[18] *Sung-shih* 48.1a-3a; *Yüan-shih* 48.1a-2b; *Ming-shih* 25.1a-b.

All this is offered in order to confirm the importance of studying and recording five elements changes. In contrast to the *Sung-shih* and *Yüan-shih* prefaces, the *Ming-shih* editors are cautious and sceptical. They accept the five elements theory as sound and reasonable, but reject the interpretations which point to cause-effect relationships between certain phenomena and specific events. Therefore, they merely record the unnatural happenings but not the elaborate and forced interpretations offered.[19]

Finally, the three prefaces on finance show interesting differences. The *Sung-shih* preface is particularly long. It begins by claiming that problems of 'food and money' are all-important. They must be solved before rites can be performed, before people settle down in security, before men can appreciate righteousness, before citizens can avoid punishment for crimes, and before soldiers can fight. This is followed by a historical survey of Sung financial administration which castigates the Wang An-shih reforms and the tendency to change laws frequently, and makes a devastating comment on Confucian officials talking more than doing. The preface then goes on to express the unorthodox view that a government's administration of its finances should be like that of a big merchant and should value future profits rather than short-term effects. It ends with the orthodox proposition with which the *Yüan-shih* preface begins: that producers should be many and consumers few, and that economy in expenditure is the secret of sound financial administration. Despite the apparent orthodoxy of this quotation, the *Sung-shih* preface shows an interest in expanding 'future profits' while the *Yüan-shih* preface emphasises budget balancing in its statement 'regulating the outgoing by the incoming'. Neither of them is as orthodox as the views succinctly outlined in the *Ming-shih* preface confirming the vital importance of agriculture and sericulture.[20]

The standard histories changed little in form and in the arrangement of data, but they did show changes in function and in historical thought. I have drawn attention to the *Hsin T'ang-shu* and the *Hsin Wu-tai shih* as better introductions to T'ang and Wu-tai history, and the *Chiu T'ang-shu* and *Chiu Wu-tai shih* as better collections of authentic documents. The later five histories are quite inadequate as repositories of historical data because many more contemporary collections have survived. The *Ming-shih* does provide a fine introduction to the dynasty's history, but the other four do not even serve as that. Only the *Liao-shih*, despite its faults, is a vital work on the period it covers because so little else has been preserved for the Liao dynasty. Nevertheless, the three continuous and 'legitimate' histories covering the 700 years from the beginning of Sung to the end of the Ming (960-1644) do reflect changes in historical thinking and, indirectly, also of political and philosophical assumptions. And they do this by showing how unprogressive

[19] *Sung-shih* 61.1a-2b; *Yüan-shih* 50.1a-2b; *Ming-shih* 28.1a-b.
[20] *Sung-shih* 173.1a-3a; *Yüan-shih* 93.1a-2b; *Ming-shih* 77.1a-b.

historiography really was and how historical change was seen as different permutations and combinations of a few basic concepts drawn from different periods of history themselves.

BIBLIOGRAPHY

The following select list is complementary to the notes for K.H.J. Gardiner's 'Standard Histories, Han to Sui' in this volume. There are many editions of the nine histories covered here; the most valuable is still the Po-na which I have used.

Beasley, W.G., and Pulleyblank, E.G., eds., *Historians of China and Japan*, London, 1961.

Chan Hok-lam, *The Historiography of the Chin Dynasty: Three Studies*, Wiesbaden, 1970.

Chao I, *Nien-erh shih cha-chi*, 1795, edition of 1899.

des Rotours, R., *Le Traité des examens*, Paris, 1932.

——, *Traité des fonctionnaires et Traité de l'armée*, 2 vols., Leiden, 1947.

Feng Chia-sheng, 'Liao-shih yüan-liu k'ao', in *Liao-shih cheng-wu san-chung*, Shanghai, 1959.

Fujieda Akira, *Chūgoku shigaku nyūmon*, Tokyo, 1951.

Gardner, C.S., *Chinese Traditional Historiography*, Cambridge, Mass., 1938.

Hsü Hao, *Nien-wu shih lun-kang*, n.p., 1947.

Naitō Torajirō, *Shina shigaku shi*, Tokyo, 1920.

Solomon, B.S., *The Veritable Record of the T'ang Emperor Shun-tsung*, Cambridge, Mass., 1956.

Wang Ming-sheng, *Shih-ch'i shih shang-ch'üeh*, 1787. Ts'ung-shu chi-ch'eng ed.

Wittfogel, K.A., and Feng Chia-sheng, *History of Chinese Society, Liao (907-1125)*, Philadelphia, 1949.

史 VII: Universal Histories

Shih-chi *and* T'ung-tien

In his *Shih-chi*, Ssu-ma Ch'ien (145-86 B.C.?) of the Former Han dynasty made the first conscious attempt to compile a history of the Chinese world from the earliest times to his own day. His work was planned in the tradition of the Confucian school: to use the material of the past and the accounts of great men as a guide to conduct and an inspiration to the people of his own time and to men of the future. As a Chinese historian, Ssu-ma Ch'ien was at once a recorder, a moralist, and an administrator. Many of his biographies (*lieh-chuan*) are based on literary and legendary material from the great schools of philosophy, and as such need to be treated with care. In his practical material, however, annals (*chi*), tables (*piao*), and treatises (*chih*), Ssu-ma Ch'ien was careful with his sources and concerned for their reliability. It is hard to judge now what records were available to Ssu-ma Ch'ien, though it may be important to note that the First Emperor of Ch'in in 213 B.C. had had proscribed all works of history other than those of his own state.[1] Some texts certainly survived the burning of the books, but it seems most likely that the Ch'in version of history was in better shape than its rivals, and that many of these others suffered from mutilation and forgery. Despite his personal preference for the Confucian school and for the philosophers and literary men of the eastern states, Ssu-ma Ch'ien's information was inevitably influenced by the restricted nature of his official sources.

For almost 1,000 years, while scholars admired the work of Ssu-ma Ch'ien and followed his sectional arrangement of history, few were prepared to break the dynastic framework established so successfully by the *Han-shu* of Pan Ku and no one made any serious attempt to compile any work of comparable scope. With the reunification of China by the T'ang dynasty, and under the patronage of Emperor T'ang T'ai-tsung and his successors, there was immense development in historical writing; great numbers of dynastic histories were commissioned, edited and annotated, and by the eighth century A.D., in his great theoretical work *Shih-t'ung*, the historian

---

[1] *Shih-chi* (Po-na ed.) 6.22bf, translated by Chavannes, *Les mémoires historiques de Se-ma Ts'ien*, vol. 2, p. 172.

Liu Chih-chi (661-721) had urged a broader view and a wider approach.[2] A work called *Cheng-tien* had already attempted to survey the forms of administration from the legendary age of Yao and Shun, but it was the great compilation, *T'ung-tien* by Tu Yu (735-842), that presented the first complete historical study of political institutions and their organisation.

Tu Yu took thirty-six years to compile his *T'ung-tien*, or *Comprehensive Statutes*. The material is now divided into nine sections, on economics (*shih-huo*), examinations (*hsüan-chü*), the official system (*chih-kuan*), rites (*li*), music (*yüeh*), military administration (*ping*), law (*hsing*), administrative geography (*chou-chün*), and frontier policy (*pien-fang*). Each section has an introduction, and each deals with the time from the reign of the legendary Yellow Emperor to 755 A.D., adding notes on some details of the period 755-801 A.D. Within the sections, topics are discussed item by item, with major interest given to the section on rites, and with valuable early commentaries there to the Confucian classics *Shang-shu* and *Chou-li*.

The most important point about *T'ung-tien* is that it clearly reflects Tu Yu's own interpretation of his material. The main part of each section is in the form of a general essay, with quotations linked by Tu Yu's own writing, and at the end of each part there are additional comments by other scholars, selected by Tu Yu from memorials and speeches to the throne or from essays and other collections. *T'ung-tien* is a major source for early Chinese history, and there are several items of information which survive only in this work, but, where comparison is possible, it may sometimes be found that quotations have been removed from their former context, and have been used to support the opinion of a fine T'ang scholar rather than the true intention of the original author.

Tzu-chih t'ung-chien *and Related Works*

Shih-chi and *T'ung-tien* present two different methods of dealing with the history of earlier periods; *Shih-chi* by a form of analysis now generally accepted by all compilers of dynastic histories; *T'ung-tien* by encyclopaedic collection of material and essays of opinion on particular topics of politics and administration. It was not until the Sung dynasty, however, that the scholar and official Ssu-ma Kuang (1019-86), perhaps the greatest of all Chinese historians, attempted the massive task of presenting the whole history of China, from the Chou dynasty to his own day, within the framework of a continuous narrative.

Tzu-chih t'ung-chien, presented to the throne in final form in 1085, is a chronicle of the years from 403 B.C., when the formal division of the ancient state of Chin marked the beginning of the rise to power by the empire of Ch'in, to 960 A.D., the end of the Five Dynasties and the beginning of Sung.

---

[2] Pulleyblank, 'Chinese Historical Criticism: Liu Chih-chi and Ssu-ma Kuang', pp. 135ff.

In his analysis of the section dealing with the years 220-65, Achilles Fang has demonstrated Ssu-ma Kuang's technique of selection and reorganisation, and has shown, in particular, that the greater part of the material can readily be traced back to passages in the standard histories.[3] The same cannot be said, however, for his treatment of the Period of Division or T'ang. There he has used many sources apart from the standard histories and the value of his work is enhanced by the fact that many of the books upon which he has relied are no longer extant.

The most important aids to the study of Chinese history through the *Tzu-chih t'ung-chien* are the *k'ao-i* commentary by Ssu-ma Kuang himself, which compares variant statements in his sources and explains his reasons for choosing one or the other,[4] and the general commentary by Hu San-hsing (1230-1302), which includes, however, a great quantity of material already available in the commentaries to the standard histories. As a guide to the history, the Southern Sung scholar Yüan Shu (1131-1205) compiled the *Tzu-chih t'ung-chien chi-shih pen-mo*, which extracted all the material on 239 different topics and arranged it in chronological order. The text of each section is taken straight from *Tzu-chih t'ung-chien* without alteration, and it is useful primarily as a guide to particular sequences of events without the scattering of extraneous information implicit in strict chronicle form. The example of Yüan Shu's work has been applied to later histories with similar masses of material.

Of equal fame with the *Tzu-chih t'ung-chien*, but of far less use to the historian, is the *Tzu-chih t'ung-chien kang-mu*, often known as *T'ung-chien kang-mu*, an abridgement of Ssu-ma Kuang's work by the philosopher Chu Hsi (1130-1200) and his disciples. As Otto Franke has remarked, Chu Hsi saw himself as the compiler of a new *Ch'un-ch'iu*, and he gave praise and blame like a second Confucius.[5] No new material is added, and in several places Ssu-ma Kuang's objective view as a historian has been altered to fit the moral opinions of the philosopher. The work, however, is convenient to use, and this abridged and slanted chronicle has been the basis for several major works in Western languages: notably the eighteenth-century *Histoire générale de le Chine* by the Jesuit Father de Mailla, Henri Cordier's close imitation of the same name, and the semi-translation entitled *Textes historiques* by Father Léon Wieger. In contrast, the monumental *Geschichte des chinesischen Reiches* by Otto Franke takes much of its material from *Tzu-chih t'ung-chien*.

[3] *The Chronicle of the Three Kingdoms*, Harvard-Yenching Institute Studies VI, 2 vols. (Cambridge, Mass., 1952, 1965).
[4] The value of this work for the mid-T'ang period is explained by Pulleyblank in 'The Tzyjyh Tongjiann Kaoyih and the Sources for the History of the Period 730-763', *Bulletin of the School of Oriental and African Studies* XIII (1950), pp. 448-73.
[5] See 'Das *Tse tschi t'ung kien* und das *T'ung kien kang mu*, ihr Wesen ihr Verhaltnis zueinander und ihr Quellenwert', p. 126.

T'ung-chih *and* Wen-hsien t'ung-k'ao

T'ung-chih, compiled by the Sung historian Cheng Ch'iao (1104-62), attempts to emulate the *Shih-chi* of Ssu-ma Ch'ien and tell the history of China from the earliest times to the periods of Sui and T'ang. Like *Shih-chi*, the work is divided into annals (*chi*), chronological tables (*p'u*), monographs (*lüeh*) and biographies (*chuan*). The annals and biographies describe events only to the end of the Sui dynasty, but the tables and monographs include material to the end of T'ang.

Despite Cheng Ch'iao's intentions, his work is known now rather for the monographs than for any other section. He believed it a mistake to divide history into arbitrary periods of dynasties and states, and the scope and continuity of his work established his point, but most information on specific periods is more readily found in the pages of the standard histories. The twenty monographs, however, represented an attempt to summarise all that was known about the various subjects, and the discussion of the material, in much the same format as *T'ung-tien*, is better organised than in any comparable work. The subjects are: family and clan (*shih-tsu*), philology (*liu-shu*), phonetics (*ch'i-yün*), astronomy (*t'ien-wen*), geography (*ti-li*), political subdivisions (*tu-i*), rites (*li*), posthumous titles (*shih*), ceremonial vessels and robes (*ch'i-fu*), music (*yüeh*), the official system (*chih-kuan*), examinations (*hsüan-chü*), legal system (*hsing-fa*), economics (*shih-huo*), bibliography (*i-wen*), collation of books (*chiao-ch'ou*), charts and tables (*t'u-p'u*), inscriptions on metal and stone (*chin-shih*), omens of good or bad fortune (*tsai-hsiang*), plants and insects (*k'un-ch'ung ts'ao-mu*).

Inevitably, a great part of the information for the period up to the middle of T'ang follows very closely that already in *T'ung-tien*, but the first three sections, the last, and the section on political sub-divisions, have not been treated independently in any earlier work. In particular, the sections on bibliography, on the collation of books, on charts and tables, and on inscriptions provide valuable and comprehensive lists of written material from the T'ang and pre-T'ang periods which was extant in Cheng Ch'iao's lifetime.

The *Wen-hsien t'ung-k'ao*, commonly referred to simply as *T'ung-k'ao*, was compiled by Ma Tuan-lin of the late Sung and early Yüan dynasties. The 324 chapters are divided into twenty-four sections, each dealing with material on a particular topic from the earliest times up to the year 1224. As *T'ung-chih* imitates *Shih-chi*, so the arrangement of *Wen-hsien t'ung-k'ao* follows *T'ung-tien*, and all but four of the subjects treated have a counterpart in one of the nine sections of that earlier work. In the list following, these four new sections are marked by an asterisk: land tax and grain tribute (*t'ien-fu*), coinage (*ch'ien-pi*), population (*hu-k'ou*), poll tax and corvée service (*chih-i*), revenue (*cheng-ch'üeh*), price-control and grain-storage (*shih-ti*), production (*t'u-kung*), finance (*kuo-yung*), examination system (*hsüan-chü*), education and schools (*hsüeh-hsiao*), official system (*chih-kuan*), sacrifices (*chiao-she*), imperial temples (*tsung-miao*), imperial rites (*wang-li*), music (*yüeh*), military system (*ping*), law (*hsing*), bibliography (*ching-chi*), imperial genealogies* (*ti-hsi*), enfeoffment* (*feng-chien*), astronomy* (*hsiang-wei*), unusual phenomena* (*wu-i*), geography (*yü-ti*), foreign countries (*ssu-i*). For material on the period up to the outbreak of the An Lu-shan rebellion in 755, *Wen-hsien t'ung-k'ao* follows *T'ung-tien* very closely, but material on late T'ang and Sung was collected by Ma Tuan-lin himself from various sources, and includes considerable information which does not appear in the standard history *Sung-shih*.

For each section, Ma composed an introduction, explaining his approach to the material and giving a short survey of the whole topic. The main body of the section contained first factual quotations, then memorials to the throne and other essays of criticism and opinion, and finally Ma's own conclusions. It is generally accepted that the most important parts of the whole work are Ma Tuan-lin's own writings, and his introductions, in particular, were learnt by heart, in full, by many candidates for the imperial civil service examinations of Ming and Ch'ing.

Chinese scholars commonly group the three works *T'ung-tien*, *T'ung-chih*, and *Wen-hsien t'ung-k'ao* and refer to them as the *San-t'ung*. Of the three, it is generally agreed that the two more strictly encyclopaedic works are the most valuable and successful, *T'ung-tien* as the original repository of so much material that would otherwise be lost, and *Wen-hsien t'ung-k'ao* for the critical notes of Ma Tuan-lin. *T'ung-chih*, as we have seen, is regarded chiefly for its monographs, and it may be noted that the Ssu-pu pei-yao collection has printed them as a separate work, in fifty-two chapters, entitled *T'ung-chih lüeh*.

Continuations

If the T'ang dynasty was the great age of compilation for the standard histories, and the Sung dynasty, with Ssu-ma Kuang, Cheng Ch'iao, and Ma Tuan-lin, the period of universal histories, the scholars of the Ch'ing dynasty (particularly those of the Ch'ien-lung period) made a valiant attempt to bring the ancient encyclopaedias up to date. On the whole, their work is of less value than that of their predecessors, not necessarily because they themselves were inferior in scholarship or in diligence, but because the original sources for much of the material are still preserved, and we are to that extent less dependent on their compilations for texts which would otherwise be lost.

Apart from the encyclopaedists of Ch'ien-lung, we may first note two other continuations of the earlier historical works. The Ch'ing scholar Pi Yüan (1730-97) compiled a *Hsü Tzu-chih t'ung-chien* in 220 chapters, covering the period from the beginning of Sung in 960 to the first years of the Ming dynasty. His sources were for the most part taken from the standard dynastic histories, with additions from other contemporary writings, histories and essays, and he included a *k'ao-i* commentary on variant texts, in emulation of Ssu-ma Kuang. The work is detailed and clear, and of some value on particular points of the period that it covers, but it has never received the respect and admiration shown to the original.

In 1586, the Ming scholar Wang Ch'i completed his compilation of a *Hsü Wen-hsien t'ung-k'ao*, in 254 chapters, with material covering the later Sung, and the Liao, Chin, Yüan and Ming dynasties, arranged in the same fashion as that of Ma Tuan-lin. Some new sections and topics are discussed, and the work is most valuable for its preservation of material on law cases of the Ming period and on relations with foreign countries.

Under the Ch'ien-lung Emperor, scholars were commissioned to prepare continuations of *T'ung-tien*, *T'ung-chih*, and *Wen-hsien t'ung-k'ao*. The works are: *Hsü T'ung-tien*, 150 chapters, commissioned 1767; *Hsü T'ung-chih* (monographs only), 640 chapters, commissioned 1767; *Hsü Wen-hsien t'ung-k'ao*, *Ch'in-ting*, 250 chapters, commissioned 1747; *Huang-ch'ao T'ung-tien*, 100 chapters, commissioned 1767; *Huang-ch'ao T'ung-chih* (monographs only), 126 chapters, commissioned 1767; *Huang-ch'ao Wen-hsien t'ung-k'ao*, 300 chapters, commissioned 1747.

Of these works, the first three deal with the period up to the end of the Ming dynasty, and the last three, the first characters of their titles being now sometimes written *Ch'ing-ch'ao*, cover the years from the beginning of the Ch'ing dynasty to 1785. It will be observed that the *Hsü Wen-hsien t'ung-k'ao*, *Ch'in-ting* duplicates the work of Wang Ch'i. This was done partly for the sake of completion, and partly because it was believed that the earlier work had been poorly arranged. The two rival books are best consulted together, for although Wang Ch'i certainly tended to mingle his own commentary among the original quotations, the Ch'ing work is largely composed of extracts and abridgements from Wang Ch'i's work, and does not give such full quotations from the original sources.

A work entitled *Huang-ch'ao* (or *Ch'ing-ch'ao*) *Hsü Wen-hsien t'ung-k'ao*, compiled by Liu Chin-tsao of the Republic, preface dated 1921, presents a supplement to the continuations of the Ch'ien-lung period, and deals with the years 1786-1911. Teng and Biggerstaff describe the book as giving a reasonably reliable picture of the second half of the Ch'ing dynasty, though not of the same standard as the earlier encyclopaedias.[6]

It is fair to say that all these works of continuation are of secondary value for historical research: they may provide a general guide to particular subjects and periods, and they can be useful supplements to basic texts, but they do not often contain original material which cannot be found elsewhere, and as a result they can seldom be considered primary authorities.

---

[6] *An Annotated Bibliography of Selected Chinese Reference Works*, p. 114.

The text history of *Shih-chi* is too widely known to need detailed discussion or reference. The most useful editions are in the Po-na collection of the Commercial Press, reproducing a Sung dynasty block-print of 1195-1200, and the Japanese work *Shiki kaichū kōshō* of Takigawa Kametarō, first published in Tokyo in 1934, which has detailed punctuation and modern commentary. No. 40 of the Harvard-Yenching Institute Sinological Index Series, published in 1947, is an index to the Shanghai Wu-chou t'ung-wen shu-chü edition, which is itself based on the Palace edition (Wu-ying tien) of 1739.

The two major translations are by Edouard Chavannes, *Les mémoires historiques de Se-ma Ts'ien*, 5 vols. (Paris, 1895-1905; reprinted Leiden, 1967), which renders the first forty-seven chapters, and by Burton Watson, *Records of the Grand Historian of China, from the Shih chi of Ssu-ma Chi'en*, 2 vols. (New York, 1961), which deals largely with the Ch'in and Han period, and includes a finding list at the end of vol. 1.

For descriptions of the various historical encyclopaedias, from *T'ung-tien* to the continuations of the Ch'ing scholars, the essential text is Ssu-yü Teng and Knight Biggerstaff, *An Annotated Bibliography of Selected Chinese Reference Works*, Harvard-Yenching Institute Studies II (third ed., Cambridge, Mass., 1971), especially pp. 107-14. The most useful edition is the Shih-t'ung of the Commercial Press (Shanghai, 1936), which gives the texts of the *San-t'ung*, the *Hsü Wen-hsien t'ung-k'ao* compiled by Wang Ch'i, and the six continuations of the Ch'ien-lung period. The last of the twenty volumes contains a four-corner index to all ten works.

For *Tzu-chih t'ung-chien* and its allied works, the *locus classicus* of text criticism is the article by Otto Franke, 'Das *Tse tschi t'ung kien* und das *T'ung kien kang mu*, ihr Wesen, ihr Verhaltnis zueinander und ihr Quellenwert', in *Sitzungsberichte der (königlichen) preussischen Akademie der Wissenschaften: philosophisch-historische Klasse* (Berlin, 1930), pp. 103-44. An important recent article is that of E.G. Pulleyblank, 'Chinese Historical Criticism: Liu Chih-chi and Ssu-ma Kuang', in W.G. Beasley and E.G. Pulleyblank, eds., *Historians of China and Japan* (London, 1961), pp. 135-66. The translation by Achilles Fang, entitled *The Chronicle of the Three Kingdoms*, Harvard-Yenching Institute Studies VI, 2 vols. (Cambridge, Mass., 1952, 1965), gives chapters 69 to 78 and analyses the method by which Ssu-ma Kuang compiled his work from the texts of earlier histories. My work, *The Last of the Han*, Monograph 9 of the Centre of Oriental Studies, Australian National University (Canberra, 1969), translates chapters 58-68 and includes an introduction on the text history of *Tzu-chih t'ung-chien*. The most useful and reliable edition of *Tzu-chih t'ung-chien* is that of the Ku-chi ch'u-pan she (Peking, 1956). In 1957, the same company also published an edition of the *Hsü Tzu-chih t'ung-chien* of Pi Yüan, and a further scholarly edition, *Tzu-chih t'ung-chien chin-chu*, was published by Chung-hua ts'ung-shu wei-yüan hui, Taipei, 1956.

史　VIII: Local Gazetteers

D. D. LESLIE

Already by the Sung, several hundreds of *fang-chih* (or *ti-fang chih*) had been compiled by the local gentry under the auspices of the local authorities, for province *sheng* (*t'ung-chih*), prefecture *fu*, subprefecture *chou*, and district (or county) *hsien*. Chang Kuo-kan lists over 2,000 dating from before the Ming, of which fewer than fifty are now extant.[1] During the Ming, local gazetteers were compiled to provide information for the 1461 general gazetteer, the *Ta-Ming i-t'ung chih*. Thereafter, these were continually revised and re-edited. Altogether, several thousands of Ming editions were published, of which nearly 1,000 are still extant. During the Ch'ing, completely new editions for almost all areas were compiled, running to many thousands, of which a large proportion, perhaps 5,000, are extant. The twentieth century has seen a further burst of production of new local gazetteers, together with the reprinting of many earlier ones.

Most gazetteers extant today were compiled in the central and eastern provinces. Those of the Sung and Yüan were largely *fu-chih* (in particular of Chekiang). Those of the Ming, mostly compiled during Chia-ching (1522-66) and Wan-li (1573-1619), were mainly *fu-chih, chou-chih, hsien-chih,* and some *t'ung-chih,* of Nan Chih-li (approximately Kiangsu), Pei Chih-li (Hopeh), Honan, Chekiang, and Shantung. During the Ch'ing, a vast number of *hsien-chih* were compiled, but so also were *t'ung-chih, fu-chih, chou-chih,* and, towards the end of the dynasty, *hsiang-t'u chih* (village gazetteers). The provinces best covered were Chih-li (Hopeh), Kiangsu, Szechwan, and Shantung. Minor categories of gazetteers covering smaller areas are also found, composed mainly during the Ch'ing. These include *t'ing-chih, wei-chih, kuan-chih, shih-chih,* and *chen-chih.* The compilation of *hsiang-t'u chih* and *hsiang-chen chih* was commenced only towards the end of the Ch'ing.

The main collections are found in Peking, Tokyo, Shanghai, Nanking, and Taipei. The 1958 union list by Chu Shih-chia covers mainland China,[2] and we also have a union list for Taiwan made by the National Central

---

[1] See Introduction to *Chung-kuo ku fang-chih k'ao.*
[2] See *Chung-kuo ti-fang chih tsung-lu.*

Library in 1960,[3] and a 1969 one for Japan made by the National Diet Library. The main collections available outside mainland China are in the Tōyō bunko, Tokyo; Jimbun kagaku kenkyūjo, Kyoto; Tenri (University) Library, Tenri; Naikaku bunko, Tokyo; National Diet Library (including the Ueno Library), Tokyo; Academia Sinica, Taipei; National Central Library, Taipei; National Palace Museum (the Ku-kung), Taipei; Library of Congress, Washington. Other American libraries with goodish collections are Harvard-Yenching, Cambridge, Massachusetts, and Columbia University, New York. European holdings are given in the 1957 union list by Y. Hervouet.[4]

For the Ming, the best holdings are in the Peking National Library, Peking; the T'ien-i ko, Ning-po; the National Central Library, Taipei (which now holds the original collection of rare books formerly in the Peking National Library). Yamane Yukio has listed Ming gazetteers held in Japan.[5] The Naikaku bunko, Sonkeikaku bunko, and Ueno Library, together with the Tōyō bunko, are comparatively rich in Ming editions. The microfilm collection of the rare books of the Peking National Library, made by the Library of Congress during the war, includes over 300 Ming gazetteers, and is available in several Western libraries.

Recent reprints, published mainly in Taiwan, have made available quite a number of local gazetteers, of province, *fu*, and *hsien*. We may note in particular: Chung-kuo fang-chih ts'ung-shu (well over 100); Pien-chiang fang-chih (well over 100); Chung-kuo pien-chiang ts'ung-shu; Chung-kuo sheng-chih hui-pien; Chung-kuo shih-hsüeh ts'ung-shu (in particular, the Ming-tai fang-chih hsüan).

A comparison of the *hsien*, *fu*, and provincial gazetteers shows that the most important material in the first is included, though often summarised, in the second, which in its turn is incorporated, summarised, in the third. For a quick survey, the provincial *t'ung-chih* is sufficient (and for most purposes, the Ku-chin t'u-shu chi-ch'eng of 1725 covers the ground), but for full information the relevant *hsien-chih* must be found. For the Ming, the later Ch'ing editions are sometimes unreliable or too summary, and one must search for the earliest. But later editions, and even *fu* or provincial gazetteers, occasionally contain facts not given earlier or in the *hsien* gazetteer. One must also watch out for minor changes or extra prefaces in supposedly identical works.

The contents of local gazetteers are similar to those of the dynastic histories, encyclopaedias, and other national works, but the far greater detail about local affairs, and also the monograph (and uniform) arrangement and statistical tables, make them essential reading for many topics.

---

[3] *T'ai-wan kung-ts'ang fang-chih lien-ho mu-lu.*
[4] *Catalogue des monographies locales chinoises dans les bibliothèques d'Europe.*
[5] *Nihon genzon Mindai chihōshi mokuroku.* Cf. also W. Franke, *An Introduction to the Sources of Ming History.*

Some of the material they contain is unique, both for historical geography and for geographical history. Gazetteers deal with local topography and maps, rivers, passes, bridges, fords, mountains, scenery, etc.[6] They are also invaluable for meteorology and climate, local plants and animals, mineralogy and phenology, astronomy, and technology. More significant for historical purposes are the sections on irrigation and waterways, floods and dykes, the hydraulic system and communications, transportation and posts, city walls, and other antiquities.

Economic considerations are well supplied. Basic information is available for taxes and revenue, salt tax and border customs, markets and production, population, and local products. Gazetteers are also fundamental sources for all manner of sociological studies, local customs and festivals, Confucian ancestral shrines (*miao*), and Buddhist and Taoist temples (*ssu-kuan*). Administrative structure, civil, military, legal and commercial, institutional, and boundary changes, public offices and buildings, schools and academies, all are dealt with.

Local gazetteers are of special value for information about individuals, both local degree-holders (*hsüan-chü* chapters) and officials (from other areas) (*chih-kuan* chapters). Information about appointments is more detailed than that to be found in national histories. Biographies for eminent officials (*ming-huan* chapters) and for local worthies (*jen-wu* chapters) sometimes go into considerable detail. These chapters include sections on martyrs, filial sons, officials, soldiers, scholars, hermits, Taoists, Buddhists, magicians, book-collectors, artists, physicians, and virtuous women. There are invaluable name indices to the 1934 Commercial Press edition of the provincial gazetteers (*t'ung-chih*) of Kwangtung, Shantung, Hunan, Hupeh, Chekiang, and Hopeh (Chi-fu); Chu Shih-chia published in 1963 an index to biographies in Sung and Yüan extant gazetteers;[7] and Yamane Yukio, with others, published in 1964 a draft index of biographies of (299) Ming gazetteers extant in Japan.[8] Slowly one can build up genealogies, and the rise and fall of great families traced in the *chia-p'u* can be confirmed from the local gazetteers.

Local gazetteers are also of special value for military affairs. The provincial gazetteers, and some others, include changes in establishments with lists of appointments of officers, from general down to company commander, captain-adjutant, and even lieutenant (*tu-ssu, shou-pei, ch'ien-tsung*). Military campaigns, especially against rebels and local bandits, are described in detail. The local military camps, sea, river, land, and border defences and fortifications are also described.

[6] For their geographical worth, see Chen Cheng-siang, *Chung-kuo fang-chih ti ti-li hsüeh chia-chih.*
[7] *Sung-Yüan fang-chih chuan-chi so-yin* (Peking, 1963).
[8] *Nihon genzon Mindai chihōshi denki sakuin kō* (Tokyo, 1964).

There are many chapters to inspect. The prefaces and lists of editors and assistant editors may provide unsuspected facts; the chapter on omens includes military revolts; the *i-wen* sections of belles-lettres of various kinds are a mine of information, not merely of bibliographical and literary import, not found elsewhere (and the contents of the *hsien-chih* and *fu-chih* for these chapters are quite distinct from one another). Tombstone and other inscriptions are basic. Public addresses, official letters, memorials, and funeral eulogies cannot be overlooked. In all chapters, we may cut across the career of individuals, officials, and local men.

Thus, though local gazetteers do not have the national authority of the dynastic histories, and the quality of their compilation varies from locality to locality, their closeness to their material usually gives them the edge over all other sources for the detailed year by year history of localities and individuals.

BIBLIOGRAPHY

Chang Kuo-kan, *Chung-kuo ku fang-chih k'ao*, Shanghai, 1962.
Chen Cheng-siang (Ch'en Cheng-hsiang), *Chung-kuo fang-chih ti ti-li hsüeh chia-chih*, Hong Kong, 1965.
Chu Shih-chia, *Chung-kuo ti-fang chih tsung-lu*, Shanghai, 1958 (largely replaces 1935 work).
——, *A Catalogue of Chinese Local Histories in the Library of Congress*, Washington, 1942.
Dow, Francis D.M., *A Study of Chiang-su and Che-chiang Gazetteers of the Ming Dynasty*, Canberra, 1969.
Franke, Wolfgang, *An Introduction to the Sources of Ming History*, Kuala Lumpur, Singapore, 1968.
Hervouet, Yves, *Catalogue des monographies locales chinoises dans les bibliothèques d'Europe*, Paris, The Hague, 1957.
Hung Huan-ch'un, *Che-chiang ti-fang chih k'ao-lu*, Peking, 1958.
Leslie, Donald and Davidson, Jeremy, *Catalogues of Chinese Local Gazetteers*, Canberra, 1967.
National Central Library, *T'ai-wan kung-ts'ang fang-chih lien-ho mu-lu*, Taipei, 1957, almost identical in *Chinese Culture* III, 1 (Oct. 1960), pp. 155-212, III, 2 (Dec. 1960), pp. 157-224.
Suzuki Heihachirō and others, *Chūgoku chihōshi sōgō mokuroku*, Tokyo, 1969 (replaces draft *kō* of 1950-64).
Yamane Yukio, *Nihon genzon Mindai chihōshi mokuroku*, Tokyo, 1962.

史　ix: Unofficial Regional Records

COLIN MACKERRAS

The great majority of pre-Republican works devoted to one particular area are regional gazetteers (*ti-fang chih*). These were officially approved by the local authorities and compiled by groups of scholars according to a stereotyped pattern not unlike that of the standard histories. We also find in the vast body of Chinese literature other works dealing with specified areas. Some of these books are diaries—the private records of scholars who travelled through a region—but this chapter will be devoted mainly to those works which are the result of personal experience and research over an extended period.

Unofficial regional records of this type are classified in Chinese catalogues under the headings 'notebooks' (*pi-chi*) or 'various records' (*tsa-chi*). The majority are therefore contained in larger collections (*ts'ung-shu*), but separate editions have been made for the most important examples. Notebooks and various records were already established as a *genus* of literature well before the Sung dynasty (960-1279), but the number written increased greatly at that time, and continued to grow in later centuries.

Unlike the *ti-fang chih*, the books under discussion here were usually each the work of one scholar. Although eminent officials did occasionally turn their hands towards describing their home-towns or the places where they worked, it was usually left to authors with little or no reputation as government administrators to write privately about cities or regions they loved. Some of them are known only by their pen-names and it is possible to construct detailed biographies for only a few of them.

These men were concerned to fill in colourful details usually omitted from the official regional gazetteers. It is not surprising, therefore, that they directed most of their attention towards the great cities of their day—K'aifeng in the Northern Sung (960-1127), Hang-chou in the Southern (1127-1279), and Nanking, Yang-chou, and Peking in the Ming (1368-1644) and Ch'ing (1644-1911). From the sixteenth century on, scholars wrote far more on the great urban centres of Kiangsu and Chekiang than on those of any other province, simply because these two were culturally the most advanced in China and could boast the most fascinating towns outside Peking. Though most concern cities, there are some regional *pi-chi* and *tsa-chi* which describe whole regions or entire provinces. Here again, more material is available for the south than the north. Kiangsu, Hupeh, and Kwangtung, for instance, are much better covered than Shensi or Honan.

A number of salient characteristics flow from the fact that these works were unofficial. In some respects they are vastly inferior as sources to the *ti-fang chih*. Because they were not sponsored by the authorities they are comparatively few in number. Provincial and local officials encouraged the compilation of gazetteers and these survive in large numbers from all over the country, even though some regions are much better represented than others. The writing of notebooks and various records was much more haphazard. No government official cared whether they were written, or survived long after publication. The research worker seeking information on such matters as the biographies of eminent local officials, fiscal administration, or ancient relics will find much more copious and thorough material in the *ti-fang chih* than in the local *pi-chi* or *tsa-chi*.

On the other hand, the unofficial records can offer a great deal of exclusive material and many valuable insights. There are quite a few aspects of local life which are treated scantily or not at all in the gazetteers, and in matters pertaining to daily life or popular entertainment, the privately written works are very much more useful. Local music and art, puppet shows, operas, the activities of wandering story-tellers or actors, all these cultural and social phenomena were considered rather outside the scope of detailed treatment in official records. The scholars who wrote the *pi-chi* and *tsa-chi* were interested in such things. Those of them who had no great official reputation to preserve could well afford to undertake research on the disreputable elements of society. The list of subjects considered at length in unofficial but not in official books is extensive and includes restaurants, shops specialising in particular goods, brothels, local dishes, and songs. Quite a few of these works are not unlike guide-books, and in some cases appear to have been written specifically for the benefit of outside visitors to the city under discussion.

One definite advantage which the 'guide-books' enjoy over the gazetteers lies in the nature of the sources used by their authors. We find a far greater concentration on personal experiences and eye-witness accounts. This is not to say that secondary material is not used, or, indeed, that the material in official gazetteers is never first-hand, but certainly the authors of the *pi-chi* and *tsa-chi* relied much more heavily than their official counterparts on what they had seen and heard in the regions they were investigating, and much less on the accounts of other books and documents. We may therefore conclude that the unofficial records are somewhat closer than the gazetteers to 'primary sources', in the strictest sense of the term. Moreover, they are less likely to be censored than the *ti-fang chih*, the authors of which had to gain official approval for their works. The regional notebooks supply us with individual and freely expressed viewpoints.

From a literary point of view, the works under consideration here are in some ways preferable to the *ti-fang chih*. They were written by men who wrote because they loved their subjects and not because their official position demanded it. Moreover, the private records of independent scholars are very diverse in form and content. They do not follow stereotyped lines such as those found in the gazetteers. There is overlap in the content of official and unofficial records, but in general one can say that it is for social and cultural history that the latter are most valuable.

Specific Examples of Unofficial Regional Records

To illustrate the general comments made let us consider a few specific works. Those chosen are, of course, only a small part of the total number, but are probably sufficient to show the types of unofficial regional records available, and to give some indication of the kinds of men who wrote such works.

A particularly famous early example is the *Tung-ching meng-hua lu*, prefaced 1147 by its author Meng Yüan-lao. It contains ten *chüan* and has been published in several surviving editions, the oldest dating from the Yüan dynasty. A number of collections contain the work,[1] and it has also been issued in Shanghai (1956) in the collection Tung-ching meng-hua lu (wai ssu-chung). The modern edition is especially useful since it is fully punctuated and the volume includes four other similar works about the Sung dynasty. These will be discussed below.

The *Tung-ching meng-hua lu* is a lengthy description of K'ai-feng in the late years of the Northern Sung, when the city was China's capital. It details the streets, shops, restaurants, and places of amusement, and gives a vivid picture of the people's everyday life. Yet, despite its vital importance for any study of urban China under the Sung, virtually nothing is known about its author. Possibly Yüan-lao was his *tzu*, rather than his *ming*, and it has even been suggested that he deliberately hid his real identity through fear that his responsibility in a certain building disaster would become widely known.[2]

Following Meng's example, four authors wrote accounts of China's capital of the Southern Sung, Hang-chou. Their works are (i) *Tu-ch'eng chi-sheng*, prefaced 1235 by its author Chao, pen-named Kuan-pu (or yüan) nai-te weng;[3] (ii) *Hsi-hu lao-jen fan-sheng lu*, written, probably in the 1250s,

[1] See details in *Chung-kuo ts'ung-shu tsung-lu*, 3 vols. (Peking, 1959-62), vol. 2, p. 544.
[2] See Meng Yüan-lao and others, Tung-ching meng-hua lu (wai ssu-chung) (Shanghai, 1956), 'Ch'u-pan shuo-ming', p. 3. It should be added, however, that some scholars have denied the suggestion noted in the text. See, in particular, Teng Chih-ch'eng, *Tung-ching meng-hua lu chu* (Peking, 1959), 'Tzu-hsü', pp. 15-16.
[3] The surname of the author of *Tu-ch'eng chi-sheng* is nowhere given in the book itself. However, in Shuo-fu 14.1a-5b, we find a work called *Chiu-jih lu* by a writer surnamed Chao of the Sung, with *hao* Kuan-yüan nai-te weng.

by an author pen-named Hsi-hu lao-jen; (iii) *Meng-liang lu*,[4] probably prefaced 1274[5] by its author Wu Tzu-mu, a native of Hang-chou; and (iv) *Wu-lin chiu-shih*, written some time after 1280[6] by Chou Mi. All four have been reprinted from editions in earlier collections[7] in the modern volume Tung-ching meng-hua lu (wai ssu-chung), where they are fully punctuated.

The longest and most important of the four are the *Meng-liang lu* and the *Wu-lin chiu-shih*. The first describes Hang-chou in the mid-thirteenth century. The second is wider in its timescope: Chou Mi has 'taken [material from] all the other [three] books mentioned, but has also relied on what he himself saw and heard'.[8] Of all the authors named so far, Chou Mi is the best known. He wrote several other works besides the *Wu-lin chiu-shih*, and was known as a *tz'u* poet; he held an official post under the Sung, but refused to serve when the Mongols came to power. Chou came originally from Chi-nan in Shantung, but spent many of his later years in Hang-chou.[9]

Though they vary greatly in length, the four works follow roughly the pattern of the *Tung-ching meng-hua lu* in the topics they treat. No research into Sung society or culture can ignore these five books. They contain a wealth of material concerning the layout of cities, administration, education, guilds, prostitution, dances, festivals, the theatre, and popular literature and entertainment. Not surprisingly, works like Jacques Gernet's *Daily Life in China on the Eve of the Mongol Invasion 1250-1276*[10] rely heavily on them for information.

A later and completely different kind of unofficial regional record is the *Chin-ling so-shih* by Chou Hui from Nanking (Wan-li period). This work contains four *chüan*, and was prefaced 1610 by the author; Chou later added four chapters. The book was reprinted in the late Ch'ing and again in Shanghai in 1936. The most recent edition is a photolithographic reproduction of the original Wan-li version and was published in Peking in 1955.

[4] In the preface to the *Meng-liang lu*, Wu Tzu-mu writes: 'Formerly, somebody was sleeping while food was being cooked, and he thought over the whole course of his official life. Then he awoke and everything was just as before his dream; and he realised that he had been dreaming. So he [wrote a story and] called it the *Huang-liang meng*. Times and affairs change. The richness of the city's moats and parks, the prosperity of customs and the literary people, all these I should like to preserve forever. So I have thought over past things, just as in a dream, and called my work "Dreaming of Millet".' The *Huang-meng liang* is a short story of the T'ang. It has been translated by E.D. Edwards in her *Chinese Prose Literature of the T'ang Period A.D. 618-906* (Probsthain's Oriental Series, Vols. XXIII-IV, London, 1937-8), vol. 2, pp. 212-15.

[5] The preface of the *Meng-liang lu* is dated as the year *chia-hsü*. This could be 1274 or 1334. The former is the more likely date. See Tung-ching meng-hua lu (wai ssu-chung), 'Ch'u-pan shuo-ming', pp. 4-5.

[6] Ibid., p. 5.

[7] For details, see *Chung-kuo ts'ung-shu tsung-lu*, vol. 2, pp. 537-8.

[8] Sun K'ai-ti, *K'uei-lei hsi k'ao-yüan*, Chung-kuo hsi-ch'ü li-lun ts'ung-shu (Shanghai, 1952), p. 43.

[9] A biography of Chou Mi may be found in *Hsin Yüan-shih* 237.

[10] The original title of this work is *La vie quotidienne en Chine à la veille de l'invasion mongole 1250-1276* (Paris, 1959). It was translated into English by H.M. Wright and published in London in 1962 as no. 7 of the Daily Life Series.

Chou Hui has something to tell us about customs and life in Nanking, and, although he sometimes quotes from older books, his notes are largely based on his own experiences and stories he heard in the city. Yet his approach differs radically from that of the authors mentioned earlier. His interest seems to have rested much more in cultural than social matters. For instance, he devotes the whole of his second *chüan* to the calligraphers, dramatists, poets, and painters of Nanking, and elsewhere gives us a fairly lengthy biography of the painter Wu Hsiao-hsien.[11] He delights in anecdotes about cultural figures and his own experiences with them. He himself does not appear to have been especially famous and not much is known about him.[12]

One of Chou's friends, Ku Ch'i-yüan (1565-1628), wrote a work on Nanking which is, in many ways, not unlike the *Chin-ling so-shih*. This was the *K'e-tso chui-yü* in ten *chüan* contained in the Chin-ling ts'ung-k'e.[13] It is prefaced 1617 by the author and was therefore written only a few years after the work discussed above. Indeed, Ku expresses his great admiration for the *Chin-ling so-shih* in his own book,[14] and it is very likely that he was influenced by his friend in writing it.

Ku was a native of the city he describes and passed the *chin-shih* examinations in 1598. He held minor official posts, including one in Nanking, but resigned and spent his later years in retirement at home.[15] His positions gave him some insight into official life and he writes of it, none too favourably, in his *K'e-tso chui-yü*. He describes the corruption of Nanking's bureaucrats and attacks the incompetence of their administration.

The work goes far beyond such matters in its scope. Ku deals at some length with popular customs in his city and considers the characteristics of the dialects spoken there. He also has a great deal to say about popular literature. Not only does he list in detail some popular tunes, but also provides valuable information on popular stories and dramas. Even the theatre of the gentry is discussed and we read of the kinds of opera favoured by the richer classes at their banquets. Ku's work is an important source for the social, cultural, and administrative history of Nanking early in the seventeenth century.[16]

---

[11] *Chin-ling so-shih* (Peking, 1955) 3.296-303. This painter's *ming* was Wei, his *hao* Hsiao-hsien. He was famous only in Nanking.

[12] For details and references for this work and its author, see Wolfgang Franke, *An Introduction to the Sources of Ming History* (Kuala Lumpur, Singapore, 1968), p. 117.

[13] This collection was compiled in Nanking by Fu Ch'un-kuan over the years 1897 to 1905.

[14] *K'e-tso chui-yü* 9.15b-16a.

[15] For further material and references on Ku Ch'i-yüan and his work, see Franke, *An Introduction*, p. 117 and Hsieh Kuo-chen, *Ming-Ch'ing pi-chi t'an-ts'ung* (Peking, 1960, 1962), pp. 28-31.

[16] Other unofficial regional records of the Ming are listed in Franke, *An Introduction*, pp. 115-18. The first and among the most important of the books mentioned by Franke is the *Wan-shu tsa-chi* by Shen Pang, prefaced 1592 by its author. I have not dealt with it here, because it is very similar in format and content to a *ti-fang chih*.

Among the most fascinating of all the unofficial regional records is the *Yang-chou hua-fang lu*, a description of Yang-chou in the eighteenth century. The work is prefaced 1794 by Yüan Mei,[17] possibly eighteenth-century China's greatest poet, and 1796 by the author himself, Li Tou. It was printed originally in the latter year and reprinted several times in the nineteenth century.[18] In 1960 a punctuated edition was published in Peking as part of the Ch'ing-tai shih-liao pi-chi ts'ung-k'an and in 1963 an identical version was printed in Taipei as the second volume (*ts'e*) of the first collection (*ch*) of the Ta-lu ko-sheng wen-hsien ts'ung-k'an.

The author, Li Tou, was not a success as an official, and he is mentioned but scantily in contemporary records. He loved to travel and his wanderings took him as far afield as Peking, Fukien, and Hupeh.[19] He spent most of his life, however, in Yang-chou, which was his native city and where he had many friends. He wrote several other works besides the *Yang-chou hua-fang lu*, including some dramatic pieces.[20]

Li Tou began collecting material for his work in 1764 and spent some thirty years on the task.[21] The long time was necessary, for Yang-chou was a singularly colourful city at the time. It was a very important cultural centre and the hub of an enormous salt industry, which began to decline at the end of the eighteenth century.[22] Li took the various regions of the city and described them one by one. He paid attention to a wide range of subjects, detailed the history and prominent features of ancient monuments and temples, discussed the biographies of salt merchants, eminent officials, and cultural figures, and described in detail the customs and life of the people. Some space is given to the city's gay quarters, its festivals, products, and streets. Li Tou also appears to have been very interested in the theatre, to which he devoted the whole of his fifth *chüan*.

This work combines the virtues of a history and a colourful guide-book. Li Tou has based his information on other books, including some rare ones, but his principal qualifications to write on Yang-chou were his personal knowledge of and great love for his native city, and his many friends and contacts there. As a source for a single city, few works can rival this one.

In view of Peking's importance as China's capital under the empire's last three dynasties, it is not surprising that the city attracted a good deal of attention from scholars. Apart from official records, the two most impor-

---

[17] For a full-length biography in English of Yüan Mei, see Arthur Waley, *Yuan Mei, Eighteenth Century Chinese Poet* (London, 1956).

[18] For details, see *Chung-kuo ts'ung-shu tsung-lu*, vol. 2, p. 536.

[19] *Yang-chou hua-fang lu* (Peking, 1960), 'Tzu-hsü', p. 10.

[20] On Li Tou and the *Yang-chou hua-fang lu*, see also Hsieh Kuo-chen, *Ming-Ch'ing*, pp. 142ff.

[21] *Yang-chou hua-fang lu*, 'Tzu-hsü', p. 10.

[22] The most important contribution in English on the salt merchants of eighteenth-century Yang-chou is Ho Ping-ti, 'The Salt Merchants of Yang-chou: A Study of Commercial Capitalism in Eighteenth-Century China', *Harvard Journal of Asiatic Studies* XVII (1954), pp. 130-68.

tant Ch'ing works are the *Ch'un-ming meng yü-lu* in seventy *chüan* by Sun
Ch'eng-tse (1593-1675)[23] and the *Jih-hsia chiu-wen k'ao* in 160 *chüan* by Chu
I-tsun (1629-1709) and others.[24] These works are concerned principally
with Peking's history and do not quite fit the category of works under
discussion in this chapter.

The most thorough treatment of contemporary life in Peking is a series
of books, collectively called *Tu-men chi-lüeh*, published on the customs and
sights of Peking during the nineteenth century. The earliest, entitled *Tu-men
chi-lüeh*, was written in 1845 by Yang Ching-t'ing of T'ung-chou near Peking.
Many later expanded and altered editions followed that of 1845. There are
updated versions for 1851, 1864, 1872, 1876, 1880, 1887, and 1907. Possibly
the most readily available are the 1864 and 1907 editions, which are called
Tu-men chi-lüeh, and that of 1887, named *Ch'ao-shih ts'ung-tsai*. Yang Ching-
t'ing was not a spectacular person; he was modest and in worldly terms a
failure. Yet he was deeply familiar with the city of Peking and knew the life
of its ordinary people intimately.

The *Tu-men chi-lüeh* explain the positions of Peking's theatres, shops, and
other places of interest, and give accounts of local customs, dress, food, and
drink. There are long lists telling which actors could perform which roles
in which dramas. Information is also provided on the various forms of story-
telling in the markets of Peking.[25] The many sections on the Peking Opera
of all versions but those of 1851 and 1872 have been collected together into
one book: the *Tu-men chi-lüeh chung chih hsi-ch'ü shih-liao* by Chou Chih-fu,
published in Shanghai in 1932 as no. 1 in the series Chi-li chü hsi-ch'ü
ts'ung-shu.

Of all the books I have mentioned here, the *Tu-men chi-lüeh* series bears
the fewest signs of having been written as a literary contribution. The fact
that the original book of 1845 was so constantly brought up to date suggests
that the *Tu-men chi-lüeh* were designed for the benefit of people coming to
the city and not familiar with it. They were in fact a kind of advertisement.
The unofficial regional records had come as close as any work written in the
Chinese traditional vein to the modern Western guide-book.

[23] This work deals, among other things, with the palaces, gardens and public buildings of
Peking in the Ming dynasty. For further details and references on the work and its author,
see Franke, *An Introduction*, p. 116, and Arthur Hummel, ed., *Eminent Chinese of the Ch'ing
Period (1644-1912)*, 2 vols. (Washington, 1943), vol. 2, pp. 669-70.

[24] This work was completed in 1687 by Chu I-tsun under the title *Jih-hsia chiu-wen* and
supplemented by his son K'un-t'ien. In 1774, additions and revisions were made on the
order of the Emperor Ch'ien-lung, and the work was printed some years later under the
title *Jih-hsia chiu-wen k'ao*. It contains an enormous amount of information on the history of
Peking. See Hummel, *Eminent Chinese*, vol. 1, p. 183.

[25] See a discussion of the *Tu-men chi-lüeh* in Hsieh Kuo-chen, *Ming-Ch'ing*, pp. 125-7. The
works are there called collectively *Tu-men tsa-chi*. A more comprehensive treatment of the
authors and versions of 1845, 1864, 1876, 1880, 1887, and 1907 may be found in Chou
Chih-fu, *Tu-men chi-lüeh chung chih hsi-ch'ü shih-liao*, pp. 1-8.

BIBLIOGRAPHY

The following is a short list of unofficial regional records which, needless to say, does not purport to be comprehensive. The place given is that to which the work refers, not necessarily that of publication. For further information on these works see especially *Chung-kuo ts'ung-shu tsung-lu*, which details the collections where they can be found, Hsieh Kuo-chen, *Ming-Ch'ing pi-chi t'an-ts'ung* and Franke, *An Introduction to the Sources of Ming History*, pp. 116-18.

Anon., *Yen-ching tsa-chi*, nineteenth century. Peking.

Ch'ai Sang, *Ching-shih ou-chi*, 1701. Peking.

Chou Hui, *Chin-ling so-shih*, 1610. Nanking.

Chou Mi, *Wu-lin chiu-shih*, c. 1280. Hang-chou.

Ch'ü Ta-chün, *Kuang-tung hsin-yü*, c. 1680. Kwangtung (mainly Ming period).

Fan Lien, *Yün-chien chü-mu ch'ao*, 1593. Hua-t'ing, Kiangsu.

Fan Tsu-shu (fl. 1863), *Hang-su i-feng*. Hang-chou.

Hsi-hsi shan-jen, *Wu-men hua-fang lu*, 1806. Courtesans of Su-chou.

Hsi-hu lao-jen, *Hsi-hu lao-jen fan-sheng lu*, c. 1250. Hang-chou.

Huang Wei, *P'eng-ch'uang lei-chi*, 1527. Su-chou.

Kan Hsi, *Pai-hsia so-yen*, mid-nineteenth century. Mostly Nanking.

Ku Ch'i-yüan, *K'e-tso chui-yü*, 1617. Nanking.

Ku Lu, *Ch'ing-chia lu*, 1830. Su-chou.

Ku Ts'ai, *Jung-mei chi-yu*, c. 1703. Ho-feng, western Hupeh.

Kuan-pu nai-te weng, *Tu-ch'eng chi-sheng*, 1235. Hang-chou.

Li Hsiu-fang (1794-1867), *Chen-chou feng-t'u chi*. Chen-chou, near Yang-chou.

Li Tou, *Yang-chou hua-fang lu*, 1796. Yang-chou.

Liu Ch'ing, *P'ien-k'e yü-hsien chi*, 1754. Fukien, Taiwan.

Liu Hsien-t'ing (1648-95), *Kuang-yang tsa-chi*. Hunan, Hupeh.

Lu Ts'an, *Keng-ssu pien*, c. 1520. Southern Kiangsu.

Meng Yüan-lao, *Tung-ching meng-hua lu*, 1147. K'ai-feng.

Tun Ch'ung, *Yen-ching sui-shih chi*, 1900. Festivals of Peking. This work has been translated into English by Derk Bodde in *Annual Customs and Festivals in Peking as Recorded in the* Yen-ching Sui-shih-chi *by Tun Li-ch'en*, Peiping, 1936; Hong Kong, 1965.

Wang Lin-heng, *Yüeh-chien pien*, 1601. Kwangtung.

Wu Ch'ang-yüan, *Ch'en-yüan shih-lüeh*, 1788. Peking.

Wu Tzu-mu, *Meng-liang lu*, c. 1274. Hang-chou.

Wu Ying-chi, *Liu-tu chien-wen lu*, c. 1644. Nanking.

Yang Ching-t'ing, *Tu-men chi-lüeh*, 1845. Peking.

——, and others, *Ch'ao-shih ts'ung-tsai*, 1887. Peking.

Yeh Meng-chu, *Yüeh-shih pien*, late seventeenth century. Sung-chiang.

Yü Huai, *Pan-ch'iao tsa-chi*, c. 1650. Courtesans of Nanking. This work has been translated into English by Howard S. Levy in *A Feast of Mist and Flowers, The Gay Quarters of Nanking at the End of the Ming*, Yokohama, 1966.

史 x: Genealogical Registers

OTTO BERKELBACH van der SPRENKEL

The aim of this chapter is, first, to give an account of the documents known as *tsung-p'u*, the so-called 'genealogical registers'; and second, to evaluate their usefulness as a source for Chinese social history. Their name is more accurately rendered as 'lineage' or 'family' registers:[1] the commonly used name is justified by the fact that, whatever else they may or may not contain, the greater part of their content consists of genealogical tables. These tables give information about the generations of a lineage, here defined as a group 'composed of the male agnatic descendants of a single ancestor together with their unmarried sisters and wives'.[2]

Such registers, in manuscript or privately printed, were both the products and embodiments of kin solidarity. Their contents were 'private' in that they concerned, and primarily interested, members of the lineage whose generations they chronicled. Their possession was at once a privilege and a responsibility, and reflected the holder's status in the lineage. It is therefore not surprising that very few of these documents passed into the hands of outsiders until the 1930s, when the kinship structure that had produced them and given them meaning was disintegrating under the impact of Westernisation and war.

During the last thirty years a few libraries have built up collections of *tsung-p'u*. In 1960 Taga Akigorō listed almost 3,000 which were then accessible to students in the following libraries: Japan, 1,510, of which 816 were in the Tōyō bunko, 436 in the Diet Library, and 237 in the Tokyo University Library; the United States, 933, of which 926 were in the East Asiatic Library of Columbia University; and China, 483, of which 353 were in the Peking National Library.[3] In other words, about 2,780 out of approxi-

---

[1] Other names often used are *tsu-p'u* and *chia-p'u*. From a formal point of view the terms *tsung*, *tsu* and *chia* should indicate lineages in decreasing order of magnitude, but they cannot be always so interpreted in register titles. A rough count of the 1,200 odd registers on pp. 80-185 of Taga's *Sōfu no kenkyū* shows nearly half (571) are called *tsung-p'u*; just under 200 are described as *tsu-p'u*; 225 have either *chia-p'u* or *chia-ch'eng* in their titles; 90 are designated *chih-p'u*, showing that the register covers one branch only of the lineage concerned; *shih-p'u* 世譜 , *shih-p'u* 氏譜 , and *fang-p'u* are used, but less often.

[2] See Maurice Freedman, *Chinese Lineage and Society: Fukien and Kwangtung*, p. 1.

[3] Taga makes no reference to the Library of Congress. See his *Sōfu no kenkyū*, pp. 72-189, 314-452. As far as I have been able to find out in the course of a brief search of the Librarian's

83

mately 3,000 (93 per cent) of *tsung-p'u* in the public domain in 1960 were held in the libraries of only three cities. This has to some degree inhibited their exploitation and has meant, as well, that much of the pioneering work in this field has of necessity been done intensively, using only one or two registers, rather than extensively, using a number large enough to enable well-founded conclusions to be drawn as to their norms of content and presentation. Fortunately, thanks to the development of photo-copying techniques, the concentration of holdings no longer restricts the generalised study of these documents to Tokyo, Peking, and New York.

The 3,000 or so *tsung-p'u* presently available for research surely represent a mere fraction of what existed a generation ago.[4] What we now have can be regarded only as a sample. There must have been a great deal of destruction of family records during the civil and foreign wars that afflicted China during the crucial years 1910 to 1950; and the Communist régime has demonstrated hostility to the propertied gentry lineage as an institution and to all its works, including genealogical registers. For these reasons it is unlikely that existing holdings of this type of literature will be much increased by new finds.

The Nature of Extant Registers

If we wish to use this material and draw from it conclusions about population changes, life expectancy, marriage and the family, etc., we should be quite clear about the nature of our sample, its qualities, and, especially, its limitations. As regards the latter, there are several points to be made.

Firstly, a lineage that desires, and can afford, to produce a printed register is clearly one that is well-to-do,[5] possesses a measure of corporate consciousness,[6] and reckons men of education among its members. These registers therefore reflect the circumstances and customary behaviour of the

---

Annual Reports, the *Quarterly Journal of Acquisitions,* etc., the library had no significant holding of *tsung-p'u* in 1960, and appears not to have acquired one since then.

[4] Hu Hsien-chin's assertion (*Common Descent Group,* p. 41) that 'nearly all *tsu* have a genealogy' is surely an overstatement. However, the total number of lineage registers produced, allowing for periodic revisions, and reckoning the size of editions at about 100 copies, must have been very large indeed.

[5] Production of a genealogical register would normally entail widespread support and active participation from *tsu* members, and a considerable financial outlay. For example, the cost of producing 100 copies of the 1771 revision of the *Tung-t'ing Wang-shih chia-p'u* (Wu county, Kiangsu), 26 chapters in 30 volumes, was 716 taels. The fourth revision, in 1900, of the *Hsiang-hsiang Tseng-shih ssu-hsiu tsu-p'u,* 1,744 leaves and 16 volumes, involved the co-operation of 109 members of the *tsu,* and cost $5,469. The size of the edition is variously given as 114 and 123 copies.

Father Ravary, about a century ago, wrote: 'La réimpression des *Kia-pou* entraine de fortes dépenses. En moyenne, chacun des volumes qui les compose, coûte de 120 à 150 piastres (720 à 950 francs).' 'Les tablettes des ancêtres et les registres de la famille en Chine', p. 766.

[6] Johanna Meskill raises the interesting question whether the lineage produces the register, or the register the lineage. Her argument is worth quoting: 'It may be that, far from having to be well organized to produce a genealogy, a lineage need barely exist. In the case of many

well-off rural gentry, the urban bourgeoisie, or combinations of the two: they will not yield information about Chinese society as a whole.

Secondly, our sample is restricted spatially as well as socially. As regards geographical coverage, some parts of China are extremely well represented; others hardly at all. For example, Taga's catalogue of 1,197 geographically assignable Chinese *tsung-p'u* in Japanese libraries lists 433 registers from Kiangsu, 378 from Chekiang, and 118 from Anhwei. In other words, 929, or more than three-fourths of the whole, come from three provinces comprising, roughly, the Yangtze delta region. The rest of China together contributes less than a quarter of the material. Apart from the three provinces mentioned, the only others which show significant numbers of registers are Kiangsi (43), Kwangtung (40), Shantung (40), Hopeh (34), Hunan (20), and Shansi (18).[7] It seems incredible that these figures could be due simply to the prevalence or otherwise of lineages in the various provinces of the empire. One would of course expect high totals from the riverine provinces of the lower Yangtze—on such grounds as general prosperity (it is one of Chi Ch'ao-ting's 'key economic areas');[8] the scholarly tradition which is particularly strong there, as witnessed by the region's high incidence of *shu-yüan* (literary academies);[9] and its outstanding record as an exporter of officials, especially in the Ming and Ch'ing periods.[10] Such considerations,

first editions of genealogies, at any rate, the editing and printing of a genealogy created the organized kinship group rather than vice versa. That is, making a formal genealogy may have been the first step on the road that led an agnatic group to incorporate property and thus to create itself a lineage. Even updated editions of older genealogies, except for those printed at frequent intervals, do not necessarily presuppose that a highly organized lineage maintained itself in the interval between editions. In many instances, all it seems to have taken to produce a first or later edition of a genealogy was a few wealthy individuals who could defray the printing and other expenses' ('The Chinese Genealogy as a Research Source', p. 141). This hypothesis seems not impossible, at least as far as the initial production of a register is concerned, though even then I think the sequence of events she suggests would be the exception and not the rule. On the other hand, when a register is kept up to date (which implies that workable arrangements made by the lineage for doing this exist and are made use of), and is periodically revised, printed and distributed, it seems unreasonable to imagine that the lineage would or could cease to exist as a self-conscious entity during the intervals between revisions, even when these were as long as 60 or 100 years. See also note 13 below.

[7] Taga, *Sōfu*, pp. 190-219, together with dot map and table, pages 62-3.

[8] Chi Ch'ao-ting, *Key Economic Areas*, pp. 124-9, 146-50.

[9] See Tilemann Grimm, *Erziehung und Politik im konfuzianischen China der Ming-Zeit* (Hamburg, 1960), p. 117. Grimm, using information taken respectively from Wang Ch'i's *Hsü Wen-hsien t'ung-k'ao* and the Wan-li edition of the *Ta-Ming i-t'ung chih*, gives the number of *shu-yüan* towards the end of Ming in southeast China as 258 and 293; and those in five northern provinces (Chingshih, Shantung, Honan, Shansi, Shensi) as 63 and 68. In Szechwan there were 19 or 21 and in Kwangsi 7 or 11; none was recorded for Yunnan or for Kweichow.

[10] See my article on 'The Geographical Background of the Ming Civil Service', *Journal of the Economic and Social History of the Orient* IV (1961), pp. 302-36. Chekiang, Kiangsi and Fukien, clustering together around the lower Yangtze region of Southeast China, make up together only a fifth of the country's population (20·85 per cent). Men from these three provinces, however, account for well over a third of the personnel of the upper civil service (35·5 per cent).

however, do not appear to provide a sufficient explanation of the very severe disparities in the numbers of extant registers from the different provinces; and it is, for example, disconcerting to find that Fukien, where gentry kinship structures were important, can muster only eleven *tsung-p'u*, and that an area as large and populous as Szechwan contributes only six. These facts impose another limitation on our use of this material: namely, that findings based on quantitative studies of *tsung-p'u* from the lower Yangtze region cannot, without further supporting evidence, be held valid for other parts of China.

Finally there is the question of the temporal span for which the registers provide reliable data. While the view of Chao I (1727-1814) that the construction of genealogies goes back to China's high antiquity is clearly unacceptable, there is no reason to question his assertion that they first became socially important in the third century A.D. with the introduction of the *chiu-p'in chung-cheng* system (the 'Nine categories and the Impartial and Just') for classing candidates for public office.[11] No genealogies, however, have come down to us from those early times: there are indeed very few still extant that go back to before the sixteenth century. A useful guide to the temporal distribution of presently available genealogical registers is provided by another of Taga's tables, which classifies 1,550 *tsung-p'u* according to the periods in which they were compiled.[12] This gives the following results: Yüan, 1; Ming, 13; Ch'ing, 1,214 (of which the first four reigns, from 1644 to 1795, account for only 88, and the Kuang-hsü and Hsüan-t'ung reigns, from 1875 to 1911, for 473); and the Republic, 322.

The position is in fact both better, and worse, than these figures would suggest. Better, because genealogical registers were constantly revised and reprinted, the most recent editions almost always preserving material taken from the earlier ones. For example, my edition of the *Ju-kao Yu-shih tsung-p'u*, the register of the Yu lineage of Ju-kao, Kiangsu, is dated 1849, but much of the information it contains is repeated from the first edition of 1532, and the revisions of 1611 and 1727. A large proportion of the late Ch'ing and Republican *tsung-p'u* are in fact revisions that bring up to date earlier editions of the register of the same lineage, and all of these will include some material going back to the time of the original compilation.[13]

---

[11] For this system see the excellent study by Donald Holzman, 'Les débuts du système médiéval de choix et de classement des fonctionnaires: les Neuf Catégories et l'Impartial et Juste', *Mélanges publiés par l'Institut des Hautes Études Chinoises* I (1957), pp. 387-414. Hsiao Kung-ch'üan (*Rural Control*, p. 665) writes: 'During the Six Dynasties (fourth to sixth centuries), when the line between "high" families and commoners became quite rigidly drawn, acquaintance with the *p'u-tieh* (genealogical records) attained the dignity of an independent branch of "learning".'

[12] Taga, *Sōfu*, pp. 220-49.

[13] To quote again from Ravary's interesting article: 'Après un temps plus ou moins considérable, quarante, cinquante ou soixante ans, les volumes, formant un *Kia-pou*, sont réimprimés'

But the position is also rather worse than it appears to be for two reasons. The first, and less important, is that information given in the registers for the period after, say, 1880-90, is unusable for certain lines of inquiry, e.g., the working out of life expectancy tables.[14]

The second reason is more serious, and concerns the reliability of the data supplied by the registers for the earliest generations figuring in the lineage history. It is an unfortunate fact that almost all the genealogical records presented in *tsung-p'u* comprise earlier fictional and later factual parts. The *Tseng-shih ssu-hsiu tsu-p'u* used by Hu Hsien-chin offers a good example. She writes:

> The *tsu* of Tsêng in Honan believes it can trace its descent from a prince of the Hsia dynasty, whose father reigned from 2218-2168 B.C., and from Tsêng Shên, the disciple of Confucius. They point out a fifteenth-generation descendant of Tsêng Shên, who lived around 10 A.D., and record the separation of three brothers in the nineteenth generation, one of whom moved from his native Shantung to Kiangsi, from which province a branch migrated to Honan around 1460 . . . These attempts to trace the origin of one's *tsu* to some important personage and to claim this or that famous individual as one's ancestor have interest as a sociological phenomenon rather than for historical accuracy.[15]

Such attempts fill the pages of the fictional part of the genealogy. It goes without saying that most of the information presented in this part is quite untrustworthy. Eberhard's statement that 'after A.D. 1000, family genealogies yield abundant material, which has not yet been used' would appear (for quantitative studies certainly) to be unacceptable.[16]

What I have called the factual part of the genealogy begins with the man who first established the lineage in the place where (according to the register) it now exists, and who moved there from a district where his own forefathers were settled. This man is described as the *shih-ch'ien tsu*, the 'first ancestor who moved', and the record of his descendants is usually fuller,

---

('Les tablettes des ancêtres', p. 766). Hu Hsien-chin writes: 'Genealogies are printed and revised from time to time, ideally every thirty years at least, but actually at irregular intervals' (*Common Descent Group*, p. 41). She gives the following examples: *Huang-shih ch'ung-hsiu tsu-p'u* (of Chiang-tu in Kiangsu), fourteen editions from 1618 to 1920, or every twenty-three years; *T'an-shih hsü-hsiu tsu-p'u* (Kiangsi), twelve editions from 1423 to 1921, or every forty-five years. The register of the Yu lineage mentioned above was revised four times from 1532 to 1849, or roughly every century.

[14] For example, a register in which no deaths are recorded that took place after 1930 cannot provide full information for the quinquennial cohort born between 1876-80. Members of this group who died before reaching fifty to fifty-four will be recorded, but the register cannot tell us at what age the others died. Statistics based on this incomplete information would necessarily understate the life expectancy of this (not to mention later) cohorts, and all births after about 1850 or 1855 would have to be excluded.

[15] Hu Hsien-chin, *Common Descent Group*, pp. 45-6.

[16] Eberhard, *Settlement and Social Change*, p. 39.

more detailed and more accurate than that provided for the generations before his own.[17]

The point of transition from fiction to fact is usually quite clearly marked. A good example, which also demonstrates a more sophisticated approach to lineage history than is commonly found, is an essay on the history of the Ts'ao lineage of Shanghai, contributed to the 1721 edition and reprinted in the 1925 edition of the *Shang-hai Ts'ao-shih tsu-p'u*. This is by Ts'ao I-shih (1678-1736, *chin-shih* in 1730), and is divided into three recognisably distinct sections. The first begins with a certain Ts'ao An, 'the first to bear the Ts'ao surname', whose forebears are traced back to the Yellow Emperor, and whose descendants were enfeoffed at the time of the Chou conquest. This section concludes with the remark: 'Of the later fate of this family nothing is known'. Reference is then made to another Ts'ao lineage, taking its origin from Chen-to, the younger brother of Chou Wu-wang, who became lord of the domain of Ts'ao and was the progenitor of, among others, Ts'ao Hsü, 'who personally attended Confucius'. Again we are told that 'the line of descent . . . cannot be ascertained'. Other bearers of the surname are mentioned from the Han and Six Dynasties periods, but with the words, 'their parentage is not recorded'. This first section closes with the observation that 'during the Sui and T'ang the Ts'ao produced no illustrious sons'; and the writer further notes that 'the disorders of the later T'ang and the changes of the Five Dynasties saw a decline in the practice of keeping family registers'.

The second, quasi-historical section, opens with the Sung. The author mentions a number of historical figures with the name Ts'ao, and notably Ts'ao Pin (931-99), who eventually rose to be Chief of the Imperial Chancellery. Most of the persons named held high official posts, and, we are told, 'when [Sung] Kao-tsung crossed to the south [of the Yangtze, in 1127], members of the Ts'ao clan followed and also came south'. I-shih mentions several lineages holding themselves to be descended from one or other of

---

[17] For prestige reasons, and to give greater 'depth' to the generation record, a lineage will sometimes take as its *shih-ch'ien tsu*, not the man who first transferred the lineage to its present location, but the leader of an earlier removal. For example, the Yu lineage of Ju-kao regards as its 'first ancestor who moved' a certain Yu Ch'eng (born *c*. 1000), who moved away from the Yu's earlier home in Chin-chiang county, Fukien, to establish a new branch in Ku-su county, Kiangsu. The *Yu Register* is unable to give either the exact birth and death dates of Yu Ch'eng or the year of the removal. Yu Ch'eng's descendant in the thirteenth generation was Yu Nan-hu (1373-1451), and he it was who left Ku-su for Ju-kao county (also in Kiangsu) in early Ming. For the Ju-kao branch of the lineage, Yu Nan-hu has every right to be regarded as their *shih-ch'ien tsu*; but to accept him as 'founder' and reckon the first generation from him would restrict the ancestral record to only fifteen generations, a much less impressive total than the twenty-seven that result from taking Yu Ch'eng instead. It was therefore the spirits of Yu Ch'eng and his wife née Chang that were invoked at the spring and autumn ancestral services in the lineage temple as 'first ancestors'. On the other hand, of the 502 pages of genealogical tables set out in the register, only thirty-two are devoted to the descendants of Yu Ch'eng in the direct line to Yu Nan-hu, while 470 record the many descendants of the latter.

these notabilities, and in particular a certain group that gradually made its way to Chia-ting county in Su-chou, and later moved from there to Shanghai. This, he declares, is the only group entitled to claim descent from Ts'ao Pin. It is of interest that he earlier states that Ts'ao Pin himself could not trace his own ancestry further back than his father. I-shih also writes:

> In the disorders that marked the end of the Sung, genealogies were lost. With the coming of the Yüan . . . the descendants [of Ts'ao Pin in south China] all chose to live in seclusion, and were no longer seen [in the world of affairs]. Yet the Ts'ao family of Shanghai knows that it is descended from Ts'ao Pin. This is because the line of descent has been orally transmitted [in a family that] has not dared to forget its ancestral sacrifices. From the later years of the Yüan down to early Ming the order of generations and the names [of individuals], and even of the ancestor who was the first to move to Chia-ting, cannot be ascertained. Alas! Alas!

This cry fittingly ends the second section.

The concluding section of this historical sketch is completely factual, and is written in a homely and anecdotal style that contrasts strongly with the consciously scholarly style of the earlier parts. It begins with I-shih's 'grandfather's great-great-grandfather', Ts'ao Meng-ch'un, who is revered by the Shanghai Ts'ao lineage as its *shih-ch'ien tsu*. He left the family home in Chia-ting, and moved into the house of his mother's parents, where he received some training in medicine. 'When he had achieved modest success [as a doctor] he moved to the sea coast [i.e. to Shanghai], and soon after this he died.' Meng-ch'un's birth and death dates are not given; nor the year he established himself at Shanghai. The real 'founder' of the lineage was clearly his son, Ts'ao Shou-yü (1511-1600), who not only achieved longevity (ninety *sui*) but sired four sons. Nevertheless, the genealogical tables of the register begin with Meng-ch'un as representative of the first generation. Ts'ao I-shih belonged to the seventh generation; and the 1925 recension of the register is able to record members of the fifteenth generation.[18]

In assessing the value of these documents as sources, it is essential to be quite clear as to the reliability of the information they contain. From the above discussion it seems fair to accept as generally reliable the data provided

---

[18] Translated from *Shang-hai Ts'ao-shih tsu-p'u* 1.26a-30b. What is particularly interesting about this essay is the openly sceptical attitude which I-shih displays about the relation of his own lineage to the illustrious personages that bore the name Ts'ao in China's distant historical and legendary past. Such expressions as 'of this family nothing is known' or 'their parentage is not recorded' are unusual in writings of this kind, in which piety is generally more in evidence than regard for historical accuracy. The only point on which Ts'ao I-shih is absolutely insistent is the validity of the line of descent of his own Shanghai lineage branch of the Ts'ao clan from Ts'ao Pin. All this is in contrast with, for instance, the claims of the Tseng lineage of Honan, described by Hu Hsien-chin.

A feature, characteristic for very many southern lineage histories, is the reference to 'crossing the Yangtze' in 1127 in the train of emperor Kao-tsung—the event that marks the division between the Northern and Southern Sung dynasties—when, in historical fact, great numbers of northern families later migrated south to escape the Mongols.

by the registers, always bearing in mind the three limitations previously pointed out: first, that the registers relate to a particular social class and not necessarily to Chinese society as a whole; second, that they relate to certain regions of China and not necessarily to the country as a whole; and third, that their genealogical tables can usually be accepted as accurate only for the generations subsequent to that of the 'first ancestor who moved' to the present site of the lineage in question.

Arrangement and Content of the Yu-shih tsung-p'u

It may be useful at this point, before proceeding to a more detailed examination of the genealogical tables, to give some account of general arrangement and the content of a representative lineage register,[19] the 1849 *Yu-shih tsung-p'u*. It consists of some preliminary matter, followed by twelve chapters, and is bound up in seven volumes (*ts'e*). The preliminaries comprise: (a) several prefaces to the 1849 edition, contributed by local notabilities (of other surnames) and by the chief compiler and his assistants; (b) the collected prefaces to the earlier editions, beginning with that of 1532; (c) reproductions of inscriptions on the tablets in the ancestral temple; (d) instructions to the reader explaining the plan of the work and the rules followed in its compilation; (e) a list, with names and titles, of the editors and assistant compilers of the present and earlier editions; (f) a detailed table of contents.

The first chapter is taken up with a recital of 'gracious decrees manifesting Imperial favour' awarded to members of the lineage. A dozen or more of these are handsomely reproduced, the earliest dating from 1182 and the last from Hsien-feng eighth year, the ninth day of the second lunar month (23 March 1858).[20] They are followed by three reproductions of the imperial signature.

Chapter 2 begins with an illustrated section, which includes: (a) a series

---

[19] Very different from the genealogical registers discussed in this chapter, which all relate to a single lineage or segment of a lineage, are the 'giant genealogies' of 'clans' constructed by discovering (or sometimes fabricating) relations between lineages with a common surname. These lineages, regarded as 'houses' of the clan, may be scattered geographically over an area large enough to include one or more provinces. The evidential value of these works is high for certain types of material, low for others. Eberhard's *Social Mobility in Traditional China* is largely based on data drawn from two such works: the *Ling-nan Wu-shih tsung-p'u*, and the *Jung-shih p'u-tieh*; and his book gives a good descriptive account of these works and their contents. See, however, the very pertinent remarks of Freedman in *Chinese Lineage and Society*, pp. 26ff. It hardly needs saying that the *Yu-shih tsung-p'u* is representative of the 'lineage' and not of the 'clan' register.

[20] The last preface of the *Yu-shih tsung-p'u* is dated 1849, and this year is properly taken as the date of the edition. It is clear, however, that the printing of the volumes was held up for more than a decade, and that the editors took advantage of the delay to insert later material. The Imperial decree of 1858 is an example. Furthermore, the births of children are recorded for 1855, 1858, and 1860. The outbreak of the Taiping rebellion was probably the reason why the production of the register was postponed.

of rather conventionalised ancestor portraits; (b) pictorial maps showing the mansions and lands of the lineage in Ju-kao county; (c) the entrance and front elevation of the ancestral temple; and (d) the lineage burial grounds, showing the positions of individual graves. This last group includes seventeen maps, all drawn in considerable detail. The section is followed by two others, devoted to family instructions (*tsu-hsün*) and admonitions (*tsu-chieh*). The former, twenty in all, begin by stating the principles that should guide the conduct of officials, of children and parents, wives and husbands, younger and elder brothers, and friends (the traditional Confucian five relationships). Other topics include entry into adulthood, marriage, the performance of sacrifices, the ritual conduct of interviews, food, and dress. These exhortations to right behaviour are then supplemented by warnings against wrong behaviour. The second list is a short one, with only ten items, amongst which are those warning that lineage members should avoid pride and extravagance, but equally eschew meanness and pettiness; they should never be disrespectful or impudent, but equally eschew fawning and toadying. Other admonitions are against quarrelling, drinking to intoxication, gambling, and lewd indulgence. Characteristically, there is also a warning against engaging in litigation.[21] The chapter ends with two further sections, the first on the *tzu-p'ai* system, by which particular characters are chosen by the lineage to use in a certain order in the personal names of male members so as to indicate the generation to which they belong, and the second setting out the form of service to be observed in the ancestral sacrifices (*chi-li*) in the temple.

The main part of the register, comprising chapters 3 to 10, contains the genealogical tables. The first twenty generations are quickly gone through in chapter 3; generations twenty-one to twenty-five occupy chapters 4 to 7; and space is allowed for generations twenty-six to thirty in chapters 8 to 10. The latest generation for which information is more or less completely given in the printed text is the twenty-sixth, though there are a few entries for the twenty-seventh, and one or two births are even recorded for the twenty-eighth. The extra pages provided for generations twenty-nine and thirty clearly show that the volumes as printed were intended to be added to in handwriting by their possessors for two or more generations to come.

The last few pages of chapter 10 contain the names of members of the lineage who achieved official rank or were awarded special honours. Altogether 105 persons are mentioned: twenty of them in the twelve generations before this branch of the lineage was established in Ju-kao; fourteen in the eight succeeding generations; and seventy-one in the twenty-first and later generations. Chapter 11 is devoted to biographies, *lieh-chuan*, of which

[21] For a comprehensive treatment of this aspect of *tsung-p'u* studies see the pioneering work of Liu Hui-chen (Wang), *The Traditional Chinese Clan Rules*. Cf. also Hu Hsien-chin, *Common Descent Group*, pp. 59ff.

fifty-four recount the lives of male members (two of them include wife as well as husband), while eight are biographies of wives only. The final chapter has the title *i-wen*, 'literary productions', and consists mainly of poetry written either by members of the Yu lineage or by poets who were their close friends.

The entries in the *Yu-shih tsung-p'u*, as in most other registers, follow a standard pattern. Below are the items recorded, in the order in which they appear. Two comments are needed: first, that for many members of the lineage, there will be items that do not apply (it even happens, occasionally, that if nothing else is known about a man, only his personal name and his father's name are recorded); and second, that a good deal of variation exists between different *tsung-p'u* in the kind and amount of information they provide: in general, more is given in a 'lineage' or 'branch' register than in a 'clan' register.[22]

1 The subject's personal name (*ming*) and, if there has been a change of name, his later name.

2 His relationship to his father, i.e., biological or adopted son; his position in the family, i.e., eldest (or second, third, etc.) son; and his father's personal name.

3 His 'style' (*tzu*) and, where necessary, his 'literary appellation' (*hao*).

4 His education (e.g. attendance at the county or prefectural school); his highest examination success (degree gained, with date); his highest official post; titles and honours.

5 His date of birth, given in the form: reign-period (*nien-hao*) with the

---

[22] W. Eberhard, who deserves credit for his early realisation of the importance of this type of source, would hardly, if he had been able to consult and compare with one another a reasonably wide range of registers (including 'lineage' as well as 'clan' registers), have committed himself to the following statements: 'The genealogies ... (a) usually do not mention the daughters of the family, so that any conclusions on changes of fertility have to be made on the basis of the assumption that there were as many daughters born as were sons (an assumption which, however, seems to be a safe one), (b) they very often do not mention the wives and their origin, so that we cannot draw clear conclusions upon polygamy and intermarriage systems ... (c) they do not mention babies who died shortly after birth, nor even, it seems, sons who lived less than to the age of at least 15. Perhaps only those who married were mentioned' ('Mobility in South Chinese Families', p. 18). In the dozen or so registers I have personally examined, births of daughters are generally recorded, certainly for the six or seven most recent generations, while in many the marriages of daughters out of the lineage and the surnames of the bridegrooms are noted. Far from it being the case that 'very often' wives are not mentioned, I have not so far seen a register that omits them. Sons who died young are certainly recorded: the character *shang* is often used where a person has died before reaching marriageable age, and seems to indicate death in or before the fourteenth year. The character *yao* often appears against the names of sons that died in infancy: in one register, the *Ts'ao-shih tsu-p'u* already mentioned, *yao* is defined as meaning 'to die before completing the sixth year'. Finally, a statistical survey of the same Ts'ao lineage showed that, of 465 males listed, 92 died unmarried (most of whom lived into middle or old age). This disposes of the suggestion that 'only those who married' were recorded.

sexagenary cyclical characters which fix the year, followed by the number of the day, and the horary character for the hour.

6 His date of death (given in similar detail).

7 If he enjoyed exceptional longevity, his age at death by Chinese reckoning (*sui*).

8 His wife's surname. If the wife's father held official rank, his full name (exceptionally, in other instances as well).

9 Any meritorious title conferred on the wife (instances of wives who were widowed at an early age and did not remarry are specially noted, particularly if a *p'ai-lou* or honorific arch was decreed to reward their constancy).

10 The wife's birth date in full (as for 5 above).

11 The wife's death date in full.

12 If the wife enjoyed exceptional longevity, her age at death by Chinese reckoning (see 7 above).

13 If, after the death of his first wife, the husband marries again, some or all of the information under 8 to 12 for the second (third, etc.) wife. Should the husband, having a principal wife living, marry a secondary wife, the same information for her.

14 The exact situation of the graves of husband and wife (or wives) in the lineage burial grounds.

15 The sons born to the marriage, listed by name. Whether a son died in infancy. Where a son is adopted in, the name of the biological father, identification of the child as the eldest (or second, third, etc.) son of his biological father. If a son is adopted and becomes the adopted son of another member of the lineage (perhaps moving from his own to another branch of the lineage), the name of the person adopting him, and the relationship of the adoptive father to the biological father. Cases of 'joint heirship' (in which a boy is adopted by, for example, a childless uncle as his son and heir, while at the same time remaining the son and heir of his biological father).

16 The daughters born to the marriage, enumeration, personal names not given. For daughters who married, the husbands' surnames (exceptionally, their personal name and their fathers' names).

17 If the subject had children by more than one wife, the child's biological mother (for daughters as well as sons).

18 If the subject entered religion, becoming a Taoist or Buddhist monk, the expression *ch'u-chia* (literally, 'left the family'), immediately after his personal name (then, as he no longer has any connection with the lineage, his entry is terminated).

How reliable is the information given in these genealogical tables? We will endeavour to answer this question, first, in general terms; second, by reference to a number of particular points. Speaking generally, my own view tallies exactly with that of Maurice Freedman, who writes: 'I am still under the same impression . . . that the written genealogy of a local lineage (but not of a higher-order lineage or clan) was more or less immune to fudging . . . A written genealogy may commit many sins of omission (consigning ignominious men to oblivion), but it is unlikely in the case of a local lineage to be allowed to carry a positive statement of untruth'.[23]

Of special points relating to the reliability of the information these documents contain, I will raise here only three. Firstly, most registers show evidence of the extreme care taken by the editors to achieve an accurate record. Chinese books, like those of other countries, have their share of misprints. In some registers these have been picked up, and correct characters, hand-stamped in red, have been inserted. I have also seen text corrections written in with the brush. Once even, in a copy of the Yu Register, I discovered that two double pages in Chapter 5 (23ab and 24ab) had been re-engraved to correct a serious mistake (two persons confused with each other), and by oversight both versions had been bound into the volume. Since *tsung-p'u* were highly prized as 'correct records' of the life of the lineage, it is not surprising to find such care lavished upon them.

Secondly, accurate birth and death dates are essential for studies of life expectancy, fertility, etc. As far as the *tsung-p'u* are concerned, a quite extraneous circumstance goes far to guarantee their reliability. This is the practice of exchanging the *pa-tzu* or eight characters, i.e. the four pairs of cyclical characters denoting the year, month, day and hour of birth, of the two parties to a betrothal. These were necessary for the drawing of horoscopes, and the compatibility or otherwise of the horoscopes often determined whether negotiations for the marriage would be pursued. It was therefore essential that the exact time indicated by the *pa-tzu* was correct.[24]

Thirdly, relevant to the question of the use of *tsung-p'u* for demographic studies, for example, is the fact that not all descendants necessarily appear in the genealogical tables, as 'omission from the genealogy' was a punishment sometimes inflicted on a lineage member for notorious and repeated bad behaviour. Such omissions can, however, sometimes be discovered and made good. Hu Hsien-chin quotes the following from the rules concerning this punishment in the register of the Yang lineage of Wan-t'ung:

> A man who disgraces his ancestors, or one whose offences are well-known, even though he is not tried in court, is to have his name omitted from the genealogy. If such a person should have a son, it should be mentioned

---

[23] Freedman, *Chinese Lineage and Society*, p. 42.
[24] See e.g., Justus Doolittle, *Social Life of the Chinese* (New York, 1865), Vol. I, pp. 65–6. Despite its now centenarian status, this is still an excellent, and readable, work of reference.

under the names of his parents: their grandson is so-and-so. Again under the name of the son of the criminal, it is to be noted: his mother was so-and-so. His birth dates should be correctly stated.[25]

So, provided only that the man omitted from the genealogy had become the father of a son before incurring this punishment, his absence from the genealogical table would be clearly, if silently, indicated.

Usefulness of the Registers

It remains only to note some of the areas of research into which lineage registers can be made to throw light. Naturally, the material in the *tsung-p'u* will usually need 'processing' before becoming exploitable to maximum advantage. Further, much of the material, though by no means all, calls for quantification if best results are to be obtained. Following are some suggested problems, the investigation of which could be significantly advanced by making use of the data in lineage registers.

First, life-tables: the *tsung-p'u* constitute a documentary source for population history which no other people can match. The only comparable material in Europe relates to the genealogies of royal and noble families; material which is both much less voluminous and also refers to a smaller and more atypical social group. All *tsung-p'u* contain birth and death dates for (virtually) all the male members of the lineage, and for the women who married into the lineage. By exploiting reasonable numbers of registers it is quite possible to assemble numerically large quinquennial cohorts from at least 1700 on (possibly from 1650) down to about 1860 and 1870.[26]

Second, marriage and the family: there is a whole complex of problems associated with marriage and the family which the *tsung-p'u* can help to clarify. Among them are: (a) the proportion of males, surviving to and beyond marriageable age, who do not in fact marry (my own investigations show that this figure could be as high as 20-25 per cent); (b) the size of the biological family; (c) the number of first marriages (or second, etc.) that are either childless, or fail to produce a male heir; (d) the number of families that have one, two, three, etc. children, and the distribution of boys and girls among them (the answers to this last problem, especially if we take our figures only from the more recent generations in the genealogical tables, which regularly list daughters as well as sons, make it possible for us to measure the prevalence of female infanticide in the lineages, and for the periods, concerned); (e) the lower and upper age-limits of child-bearing

---

[25] *Common Descent Group*, pp. 136-7. The quotation is from the *Wan-t'ung Yang-shih tsung-p'u* (1872) 1.5b.

[26] This kind of work can also produce results of interest to people other than demographers. My own preparation of life tables from a number of registers from the lower Yangtze region showed a very marked impact of the Taiping rebellion on the life expectancy of cohorts from about 1805-9 on.

among the mothers of these families (exact answers to this question can perhaps not be given, as still-births are almost certainly never entered on the genealogical tables, and nor are the births of children who died before completing their first, or second, even third, fourth year—even so, with the material we have, it is possible to arrive at useful approximations); (f) the way in which patterns of life expectancy vary between men and women, and in which the pattern for women is affected by the frequency of death in childbirth; (g) the proportion of men who marry more than once, and the degree to which the taking of a secondary wife while the principal wife is still living is associated with the absence of an heir to continue the line; (h) the frequency with which widows remarry; (i) the patterns of adoption (are eldest sons of a junior branch most often selected for adoption into a senior branch, and conversely?); (j) the frequency of cases of 'joint heirship', and the circumstances in which this device is most likely to be made use of. These are only some of the problems to which answers could certainly be found if a sufficiently large-scale investigation of *tsung-p'u* genealogical tables were undertaken.

Third, inter-lineage relations: the genealogical tables have little contribution to make to what Freedman calls 'the system of violence within which lineages stood opposed and allied'.[27] On the other hand, they contain an immense amount of material on marriage links between lineages. In the *Shang-hai Ts'ao-shih tsu-p'u*, for example, the surnames are given for 577 wives of men of the lineage: most of them relating to generations 6 to 14, the latest in the register. The eight surnames that occur most often are, in descending order of frequency: Chang, Wang, Chu, Hsü, Ch'en, Li, Lu, and P'an. There are also 326 surnames recorded for the husbands of women who married out of the Ts'ao lineage in the same generations. The six most frequent are: Chu, Chang, Wang, Lu, Shen, and Hsü. This is reasonably good evidence for the existence of reciprocal marriage links between Ts'ao, Chu and Lu lineages (Hsü might perhaps be added); but the surnames Chang, Wang, and Li are so extremely common that the mere fact of their presence in the lists means very little, and there are likely to be several quite unrelated lineages of those names living in the area. Another register, the *Li Wen-chuang kung chia-ch'eng* (edition of 1902),[28] records 3,284 marriages of male members of the lineage (giving the surnames of all but thirty of their spouses), and 1,853 marriages of females of the lineage (giving in every case the surname of the husband). Fairly full information about the births and marriages of daughters seems to be given from the twenty-first generation to the twenty-seventh, the last in the register (approximately from about the middle of the seventeenth century on). The most frequently appearing

---

[27] Freedman, *Chinese Lineage and Society*, p. 97.
[28] This impressive work chronicles the descendants of Li Ch'iao-mu of the Southern Sung (died 1147).

surnames of the women marrying into the lineage (with the number of times they occur) are: Liu 220, Yang 182, Chou 170, Chang 149, T'ang 139, Wang 124, T'an 123, and Huang 115. The nine most frequently appearing surnames of the husbands of Li women marrying out are: Yang 137, Liu 119, T'ang 97, Chou 85, Chang 78, Wang 73, Ch'eng 66, Huang 61, and T'an 61. The correspondences are striking.

Studies along these lines could be carried out most effectively if (a) several *tsung-p'u* relating to lineages all living in the same area were looked at together, such a group being now able to be selected quite easily (though mainly for the lower Yangtze region) thanks to Taga's list of *tsung-p'u* classified by area;[29] and (b) use were made of the relevant *hsien* gazetteers, in particular of the tables of local examination successes, and of the biographies of local worthies.

Finally, as some sort of corrective to the general drift of suggestions here put forward as to how the genealogies can best be turned to good account— a drift that naturally enough reflects the present writer's own interests and competencies—let me quote, and end with, the following stirring text: it illustrates, I believe, not a competing, but a companionable approach:

> The study of Chinese clan and lineage genealogies from a sociological point of view has barely begun. The few people engaged in exploiting the material tend to look at genealogies merely as sources of demographic, institutional and biographical data—in short, as texts of social history. A genealogy is much more than that, as we can see. It is a set of claims to origin and relationships, a charter, a map of dispersion, a framework for wide-ranging social organization, a blue-print for action. It is a political statement—and therefore a perfect subject for the anthropologist.[30]

BIBLIOGRAPHY

Baker, Hugh D.R., 'The Five Great Clans of the New Territories', *Journal of the Hong Kong Branch of the Royal Asiatic Society* VI (1966), pp. 25-47.

——, *A Chinese Lineage Village, Sheung Shui*, London, 1968.

Chi Ch'ao-ting, *Key Economic Areas in Chinese History as Revealed in the Development of Public Works for Water Control*, London, 1938.

Eberhard, Wolfram, 'Mobility in South Chinese Families', *Sinologica* VI (1959), pp. 16-24.

——, 'Research on the Chinese Family', *Sociologus* IX (1959), pp. 1-11; revised and reprinted in *Settlement and Social Change in Asia* (London, 1967), pp. 28-42.

[29] For example, in Kiangsu, seventeen registers are listed from Tan-t'u representing fourteen different surnames; eleven from Tan-yang; twenty-one from Chiang-yin; seventeen from Wu-hsien; etc.

[30] Freedman, *Chinese Lineage and Society*, p. 31.

Eberhard, Wolfram, 'Social Mobility and Migration of South Chinese Families' (paper read in 1961), reprinted in *Settlement and Social Change in Asia* (London, 1967), pp. 136-49.

——, *Social Mobility in Traditional China*, Leiden, 1962.

Freedman, Maurice, *Lineage Organization in Southeastern China*, L.S.E. Monographs on Social Anthropology 18, London, 1958.

——, *Chinese Lineage and Society: Fukien and Kwangtung*, L.S.E. Monographs on Social Anthropology 33, London, 1966.

Friend, Hilderic, 'Tsung-tsuh-chi-lai-tih, Extracts from an Essay on Clans, Read before the Canton Missionary Conference, June 5th, 1878', *Chinese Recorder* IX (1878), pp. 299-304, 379-85.

Hsiao Kung-ch'üan, *Rural China, Imperial Control in the Nineteenth Century*, Seattle, 1960.

Hu Hsien-chin, *The Common Descent Group in China and its Functions*, Viking Fund Publications in Anthropology, no. 10, New York, 1948.

Liu Hui-chen Wang, *The Traditional Chinese Clan Rules*, Association for Asian Studies, Monograph no. 7, Locust Valley, N.Y., 1959.

Lo Hsiang-lin, *Chung-kuo tsu-p'u yen-chiu*, Hong Kong, 1971.

Makino Tatsumi, 'Mei Shin zokufu kenkyū josetsu', *Tōhōgakuhō* VI (1936), pp. 261-88.

——, *Kinsei Chūgoku sōzoku kenkyū*, Tokyo, 1949.

Meskill, Johanna M., 'The Chinese Genealogy as a Research Source', in Maurice Freedman, ed., *Family and Kinship in Chinese Society* (Stanford, 1970), pp. 139-61.

P'an Quentin Kuang-tan, 'Chung-kuo chia-p'u hsüeh lüeh-shih', *Tung-fang tsa-chih* XXVI (1933), pp. 107-20.

Ravary, François, S.J., 'Les tablettes des ancêtres et les registres de la famille en Chine', *Études* XIII (1874, ii), pp. 762-8.

Taga Akigorō, *Sōfu no kenkyū*, Tokyo, 1960.

Twitchett, Denis C., 'The Fan Clan's Charitable Estate, 1050-1760', in D. Nivison and A.F. Wright, eds., *Confucianism in Action* (Stanford, 1959), pp. 97-133.

Yuan I-chin, 'Life Tables for a Southern Chinese Family from 1365 to 1849', *Human Biology* III (1931), pp. 157-79.

史 XI: Legal Sources[1]

DERK BODDE

From the beginning, Chinese codified written law has functioned primarily as an instrument of government, imposed from above to maintain social and political order among those below. As such, it has been overwhelmingly penal in emphasis. The strength of bureaucratic centralism has prevented the rise of a private legal profession.

Traditionally, the inscribing of 'books of punishment' (*hsing-shu*) on bronze tripods in the state of Cheng in 536 B.C. marks the beginning of Chinese publicly promulgated law.[2] However, H.G. Creel, in an as yet unpublished paper, finds considerably more 'proto-legal' activity in early Chou times than has been commonly supposed.[3]

The prototype of all Chinese codes is allegedly the *Fa-ching*, said to have been promulgated by the statesman Li K'uei about 400 B.C. However, there is good reason for doubting the validity of this tradition, at least in its details. During the last century or more of the Chou, the chief advocates of law were the statesmen and political thinkers later known as Legalists. Their opponents were Confucian scholars who viewed law as compulsive and therefore inferior to their own suasive *li* (traditional rules of civilised behaviour). This prejudice, which continued even into imperial times after the necessity for law had been grudgingly accepted, helps explain why relatively few pre-modern Chinese scholars have concerned themselves seriously with legal studies.

From 221 B.C. onwards, elaborate written codes were promulgated by all major dynasties, but none has survived from before the T'ang dynasty. On Han jurisprudence, however, Hulsewé has contributed an illuminating study.[4] Among surviving codes, the earliest is the *T'ang-lü shu-i* of A.D. 653.[5] It consists of 502 (traditionally 500) articles or statutes (*lü*), each accompanied by an officially compiled, and therefore equally authoritative, commentary.

---

[1] This discussion deals only with law in pre-Republican China.
[2] *Tso-chuan*, sixth year of Duke Chao.
[3] Herrlee G. Creel, 'Legal Institutions and Procedures during the Chou Dynasty', to appear in Jerome A. Cohen, R. Randle Edwards and Fu-mei Chen, eds., *China's Legal Tradition*, to be published by Harvard University Press.
[4] A.F.P. Hulsewé, *Remnants of Han Law*, vol. 1 (Leiden, 1955).
[5] See bibliography, Works on the T'ang Code.

The T'ang Code was perpetuated almost unchanged in the Sung Code of 963 and from there, probably with only minor changes, in the now lost Yüan Code (1323). Sharp changes in format first came with the Ming Code of 1397 and, in its wake, the Ch'ing Code (*Ta-Ch'ing lü-li*) of 1740.[6] The continuing strength even then of the T'ang tradition is indicated by an estimate that no less than 30 to 40 per cent of the statutes in the Ch'ing Code are identical with T'ang prototypes. Only at the very end of the Ch'ing (1905 onward) did the ancient legal tradition disintegrate.[7]

Besides the codes, other bodies of officially promulgated law (such as administrative law) have also existed, though few have survived from earlier dynasties. A notable exception is the *ling*, ordinances, of T'ang, which, a few decades ago, were brilliantly reconstituted by Niida Noboru.[8] Only in the Ming and Ch'ing Codes, however, was the major step taken, within the codes themselves, of supplementing the basic statutes (*lü*) by relevant additional laws known as *li*, 'precedents' or 'sub-statutes'. These *li* originated as imperial edicts (often inspired by important legal cases), which, having been circulated and acquiring the force of law, were then periodically selected for inclusion in new editions of the code. In this way the Ming and Ch'ing jurists solved the problem of bringing flexibility into what would otherwise have been an almost unchanging body of law.

Ideologically, the most important single feature of all surviving codes is their Confucianisation, which means, primarily, their emphasis on hierarchical differentiation. That is to say, it often happens that the same or almost the same offences are given differing punishments because of legally prescribed considerations concerning the particular social or family status of the wrongdoer and/or his victim, as well as other particularising circumstances. The continuity and authority of the surviving codes, their adherence to a common ethic, and the precision with which they prescribe carefully graduated penalties for each category of offence and offender, make them unrivalled instruments for measuring, dynasty by dynasty, the gradually shifting configurations of Chinese social and political values as officially defined.

Aside from the codes themselves, the best sources for studying Chinese jurisprudence in its historical development are the chapters in fourteen of the dynastic histories entitled 'Hsing-fa chih' or 'Treatises on Penal Law'. These are:[9] *Han-shu*, chapter 23;[10] *Chin-shu*, chapter 30; *Wei-shu*, chapter 111; *Sui-shu*, chapter 25;[11] *Chiu T'ang-shu*, chapter 50; *Hsin T'ang-shu*, chapter

[6] See bibliography, Works on the T'ang Code.
[7] See M.J. Meijer, *The Introduction of Modern Criminal Law in China* (Batavia, 1949).
[8] *Tōryō shūi* (Tokyo, 1933).
[9] All these treatises have been conveniently assembled and punctuated in Ch'iu Han-p'ing, ed., *Li-tai hsing-fa chih* (Ch'ang-sha, 1938).
[10] This has been translated by Hulsewé in *Remnants of Han Law*, pp. 321-50.
[11] For translation see Etienne Balazs, tr., *Le Traité juridique du 'Souei-chou'* (Leiden, 1954).

56;[12] *Chiu Wu-tai shih*, chapter 147; *Sung-shih*, chapters 199-201; *Liao-shih*, chapters 61-2; *Chin-shih*, chapter 45; *Yüan-shih*, chapters 102-5;[13] *Hsin Yüan-shih*, chapters 102-3; *Ming-shih*, chapters 93-5;[14] *Ch'ing shih-kao*, chapters 143-5.[15]

Other important sources are the legal sections in encyclopaedias, compendia on governmental institutions, and the like. There are many sections on law in the various general encyclopaedias, in the ten compendia on government collectively known as the Shih-t'ung, and in the *hui-yao* of the successive dynasties, as well as such administrative compendia as the *T'ang liu-tien* (738), the *Yüan tien-chang* (*c.* 1320), and the Ming and Ch'ing *Hui-tien*.[16]

Records of actual cases are of course all-important for comparing legal theory (codified law) with legal practice. Unfortunately, Chinese casebooks hardly go back before the Sung, and even then they usually consist of anecdotes or of answers made to often hypothetically formulated examination questions on law, rather than genuine case records.[17] Only in the late Ming and especially the Ch'ing do large classified compilations of such cases appear; they culminate in the gigantic nineteenth century *Hsing-an hui-lan*, compiled in 1834, with three similarly named sequels, dated 1840, 1886, and 1887. This work contains (with its sequels) reports of more than 9,000 actual cases as decided by the Board of Punishments, Peking, from 1736 to 1885.[18]

---

[12] The treatises in the two T'ang histories have been translated by Karl Bünger in *Quellen zur Rechtsgeschichte der T'ang-Zeit* (Peiping, 1946), pp. 73-173.

[13] Chapter 102 and part of 103 of *Yüan-shih* are translated in Paul Ratchnevsky, tr., *Un Code des Yuan* (Paris, 1937). This treatise, unlike all the others, is not a historical survey, but reproduces a code, possibly of 1331, whose relationship to the primary but now lost Yüan Code of 1323 is uncertain. See also index to Ratchnevsky by Françoise Aubin in *Mélanges publiés par l'Institut des Hautes Études Chinoises* II (1960), pp. 423-515.

[14] Chapter 93 of *Ming-shih* is translated in Frank Münzel, *Strafrechte im alten China nach den Strafrechtskapiteln in den Ming-Annalen* (Wiesbaden, 1968).

[15] The best edition of this treatise, with excellent commentary, is *Ch'ing shih-kao hsing-fa chih chu-chieh* (Peking, 1957), edited by the Legal Research Division, Bureau of Legal Affairs, Council of State.

[16] These are too numerous to be listed here. For detailed enumerations see T'ung-tsu Ch'ü, *Law and Society in Traditional China*, pp. 288-9.

[17] The *T'ang-yin pi-shih* (1211) is one of the three well-known Sung collections and consists of 144 criminal and civil cases ranging from about 300 B.C. to about 1100 A.D. Their legal value is lessened by the fact that their form is literary and anecdotal rather than juridical. The work is translated, with an excellent introduction, by R.H. van Gulik in *T'ang-yin-pi-shih*, 'Parallel Cases from under the Pear-tree' (Leiden, 1956). The *Ming-kung shu-p'an ch'ing-ming chi* dates from the late Sung dynasty and is by an unknown compiler. It consists of answers by civil service candidates, mostly from central coastal China during *c.* 1190-1230, to examination questions on either actual or hypothetical cases. As of this writing (1970), I.R. Burns is preparing a Ph.D. dissertation at Oxford dealing with this work.

[18] For translation of 190 of the cases see Derk Bodde and Clarence Morris, *Law in Imperial China, Exemplified by 190 Ch'ing Dynasty Cases* (*Translated from the Hsing-an hui-lan*), *with Historical, Social, and Juridical Commentaries*, Harvard Studies in East Asian Law 1 (Cambridge, Mass., 1967), pp. 203-489. The cases here translated are preceded by a 200-page essay on legal concepts and practices and followed by a statutory analysis. For other casebooks see T'ung-tsu Ch'ü, *Law and Society*, pp. 292-3.

In the day-to-day lives of ordinary Chinese, there is little doubt that localised customary law usually played a greater role than did the government codified law. This was especially true in such non-criminal spheres as marriage, inheritance, property relations, and the like. Unfortunately, Chinese customary law is very difficult to study, precisely because it is amorphous, often unwritten, and differs from place to place and group to group. Quite recently, however, Kroker has translated into German a large twentieth century Chinese compendium on the subject.[19]

The significance of legal sources not only for the study of Chinese law but also for the history of China itself is clear from the great importance of law in the understanding of any given civilisation. This comment carries special weight in the case of China which has an extremely long legal tradition. The importance of the legal sources in determining the changes in social and political values throughout the ages has already been pointed out. The casebooks are also of particular value for research in many areas of social history. The people who were forced to come before the tribunals belonged to a wide variety of trade, professional and other groupings, and the manner in which the officials dealt with them cannot fail to give valuable insight into their position in society. The hierarchical attitudes which dominated Chinese law are in this way of great value to the historian.

SELECTED ANNOTATED BIBLIOGRAPHY

General Studies

Ch'ü T'ung-tsu, *Law and Society in Traditional China*, Paris & The Hague, 1961. Tremendous wealth of material and a very valuable bibliography.

Needham, Joseph, 'Human Law and the Laws of Nature in China and the West', in Needham (with Wang Ling), *Science and Civilisation in China*, vol. 2, *History of Scientific Thought* (Cambridge, 1956), pp. 518-83.

Niida Noboru (1904-66), *Chūgoku hōseishi kenkyū*, Tokyo, 1959-64. Four unnumbered volumes, subtitled in English: *Criminal Law* (1959); *Law of Land and Law of Transaction* (1960); *Law of Slave and Serf, and Law of Family and Village* (1962); *Law and Custom, Law and Morality* (1964). Each volume has an English summary. The master work of this greatest of Japanese specialists on Chinese law.

Shen Chia-pen (1840-1913), *Shen Chi-i hsien-sheng i-shu, chia-pien*, Peking, n.d. [1929], reprint, 2 vols., Taipei, 1964, with continuous pagination.

[19] Edouard J.M. Kroker, tr. and commentator, *Die amtliche Sammlung chinesischer Rechtsgewohnheiten (Min shang hsi kuan tiao ch'a pao kao lu), Untersuchungsbericht über Gewohnheiten in Zivil- und Handelssachen*, 3 vols. (Bergen-Enkheim bei Frankfurt/M., 1965). The compendium here translated is of civil and commercial customary law as reported by late Ch'ing and early Republican officials from many areas of China, published by the (Kuomintang) Ministry of Justice, Nanking, 1930. See also Niida Noboru, *Chūgoku hōseishi kenkyū*, and Harro von Senger, *Kaufverträge im traditionnellen China* (Zurich, 1970).

Numerous legal studies, long and short, by a pioneer who remains the prince of Chinese legal historians.

Works on the T'ang Code of 653

Chuang Wei-ssu, comp., *T'ang-lü shu-i yin-te*, Taipei, 1965. The compiler of this very useful index is actually the American T'ang legal specialist, Wallace S. Johnson, Jr, under his Chinese name.

Deloustal, Raymond, tr., 'La Justice dans l'ancien Annam', *Bulletin de l'Ecole Française d'Extrême Orient* VIII-XIII, XIX, XXII (1908-13, 1919, 1922). A loose rendition, awkward to use because of its scattered format, of the Annamite code of the Le dynasty (1428-1786), which closely conforms to the T'ang Code.

Johnson, Wallace S., Jr, tr., 'The T'ang Code; an Analysis and Translation of the Oldest Extant Chinese Penal Code (A.D. 635), Chapters 1-3'. Ph.D. dissertation, University of Pennsylvania, Philadelphia, 1968. First portion of an ongoing translation.

Ou Koei-hing, *La Peine d'après le Code des T'ang*, Shanghai, 1935.

Tai Yen-hui, *T'ang-lü ko-lun*, Taipei, 1965. An excellent running commentary.

——, *T'ang-lü t'ung-lun*, Taipei, 1954. A topical analysis.

Works on the Ch'ing Code of 1740

Boulais, Guy, tr., *Manuel du code chinois*, Shanghai, 1924; reprint, Taipei, 1966.

Hsüeh Yün-sheng, *Tu-li ts'un-i*, Peking, 1905; revised edition, Huang Ching-chia, ed., *Tu-li ts'un-i ch'ung-k'an pen*, 5 vols., Taipei, 1970. By far the best edition of the Ch'ing Code, in which each statute and sub-statute is accompanied by a valuable discussion of its dating and origin. In the revised edition, Huang adds modern punctuation and consecutive numbering of all statutes and sub-statutes.

Philastre, P.L.F., tr., *Le Code annamite, nouvelle traduction complète, comprenant: Les commentaires officiels du Code, traduits pour la première fois; de nombreuses annotations extraites des commentaires du Code chinois*, 2 vols., Paris, 1876; 2nd ed. with 20-page index, 1909; reprint of 2nd ed., Taipei, 1967.

Staunton, George Thomas, tr., *Ta Tsing Leu Lee, Being the Fundamental Laws . . . of the Penal Code of China*, London, 1810; reprint, Taipei, 1966.

Of the three translations into European languages, Staunton is still good but translates only statutes and not sub-statutes; Boulais is considerably better because much more complete and because he reproduces the Chinese text; Philastre is the best of all both in coverage and accuracy but supplies no Chinese characters. The Annamite code of 1812 translated by him closely conforms to the Ch'ing Code.

史 XII: The Compilation and Historical Value of the Tao-tsang

LIU TS'UN-YAN

The compilation of the Tao-tsang or the Great Collection of Taoist Literature, sometimes rendered into English as the Taoist Tripitaka, was started in the early Ming, and completed in 1445. It is a work of the *ts'ung-shu* type. Published in a concertina format and distributed only sparsely to Taoist monasteries as an imperial favour, it had a total number of 5,305 *chüan*, contained in 480 *han* (wrappers) arranged in the order of the first 480 characters in the *Ch'ien-tzu wen*. A sequel, the Hsü Tao-tsang, was compiled in 1607 with an additional 180 *chüan* of new material in 32 *han*. The original and the sequel have been issued together since then. Ting Fu-pao (b. 1874) alleged that there was a pocket-sized edition of the Tao-tsang published in 1626. Modern scholars, including Yoshioka Yoshitoyo and myself, are inclined to suspect that he was confused by the fact that in that particular year a Nanking Taoist priest Pai Yün-chi (*tzu* Ming-chih, *hao* Tsai-hsü-tzu) compiled a concise catalogue of the Tao-tsang (*Tao-tsang mu-lu hsiang-chu* in four *chüan*).[1] This last work was later included in the Ssu-k'u ch'üan-shu from which a photolithographic copy was made in the early Republic.[2] During the Ch'ing dynasty it was available only in transcript and was greatly valued by bibliophiles, since the original copies, regarded as national treasures, were kept only in a few imperial and national libraries. Strangely enough, yet another concise catalogue with the same title, same number of *chüan* and more than 95 per cent of its content identical with Pai's work, was published in Ch'ing times under the name of Li Chieh (*tzu* Jo-chih) of Liao-tso (Liao tung).[3] Since the *Sun-shih tz'u-t'ang mu-lu*,

---

[1] In his preface to the Tao-tsang ching-hua lu. See also Ting's autobiography entitled *Ch'ou-yin chü-shih hsüeh-shu shih* (Shanghai, 1949), p. 59. Ting is a great bibliophile from Wu-hsi, also known for his sponsorship of numerous publications including the *Shuo-wen ku-lin* and other classical anthologies. But since most of his works were compiled with considerable help from his several assistants, similar errors can be found elsewhere. For Yoshioka, see his *Dōkyō kyoten shiron* (Tokyo, 1955), p. 174.

[2] The T'ui-keng t'ang edition. T'ui-keng t'ang is the name for President Hsü Shih-ch'ang's studio. Hsü was one of the men sponsoring the publication of the photolithographic edition of the Tao-tsang in 1923.

[3] It is included in the Tao-tsang ching-hua lu, Series I. Weng Tu-chien claimed in 1935 that there was a Ming edition of Li's Catalogue in the National Peiping Library, see *Tao-tsang tzu-mu yin-te*, Harvard-Yenching Institute (Peiping, 1935, Taipei reprint 1966), p. ii.

compiled by the great sinologue Sun Hsing-yen (1753-1818), includes Li's work bearing the same title though divided into twelve *chüan*,[4] it is difficult to deny that his could have been an independent work published during or before Sun's time. Sun also noted that Li was a Ming scholar, but he misread his name as Li Chieh-jo.

In both catalogues, the Taoist works included in the sequel to the Tao-tsang contained no bibliographical notes, while nearly every work found in the proper series is given some kind of description, varying from one double column of only two characters to six or seven double columns of approximately 300 characters.[5] In many cases, only a brief account of the contents is given, and even then discrepancies between the description and the work can still be found.[6] However, it was mainly on these two catalogues that the famous *Taoïsme*, Tome I (*Bibliographie générale*) of Dr Wieger, S.J., was based.[7]

Father Wieger was not a great expert in the history of Taoism. In the compilation of his work, though he had generally digested the accounts given by the Chinese catalogues, in many instances rewriting them not only in his own succinct style but also with his own ideas, he failed to devote his time and effort to a thorough checking of these catalogues against copies of the works from the original collection.[8] For instance, the dates of Lin Yüan, the author of *Ku-shen p'ien* (Tao-tsang, No. 119), are not mentioned in either Chinese catalogue.[9] Father Wieger writes, however, 'L'homme supérieur doit revenir, par la contemplation, de la multiplicité à l'unité, à la cause première, et s'y fixer. Par Linn-yuan, dynastie Song' (p. 65). As a matter of fact, to this particular work, two prefaces had been written, one dated 1315 and the other 1304. The last one was penned by none other

---

I have seen, however, a wooden-block edition of this work dated 1845 and published by the Pai-yün Monastery, Peking. For other copies of the Ming edition of the Tao-tsang, especially an incomplete set preserved in the Archives and Mausolea Division, Library of the Japanese Imperial Household Agency, see Yoshioka, *Dōkyō*, p. 175.

[4] *Chüan* 3, 'nei-p'ien'.

[5] There are quite a few works in Pai's Catalogue with only their titles given, and in some cases even the title is missing. Only in one or two cases has Li's Catalogue filled such gaps. For instance, the title of *Hsü-hsien chen-lu* in five *chüan* (Tao-tsang, Nos. 1086-8), not included in Pai's Catalogue (Appendix: 'Ta-ming Hsü Tao-tsang ching mu-lu', p. 4b), is found in the nearly identical work, 4.54a, published under Li's name.

[6] For instance, Pai Yün-chi's note (1.23a-b) under the *Ta-i hsiang-shu kou-shen t'u* (Tao-tsang, 70) is actually a note for a similar work on the *Book of Changes*, namely, the *I-shu kou-yin t'u* (Tao-tsang, 71).

[7] Hsien-hsien (Chihli or present day Hopeh), 1911.

[8] I need not point out the fact that Father Wieger might have had difficulties with access to this work. At any time before 1923 when a photolithographic edition of the Tao-tsang was started, a scholar who wished to familiarise himself with the Tao-tsang had to go to a Taoist monastery (such as the Pai-yün Monastery in Peking or Shanghai) where a complete set of the collection was preserved. Cf. Liu Shih-p'ei, 'Tu Tao-tsang chi' first published in the *Kuo-ts'ui hsüeh-pao* LXXV (1911) and later in *Liu Shen-shu hsien-sheng i-shu*, book 63 (1934), pp. 1a-28b. The priests did not always grant scholars permission to consult their library.

[9] Pai (1.37b) and Li (1.25a) are identical.

than Lin Yüan himself nearly thirty years after the fall of Hang-chou to the Mongols. Another example of Father Wieger's negligence may be seen in his notes on the *Hsiu-chen shih-shu* (Tao-tsang, Nos. 122-31, sixty-four *chüan* in total), which is an anthology of a number of works on self-cultivation compiled by many anonymous as well as known Taoist priests including Pai Yü-ch'an. I even have evidence that this anthology might have been compiled at one stage by some disciples of Pai Yü-ch'an, a patriarch who flourished in the early part of the thirteenth century.[10] However, Father Wieger, following merely the description given by the first out of five successive items dealing with the same anthology found in the Chinese catalogues,[11] concludes rather hastily that this work is an 'Immense compilation d'extraits et citations, sur la voie des Sien et des Tchenn, théorie, pratique, etc. Par Cheu-t'ai, dynastie Song. Avec des illustrations'.[12]

The Chinese catalogues, like the French one, were compiled before 1923, the year when it was planned to arrange a photolithographic edition taken from the extant set of the Tao-tsang preserved in the Pai-yün Monastery, Peking. This plan was carried out most successfully under the patronage of President Hsü Shih-ch'ang (1855-1939), Fu Tseng-hsiang, and others. In 1926 the photolithographic edition was completed, 1,200 *ts'e*, stitch-bound, combining two concertina leaves into one.[13] At the end of each *ts'e*,

[10] For Pai Yü-ch'an, see below. In this anthology works written by Taoist priests of Yüan times, such as the *P'an-shan yü-lu*, are also found; see Tao-tsang 130, p. 53, cf. also the *P'an-shan Ch'i-yün Wang chen-jen yü-lu*, Tao-tsang, 728.

[11] Pai (1.39a-40a) and Li (1.26a-27b) are identical except for two miswritten forms.

[12] *Le Canon (Patrologie) taoïste*, p. 67. In his preface to this work Father Wieger also writes: 'le catalogue du grand couvent taoïste Kinn-ling (depuis Nankin), au commencement de la dynastie Ming. La tradition taoïste est, que ce catalogue date de la dynastie Song, douzième siècle probablement. Longtemps manuscrit, il fut gravé durant la période Kia-tsing 1522 à 1566 des Ming, et servit depuis à dresser tous les catalogues postérieurs.' (p. 6). This information about the history of the catalogue is somewhat inaccurate. Although the Chia-ching period had nothing to do with the publication of any of these catalogues, it is known that in 1524 (the third year of Chia-ching) the Tao-tsang was at least partially reprinted, as some fragmentary copies of the collection are preserved in Professor Kubo Noritada's study at the University of Tokyo. The detailed history of the compilation of the 'Tao-tsang' at different periods before Ming times should be the topic of an independent study. Unfortunately all the other 'Tao-tsang' engraved and printed before the 1445 edition are no more extant, and I doubt very much that Father Wieger had seen the *Sung Ling-yu kung Tao-tsang mu-lu* cited in the *Pu Chin-shu i-wen chih*, compiled separately by Ting Kuo-chün (*Erh-shih-wu shih pu-pien* 111.3694) and Ch'in Jung-kuang (p. 3837).

[13] This is the number of *ts'e* often quoted by modern scholars studying this work, also the number I have used in the foregoing passages. The numbers given in Father Wieger's catalogue are in running order, following the appearance of each work in the collection. As a result his catalogue informs us that the Tao-tsang contains 1,464 works. This number is inaccurate since Father Wieger has left out some works because he followed the two Chinese catalogues faithfully. Father Wieger's catalogue also falls short when its numbers are used to consult the photolithographic edition, for in the latter, a *ts'e* may contain more than one work, or *vice versa*; a work may not be restricted to the limited space of one *ts'e*. In the *Tzu-mu yin-te* edited by Weng Tu-chien (see below), a table of conversion (xii) is given for Western readers who use Wieger's catalogue but also wish to consult the *Yin-te* index.

the original index-word following the order of the *Ch'ien-tzu wen* and a numeral denoting its number in this edition are typeprinted. Two indexes have been made since 1935 for this new edition, of which only 350 copies were printed and sold at a high price.[14] The *Tao-tsang tzu-mu yin-te*, edited by Weng Tu-chien and published by the Harvard-Yenching Institute,[15] is worth having not only as a good index, but also for some of the invaluable subsidiary materials relating to chronology and authorship.[16] The *Min Seitō bon Dōzō shomei jikaku sakuin*, edited by the library staff of the Women's University of Kyōto (Kyōto joshi daigaku) and published in 1965, is a very useful work, though wrongly titled, for it includes all the works in the Hsü Tao-tsang. The value of this little book is in its simpler arrangement of the index by number of strokes in the title (as against the Harvard-Yenching Sinological Index Series), which makes it most convenient for quick reference. Under each title, the index-word following the order of the *Ch'ien-tzu wen* is given side by side with the running numbers of *ts'e* and of wrapper and is set up in accordance with the arrangements found in the photolithographic edition of 1926. In that particular edition there are only 128 wrappers, each of which takes care of an approximately equal number of *chüan* of the Taoist texts originally engraved under four index-words (i.e. four wrappers) in the wood-block concertina edition. Names of authors are given in very small characters in double-columns. This was planned, I presume, for librarians' reference only; but there are mistakes which should be corrected.[17]

Since the late seventeenth century, a Tao-tsang on a smaller scale has been in demand from time to time. Of the edition of the Tao-tsang chi-yao alleged to have been compiled on the initiative of P'eng Ting-ch'iu (1645-1719), a scholar more Neo-Confucianist than Taoist,[18] records about its

[14] The original photolithographic edition was sold, in 1926, at 800 silver dollars per set. In the late fifties a reprint of this edition was made available in Taipei, and its present market-price as quoted by a second-hand book-dealer in Hong Kong is about HK$7,000.
[15] Cf. Note 3 above.
[16] The author index, pp. 115-40; the bibliographical records, pp. 141-216.
[17] Besides a number of typographical errors, the names of authors of some of the known works have also been left out in this index. For instance, the name Chou Wu-so on p. 31 is a misreading of a sobriquet of a Taoist priest who described himself as Chou-wu-so-chu. Chou cannot possibly be a surname in this case. Apparently the compilers inherited this error from Pai (4.17a) and Li (4.11b). Sometimes one and the same work appears in two different places, e.g., the *Li-shih i-yin* on pp. 30-1 and the *I-yin* on p. 34. This is a work of Li Chih (1527-1602), a well-known Ming philosopher.
[18] A biography of P'eng written by Rufus O. Suter can be found in Arthur W. Hummel, ed., *Eminent Chinese of the Ch'ing Period* (Taipei reprint, 1967), pp. 616-17, but nothing is said there about this Taoist compilation. Cf. *Pei-chuan chi* 44.21a-25b. In the division *kuei* of the Chi-yao, there is a work titled *Chen-ch'üan* in three *chüan* under P'eng's name, but his own colophon (dated 1710) informs us that this work was handed to him by his father. On the title-page of the book, it is recorded that the work was 'handed down by Yang Tao-sheng, alias Pao-chen-tzu, but collated by P'eng Ting-ch'iu. Whether Tao-sheng was a real name or only a pseudonym of P'eng's father (to mean the growth of his vigorous *yang*) we do not know. In the *Ssu-k'u ch'üan-shu tsung-mu* (Taipei, 1964 ed.), vol. 5, p. 2,921, there is a reference to the *Chen-ch'üan* in which only Pao-chen-tzu's name is mentioned.

compilation could have been wrong even to the extent that such a work never existed. The extant edition of the work bearing the same title and known to have been engraved between 1796 and 1820, was published under the name of its compiler, Chiang Yü-p'u, alias Chiang Yüan-t'ing (1755-1819), who was a vice-minister at the time.[19] It has for a long time been very difficult to obtain even this edition. It contains Taoist works with 173 titles, all of which can be found in the original collection of the Tao-tsang. However, between 1821 and 1900, the Tao-tsang chi-yao was engraved twice, and, in the process, ninety-six works, not included in the Tao-tsang itself, were added to these collections.[20] Since then, the Tao-tsang chi-yao has ceased to be merely a selection from the original. In 1906, yet another re-engraved edition of the Tao-tsang chi-yao was made available in Ch'eng-tu, Szechwan, under the joint editorship of two native Taoist scholars, Ho Lung-hsiang and P'eng Han-jan, while the collation and proof-reading was done by Yen Yung-ho, the Abbot of the Erh-hsien Monastery, Ch'eng-tu. The same monastery was responsible for the publication and circulation of the work. In this revised edition, another eighteen works were added to the earlier compilations, thus making the Chi-yao a collection of 287 Taoist works in all, contained in 245 *ts'e*.

The last edition of the Tao-tsang chi-yao is perhaps the most popular and is found in many libraries, hence it needs a more detailed description. The contents of this Tao-tsang chi-yao are in twenty-eight divisions according to the order of the twenty-eight constellations in Chinese astronomy, beginning with *chüeh* and ending with *ch'en*. In each division, there are a number of works subdivided further into items: *Chüeh* I, *Chüeh* II, etc. A sub-division may contain either one work or a number of works of comparatively shorter length, but in some instances a bulky work may be carried on to the next sub-division or sub-divisions. This collection is important for three reasons. Firstly, as stated already, it contains some Taoist texts and commentaries which are not found in the two collections of the Tao-tsang. Some of them were compiled after 1607.[21]

Secondly, the editors of the 1906 edition of the Tao-tsang chi-yao, Ho and P'eng, not only made some revision of the less known works in the collection, but also took the trouble to compile a *Tao-men i-ch'ieh ching*

---

[19] For a biography of Chiang, see Li Huan, *Kuo-ch'ao ch'i-hsien lei-cheng* (1884 ed., Taipei reprint, 1966), vol. 8, 94.4407. Evidence showing that Chiang had actually published the Chi-yao can be seen in many places in the collection itself. For instance, in the colophon to the *T'ai-i chin-hua tsung-chih* (division *shih*), En-hung writes, 'Kuang-hua Tzu re-edited and included it in this compilation'. Kuang-hua Tzu was Chiang Yü-p'u's Taoist style. For the English translation of the *T'ai-i chin-hua tsung-chih*, see Richard Wilhelm, *The Secret of the Golden Flower: a Chinese Book of Life* (London, 1942).

[20] See Yoshioka, *Dōkyō*, p. 176.

[21] Such as the *Wu chen-jen hsien-fo ho-tsung yü-lu* of Wu Shou-yang (1563?-1632?) included in division *pi*, vols. 1-6. For a bibliographical account of Wu and his theories, see my 'Wu Shou-yang, the Return of the Ethereal *Ch'i*' still to be published.

tsung-mu, a transcribed and combined catalogue of all Taoist catalogues available to them at the time, although some of the works cited in them might have been lost long before.[22] This *tsung-mu* has four *chüan*: it includes all the items on Taoist works taken from both the concise and the detailed catalogues of the Ssu-k'u ch'üan-shu; the complete catalogue of the Tao-tsang; the titles of the Taoist works found in some of the *ts'ung-shu*,[23] and also the sections relating to Taoist studies in several of the best known bibliographical records, such as the *Chün-chai tu-shu chih* and the *Chih-chai shu-lu chieh-t'i* of Sung times. It also contains Taoist catalogues from the famous institutional histories.[24] The part which interests me most in this *tsung-mu* is the *Kuo-ch'ao fang-k'e Tao-shu mu-lu*, or the *Catalogue of Taoist Works Published Recently*, a selective catalogue compiled exceedingly well by Ho Lung-hsiang. This catalogue serves as a guide to the reliability of the editions of Taoist works engraved in Ch'ing times, though the authors themselves might not have lived in the same period. For instance, it mentions the *Pao-chi pi-shu* in four *chüan* reprinted by Tzu-han-tzu of Yang-chou in 1857; also the *Wu-Liu hsien-tsung*[25] published by the Chi-yün li owned by Teng Hui of Chungking in 1897. However, the compiler is wrong in remarking under the 1854 edition of the Tao-yen wu-chung that this particular collection was selected by Weng Pao-kuang in 1173, since it includes the *Chin-tan ta-yao* of Ch'en Chih-hsü who flourished in the mid-fourteenth century,[26] and also the *Chin-tan chiu-cheng p'ien* of Lu Hsi-hsing, a well-known Taoist priest of Ming times.[27]

Thirdly, the detailed table of contents in this edition of the Tao-tsang chi-yao, entitled *Ch'ung-k'an Tao-tsang chi-yao tzu-mu ch'u-pien* in four *chüan* (plus an additional one), which follows immediately upon the General Table of Contents (*tsung-mu*), is also valuable. It provides information on

---

[22] For instance, some of the titles are included in the Sung catalogues. A sample case may be seen in my article 'Lun Tao-tsang pen Ku Huan chu Lao-tzu chih hsing-chih' published in the *United College Journal* VIII (1970).

[23] Noticeably the Ku-chin i-shih ssu-shih chung engraved by Wu Kuan of Hsin-an in Ming times; the Chi-ku ko catalogue and the *Fang-hu wai-shih*. The last work is the collected Taoist writings of Lu Hsi-hsing (1520-?1601) in eight *chüan*. Besides a few modern editions which were published during the Republic, some transcribed manuscripts of Lu's works can be found in the Department of Oriental Books and MSS. of the British Museum, and one manuscript is preserved in the National Central Library, Taipei.

[24] I.e., the *T'ung-chih*; the *T'ung-k'ao*, the *Hsü Wen-hsien t'ung-k'ao*, and the *Huang-ch'ao [Ch'ing] Wen-hsien t'ung-k'ao*.

[25] The best known work of the Wu-Liu Sect which regarded Wu Shou-yang and his disciple Liu Hua-yang as its founding patriarchs. For Wu, see note 21.

[26] For the dates of Ch'en Chih-hsü, see his own preface to the *Yüan-shih wu-liang tu-jen shang-p'in miao-ching chu-chieh*, Tao-tsang, 45.

[27] For Lu, see my article 'Lu Hsi-hsing, A Confucian Scholar, Taoist Priest and Buddhist Devotee of the Sixteenth Century', *Asiatische Studien* XVIII-XIX (1966), pp. 115-42; also 'Lu Hsi-hsing and his Commentaries on the *Ts'an-t'ung-ch'i*', *The Tsing-hua Journal of Chinese Studies*, New Series VII (1968), pp. 71-98; also *Buddhist and Taoist Influences on Chinese Novels*, Vol. I (Wiesbaden, 1962), pp. 254-89.

most of the works included in the collection in terms of chapters and items, sometimes even to the extent of describing arrangements that are not found in the original work. The additional *chüan* (*Chüan* 5) deals mainly with titles which have already been entered under the sub-divisions of the previous four *chüan*, although the works themselves were meant to be added only in this edition, being marked in the General Table of Contents with *hsü* (to be added) under the title of the work. No doubt this is a rather strange and complicated arrangement. Appended to this *chüan* there is yet another catalogue named *Nü-tan ho-pien* consisting of fifteen works written specially for the self-cultivation of the female by a number of Taoist forerunners, with a preface written by Ho Lung-hsiang, dated 1904.

The Tao-tsang ching-hua lu, edited by Ting Fu-pao, in ten series, each of which contains ten Taoist works, was published after the photolithographic edition of the Tao-tsang had already been circulated.[28] Although published with a rather misleading title implying that the works included in it are the most valuable texts taken exclusively from the Tao-tsang itself, the work actually contains a number of texts which are not to be found in the Tao-tsang. It even includes the writings of some late nineteenth century or contemporary scholars, such as Yü Yüeh (1821-1906) and Liu Shih-p'ei (1884-1919).[29]

Besides the collections already mentioned, there are still a few collections of works published during the Republic which bear a vague relation to the Tao-tsang. One is the Tao-tsang pen wu-tzu published by Fu Tseng-hsiang in 1918, which contains five pre-Ch'in philosophical works using the Tao-tsang as its facsimile edition. The same can be said about the Tao-tsang chü-yao printed photolithographically by the Commercial Press, Shanghai, in ten divisions, each of which contains a number of works taken from the original Ming edition of the Tao-tsang. Both works were meant for the bibliophiles. There is also the Tao-tsang ch'u-p'ien which includes only six scriptures printed in vermilion. Another is the Tao-tsang hsü-p'ien, Series I, edited by Min I-te, which contains a number of Taoist texts written by Taoist priests and laymen of Ch'ing times, including Min's own works.[30] Amongst them, the most noticeable works are perhaps those written by Liu I-ming, alias Wu-yüan-tzu (1734-*c.* 1815) from Kansu, who was active until the early-nineteenth century.[31]

Let us now turn to a more detailed history of the compilation of the Tao-tsang. Before the two collections (the Tao-tsang of 1445 and the Hsü Tao-tsang of 1607) were made, the Chinese scholars of Taoism at different times,

---

[28] By the I-hsüeh shu-chü, Shanghai, a bookstore owned by Ting.

[29] Yü's *T'ai-shang kan-ying p'ien tsan-i* is found in Series X, Liu's 'Tu Tao-tsang chi' in Series I.

[30] Published by the I-hsüeh shu-chü.

[31] Most of Liu's writings are found in his Tao-shu shih-erh chung while his *Hsiu-chen pien-nan* is also included in the Tao-shu ch'i-chung. Some forewords or introductions to the works contained in the Tao-shu shih-erh chung give dates of compilation.

with or without the support of their governments, had long been busy with the compilation of a Taoist tripitaka, vying with the Buddhists. The staunch support of their activities by some of the emperors, champions of the indigenous cause, naturally lent much prestige to such compilations. When the great Taoist scholar Lu Hsiu-ching (406-477), who often defended Taoist doctrine in public debates against Buddhist teachings, memorialised the throne in reply to an edict of the Sung Emperor Ming-ti in 471, he maintained that 'there had been 1,228 scrolls (*chüan*) of Taoist scriptures and works including prescriptions of drugs, talismans, and pictures'. He also claimed that 'of these scriptures, 1,090 scrolls had been known to the world, while the remaining 138 scrolls were still preserved in Heaven'.[32] Fantastic as this record may seem, it gives us a rough idea of the number of Taoist texts which must have been composed, transcribed, and kept reverentially in the libraries in his time. Collation of Taoist texts and compilation of new catalogues had taken place during the Liang, Northern Chou, and Sui periods, but it was not until T'ang times that the first philological dictionary of Taoist terms and the first collection of Taoist works of Tao-tsang type were successfully compiled. The dictionary, namely the *I-ch'ieh Tao-ching yin-i* in 140 (or perhaps 150) scrolls, compiled by a team of scholars including Ts'ui Chih, Hsieh Chi, Shen Ch'üan-ch'i, and Shih Ch'ung-hsüan, is no longer extant.[33] Shih was a Taoist abbot who became involved in a conspiracy planned by Princess T'ai-p'ing and was executed in the summer of 713. The great collection of Taoist texts compiled in the reign of Emperor Hsüan-tsung before 748 was named San-tung ch'iung-kang. It is also lost to us. An order was issued to make copies of it in 748 and perhaps some might actually have been made and distributed. After the rebellion of An Lu-shan, however, libraries in the two capitals (Ch'ang-an and Lo-yang) were destroyed and there could not possibly have been much left in the ruins. During the disturbances of the Five Dynasties, not even local monasteries were left intact, though there were still some enthusiastic Taoist priests and patrons in Wu-yüeh and Szechwan who were anxious to add more Taoist works to their holdings. This may explain why even the actual number of scrolls of the San-tung ch'iung-kang varies from record to record.[34]

The term *san-tung* in Taoist texts, as found in the titles of the San-tung ch'iung-kang, needs some explanation. *San-tung* stands for three categories

---

[32] In Lu's 'San-tung ching-shu mu-lu'; cf. Monk Tao-shih, *Fa-yüan chu-lin*, 55 in the Tripitaka in Chinese (Taishō shinshū daizōkyō), No. 2122, 53.704b.

[33] With the exception of two prefaces and six short chapters of introduction (Tao-tsang, 760; see also *Ch'üan T'ang-wen* 923) and some fragmentary remarks found in the *Shang-ch'ing ta-tung chen-ching yin-i*, Tao-tsang, 54, pp. 1a-2b, 3b-4b, 6a-7b, 9b-10b, and 12a.

[34] 3,744 *chüan* according to the *Wen-hsien t'ung-k'ao* (Wan-yu wen-k'u 2nd series, large-scale ed.) 224.1802 and the *Hsü Tzu-chih t'ung-chien ch'ang-pien shih-pu* 38; 7,300 *chüan* according to Tu Kuang-t'ing (850-933) in the *T'ai-shang huang-lu chai-i*, Tao-tsang, 276, 52.16b and the *Wu-shang huang-lu ta-chai li-ch'eng-i*, Tao-tsang, 283, 21.17a; 5,700 *chüan* according to the *Tao-tsang tsun-ching li-tai kang-mu* (compiled in 1275), Tao-tsang, 1056B, p. 23b.

of texts, the *tung-chen* (a thorough understanding of truth), the *tung-hsüan* (a thorough understanding of profundity), and the *tung-shen* (a thorough understanding of spirituality). At first, each of them represented a certain school of Taoist teachings, the earliest texts of which were known to have been produced between the early third and early fifth centuries. The term was first used, however, by Lu Hsiu-ching when presenting the catalogue to the court in 471.[35] From then on, the term *san-tung* was applied to Taoist priests whose vast knowledge is said to have traversed the treasures of the three categories. After the first half of the sixth century, when Taoist texts had become more numerous and their ramifications more divergent, four supplementary divisions were developed. Thus there is the *t'ai-hsüan* division to supplement the *tung-chen*, the *t'ai-p'ing* to supplement the *tung-hsüan*, and the *t'ai-ch'ing* to supplement the *tung-shen*. These three plus a fourth one, the *cheng-i*, formed the *ssu-fu*, or the four supplementary divisions, the main function of which was to keep the ever-growing Taoist works under systematic control in librarian's terms. To make the librarian's catalogue even more comprehensible, each of the seven sections (i.e., the three categories and the four supplementary divisions) was again sub-divided into twelve sub-divisions which may be roughly rendered as (i) fundamental texts; (ii) efficacious talismans; (iii) commentaries and exposition; (iv) spiritual charts and diagrams; (v) records of inheritance; (vi) orders and prohibitions; (vii) rituals; (viii) methods for self-cultivation; (ix) alchemy and magic; (x) legends and biographies; (xi) liturgies and hymns; and (xii) petitions (to the Sovereign on high).[36] The important point here is that these arrangements actually represent the sections and sub-divisions governing the contents of the Tao-tsang (1445 and 1607) under discussion.

Following the T'ang tradition when Taoism was revered as a state religion, some of the Taoist emperors of the Northern Sung cherished the same idea of compiling a new 'Tao-tsang' on a grand scale, and the first collection called the Pao-wen t'ung-lu, in seven sections (three categories and four supplementary divisions) and 4,359 scrolls, was completed in 1016. The compilation was made possible only after some preliminary collections had been made between 989 and 991, and the Taoist scriptures preserved in the Imperial Libraries as well as an incomplete collection of the T'ang Tao-tsang originally kept in the T'ai-ch'ing Monastery of Po-chou, the sanctuary for the worship of Lao-tzu, had been shipped to Hang-chou where the collation and revision were being done. It took three more years for copies of the Pao-wen collection to be transcribed. Chang Chün-fang was appointed to supervise the work, and later added to this collection yet

---

[35] See note 32 above.
[36] There are slight differences in the exact Chinese wording for these twelve sub-divisions recorded in different works. I follow here the *Tao-chiao i-shu*, Tao-tsang, 763, 2.14b. Cf. Yoshioka, *Dōkyō*, pp. 130-1.

another 206 scrolls of texts which he had chosen from more than 2,000 scrolls of copies of the old 'Tao-tsang' sent on imperial orders to Hang-chou from Su-chou, Yüeh-chou, and T'ai-chou. Among these additional materials scrutinised by Chang were some of the Manichaean texts which were then in circulation in Fukien. It is not certain, however, whether Chang included them in the new collection which was finally presented by him to the court in the spring of 1019.[37] It totalled 4,565 scrolls, in 466 *han* arranged in accordance with the order of characters in the *Ch'ien-tzu wen*, and was named the Ta-Sung t'ien-kung pao-tsang, for the wrappers of the works began with the character *t'ien* and ended with *kung*. This great collection was compiled in the reign of the Taoist Emperor Chen-tsung. Although the T'ien-kung pao-tsang is no longer extant, Chang Chün-fang fortunately compiled also a miniature collection of Taoist works in 120 *chüan* which may serve as a summary of the T'ien-kung pao-tsang and is still available in many editions. The title of this miniature collection is the Yün-chi ch'i-ch'ien.[38]

All these collections, including the T'ien-kung pao-tsang, existed only in transcripts. However, under the sponsorship of another Taoist ruler, Emperor Hui-tsung, also known as a great connoisseur of fine arts, the number of scrolls of Taoist works catalogued in the Imperial Library in K'ai-feng was increased to 5,387 between 1102 and 1106. In 1114, a bureau was set up by imperial edict for the collation of the texts and their engraving for the first time in Fu-chou.[39] Huang Shang, alias Huang Mien-chung (1043-1129), a Prefect of Fu-chou and a Taoist devotee, supervised the wood-block printing.[40] Thus, the first printed edition of the Tao-tsang of Sung times, entitled Cheng-ho wan-shou Tao-tsang and comprising 5,481 *chüan* in 540 *han*, was completed in 1116 or 1117. It is possible that copies of this edition were also bound in concertina style, but we have no definite proof of it. According to one record,[41] transcribed copies of the Cheng-ho wan-

[37] The Manichaean texts are not found in the existing Tao-tsang. For the possible inclusion of some of these texts in the 'Tao-tsang' of Sung times, see *Fo-tsu t'ung-chi*, in Tripitaka in Chinese, No. 2035, 49.431a-b. The Ming scholar Lin Chao-en (1517-98) who styled himself 'the Master of the Three Teachings' was from Fukien, and might have been influenced to some extent by Manichaeism. For Lin, see my 'Lin Chao-ên', *T'oung Pao* LIII (1967), pp. 253-78; Sakai Tadao, *Chūgoku zensho no kenkyū* (Tokyo, 1960), pp. 263-85.

[38] See Li Pi's preface to the *Ssu-shih-chiu chang ching* quoted in the *Wen-hsien t'ung-k'ao* 224.1804-5.

[39] Yüan Miao-tsung's preface to the *T'ai-shang chu-kuo chiu-min tsung-chen mi-yao*, written in 1116, mentions that he 'was appointed to work at the bureau in the seventh month of the year before last', i.e., 1114; see Tao-tsang, 986, preface 1b. Both Yoshioka, *Dōkyō*, p. 156 and Ch'en Kuo-fu (in his *Tao-tsang yüan-liu k'ao* (Peking, 1963), vol. 1, p. 136, made a mistake in maintaining that the bureau was set up in 1115 (Yoshioka and Ch'en) or 1116 (Ch'en).

[40] Huang's collected works *Yen-shan hsien-sheng wen-chi* are included in the Ssu-k'u ch'üan-shu chen-pen, 1st series (cf. 14.7a-8b, 16.10b-12b).

[41] See *Lung-ch'i hsien-chih* (1762 ed., supplemented 1877, Taipei reprint, 1967) 11.3a-b and *Chang-chou fu-chih* (1877 ed., Taipei reprint, 1965) 47.44b-45b.

shou Tao-tsang, made between 1234 and 1236 in Lung-ch'i of Chang-chou, Fukien, had been kept intact through many generations until 1864, when the monastery in which they were preserved was burnt to the ground during the Taiping war. It is to be regretted that during the protracted compilation of the Ming Tao-tsang no investigations were made with regard to this early collection.

The wood-blocks for the Cheng-ho wan-shou Tao-tsang were brought to K'ai-feng on completion of the work. In 1188, that is some seventy years after the engraving,[42] during the reign of Emperor Shih-tsung of the Jurchen Chin which ruled north China at that time, it was decreed that these blocks be sent to Peking to be preserved in the T'ien-ch'ang Monastery, which was located to the west of the present-day Pai-yün Monastery, the centre of the Ch'üan-chen Sect. Sun Ming-tao, the Superintendent of the Monastery, was entrusted with the repair of damaged blocks, and also with the dispatch of Taoist priests to different parts of north China to investigate and collect missing scriptures for a new edition of the collection. With this government support and also with the huge donations collected from many patrons, particularly from a man named Chao Tao-chen, who had taken upon himself the purchase of the logs for the wood-blocks, this new edition was eventually completed in 1191, the second year of the reign of Emperor Chang-tsung. Following the traditional practice since the T'ang dynasty, this collection of 6,455 *chüan* in 602 *han* was renamed the Ta-Chin Hsüan-tu pao-tsang. Among the 6,455 *chüan* of texts, 1,074 *chüan* were new material.[43]

The T'ien-ch'ang Monastery where the wood-blocks of the Hsüan-tu pao-tsang were kept was burnt down in 1202, and most of the blocks are believed to have been destroyed only ten years after their engraving.[44] This happened at a time when a new branch of religious Taoism had begun to flourish. This was the Ch'üan-chen Sect, led by Wang Che and his disciples with tens of thousands of followers in many provinces in the north. Since the Ch'üan-chen was perhaps the only influential Taoist sect in the north, their patriarchs even gained imperial favour, and on more than one occasion printed copies of the Hsüan-tu pao-tsang were bestowed on Taoist monasteries sponsored by this sect.[45] Because of this unusual favour shown to them throughout Chin and Yüan times, the Ch'üan-chen leaders, headed by Patriarch Ch'iu Ch'u-chi (1148-1227), began to show great interest in the compilation of another collection of the texts in accordance with the

---

[42] See Wei Po-hsiao, 'Shih-fang ta T'ien-ch'ang kuan Hsüan-tu pao-tsang pei-ming' in *Kung-kuan pei-chih*, Tao-tsang, 610.21b-22b; also 'Wei nei-han Po-hsiao' in Yüan Hao-wen's (1190-1257) *Chung-chou chi* (Peking, 1962 ed.), vol. 1, pp. 195-6.

[43] Tao-tsang, 610, pp. 23b-24a.

[44] Wang O, 'Ch'ung-hsiu T'ien-ch'ang kuan pei' written in 1296 and quoted in the *Chi-fu t'ung-chih* (1934) 178.6636, under 'Pai-yün kuan'.

[45] See *Chin-lien cheng-tsung chi*, Tao-tsang, 76, 4.9a; also *Chin-lien cheng-tsung hsien-yüan hsiang-chuan*, Tao-tsang, 76, pp. 33a-38b.

great tradition. This would naturally have also given them a good chance to incorporate some of their own works into this collection, since Ch'üan-chen, unlike the southern school of Taoism[46] and the traditional Celestial Master's Church,[47] was a comparatively young growth in the indigenous beliefs.

The task was taken up by Sung Te-fang (1183-1247), a disciple of Ch'iu's, and by Sung's own disciple, Ch'in Chih-an (1188-1244). They started the work in 1237 with the Hsüan-tu Monastery at P'ing-yang, Shansi, as their centre, using the copy of the Hsüan-tu pao-tsang left complete in Kuan-chou even after the disturbances caused by the looting and the fighting of the troops during the last days of the Jurchen Chin.[48] The engraving of this collection, totalling some 7,800 *chüan* and including most of the collected works, *goruku* and biographies of the Ch'üan-chen patriarchs, took place in 1244.[49] It was also named the Hsüan-tu pao-tsang, and its numerous newly engraved wood-blocks were kept in P'ing-yang.

The great debate between the Buddhist and Taoist leaders at the court of Emperor Hsien-tsung (Mangu) in 1258 over the authenticity of the *Lao-tzu hua-hu ching*, a Taoist scripture possibly of the third century and aimed at ridiculing foreign beliefs, resulted in the burning by imperial decree of a number of wood-blocks dealing with the Taoist scriptures which were considered to be apocryphal. Another edict to prohibit their circulation and to destroy more Taoist works was issued by Kubilai Khan in 1281 when even the wood-blocks of the second Hsüan-tu pao-tsang were burnt.[50] This may be one of the reasons why the Ming Tao-tsang of 1445 has a smaller number of *chüan* than its two predecessors. A comparison of the available stocks by the Ming compilers with the Yüan records resulted in the compilation of a catalogue of lost Taoist texts which was included in the Tao-tsang, No. 1056. This also explains why the compilation of the Ming Tao-tsang took more time.

The compilation of the Ming Tao-tsang was begun as early as 1406 when Chang Yü-ch'u, the forty-third Celestial Master of the Cheng-i Taoist Church, was entrusted by Emperor Ch'eng-tsu with this task.[51] Chang was

[46] The school led by Chang Po-tuan of Sung times, see below.
[47] For quick reference to the history of this particular sect, see Ch'en Kuo-fu, *Tao-tsang*, vol. 2, pp. 308-69; Sun K'o-k'uan, *Yüan-tai Tao-chiao chih fa-chan* (Taipei, 1968), pp. 1-74; Holmes Welch, 'The Chang T'ien-shih and Taoism in China', *Journal of Oriental Studies* IV, 1-2 (1957-8), pp. 188-212.
[48] See Yüan Hao-wen's *I-shan hsien-sheng wen-chi* (Ssu-pu ts'ung-k'an ed.) 31.12a-14b; also Li Tao-ch'ien's *Chung-nan shan tsu-t'ing hsien-chen nei-chuan*, Tao-tsang, 604B, p. 22b.
[49] See the *Tao-tsang tsun-ching li-tai kang-mu*, Tao-tsang, 1056B, p. 23b.
[50] For detailed account see, among other places, Monk Hsiang-mai, *Pien-wei lu*, Ch. 1, Tripitaka in Chinese, No. 2116, 52.752; ch. 2, ibid., p. 764; Ch'en Yüan, *Nan-Sung ch'u Ho-pei hsin Tao-chiao k'ao* (Peking, 1962), pp. 55-8; and Nogami Shunjō, 'Gendai Dōbutsu nikyō no kakushitsu', *Ōtani daigaku kenkyū nenpō* II (1943), pp. 213-75.
[51] *Huang-ch'ao en-ming shih-lu*, Tao-tsang, 1065, 3.4a-b; *Tao-men shih-kuei*, Tao-tsang, 988, p. 2a.

quite a learned scholar,[52] though his knowledge of the history of many other branches of the religion may have been limited.[53] After his death in 1410, his mantle as the chief compiler of the Tao-tsang presumably fell on his younger brother and successor Chang Yü-ch'ing who died in 1426, the second year of the reign of Emperor Hsüan-tsung; the work might have been interrupted then for a short period for want of a leader. However, the great collection was finally published in 1444 or 1445, while Shao I-cheng, the Titled Immortal in charge of the Taoist Church in Peking, was made Superintendent of the Publication of the Taoist Tripitaka only in 1444.[54] The second collection, the Hsü Tao-tsang, compiled and published under the supervision of Chang Kuo-hsiang, the fiftieth Celestial Master, was completed in 1607 after Emperor Shen-tsung's edict of the same year. The 121,589 wood-blocks of both collections, originally kept in the imperial palaces of Peking,[55] were destroyed by foreign troops during the Boxer rebellion.

The contents of the Tao-tsang have been criticised as too heterogeneous ever since 1784, when Chi Yün (1724-1805) and other compilers of the *Ssu-k'u ch'üan-shu tsung-mu* discussed them in their review of Pai Yün-chi's *Catalogue of the Tripitaka*.[56] The indiscriminate nature of the Tao-tsang is explained by its all-embracing contents ranging from works on pre-Ch'in philosophy, divination, alchemy, medicine, astronomy, and astrology to the collected works of many individual writers who happened to have lived between the third and sixteenth centuries. I need not emphasise the very large number of Taoist scriptures contained in it, some of which were written in imitation of the Buddhist texts introduced to China through translation from the Sanskrit,[57] nor the biographical and topographical records, most of which are legendary and the fruits of the authors' imaginations. However, in view of its long period of transmission during which the texts were transcribed and engraved in a most solemn and reverential manner characteristic of a religious tradition, and the enormous number of volumes it comprises, including some reasonably reliable biographies and epitaphs, historical accounts of monasteries, and even local gazetteers, scholars of all times have long cherished the belief that there is gold in the sands.

Their view was confirmed by the scholars of the Ch'ing, well-known as the best in the field of textual criticism. In collating a text, the elder scholars

---

[52] A number of his writings including some commentaries on Taoist texts are found in the Tao-tsang, 41-2; 988; 1018-21.

[53] See *Tao-men shih-kuei* in Tao-tsang, 988, pp. 7b-8b, also 11a. In this work Chang fails to give accounts of many other sects which were quite active in the south.

[54] There is a short statement on Shao in the *Ming-shih* (Po-na ed.) 299.23a-b, under the biography of Liu Yüan-jan. Cf. also Ch'en Kuo-fu, *Tao-tsang*, p. 176.

[55] Liu Jo-yü, *Ming kung-shih*, *t'u* Series (Peking, 1963), p. 93; also Hsüeh-chin t'ao-yüan ed., Series 8.

[56] *Ssu-k'u ch'üan-shu tsung-mu* 146, vol. 5, pp. 2895-6.

[57] See my monograph 'Ming-ju yü Tao-chiao', *New Asia Journal* VIII, 1 (1967), pp. 259-96.

of the Ch'ien-lung and Chia-ch'ing periods (1736-1820) spared no effort to gather all the related editions for comparison, and the edition laboriously copied from the Tao-tsang (the Tao-tsang pen) was sometimes considered as valuable as a Sung wood-block edition of the same work, for it may have been derived from a transcribed copy of a Sung text. The great sinologist Sun I-jang (1848-1908) also laid stress on the Tao-tsang text when compiling his *Mo-tzu chien-ku*.[58] Another scholar, Liu Shih-p'ei, decided to stay at the Pai-yün Monastery for several months in the winter of 1910 in order that he might have access to the tripitaka. As a result, he later published thirty-seven bibliographical notes on the Tao-tsang. Two of them deal with some diagrams on the *Book of Changes*, and one deals with the famous *Mu t'ien-tzu chuan*, a geographical work. The two classified catalogues of Taoist materials from Tun-huang published by the Japanese professors Ōbuchi Ninji and Yoshioka Yoshitoyo in 1960 and 1969 respectively[59] have not only confirmed the authenticity of the earlier Taoist texts included in the Tao-tsang, but have also shown how impossible present research in several fields would be without the existence of this great collection of Taoist literature.

Not as basic as their work of textual criticism was the study by Ch'ing scholars of some historico-geographical works of an earlier dynasty, using the unique material discovered in the Tao-tsang. The most outstanding case of this is perhaps the pioneering study of the *Ch'ang-ch'un chen-jen hsi-yu chi*, or *The Travels of an Alchemist*, as Arthur Waley puts it,[60] by the famous historian Ch'ien Ta-hsin (1728-1804). Ch'ien discovered this record in a copy of the Tao-tsang in the Hsüan-miao Monastery of Su-chou in 1795.[61] The story of Ch'iu Ch'u-chi's travels to the western region for an audience with Genghis Khan on the northern bank of the Hindu Kush in 1222 was translated first into Russian by Palladius, whose version was published in the *Proceedings of the Russian Orthodox Mission in Peking*, 1866.[62] A recent work on this subject is Cheng-siang Chen's *Ch'ang-ch'un chen-jen hsi-yu chi ti ti-li hsüeh p'ing-chu* published in 1968.[63] There are other scholarly works, notably Maspero's and Stein's discussions on the *T'ai-ch'ing chin-yeh shen-tan ching*,[64]

[58] The Chung-hua edition (Peking, 1957) is a reprint of the popular Kuo-hsüeh chi-pen ts'ung-shu edition published by the Commercial Press before the war.

[59] Ōbuchi Ninji, *Tonkō Dōkyō mokuroku* (Kyoto, 1960) and Yoshioka, *Sutain shōrai Daiei hakubutsukan zō Tonkō bunken bunrui mokuroku* (Tokyo, 1969), section on Taoism.

[60] Translated by Arthur Waley (London, 1931).

[61] Ch'ien, *Ch'ien-yen t'ang wen-chi* (Ssu-pu ts'ung-k'an ed.) 11.15b-16b.

[62] IV (1866), pp. 259-434.

[63] Research Report No. 8, Geographical Research Centre, Graduate School, Chinese University of Hong Kong, 1968.

[64] Tao-tsang, 582A, pp. 1a-18a. The last *chüan* of this scripture is attributed to Ko Hung (283-343). For a reliable account of Ko, see Ch'en Kuo-fu, *Tao-tsang*, pp. 95-8; cf. J.R. Ware, *Alchemy, Medicine and Religion in the China of A.D. 320* (Cambridge, Mass., 1966). For Stein's and Maspero's discussions, see R.A. Stein, 'Remarques sur les mouvements du taoïsme politico-religieux au IIe siècle ap. J.-C.', *T'oung Pao* L (1963), pp. 1-78; H. Maspero, 'Un texte taoïste sur L'Orient Romain' in his *Études historiques* (Paris, 1950), pp. 95-108.

a scripture on alchemy which also shows some knowledge of ancient geography in its reports about the *Océan Méridional* and the western region.

Following the footprints of his predecessors, Shen Tseng-chih (1851-1922) combed the whole tripitaka for the Taoist texts and left us with a collection of miscellaneous jottings which are terse, but stimulating.[65] Another contemporary scholar, Ch'en Yüan, known for his studies on Buddhist history and other historical works, published in the early forties the history of the Ch'üan-chen Sect in which he verified most of the Taoist records gathered from the Tao-tsang with his personal collection of rubbings taken from tablets of epitaphs, producing thus the first reliable account of religious activities in north China between the early part of the Southern Sung, and the rise to power of the Mongol Yüan.[66] The Taoist activities of the Southern School scholars have so far been overlooked, though not without reason, for the accounts of them in the Tao-tsang are scattered, and appear to be contradictory. For instance, the dates of Chang Po-tuan, one of the Five Patriarchs of the south, have been given traditionally as 987-1082.[67] In one of my essays on Taoism, I have refuted these dates on the strength of a record I have discovered in the *Tzu-yang chen-jen wu-chen chih-chih san-ch'eng pi-yao* which asserts that Chang had met a court minister named Huang Mien-chung in Yen-p'ing, Fukien, between 1111 and 1117, or some thirty to thirty-five years after Chang would have died according to the conventional dates. Huang Mien-chung or Huang Shang, who was the one entrusted with the engraving of the wood-blocks of the Cheng-ho wan-shou tao-tsang, is known to have been in Fukien at this time. This tallies again with my hypothesis that Chang might have been born in 1076.[68] Detailed studies of this kind could help to stir up interest among scholars whose main field of research is not religious, but historical.

Although there have been hundreds of Japanese scholars working on the Taoist tripitaka since the War, and Taoist studies in terms of religious cultivation and alchemy have been in vogue in Europe as well as in the United States,[69] much valuable information remains comparatively little known: for instance that some of the lost essays written by one of the earliest Taoist masters Lu Hsiu-ching are actually hidden in the Tao-tsang, in a ritual work dealing with the lighting up of a candle;[70] and that in the same collection there are materials related either to the construction of a clepsydra,

[65] *Hai-jih lou cha-ts'ung* (Peking, 1962 ed.) 6.

[66] *Nan-Sung ch'u Ho-pei hsin Tao-chiao k'ao*, cf. Note 49.

[67] *Tzu-yang chen-jen wu-chen p'ien chu-shu*, Tao-tsang, 62, 5.11b.

[68] 'Tao-tsang pen wu-chen p'ien san-chu pien-wu', *Tung-hsi wen-hua* XV (Sept. 1968), pp. 33-41; cf. Tao-tsang, 64, pp. 15a-16b.

[69] For the study of alchemy and medicine, see Nathan Sivin, *Chinese Alchemy Preliminary Studies* (Cambridge, Mass., 1968); Ho Peng-yoke and Su Ying-hui, 'Tan-fang ching-yüan k'ao', *Journal of Oriental Studies* VIII, 1 (1970), pp. 1-23.

[70] See *Tung-hsüan ling-pao chai-shuo kuang-chu chieh-fa teng-chu-yüan-i*, Tao-tsang, 293, pp. 1a-7b.

or to a mechanical device to forecast the weather.[71] Dozens of examples of a similar nature remind us how much work remains to be done before justice can be done to this great tripitaka, of which no reliable bibliographical catalogue has yet been made since its last publication nearly 400 years ago.

BIBLIOGRAPHICAL NOTES

Bibliography for the study of the Tao-tsang is extremely difficult to list. Yoshioka Yoshitoyo, in his *Dōkyō kyoten shiron* mentioned above, has given twenty-three books and monographs relating to this subject. Ch'en Kuo-fu's history of the Tao-tsang should be recommended in its 1962 revised edition rather than the first edition of 1949. In addition, the new publications on religious Taoism by Yang Lien-sheng, Wang Ming, Ch'en Shih-hsiang, Jao Tsung-i, Yen Ling-feng, Chang Chung-yüan, Ho Peng-yoke, Sun K'o-k'uan, Yoshioka Yoshitoyo, Fukui Kojun, Kubo Noritada, Ōbuchi Ninji, Sakai Tadao, R.A. Stein, Max Kaltenmark, Arthur Wright, Hellmut Wilhelm, Holmes Welch, Nathan Sivin, Werner Eichhorn, Marcel Granet, Anna Seidel, Kristopher Schipper, Jean Filliozat and many others should be noted. A selected bibliography of Chinese and Japanese works on Ming Taoism compiled by me in 1966 and published in the *Chung-chi Journal* VI, 2 (1967), and the 'Bibliographie du Taoïsme: étude dans les occidentales' compiled by Michel Soymié and F. Litsch and appearing in the third volume of the *Dōkyō kenkyū* (Tokyo, 1968) may also be mentioned.

---

[71] The *Ch'üan-chen tso-po chieh-fa*, Tao-tsang, 988, pp. 1a-4b and the *Yü-yang ch'i-hou ch'in-chi* and the *P'an-t'ien ching* both in Tao-tsang, 1004, pp. 1a-16b and 1a-15b respectively.

119

史 XIII: The Tun-huang Manuscripts

FUJIEDA AKIRA

About 1900, a small cave-temple was found behind the right-hand side wall of the corridor to the main hall of cave No. 16 (as numbered by the Tun-huang Institute) which is one of the biggest of the famous Ch'ien-fo Caves in Tun-huang. The small cave discovered was filled with old Chinese manuscripts in scroll form and Tibetan manuscripts in scroll and *pothi* forms, as well as numerous broken Buddha images, paintings on paper, silk, and hemp, and other decorations of Buddha halls. A decade later, successive expeditions to Central Asia, sent by the Indian and British governments (led by Aurel Stein), France (Paul Pelliot), Japan (Ōtani Kōzui), and Russia (Sergei F. Oldenburg), visited the place and bought thousands of manuscripts and other objects from the Taoist monk who dwelt in one of the caves and had found the hidden library. The Chinese government, surprised by the news of these foreign expeditions, ordered the local office to bring all the remaining Chinese manuscripts to Peking. There still remained a large number of manuscripts, mostly in Tibetan, and they were said to have weighed more than a ton.

These manuscripts were sent to the central libraries and museums of the home countries of the expeditions. They were catalogued and some of them were photographed, edited and studied. All the manuscripts of the first series of both the Stein and Peking collections, each nearly 10,000 in number, have been microfilmed. We now have access to the corpus of manuscripts, which has been scattered to various parts of the world. This paper will deal with the manuscripts in Chinese only.

The Stein and Peking collections are somewhat similar in content, the majority of the manuscripts being Buddhist texts. There are a small number of Taoist and Confucian texts and documents. Pelliot did not choose the usual Buddhist texts but picked up unusual ones and texts other than Buddhist. The Japanese expedition acquired only a small number of manuscripts, since it went to Tun-huang after the Chinese government had taken away the bulk of the remaining manuscripts. The Russians went there last of all and they collected mostly fragments, although their collection is large in its number of manuscripts.

There are many small collections besides the five mentioned above, varying from several hundred to a few scrolls. Most of these manuscripts are said to have been lost from the main body on their way from Tun-huang to the Peking National Library, but as far as I have seen, the manuscripts of these minor collections are not genuine.

Formal Characteristics of the Manuscripts and their Dating

Most of the manuscripts in Chinese are in scroll form. This had been in use for ordinary books since the invention of paper and remained so for nearly eight centuries before printed books became dominant. Again the greater number of scrolls are in the standard form, others are in irregular forms.

The common rule for the standard form of scrolls is as follows: the manuscripts are written on a certain quality of paper, one foot in width; each scroll is covered with a frontispiece of a thick sheet or double-sheet of paper, on which a title, serial number and other library marks are given; the text starts with a full title and usually closes with an abridged one, sometimes with a colophon attached; each column is divided by very thin lines and contains seventeen characters; the characters are in the very upright handwriting of professional scribes.

Nearly 1,000 manuscripts bear a dated colophon, and documents are normally dated. The dates of some others are identifiable. The earliest of them is a Vinaya text, S.797, which bears a colophon dated 406 A.D., while the latest is a document in the Leningrad collection which is dated 1002 A.D. Only a few manuscripts seem to have been written earlier than 406 and probably none is later than 1002. The dated manuscripts are numerous enough and close enough in succession to enable us to date other manuscripts.

Roughly speaking, we can divide the change of the form of the manuscripts into three stages, fifth-sixth centuries, seventh-eighth centuries, and ninth-tenth centuries. We may take the manuscripts of the second stage as the standard type, the first as the early type, and the third as the later or corrupt type. This division is concerned not only with the form of the manuscripts but has a definite importance for the nature of the text.

The formal characteristics of the scrolls of the standard type from the second period are as follows.

They are written on *ma-chih* or hemp paper, thick and very fine in texture, made from used hemp cloth, about 25-6 cm in width, dyed in brown colour with the juices of certain kinds of vegetable. The handwriting of this period may be regarded as the typical *k'ai* style, written with a brush made of a bamboo holder and rabbit hair. Typical of the scrolls of this stage are the series of manuscripts of the *Lotus Sūtra* and the *Diamond Sūtra* which were copied at the T'ang court in the years 671-7. Many other copies were made after the model of these imperial manuscripts to keep at local libraries. Some manuscripts of Taoist and Confucian texts were also written in Ch'ang-an, according to their colophons, and are outstanding in appearance.

The first stage can be divided into two parts. The manuscripts of the earlier part were written on very coarse paper, 1-2 cm narrower than that of the second stage, sometimes dyed in light brown. The handwriting is something between the *li* and the *k'ai* styles and we may regard it as the transition stage between the two. It is obviously written with a different kind of brush from that of the *k'ai* style. It must have been made of deer hair and a wooden holder, which had been invented for writing the *li* style characters on a wooden tablet. A column does not always contain seventeen characters in the manuscripts written in the oldest style of handwriting. As time went on, the paper became finer and the handwriting closer to the typical *k'ai*.

This type of paper was gradually replaced by another kind in the second half of the sixth century, and finally disappeared from Tun-huang about 600 A.D. The later type of paper is very thin and much finer in texture, dyed in beautiful lemon-yellow. The typical *k'ai* style first appeared in Tun-huang on this kind of paper at the end of the sixth century, that is after the unification of China by the Sui dynasty. A manuscript in the Stein collection coming from south China in 513 A.D. is written on this type of paper and in handwriting very close to the *k'ai* style. We can trace the lineage of this type of manuscript to as early as the fifth century, because a fragment in the Turfan collection of Berlin, which was also written in south China in 476, is of the same type. We may conclude that the paper and the handwriting of this type were an invention from south China. The paper was replaced by the hemp paper mentioned above in the middle of the seventh century, that is at the beginning of the T'ang rule.

At the end of the eighth century the area of Tun-huang was occupied by the Tibetans, and the Chinese people there could not obtain writing material from China proper. At first both they and the Tibetans wrote their manuscripts on the reverse side of used paper with a reed or wooden pen. They then began to produce paper by themselves in Tun-huang early in the ninth century. This paper is very thick and coarse in texture, about 32 cm in length and must have been intended to make a regular T'ang foot (30 cm) when the margins were cut to make a scroll. They sometimes retouched the strokes to imitate the touch of brush writing. A brush was very seldom used even after the Chinese had recovered Tun-huang in the middle of the ninth century.

The scrolls in irregular forms were often written on paper of a kind different from the normal type of each period and often on the reverse side of used paper. They are usually not in an upright writing style and a column contains more than seventeen characters.

New types of books, in forms other than scroll, appeared in the third period. They are *pothi*, accordion-shaped books and booklets, but the remaining examples are not very numerous. They were always written with a reed pen on thick, coarse paper made in Tun-huang. The manuscripts in other than the regular scroll form normally contain texts of a kind different from those entered in the standard Buddhist, Taoist, and Confucian catalogues: commentaries to a regular text, exercise books, apocryphal works, glossaries, and other texts for personal use.

Buddhist Texts—Canonical

The Buddhist texts which are entered in imperial catalogues are normally written in the standard form. Each text is usually represented by a few copies. The library marks on the covers of the scrolls imply that they belonged to a few sets of the Tripitaka in monastic libraries before they were brought to the cave library and had been arranged in the order of the *K'ai-yüan Shih-chiao lu.*

There are many copies of a few texts. The most common is the *Diamond Sūtra* with nearly 2,000 copies in various collections. The second is the *Lotus Sūtra*, a copy of which consists of seven (in older times eight or ten) scrolls, more than 1,000 scrolls in all. Chapter 25 of this text was very often copied separately with another title at the end: *Kuan-yin ching.* The *Kuan-yin ching* was often copied in irregular forms in the third period. The next most common are the *Wei-mo-chieh ching* or *Vimalakīrti Sūtra* and the *Chin-kuang-ming tsui-sheng-wang ching* or *Suvarnaprabhāsottamarāja Sūtra,* each of which is represented by nearly 100 copies. These scrolls were, according to the colophons to some of them, donated by religious and lay people to a monastery in addition to the regular set of the Tripitaka.

Some texts, such as Buddhabhadra's version of the *Hua-yen ching* (*Buddhāvataṃsaka Sūtra*), were copied in the first period and the early part of the second; obviously this work was replaced by a new version in a set of the Tripitaka. At the same time, various versions of other texts, such as the *Chin-kuang-ming ching,* were copied in parallel. For some texts, such as the *Wei-mo-chieh ching,* only one version was copied through the three stages.

These old manuscripts contain, as a matter of course, a number of textual variants from the present edition of the Tripitaka, which is based on the Korean edition. The manuscripts from the first period are especially rich in preserving old forms of the texts, not only in the characters but in the division of the scrolls, chapters and paragraphs.

Buddhist Texts—Non-Canonical

Besides those texts which are entered in imperial catalogues, there are a number of texts not. Most of them had been lost or previously unknown in China and were discovered in the Tun-huang collections, which are consequently of prime importance for our knowledge of Chinese Buddhism. Yabuki Keiki studied some of them, mainly those of the Stein collection, and they have been edited in the Taishō Tripitaka, vol. 85, but we now have more material than he had fifty years ago.

The texts excluded from imperial catalogues were mostly written in the first and third periods, very few in the second. They include different versions from those entered in the standard Tripitaka; apocryphal works; commentaries to ordinary texts; Buddhist works written by Chinese; exercise books for monks and nuns; and Buddhist works for laymen. There is a considerable difference between the natures of those from the first period and those from the third.

First, let us look at the different versions. Many Buddhist texts were translated into Chinese in the fourth and fifth centuries, but some of them had very limited circulation, since north China was divided at that time into several states. A Buddhist catalogue, *Ch'u san-tsang chi chi*, mentions some of them which the compiler had not seen himself. A few such versions survive in the Tun-huang collections, such as that of the *Shih-sung lü*, the oldest dated manuscript. Under the rule of the Tibetans (781-848 A.D.), a number of Buddhist texts, such as the *Ta-sheng wu-liang shou ching* and *Tao-kan ching*, were translated into Chinese in Tun-huang and adjacent cities. Some of them, such as the *Chu-hsing-mu t'o-lo-ni ching* and the *Sa-po-to-tsung wu-shih lun*, are attributed to Fa-ch'eng (Tibetan Chos-grub), a bilingual master translator who came from the Wu family of Tun-huang. The translators of other texts are unknown, though some scholars attribute them also to him.

Second, there are the apocryphal works: each catalogue of Buddhist texts in Chinese contains a list of apocryphal books for which there are no Indian originals but which were composed in China claiming to be translations. These lists differ from one another in the contents of the texts, but finally had a fixed list in the *K'ai-yüan Shih-chiao lu*. Those listed there are no longer included in a regular set of the Tripitaka and most of them disappeared in China. Some of these texts were discovered at Tun-huang. They are mostly written in the first and third periods, with very few in the second. Those from the first period were later excluded from the imperial catalogue but apparently included in an ordinary monastic library. They are always in the regular form and written in a hand of the sixth and early-seventh centuries. Some examples are the *Ta-t'ung fang-kuang ching*, the *Ching-tu san-mei ching*, the *T'i-wei po-li ching*, the *Buddhanāma Sūtra* in sixteen scrolls, and several texts of the San-chieh Sect. Those from the second and third periods are somewhat different in nature from the earlier ones, being a mixture of Buddhism and vulgar faiths. They are very often in an irregular form, apparently not intended for a monastic library. Some manuscripts from the second period are in a regular form but written with a wooden pen.

Third, there are a number of manuscripts of commentaries to some Buddhist texts written in the first period, some of them bearing dated colophons. These commentaries were all unknown before the discovery of the Tun-huang manuscripts. The reason why they disappeared is obvious. After the unification of China by the Sui dynasty, the southern school of Buddhist studies superseded that of the north, and only the commentaries of the southern school were preserved. We find many passages of these northern commentaries quoted in later works, however, without mention of the original author. These manuscripts are indeed a rich store of source-material for reconstructing Buddhist studies under the Northern Dynasties. The commentaries from the third period differ in nature from those of the first. They represent either some non-standard school of China proper or local works of Tun-huang.

Some of the commentaries were written by the monk T'an-k'uang. He was born a few hundred miles east of Tun-huang, spent his youth at the Hsi-ming monastery in Ch'ang-an, and then went back to Ling-chou, one of the important cities in the westernmost part of China. He was soon forced to flee to Tun-huang, owing to the Tibetan invasion at the end of the eighth century, and introduced there the teachings of the Hsi-ming Monastery school which had been led by Yüan-ts'e, a disciple of the great master Hsüan-tsang. He composed commentaries to the *Ta-sheng ch'i-hsin lun*, the *Pai-fa men-ming lun*, the *Diamond Sūtra*, and other Buddhist works.

Fa-ch'eng, the bilingual master mentioned above, also left some commentaries, such as those to the *Tao-kan ching* and *Ta-sheng ssu-fa men lun*. His most outstanding work is the commentary to the *Yü-chia shih-ti lun* (*Yogācāryabhūmi śāstra*), which is represented by more than 100 scrolls. These manuscripts show that his commentaries were given in lectures and copied down on uniform scrolls by six of his disciples. Their work continued from 854 A.D. to 858, probably about the time of Fa-ch'eng's death. By then they had completed fifty-nine of the 100 or so scrolls. Besides these two masters, there must have been a few more who had written other commentaries, but they are left for future research.

A fourth kind of text comprised formulae for prayers, vows, confessions, and other rituals serving as exercise books for monks and nuns. An exhaustive collection of such formulae was compiled by Tao-hsüan in the T'ang period and is edited in the present Tripitaka. Various kinds of such collections had been in use in the first period, or before the collection of Tao-hsüan appeared, while various excerpts from Tao-hsüan were copied in the third period. They were generally in irregular forms, since they were not intended for a monastic library but for personal use. Some of them from the third period are written in the very poor hand of a small boy, apparently copied at a monastic school as described below. Some texts of this kind seem to have been translated from Tibetan. Chinese texts were often transcribed in Tibetan letters, and the pronunciation of each Chinese character is given on some of these manuscripts. Tibetan letters were apparently easier to read for the Chinese of Tun-huang under Tibetan rule.

Miscellaneous theoretical works such as essays, discussions, dialogues, and compositions have been found, dating mainly from the third period. Those which were derived from the debate carried out by the Chinese and Indian monks, such as the *Tun-wu ta-sheng cheng-li chüeh* and the *Ta-sheng nien-erh wen pen*, stand out among these manuscripts, and have been studied by Demiéville and Ueyama respectively. Many Japanese scholars of Zen (Ch'an) Buddhism are interested in the texts of their sect, such as the *Leng-chia shih-tzu chi* and the *Shen-hui yü-lu*. Some of them were brought to Tun-huang from China proper, apparently late in the eighth century, but most were copied in Tun-huang, many of them being made there under Tibetan rule.

Finally there were Buddhist writings for laymen. The manuscripts mentioned above were mostly intended for monks, nuns, and monastic libraries. Besides these, there are some kinds of manuscripts written by laymen, such as prayers and confessions, which differ from those of religious people, and some others which were intended for propaganda among laymen. They are miracle stories about certain deities and a certain scripture, eulogies in verse often in the spoken language, and a certain kind of story which used prose and verse alternatively. The last type is called *pien-wen*; it had been forgotten in China until the discovery of the library and may be regarded as the most outstanding revelation of the Tun-huang manuscripts today. This kind was also called *chiang-ching wen*, and each was originally an interpretation of a Buddhist text composed in combination with a *pien-hsiang*, or painting describing the stories of the text.

Monastic Documents

There were nearly twenty monasteries and convents in Tun-huang in the eighth to tenth centuries, and several hundred, sometimes more than a thousand, monks and nuns dwelt in them. The monasteries and convents had to administer large estates for the livelihood of so many people, and to organise a hierarchy to manage them. In connection with this huge religious order, laymen organised societies (*she*) to carry out religious activities. The cave-library contained various kinds of documents concerning the administration and finance of monasteries and lay societies, as well as confessions and other documents of Buddhist ritual written by laymen. However, these documents were stored in the library not for the purpose of preserving them as an archive, but because some other Buddhist writings had been written on the reverse side of the paper after they had been discarded at the monastic office. For this reason, the documents are too fragmentary to reconstruct the details of religious organisation satisfactorily, but not too scanty to give up. A number of scholars have studied the monastic history of Tun-huang, making use of this material.

Each monastery and convent had a school to educate lay children, who were called *hsüeh-shih-lang*. A large part of the non-Buddhist manuscripts discovered in the cave-library can be regarded as having been used at these monastic schools. Some of them are written in the poor hand of schoolboys, and punctuated in red, often with the colophon of a *hsüeh-shih-lang*. These are Confucian texts, anthologies from Chinese Classics, summaries or excerpts of a classical text, glossaries, dictionaries of phonetics, letter-writing models and other models of compositions, or calligraphic exercises of the *Ch'ien-tzu wen*.

Non-Buddhist Manuscripts

Besides the Buddhist manuscripts and those concerned with Buddhist institutions, there is a considerable number of non-Buddhist manuscripts, such as Taoist and Confucian texts or governmental documents. They do not account for more than 5 per cent of the total corpus of Tun-huang manuscripts. Yet, especially in the early stage, they attracted by far the most attention from scholars, owing to the keen interest of sinologists.

In all there are nearly 500 Taoist texts. With only a few exceptions, they are written on uniform scrolls of the regular type of the second period, and most in a very good hand. Some of them bear colophons written in Ch'ang-an. There are several fragments of colophons to Confucian texts which were written at an imperial library of the T'ang. The governmental documents of the T'ang are written on *ch'u-chih* or mulberry paper, 31 by 46 sq. cm., and bear a few governmental seals on each sheet. The reverse side of many of these manuscripts has been used for other purposes, mainly for writings in Chinese, Tibetan, and Khotanese of the late eighth and early ninth centuries or the early period of Tibetan rule in Tun-huang. The manuscripts must originally have been kept either at a Taoist monastery under the patronage of the T'ang government, a governmental school, or a local governmental office under T'ang rule. They were lost by their owners as a result of the Tibetan occupation. The Buddhists in Tun-huang, both Chinese and Tibetan, had used these manuscripts as their writing material before they began to make paper by themselves in Tun-huang, apparently in the second quarter of the ninth century. In other words, they have been preserved in our cave-library for a similar reason to that of the monastic documents treated above. We should be very careful in making use of these governmental and monastic documents as material for Chinese history, because most of them, though in Chinese and dated with a *nien-hao*, were written outside Chinese rule.

Conclusion

We have surveyed all types of manuscripts in Chinese from Tun-huang which have now been scattered to various parts of the world. It is noteworthy that very few of them have been preserved complete. They had been stored with a bulk of manuscripts in Tibetan which must have been nothing more than waste paper for the Chinese of Tun-huang when the cave-library was walled up some time very early in the eleventh century. Moreover, they had been stored together with broken Buddha images and other discarded religious objects. Stein, the first visitor to this cave-library, describes it as a 'deposit of sacred "waste" '. All the manuscripts from the first period are fragmentary. This implies that the waste must have accumulated for a long time.

The most probable reason for such a huge accumulation of waste is that, when the printing of books became widespread in the tenth century, the handwritten manuscripts of the Tripitaka at the monastic libraries must have been replaced by books of a new type—the printed Tripitaka. Consequently, the discarded manuscripts found their way to the sacred waste-pile, where torn scrolls from old times as well as a bulk of manuscripts in Tibetan had been stored. In order to prevent it from being used for an undesirable purpose, a certain pious person walled up the sacred 'waste'. All we can say for certain is that he came from the Wu family, because the compound of the three-storied cave temples, Nos. 16-18 and 365-6, is known to have been built and kept by the Wu family, of which the mid-ninth century Bishop of Tun-huang, Hung-pien, was a member.

NOTE ON THE CATALOGUES OF THE TUN-HUANG MANUSCRIPTS

The following are the catalogues published so far:

Ch'en Yüan, *Tun-huang chieh-yü lu*, Peiping, 1931. This work catalogues the manuscripts in the Peking collection.

Giles, Lionel, *Descriptive Catalogue of the Chinese Manuscripts from Tun-huang in the British Museum*, London, 1957. Catalogue of the Stein collection.

Kantōchō hakubutsukan, 'Ōtani ke shuppin mokuroku', in *Shin Saiiki ki*, Vol. 2, Kyoto, 1937. Catalogue of the Ōtani collection.

Vorob'eva-Desiatovskaia, M., and others, *Opisanie kitaiskikh rukopisei Dun'-khuanskogo fonda Instituta naradov Azii*, 2 vols., Moscow, 1963, 1966. Catalogue of the Oldenburg collection.

Wang Chung-min, 'Po Hsi-ho chieh-ching lu', in *Tun-huang i-shu tsung-mu so-yin*, Peking, 1962. Catalogue of the Pelliot collection.

A substantial portion of the non-Buddhist manuscripts, mainly from the Pelliot collection, has been described by Wang Chung-min in *Tun-huang ku-chi hsü-lu* (Peking, 1958). The detailed catalogue of the first 500 manuscripts of the Pelliot collection, which had been awaited for many years, appeared in *Catalogue des manuscrits chinois de Touen-houang (Fonds Pelliot chinois)*, vol. I, nos. 2001-500, Paris, 1970. For the remainder of the collection, however, the provisional catalogue noted above is the only one available at present.

史 xiv: Tibetan Sources

JOSEF KOLMAŠ

The sense that seems to be inherent in almost all Chinese of minutely recording the various facts and events having a bearing upon the history of their own country, and of carefully keeping their archives, is well known and can easily be attested: the contributions for the present volume provide the most striking testimony of it. Similarly well-known—even though less profoundly studied or evaluated in the West—are the Chinese records of the countries on the periphery of China's political and cultural influence. It is known that some of these countries became fully amalgamated into China's political, cultural, and other institutions, and have to all practical purposes disappeared from the scene of history. Some countries, however, managed to maintain their own specific features, their language, culture, and religion, even if they were forced to abandon their political freedom and independence. Tibet, one of the culturally most developed and politically most nation-conscious dependencies in China's 'Far West', belongs to the latter group. Were the theme of my contribution for the present volume Chinese sources on Tibet, my task would perhaps be more attractive, though not necessarily easier, and the information gathered might well be richer and more representative.[1]

Nevertheless, the reader should not automatically deduce that the contribution of the Tibetan native historiography to the knowledge of the 'Great Country' in the East, China, does not exist at all, or is hardly worth noticing. If anything, it is precisely that historiography which represents the strong side of the Tibetan culture and which has already a century-old tradition in that country.

China's history is so interwoven with Tibetan and *vice versa*, that we can find mention of China (and also of Mongolia and the country of the Tanguts) in almost every important historical composition by Tibetan authors, or by Mongol authors who wrote their histories in Tibetan. This

---

[1] For Chinese works on Tibet (including the former Sikang Province), see Teng Yen-lin, *Chung-kuo pien-chiang t'u-chi lu* (Shanghai, 1958), especially pp. 205-21. For a list of other important translations of Chinese sources on Tibet, see, e.g., my '*Ch'ing-shih-kao* on Modern History of Tibet (1903-1912)', *Archiv orientální* XXXII (1964), pp. 77-8, note 1. So far no comprehensive study is available on Tibet in Chinese dynastic histories.

they usually do in the form of a special chapter (or chapters) devoted to the political history of China in general, commencing from time immemorial and reaching roughly the date of composition of the work concerned; to a detailed discussion of Sino-Tibetan relations in the T'ang (618-907), the period that marked the beginning of mutual contacts between the two countries; and to the religious history of China, being mainly the history of the spread of Buddha's doctrine in China.

Let us put aside in this connection the relatively small and so far little explored treasure of ancient Tibetan epigraphs dating from the eighth to the ninth century. Of these stone inscriptions only the bilingual text of the Sino-Tibetan treaty of 821-2, preserved on a pillar in Lhasa, has a direct bearing upon the history of T'ang China, containing important material for the study of the relations between these two countries in the early ninth century.[2]

The so-called Tun-huang chronicles and other Tibetan texts discovered in Chinese Turkestan by Sir Aurel Stein and Paul Pelliot at the beginning of this century cover the period in Tibetan history between the last half of the seventh and the first half of the eighth century. These texts and documents represent the most ancient monuments of Tibetan literature, and by coincidence, at least some of them are of importance for the study of Chinese history, especially the question of Sino-Tibetan relations. We read, for instance, about frequent clashes between the Tibetans and the Chinese, the occupation of Chinese fortresses by the Tibetan troops, the audiences of Chinese envoys at the court of the Tibetan kings, the arrival in Lhasa (in 710 A.D.) of the Chinese Princess Chin-ch'eng to marry a Tibetan king, etc. The character and form of these annals (the events are registered in order of years) lead us to presuppose that their anonymous compiler(s) might well have known and studied the standard works of official Chinese historiography. However, for the history of China in the strict sense of the word, the value of these and related sources is rather limited.[3]

The study of Tibetan works such as *Li-yul lung-bstan-pa* or *Prophecy of the Li Country*, and *Li-yul chos-kyi lo-rgyus* or *Religious Annals of the Li Country* (both dating approximately from the ninth to the tenth centuries) is quite indispensable for a better knowledge of the ancient, pre-Islamic history of

---

[2] The text of the Sino-Tibetan Treaty of 821-2, together with a translation, has been published by Li Fang-kuei, 'The Inscription of the Sino-Tibetan Treaty of 821-822', *T'oung Pao* XLIV (1956), pp. 1-99. Studies on the Sino-Tibetan Treaty have been summarised and reviewed by Taishun Mibu in *Shūkyō bunka* XIII (December 1958), pp. 55-64, and by Hisashi Satō, *Kodai Chibetto shi kenkyū* (Kyoto, 1959), vol. 2, pp. 874-931.

[3] Tibetan texts from Tun-huang and other parts of Chinese Turkestan have been translated, with commentary, by J. Bacot, F.W. Thomas, and Ch. Toussaint, *Documents de Touen-Houang relatifs à l'histoire du Tibet*, and especially by F.W. Thomas, *Tibetan Literary Texts and Documents concerning Chinese Turkestan*. The Hungarian scholar Géza Uray has devoted many of his learned articles, published in *Acta Orientalia Hung.*, to an examination of the various aspects of this valuable historical material.

present-day Yü-tien (known as Khotan; Li-yul or the Li country in Tibetan) in the Uighur Autonomous Region of Sinkiang. Both works are incorporated in the Tanjur section of the Tibetan Buddhist canons.[4]

The proper development of the traditional Tibetan historiography, accompanied by an increase in the number of representative works of Tibetan historical literature, must be linked with the names of Lamaist authors beginning with the thirteenth/fourteenth century. Their *chos-'byung* (records of the origin and spread of Buddha's doctrine), or *rgyal-rabs* (genealogies of the kings), as these standard histories of the Lamaist period are commonly known, naturally lay the main stress on religious history (introduction and spread of Buddhism, foundation of monasteries, birth and death of leading lamas, arrival in Tibet of famous masters, etc.), the events of purely political history and other worldly developments occupying a secondary position only. Nevertheless, since they are based on other earlier and contemporary sources, some of which have not survived, or on reliable oral tradition, and sometimes on personal observation and evaluation of historical events by the authors themselves or by their contemporaries, these works are our most valuable source of information.[5]

As far as passages devoted to China are concerned, such books mostly contain information of a rather general character, taken from various official Chinese sources. Their value as original sources for China is therefore questionable if not negligible. At the most, they may testify to what was known to the respective author from the field of Chinese historical literature, or what was available to him at the moment either in the original or in translation, and how he had mastered and interpreted his sources. From the chronological aspect, the indigenous Tibetan sources are definitely inferior to the Chinese, and they cannot serve as a reliable guide. For these reasons, and also because my space is restricted, I shall limit myself in the following bibliographical sketch to those works which—as regards China— are most representative and easily accessible to non-Tibetologists. In discussing Lamaist sources on China, I have adhered to chronological order.

Amongst the oldest and most representative works of Lamaist historiography, frequently quoted in later historical literature, is Bu-ston's (1290-1364) *Chos-'byung* or *History of Religion* (i.e. Buddhism), written in 1322. However, being mainly concerned with Indian Buddhism and the history

---

[4] The contents of these and related works was first given by W.W. Rockhill, *The Life of the Buddha . . . Followed by Notices on the Early History of Tibet and Khotan* (London, 1884), pp. 230-48. For text editions and translations, see F.W. Thomas, *Tibetan Literary Texts*, part 1, pp. 89-136 and 303-23, and R.E. Emmerick, *Tibetan Texts concerning Khotan.*

[5] The question of the validity of Tibetan historical tradition in the works of the Lamaist authors in general, and especially in the light of, or with regard to the more ancient chronicles discovered in Tun-huang, is discussed by G. Tucci in his contribution for the *India Antiqua*, pp. 309-22.

of Buddhist canonical literature in Tibet, this work contains but a few pages on the history of Tibet with only sporadic mention of T'ang China.[6]

As far as I know, the first coherent and systematic discussion of China's history in the works of Lamaist authors is to be found in the little known chronicle called the *Deb-ther dmar-po* or *Red Annals*, composed by Kun-dga'-rdo-rje in 1346. This old work, considered a bibliographical rarity until recently, was republished by the Namgyal Institute of Tibetology, Gangtok, in 1961.[7] The author devotes the whole of Chapter 2 in his work (Sikkim edition, pp. 6a-12b) to an interesting description of the political history of China from the Chou dynasty in the ancient past to the Yüan dynasty (1280-1367), laying particular stress on Sino-Tibetan relations in the T'ang. His work is based on information collected from Chinese sources variously styled *rGya-nag-po'i yig-tshang* (*Chinese Archives*), *rGya'i deb-gter rñing-pa* (*Ancient Book on China*), and *Thang-śu thu-han* or *Thang-źu thu-hwen*—evidently this is the T'u-fan chapter of the *T'ang-shu*. It should be pointed out, however, that Kun-dga'-rdo-rje did not have direct access to the original Chinese text(s), but compiled his *deb-ther* from the material translated by a Chinese called Ba-hu-gyang-ju (or 'U-gyang-dsu according to other sources) in 1285 and later (1325) edited with some adaptations by Lama Rin-chen-grags. This statement is based on Kun-dga'-rdo-rje himself (Sikkim edition, p. 12a) and was later on confirmed also in the *Blue Annals* (see below).

However, according to a later chronicle, the *rGyal-rabs gsal-ba'i me-long* (Kuznetsov's edition, p. 22; about this chronicle, see below), Kun-dga'-rdo-rje's main source of information was the material translated by a certain Śes-rab-ye-śes, an authority on Chinese and Mongolian historical sources, who has remained so far unknown to modern philology. The Tibetan historiographers of the later period made frequent use of the *Red Annals*, from which, as a rule, they took over their accounts of Chinese and Mongol emperors.[8]

So far untranslated and almost untouched by Western scholars is another work of Tibetan historiography of this early period. This is Śrībhūtibhadra's (dPal-'byor-bzang-po?) *rGya bod yig-tshang* or *Archives on China and Tibet*,

---

[6] Bu-ston's work is available in an English translation by E. Obermiller, *History of Buddhism* (*Chos-hbyung*) *by Bu-ston*. The section dealing with the history of Tibet is to be found in part 2, pp. 180ff.

[7] *The Red Annals*. Part One (Tibetan Text). Published by the Namgyal Institute of Tibetology, Gangtok, Sikkim, 1961. Cf. also *The Red Annals* (*recensio nova* from an incomplete manuscript in the library of Rai Bahadur T.D. Densapa, Gangtok, Sikkim), reproduced by Prof. Dr Lokesh Chandra, International Academy of Indian Culture (New Delhi, 1968), 33 pages.

[8] So far there is no translation of *The Red Annals* into any of the Western languages. An English translation by G. Tharchin with notes by N.C. Sinha is to be published by the Namgyal Institute of Tibetology in Gangtok, Sikkim. A Japanese translation, *Hūran-Teputeru* (*Hu Lan Deb Ther*)—*Chibetto nendaiki*, by S. Inaba and H. Satō appeared in Kyoto in 1964. The chapters on China and those on the dynasties of Mi-ñag (Tangut) and Mongolia are translated on pp. 46-75 and 76-88 respectively.

also known as *Yig-tshang mkhas-pa dga'-byed*, composed in 1434. Though explored already in 1904,[9] the work was first thoroughly examined and evaluated only in recent years.[10] Chapters 6 and 7 are devoted entirely to the genealogies of the kings of China and Mi-ñag (Tangut).

Of outstanding importance amongst the Tibetan historical sources in general is the *Deb-ther sngon-po* or *Blue Annals*, composed by gŹon-nu-dpal (1392-1481) between 1476 and 1478. Based on an extensive use of former Tibetan chronicles, such as the little known *sBa-bźed* or *Affirmation of sBa* of the eleventh century,[11] Bu-ston's *History of Religion*, Kun-dga'-rdo-rje's *Red Annals*, etc., this work is invaluable for its attempt to establish an exact chronology of events in Tibetan history. Book 1 contains, among other things, a list of Chinese emperors and a genealogical table of the Mongol rulers, borrowed almost verbatim from Kun-dga'-rdo-rje's work discussed above.[12]

There are certain doubts as to how to date correctly the work known for short as the *rGyal-rabs gsal-ba'i me-long* or *Clear Mirror of Royal Genealogies*, composed by the Sa-skya-pa monk bSod-nams-rgyal-mtshan (1312-75). As the earliest date of its origin, the year 1327 is given (corrected to 1328), and one occasionally comes across other dates, viz. 1368, 1373, 1388, 1478, and 1508. This work, called 'the model of future historiography' by G. Tucci[13] and 'the history of Tibet par excellence' by L. Petech,[14] is somewhat imperfect from a strictly historiographical point of view, since the material is buried under a mass of confused legends and other folk stories. In fact, only Chapter 18, the last and longest, is of a historical nature. Nevertheless, the chronicle as a whole does enjoy an extraordinary popularity among the Tibetans and is of great interest to Tibetologists as well. As regards material on China, the work does not contain anything new. The author deals with China in two places: the general history of China (from the Chou dynasty down to the beginning of the Ming period in 1368), together with a history of the Tangut (Mi-ñag) and Mongolia (Hor), is treated in Chapter 3; the story of Sino-Tibetan relations, together with other events of Tibetan history from the seventh century onwards, is related in more detail in Chapter 18. As the main source of his information, the author quotes

---

[9] See S.C. Das, 'Tibet under the Tartar Emperors of China in the 13th Century A.D.', *Journal of the Asiatic Society of Bengal* LXXIII, 1 (1904), pp. 94-102.
[10] See A. Macdonald, 'Préambule à la lecture d'un Rgya-Bod yig-chaṅ', *Journal asiatique* (1963), pp. 53-159. A translation of this Tibetan work is not yet available.
[11] Tibetan text, edited with a French résumé and several indexes by R.A. Stein, *Une chronique ancienne de bSam-yas: sBa-bźed* (Paris, 1961).
[12] gŹon-nu-dpal's work was translated into English by G.N. Roerich, *The Blue Annals*, and published in The Royal Asiatic Society of Bengal, Monograph Series, Calcutta, vol. 7, part 1 (1949), part 2 (1953). The chapter on the royal chronologies of China and Mongolia is to be found in part 1, pp. 47-60.
[13] *Tibetan Painted Scrolls*, vol. 1, p. 142.
[14] *A Study on the Chronicles of Ladakh*, p. 89.

Kun-dga'-rdo-rje's *Red Annals* (for Chapter 3) and Rin-chen-grags's revised edition of the account of the T'u-fan in the *T'ang-shu* (for Chapter 18).[15]

The sixteenth and following centuries bring a whole range of outstanding historical works by Tibetan authors, of which, unfortunately, only a minor part is easily accessible to non-Tibetologists. Thus in 1564 there was completed a work metaphorically called *mKhas-pa'i dga'-ston* or *Feast of the Sages*, written by dPa'-bo gTsug-lag-phreng-ba (1504-66). Divided into five major parts, the work comprises, among other things, a fairly full history of China, Mongolia and Mi-ñag, mostly taken from the *Red Annals* of Kun-dga'-rdo-rje.[16]

Of the works produced during the seventeenth century, mention should be made of a famous *Chronicle of the Fifth Dalai Lama* (1617-82), *rDsogs-ldan gžon-nu'i dga'-ston*, completed in 1643.[17] Its specific contribution for the study of the history of China is practically negligible, and the work is valued by the Tibetans mainly for its stress on political history. So far as the history of Sino-Tibetan relationships is concerned, it follows mainly the *rGyal-rabs gsal-ba'i me-long*.

The foremost place amongst the Lamaist historiographers of the eighteenth century undoubtedly belongs to a Mongol (not Tibetan, as often stated erroneously by earlier writers), Ye-śes-dpal-'byor (1704-88), better known by the name of Sum-pa mkhan-po. He became known mainly for his book on the history of Buddhism in India, Tibet, China, and Mongolia, called conventionally the *dPag-bsam ljon-bzang* or *Paradise of Cogitation*, composed in 1748. This bulky work consists of four major parts, of which Part 3 is devoted to China. After briefly sketching China's geography, the author proceeds to describe in some detail the genealogies of the Chinese emperors starting from the fabulous ages of the Three Sovereigns (*san-huang*) and Five Emperors (*wu-ti*) down to the accession of Ch'ien-lung (Khēn-lung in Tibetan) in 1736; and the history of Buddhism in China. The same plan is adopted for Mongolia (Part 4).[18]

[15] The work was first introduced to Europe in 1829, by I.J. Schmidt, who provided his German translation of Sanang Setsen's chronicle, *Erdeni-yin tobči* of 1662, with notes containing extensive extracts from the Kalmuk work named *Bodhimör*, which in itself represents a fairly faithful translation of the *rGyal-rabs gsal-ba'i me-long* (cf. his *Geschichte der Ost-Mongolen und ihres Fürstenhauses*). It has also been translated twice into Chinese; by Jen Nai-ch'iang, 'Hsi-tsang cheng-chiao shih-chien' and by Wang I-nuan, *Hsi-tsang wang-t'ung chi*. There is a partial translation into Russian by Kuznetsov, *Tibetskaia letopis'* "*Svetloe zertsalo tsarskikh rodoslovnykh*". The chapter on Sino-Tibetan relations is available also in an English translation by Tucci, *The Tombs of the Tibetan Kings*, pp. 24-8. For further details, see Kuznetsov, ed., *Rgyal rabs gsal ba'i me long* (*The Clear Mirror of Royal Genealogies*); and a review of it by J. Kolmaš, *Archiv orientální* XXXV (1967), pp. 467-76.
[16] Tibetan text edited by Lokesh Chandra in the Śata-piṭaka Series, vol. 9, parts 1-4 (New Delhi, 1959-62). No translation into a Western language is as yet available.
[17] A handy Peking edition of the Fifth Dalai Lama's Chronicle (1957) bears the Chinese title, *Hsi-tsang wang-ch'en chi*. It has been announced that an English translation by G. Tucci and L. Petech is being prepared for the Serie Orientale Roma.
[18] In 1908, S.C. Das published in Calcutta an incomplete edition and translation of the *dPag-bsam ljon-bzang* [*Pag Sam Jon Zang*, part 1: *History of the Rise, Progress and Downfall of*

Another work by the same author, having special significance for the local history of the present-day Chinghai Province and adjacent regions, is his semi-poetical composition, *mTsho sngon-gyi lo-rgyus* or *Annals of Kuku-nor*, written in 1786. In it, the author deals, among other things, with the folk traditions concerning the origin of the Ch'ing-hai or Blue Lake (mTsho sngon-po in Tibetan, Kuku-nor in Mongolian), and tells the history of the Chinghai region, concentrating predominantly on seventeenth and eighteenth century political events (e.g., the anti-Manchu revolt of the Kuku-nor Mongols in 1723-4).[19]

When speaking of Tibetan historiography, it is necessary to mention, even if only in passing, some works treating the history of regions that were either originally part of the Chinese empire, but gained their independence in later times (as was the case with Mongolia, for example), or were formerly subject only to a loose control by the Chinese central authorities, but later became an integral part of the Chinese state. This, for instance, is the case with Amdo (mDo-smad), the present Chinghai Province, or with Khams, the former Sikang Province, etc. These 'local histories' can be considered as sources for the history of China (in a broader sense), though limited materially to the respective territory and its local problems.

Apart from the *Annals of Kuku-nor* mentioned above, at least three should be added to this group. The first is the work by Blo-bzang-tshe-'phel (alias 'Jigs-med-rig-pa'i-rdo-rje) entitled in short the *Hor chos-'byung* or *History of Buddhism in Mongolia* from the year 1819. Its first part (Huth's translation, pp. 3-78) is devoted to an examination of the political history of the country from its mythological beginnings down to the period of the Ch'ien-lung emperor (1736-96). The rest of the work deals with the history and spread of Buddhism among the Mongols.[20]

Certain material for the local history of the former Sikang Province

---

Buddhism in India (Tibetan text newly edited by the Mongolian Tā bla-ma rNam-rgyal-rdo-rje, *Sumpakhampo's History of India*, Delhi, 1964); part 2: *History of Tibet from Early Times to 1745 A.D.*]. Part 3, containing a history of Buddhism in China and Mongolia, preceded by the *re'u-mig* or chronological tables, was edited by Lokesh Chandra in the Śata-piṭaka Series, vol. 8 (New Delhi, 1959). Apart from S.C. Das's translation, only parts of the work have been translated by later scholars. R.E. Pubaev, of Ulan-Ude in Buryat Mongolia, is said to have translated the whole text of the *dPag-bsam ljon-bzang* into Russian. Cf. B.D. Dandaron, *Opisanie tibetskikh rukopisei*, p. 8, note 2a. The best bibliographical survey of our author is J.W. de Jong's 'Sum-pa mkhan-po (1704-1788) and his Works', pp. 208-17.

[19] This work is to be found at the end (pp. 425-58) of Lokesh Chandra's edition of the *Vaidūrya ser-po*, Śata-piṭaka Series, vol. 12/2 (New Delhi, 1960). Bira, *Mongol'skaia tibetoiazychnaia istoricheskaia literatura*, p. 29, mentions an unpublished Mongol translation by Gelegzhamtso made in 1932. B.D. Dandaron has allegedly translated the same work into Russian (*Opisanie tibetskikh rukopisei*, p. 24). See also Yang Ho-chin, ed., *The Annals of Kokonor* for a translation into English.

[20] Tibetan text edited together with a German translation by G. Huth, *Geschichte des Buddhismus in der Mongolei*, 2 vols. (Strassburg, 1892 and 1896). Huth incorrectly gives the author's name in the form of 'Jigs-med-nam-mkha'. A Japanese edition of the Tibetan text was prepared by Hashimoto Kōhō, *Seizōbun Mōko Ramakyō shi* (Tokyo, 1940).

(Eastern Tibet or Khams) in the early Manchu period can be found in the work generally known by its short title, *sDe-dge'i rgyal-rabs* or *Genealogy of the Kings of Derge*, composed in 1828 by Tshe-dbang-rdo-rje-rig-'dsin, the chief representative of the forty-third generation of the Derge ruling house (1786-?).[21] Derge (Te-ke on the Chinese maps) was once the most powerful principality in the Sino-Tibetan marches, enjoying the reputation of a political and cultural centre for the whole of Eastern Tibet.

Thirdly, the history of Amdo or Chinghai is described by dKon-mchog-bstan-pa-rab-rgyas (born in 1801) in his *Deb-ther rgya-mtsho* or *Ocean-wide Annals*, from the year 1865. Much valuable material about Amdo can be gathered from the extensive Volume 1 of the *Deb-ther rgya-mtsho* (412 folios of xylographed print) dealing with the history of the Amdo region as illustrated in the histories of numerous monasteries located in its territory.[22]

Tibetan texts may occasionally throw light on other aspects of China, apart from historical events. Thus, for instance, information on various philosophical systems in China and the development of Chinese Buddhism can be found in Chapters 10 and 11 of a work called *Grub-mtha' šel-gyi me-long* or *Crystal Mirror of the Philosophical and Religious Systems*, composed in 1802 by Thu'-bkwan Blo-bzang-chos-kyi-ñi-ma (1737-1802), the abbot of the dGon-lung monastery in Amdo.[23]

Again, in sMin-grol no-mon-han's (1789-1838) geographical work, *'Dsam-gling rgyas-bśad* or *Full Explanation of the World* (composed in 1820), there is some material relevant to China. Being a geography of the world in general, based on both domestic and European (mostly Russian) sources, this work also contains special chapters on the geography of China, Tibet, and Mongolia.[24]

As far as I know, the only work so far in Tibetan historical literature that

---

[21] Edited with a summary of the contents and a genealogical table by J. Kolmaš, *A Genealogy of the Kings of Derge*, Dissertationes Orientales 12 (Prague, 1968).

[22] The work is studied by A.I. Vostrikov, *Tibetskaia istoricheskaia literatura*, pp. 104-5 and 281-4 (notes). Cf. also Bira, *O "Zolotoi knige" Sh. Damdina*, pp. 77-8. The mimeographed Chinese edition of the *mDo-smad chos-'byung* or *History of Buddhism in Amdo* (Chinese subtitle: *An-to cheng-chiao shih*) in three volumes, published by the North-western Institute for Nationalities (Lan-chou, 1958), seems to be the same text as the *Deb-ther rgya-mtsho*.

[23] Partly edited and translated, with many inaccuracies, by S.C. Das, 'Contributions on the Religion, History, etc. of Tibet', *Journal of the Asiatic Society of Bengal* L, 1 (1881), pp. 187-251; LI, 1 (1882), pp. 1-75 and 87-128. Chapters on China in Das's translation (erroneously numbered by him as chapters 9 and 10) are to be found in LI, 1 (1882), pp. 87-114. The full edition of the original Tibetan text was prepared by Chhos Je Lama and published in Sarnath, Varanasi, 1963. Bira, *O "Zolotoi knige" Sh. Damdina*, p. 75, mentions an unpublished Mongol translation done by a certain Shagzh in 1924.

[24] The Tibetan section is available in translation, by S.C. Das (1887), by V. Vasil'ev (1895), and—by far the best, provided with text and commentary—by T.V. Wylie, *The Geography of Tibet according to the 'Dzam-gling-rgyas-bshad*. Recently, Professor Wylie has published a translation of the Nepalese section as well, entitled *A Tibetan Religious Geography of Nepal*, Serie Orientale Roma XLII, Rome 1970. A translation of the Chinese section has not yet appeared.

is entirely devoted to the history, both religious and worldly, of China, is the work called in abbreviation *rGya-nag chos-'byung* or *History of Buddhism in China*, completed in 1736[25] or 1766.[26] It was written, in Tibetan, by the Mongol Gombojab (mGon-po-skyabs). The author of this chronicle came from Üjümüchin and lived in Peking in the eighteenth century, and is known to his compatriots as the 'Great Translator *(lo-chen)* who had knowledge of four languages', i.e. Mongolian, Tibetan, Chinese, and Manchu. An outstanding philologist and historian, he was soon appointed head of, and teacher at the Tibetan School (Bod-kyi bslab-grwa; Hsi-fan hsüeh) in Peking, and is also known to have taken part in many scholarly projects of that time. Thus, in 1737, he is reported among the co-authors of the *Tibetan-Mongol Dictionary for Beginners (Bod-kyi brda-yig rtogs-par sla-ba/ Töbed-ün kelen-i kilbar-iyar surqal).*[27] In 1741-2 he collaborated in the extensive Tibetan-Mongol terminological dictionary entitled *Dag-yig mkhas-pa'i 'byung-gnas*, which was compiled for the translation of the Tanjur into Mongolian.[28] From 1741 on, with a group of talented scholars, he revised the Mongol Tanjur, which was finished in 1749. Also noteworthy are several of his Chinese translations, especially the Tibetan treatise on Buddhist iconometry completed in 1742.[29]

In the field of historiography, mGon-po-skyabs became famous mainly because of his two original historical compositions: *Gangga-yin urusqal* or *Flow of the Ganges*, a genealogy of the Mongol khans (written in 1725);[30] and the already mentioned *rGya-nag chos-'byung*. The latter is known in two blockprint editions; the Lhasa edition, numbering 110 leaves, and an unidentified edition numbering 122 leaves.

The author based his compilation almost exclusively on Chinese historical sources, partly official dynastic histories and partly biographies and travel records of eminent Buddhist personalities (including, for instance, the narrative by Hsüan-tsang of his journey to India in the first half of the seventh century). From the works of Tibetan historians, he cites, among others, Bu-ston's *Chos-'byung*, gŹon-nu-dpal's *Deb-ther sngon-po*, and Tāranātha's (alias Kun-dga'-sñing-po, born in 1575) *rGya-gar chos-'byung* or *History of Buddhism in India* (written in 1608).[31]

---

[25] According to Bira, *Mongol'skaia tibetoiazychnaia istoricheskaia literatura*, p. 36.

[26] According to Heissig, *Kirchengeschichtsschreibung*, p. 194.

[27] Cf., e.g., M. Taube, *Tibetische Handschriften und Blockdrucke*, part 3, pp. 959-60, no. 2,683.

[28] Ibid., pp. 964-74, nos. 2,690-2.

[29] See Heissig, *Kirchengeschichtsschreibung*, p. 195, and a review by J.W. de Jong in *T'oung Pao* XLIII (1955), especially pp. 309-11.

[30] Heissig, *Kirchengeschichtsschreibung*, pp. 113-17.

[31] The Tibetan text, together with a German translation of Tāranātha's History, was published by A. Schiefner, *Tāranāthae de Doctrinae Buddhicae in India Propagatione Narratio* (St Petersburg, 1868), and *Tāranātha's Geschichte des Buddhismus in Indien* (St Petersburg, 1869). There is also a translation into Japanese by Teramoto Enga, *Tāranātha Indo Bukkyōshi* (Tokyo, 1928). The text and German translation by A. Schiefner were recently reprinted and published by the

It becomes evident from the analyses of Heissig and Bira[32] that the *rGya-nag chos-'byung* is divided into three parts (the number of folios in the Lhasa edition is given in parentheses). These are as follows.

Part One: Geography and History of China (pp. 2-25). After describing China's position in the world, her provinces, famous mountains, lakes, and rivers, the author proceeds to discuss China's ancient history starting from the fabulous ages of the first legendary emperors. The subsequent historic dynasties then follow one after another, the list being closed by the growth of the Manchu power early in the seventeenth century. Special attention, quite understandably, is paid to the Mongol rulers of China (Yüan dynasty), whose names are recorded both in their Mongol and Chinese forms.

Part Two: History of Buddhism in China (pp. 26-73). This section starts with a brief sketch of pre-Buddhist thinking in China, explains the various philosophical schools in ancient China (from Lao-tzu to Chuang-tzu), and then concentrates on the appearance and further development of Buddha's doctrine and its various sects in China. Of special interest are short biographies of famous monks who assisted their Indian teachers in translating Buddhist Sūtras into Chinese, and the stories of Chinese pilgrims who visited India in the course of the fourth to eighth centuries.

Part Three is a catalogue of the Chinese Tripitaka according to one of the Yüan editions (pp. 73-107).

To sum up, the *rGya-nag chos-'byung*, a history of China written in Tibetan by a Mongol author, is one of the outstanding achievements of the Lamaist historiography in the eighteenth century. In the whole mass of Tibetan historical literature, this work, devoted exclusively to the various aspects of China's secular and ecclesiastical (i.e. Buddhist) history, occupies a unique position and deserves scholarly interest even among non-Tibetologists, It is regrettable that it remains so far unknown to modern philology.[33]

BIBLIOGRAPHY

Bacot, J., Thomas, F.W., and Toussaint, Ch., *Documents de Touen-Houang relatifs à l'histoire du Tibet*, Paris, 1940-6.

Suzuki Research Foundation, Reprint Series 2-3 (Tokyo, 1963). For a synopsis of Tāranātha's History in English by Nalinaksha Dutt, see *Bulletin of Tibetology* (Gangtok, Sikkim) V, 3 (November 1968), pp. 29-35; VI, 1 (February 1969), pp. 23-35; VI, 2 (July 1969), pp. 13-38.
[32] *Kirchengeschichtsschreibung*, pp. 196-7; *Mongol'skaia tibetoiazychnaia istoricheskaia literatura*, pp. 36-42.
[33] Neither a text-edition nor a translation of the *rGya-nag chos-'byung* into any Western language is as yet available. The work is briefly mentioned by A.I. Vostrikov, *Tibetskaia istoricheskaia literatura*, pp. 103 and 279-80 (notes), and discussed in greater detail by Heissig, *Kirchengeschichtsschreibung*, pp. 194-8, and Bira, *Mongol'skaia tibetoiazychnaia istoricheskaia literatura*, pp. 35-42, from which I have taken my information. A fine copy of *rGya-nag chos-'byung* (the Lhasa edition) is found in the library of the Namgyal Institute of Tibetology, Gangtok, Sikkim.

Bira, Sh., *Mongol'skaia tibetoiazychnaia istoricheskaia literatura (XVII-XIX)*, Studia Historica, vol. 3, fasc. 1, Ulan Bator, 1960.

——, *O "Zolotoi knige" Sh. Damdina*, Studia Historica, vol. 6, fasc. 1, Ulan Bator, 1964.

Chandra, Lokesh, *Dpag-bsam-ljon-bzaṅ* of Sum-pa-mkhan-po Ye-śes-dpal-hbyor. Part III, containing a history of Buddhism in China and Mongolia, preceded by the *reḥu-mig* or chronological tables. With a Foreword by G. Tucci and a Preface by L. Petech. Śata-piṭaka Series, vol. 8, New Delhi, 1959.

Dandaron, B. D., *Opisanie tibetskikh rukopisei i ksilografov Buriatskogo kompleksnogo nauchno-issledovatel'skogo instituta*, Vypusk II, Moscow, 1965.

de Jong, J.W., (review of) W. Heissig, *Die Pekinger lamaistischen Blockdrucke in mongolischer Sprache* (Wiesbaden, 1954), *T'oung Pao* XLIII (1955), pp. 301-18.

——, 'Sum-pa mkhan-po (1704-1788) and his Works', *Harvard Journal of Asiatic Studies* XXVII (1967), pp. 208-17.

Emmerick, R.E., *Tibetan Texts concerning Khotan*, London Oriental Series 19, London, 1967.

Heissig, W., *Die Familien- und Kirchengeschichtsschreibung der Mongolen* (Teil I: 16.-18. Jahrhundert), Asiatische Forschungen 5, Wiesbaden, 1959.

Huth, G., *Geschichte des Buddhismus in der Mongolei*, 2 vols., Strassburg, 1892 and 1896.

Inaba, S. and Satō, H., *Hūran-Teputeru (Hu Lan Deb Ther)—Chibetto nendaiki*, Kyoto, 1964.

Jen Nai-ch'iang and Liu Li-ch'ien, 'Hsi-tsang cheng-chiao shih-chien', *K'ang-tao yüeh-k'an* (Ch'eng-tu) II (1940), III (1942), and V (1944).

Kolmaš, J., '*Ch'ing-shih-kao* on Modern History of Tibet (1903-1912)', *Archiv orientální* XXXII (1964), pp. 77-99.

——, *A Genealogy of the Kings of Derge* (Sde-dge'i rgyal-rabs), Dissertationes orientales 12, Prague, 1968.

Kuznetsov, B.I., *Rgyal rabs gsal ba'i me long* (The Clear Mirror of Royal Genealogies), Scripta Tibetana 1, Leiden, 1966.

——, *Tibetskaia letopis' "Svetloe zertsalo tsarskikh rodoslovnykh"*, Leningrad, 1961.

Macdonald, A., 'Préambule à la lecture d'un Rgya-Bod yig-chaṅ', *Journal asiatique* (1963), pp. 53-159.

Obermiller, E., *History of Buddhism (Chos-ḥbyung) by Bu-ston*, 2 vols., Materialien zur Kunde des Buddhismus 18-19, Heidelberg, 1931-2. Reprinted in 1 vol. by the Suzuki Research Foundation in 1964 (Reprint Series 5).

Petech, L., *A Study on the Chronicles of Ladakh (Indian Tibet)*, Calcutta, 1939.

Roerich, G.N., *The Blue Annals*, 2 vols., The Royal Asiatic Society of Bengal Monograph Series, vol. 7, Calcutta, 1949-53.

Satō Hisashi, *Kodai Chibetto shi kenkyū*, 2 vols., Kyoto, 1958-9.

Schmidt, I.J., *Geschichte der Ost-Mongolen und ihres Fürstenhauses*, St Petersburg, 1829.

Stein, R.A., *Une chronique ancienne de bSam-yas: sBa-bžed*, Publications de l'Institut des hautes études chinoises: Textes et documents I, Paris, 1961.

Taube, M., *Tibetische Handschriften und Blockdrucke*, Verzeichnis der orientalischen Handschriften in Deutschland 11/1-4, Wiesbaden, 1966.

Thomas, F.W., *Tibetan Literary Texts and Documents concerning Chinese Turkestan*, 4 vols., London, 1935-63.

Tucci, G., *Tibetan Painted Scrolls*, 3 vols., Rome, 1949.

——, *The Tombs of the Tibetan Kings*, Serie Orientale Roma 1, Rome, 1950.

——, 'The Validity of Tibetan Historical Tradition', in *India Antiqua* (A Volume of Oriental Studies Presented . . . to J. Ph. Vogel), Leyden, 1947, pp. 309-22.

Vostrikov, A.I., *Tibetskaia istoricheskaia literatura*, Bibliotheca Buddhica 32, Moscow, 1962.

Wang I-nuan, *Hsi-tsang wang-t'ung chi*, 4th ed., Shanghai, 1957.

Wylie, T.V., *The Geography of Tibet according to the 'Dzam-gling-rgyas-bshad*, Serie Orientale Roma 25, Rome, 1962.

Yang Ho-chin, *The Annals of Kokonor*, Indiana University Publications Uralic and Altaic Series 106, Bloomington, 1969.

史 xv: Manchu Sources

JOSEPH FLETCHER

Manchu sources have two main uses for historians of China. They supply information that is unavailable in Chinese, and, when both Manchu and Chinese versions of a given text exist, they provide controls for understanding the Chinese.

Archival Sources

It is uncertain how much Manchu material survives for which Chinese versions do not also exist. Of printed books and documents, there is certainly very little, but when it comes to manuscript sources, especially archival material covering the early Ch'ing, there is a great deal that is useful for unravelling the history of the Manchus as a people, their policies for controlling the Mongols, their relations with the Ming dynasty, the administrative structure of their state, and the functioning of their empire in China.

The earliest Manchu archives are the fragmentary collection known as the *Chiu Man-chou tang* or *Lao-Man-wen yüan-tang*, which is preserved in the National Palace Museum at Wai-shuang-hsi in Shih-lin, Taiwan. This covers the years from 1607 to 1636. The *T'ai-tsung Wen huang-ti shih-lu* is based on it, and the *Man-wen lao-tang*, which has been edited and published in Japan, is based on a much revised Ch'ien-lung edition of the same collection of documents.[1] Fortunately, the National Palace Museum has reproduced it by photo-offset and published it in ten volumes under the title *Chiu Man-chou tang* (Taipei, 1969), so that it is now possible to consult the original Manchu texts themselves.[2] Another collection of pre-conquest

[1] See Kanda Nobuo and others, ed. and tr., *Man-wen lao-tang*, 7 vols., Toyo Bunko Publication Series C, no. 12 (Tokyo, 1955-63). For a comparison of the *Man-wen lao-tang* with the *Lao-Man-wen yüan-tang*, see Kuang Lu and Li Hsüeh-chih, 'Ch'ing T'ai-tsu ch'ao "Lao-Man-wen yüan-tang" yü "Man-wen lao-tang" chih pi-chiao yen-chiu', *Bulletin of the China Council for East Asian Studies* 4 (June 1965), pp. 1-165 + 163 plates. See also Ch'en Chieh-hsien, 'The Value of "The Early Manchu Archives"', in Ch'en Chieh-hsien and Sechin Jagchid, eds., *Proceedings of the Third East Asian Altaistic Conference* (Taipei, 1970), pp. 58-80, and Kuang Lu and Li Hsüeh-chih, ed. and tr., *Ch'ing T'ai-tsu ch'ao Lao-Man-wen yüan-tang*, Chung-yang yen-chiu yüan Li-shih yü-yen yen-chiu so chuan-k'an, vol. 58 (Taipei, 1970).
[2] For the controversy regarding the title and other aspects of the *Chiu Man-chou tang*, see Ch'en Chieh-hsien, '"Chiu Man-chou tang" shu-lüeh', in *Chiu Man-chou tang*, vol. 1, pp. 1-56; Li Hsüeh-chih, *Lao-Man-wen yüan-tang lun-chi* (Taipei, 1971); and Ch'en Chieh-hsien, 'An Open Letter to Participants of the Fourth East Asian Altaistic Conference, and to Other Concerned Scholars in China and Abroad' (Taipei, 1971, mimeograph).

Manchu documents is at Academia Sinica in Nan-kang, Taiwan, consisting of imperial edicts and also records of oaths, promotions, and rewards.[3]

For the late seventeenth and eighteenth centuries, an enormous amount of Manchu archival material survives. Some holdings are preserved in Peking, and collections must exist in Mukden and elsewhere. The most valuable collections are in Taiwan, where the National Palace Museum has fifty boxes of *ch'i-chü chu*, forty-seven boxes of Grand Council archives, sixty-two boxes of material from the State Historiographer's Office, and many other state papers, in all totalling some 206 boxes of Ch'ing documents, as well as a large number of previously unknown Manchu documents that have recently been discovered and are not yet published.[4] At Academia Sinica also there are over a million such documents from the archives of the Grand Secretariat.[5]

Important archival collections are to be found outside China. In Tokyo, for example, the Tōyō bunko possesses over 2,000 documents concerning the administration of the Bordered Red Banner from 1723 to 1911[6] as well as records from numerous other Manchu and Mongolian banners. In the United States, the Gest Chinese Research Library at Princeton University has a voluminous Sino-Manchu documentary collection, labelled 'Ta-Ch'ing Shang-yü tsou-shih tang-chi', in 112 fascicules, containing edicts and memorials dated as late as 1864. Other libraries in the United States, Japan, the Mongolian People's Republic, the Soviet Union, Germany, and elsewhere have collections of Manchu archival material of various types drawn from a number of civil and military offices. These Manchu archives are basic sources and, especially for the early Ch'ing, essential to an understanding of the bureaucracy's inner workings. Moreover, if we are ever to learn how much the editors of such basic Ch'ing sources as the *shih-lu*, *sheng-hsün*, or the various *fang-lüeh* have cut and altered the original documents, somebody will have to study the unpublished versions of these documents in their Chinese and Manchu entirety.

Personal Records and Unofficial Accounts

Another category of Manchu source material is that written to record experiences or the satisfactory completion of official assignments. Examples of this kind of writing are Tulišen's account of his journey across Siberia to

---

[3] See Kanda, 'Present State of Preservation of Manchu Literature', p. 93.

[4] The Palace Museum's Manchu material by and about Nien Keng-yao (d. 1726) is being prepared for publication.

[5] Samples of this kind of material can be found in Li Kwang-t'ao, comp., *Ming-Ch'ing tang-an ts'un-chen hsüan-chi*, vol. 1, Chung-yang yen-chiu yüan Li-shih yü-yen yen-chiu so chuan-k'an, vol. 38 (Taipei, 1959). See also Matsumura Jun, 'The Early Manchu Tablets', in *Proceedings of the Third East Asian Altaistic Conference*, pp. 182-93, for a type of pre-conquest material found in the Grand Secretariat archives.

[6] There are plans for these documents to be published in Romanised transcription and Japanese translation.

the Volga Kalmuks in 1712-15, entitled *Laqčaχa ǰečen-de taqôraχa babe eǰexe bitxe* (in Chinese, *I-yü lu*);[7] Funingγa's reports of 1717-24 dealing with the Ch'ing empire's struggles with the Zunghars;[8] and Bališan's account of the Tungan rebellion in Ili (1864-71), entitled 'Ili-i fačuχôn-be eǰexe bitxe'.[9] Of related interest is the 'Emu tangγô orin saqda-i gisun sarkiyan' ('Pai-erh-shih lao-jen yü-lu'), written in Manchu by the Mongol Sung-yün in 1790,[10] and containing valuable information on Manchu history and culture.

In addition, there are personal accounts written in Chinese for which Manchu translations also exist, such as Li Hsien-ken and Yang Chao-chieh, *An-nan shih-shih chi-lüeh* (1669) with the Manchu title *Taqôran-de genexe oyongγo babe eǰexe bitxe*,[11] which gives an account of the Ch'ing embassy to Annam in 1668-9; and Ch'i-shih-i, *Hsi-yü wen-chien lu* (1778), with the Manchu title *Wargi ǰečeni bade bifi donǰiχa sabuχa babe eǰexe bitxe*,[12] which describes Eastern Turkestan and Zungharia. The number of works of this general type would seem to be small, and probably almost all of them are available in Chinese versions.

Officially Commissioned Bilingual Compilations

Of all Manchu sources by far the most accessible and plentiful are official works prepared in Chinese, Manchu, and in some instances also Mongolian versions. These include such basic compilations as the veritable records, or *yargiyan qooli* (*shih-lu*),[13] the *da xergen-i bitxe* (*pen-chi*),[14] and the

---

[7] See Imanishi Shunjū, ed., *Kōchū I-iki roku* (*Tulišen's I-yü-lu Revised and Annotated*) (Tenri, 1964). See also the English translation of the Chinese text by Sir George Thomas Staunton, *Narrative of the Chinese Embassy to the Khan of the Tourgouth Tartars, in the Years 1712, 13, 14 & 15* (London, 1821).

[8] MS in the West German Staatsbibliothek, Marburg/Lahn, bearing the Chinese legend 'Ching-ni chiang-chün tsou-i'. For a translation and transcription of this text, see E.S. Kraft, ed. and tr., *Zum Dsungarenkrieg im 18. Jahrhundert, Berichte des Generals Funingga* (Leipzig, 1953).

[9] MS in the Institut narodov Azii of the Soviet Academy of Sciences, Leningrad. See the catalogue by Volkova, *Opisanie man'chzhurskikh rukopisei Instituta narodov Azii*, p. 17, no. 14. Note also the more detailed variant of the same work, listed by Volkova (p. 17, no. 15) under the title 'Ili-i ba fačuχôraχa erin-i bayita-be saqdasa-i gisurexe-be donǰime eǰefi araχa bitxe'.

[10] See R.C. Rudolph, '*Emu tanggô orin sakda-i gisun sarkiyan*, an Unedited Manchu Manuscript', *Journal of the American Oriental Society* LX (1940), pp. 554-63. This work and its Chinese translation survive in a number of copies, all MSS. See Kanda, 'Present State', p. 72.

[11] This is the title of the palace edition as given in the catalogue of T'ao Hsiang, *Ku-kung tien-pen shu-k'u hsien-ts'un mu*, vol. 1, p. 3a. See the Manchu recension reproduced in E. Haenisch, ed., *Bericht von einer chinesischen Gesandtschaft nach Annam im Jahre 1668/9: Eine Mandschuhandschrift aus dem Pekinger Palastmuseum*, Bayerische Akademie der Wissenschaften, Philosophisch-historische Klasse, Abhandlungen, New Series, vol. 60 (Munich, 1965).

[12] There is an incomplete manuscript copy in both Manchu and Chinese in Leningrad. See the catalogue by Volkova, pp. 19-20, no. 18.

[13] Of particular interest is the *Dayičing gurun-i Tayizu Xorongγo Enduringge Xôwangdi-i yargiyan qooli* (*Ta-Ch'ing T'ai-tsu Wu huang-ti shih-lu*) written originally in Manchu. See Imanishi Shunjū, ed., 'Daicing gurun i Taidzu Horonggo Enduringge Hûwangdi i yargiyan kooli', *Tôhôgaku kiyô*, Tenri University, Oyasato Research Institute, Monumenta Orientalia 2 (Tenri, 1967), pp. 173-273. See also his *Ubaliyambuha suhe gisun kamcibuha Manju i yargiyan kooli*

143

main collections of Ch'ing law: the *Dayičing gurun-i uxeri qooli bitxe* (*Ta-Ch'ing hui-tien*), *Uxeri qooli-i qooli χačin bitxe* (*Hui-tien tse-li*), *Uxeri qooli-i bayita χačin bitxe* (*Hui-tien shih-li*) and *Dayičing gurun-i fafun-i bitxe qooli* (*Ta-Ch'ing lü-li*).[15]

There are the major collections of imperial edicts, including the *enduringge tačixiyan* (*sheng-hsün*)[16] of the first ten reigns, the *Dergi xese* (*Shang-yü*) of the Yung-cheng Emperor, and collected edicts to the eight banners (in Chinese, *Shang-yü pa-ch'i*), and there are books of precedents and regulations for the six boards, such as *Dorolon-i ǰurγan-i qooli χačin-i bitxe* (*Li-pu tse-li*) of the Board of Rites, and for departments of the six boards, such as the 'Xafan-i ǰurγan-i Faššan-be bayičara fiyenten-i qooli' ('Li-pu Chi-hsün ssu tse-li') of the Record Department of the Board of Civil Appointments. Similar compilations exist for other organs of the Ch'ing government—for example, the *Tulergi γolo-be dasara ǰurγan-i qooli χačin-i bitxe* (*Li-fan yüan tse-li*)[17] of the Court of Colonial Affairs and the *J̌aqôn γôsai qooli χačin-i bitxe* (*Pa-ch'i tse-li*) of the eight banners.

For many of the important military campaigns there are the detailed documentary accounts known as *bodoγon-i bitxe* (*fang-lüeh*).[18] For biographical and genealogical data there are basic collections like the 'Gurun-i suduri-i ambasai fayidangγa ulabun' ('Kuo-shih ta-ch'en lieh-chuan'), the 'Gurun-i suduri-i tondo ǰurγangγa-i fayidangγa ulabun' ('Kuo-shih chung-i chuan'), the *Uqsun-i wang gung-sai gungge faššan-be iletulere ulabun* (*Tsung-shih wang kung kung-chi piao-chuan*), the *Tulergi Mongγo Xoyise ayiman-i wang gung-sai iletun ulabun* (*Wai-fan Meng-ku Hui-pu wang kung piao-chuan*), and the *J̌aqôn γôsai Manǰusai muqôn χala-be uxeri eǰexe bitxe* (*Pa-ch'i Man-chou shih-tsu t'ung-p'u*). Of particular interest for the study of the eight banners is the *J̌aqôn γôsai tung ǰï bitxe* (*Pa-ch'i t'ung-chih*).

Other Sources

In addition to the types of material cited above, there are also other Manchu sources in which information of interest to historians may be found.

(Kyoto, 1938), recently reprinted as vol. 4 of *Ch'ing-shih tzu-liao*, Series 2, *K'ai-kuo shih-liao*, 2 (Taipei, n.d.).

[14] See Ch'en Chieh-hsien, 'Notes on the Manchu Edition of the Ch'ing Emperors' *Pen-chi* (Imperial Annals)', which will appear in the *Proceedings of the Fourth East Asian Altaistic Conference* (Taipei, 1972).

[15] See the English translation by G.T. Staunton, *Ta Tsing Leu Lee; Being the Fundamental Laws, and a Selection from the Supplementary Statutes, of the Penal Code of China* (London, 1810).

[16] Occasionally the originals of Manchu edicts sent to foreign rulers can be found abroad. See, e.g., A. Liubimov, 'Nekotorye man'chzhurskie dokumenty iz istorii russko-kitaiskikh snoshenii v XVII-m veke', *Zapiski Vostochnogo otdeleniia Imperatorskogo russkogo arkheologicheskogo obshchestva* XXI (1911-12), pp. 65-94 (esp. p. 72).

[17] A Russian translation of the Manchu text has been made by S.V. Lipovtsov, under the title *Ulozhenie Kitaiskoi Palaty vneshnykh snoshenii*, 2 vols. (St Petersburg, 1828). Unfortunately I have not been able to consult it at first hand.

[18] Samples of this type of material are reproduced in E. Haenisch, *Historische Mandschutexte*, Asiatische Forschungen, vol. 29 (Wiesbaden, 1970).

There are epigraphic texts of historical value dated as early as 1630[19] and commemorative works like the *Tayizung Xôwangdi Ming gurun-i čooχa-be Sung Šan-de ambarame efuleme afaχa bayita-be ejeme araχa bitxe* (*T'ai-tsung huang-ti ta-p'o Ming-shih yü Sung-shan chih chan shu-shih wen*), which deals with Abaχai's victory over the Ming forces at Sung-shan in 1642. The Manchu texts of treaties, as for example the Treaty of Nerchinsk (1689), provide valuable historical insights. Manchu material like the divinatory guide in the Princeton collection, labelled 'Jih-yüeh hsing-ch'en chan', can be a useful aid for the study of Chinese astrology. For the Manchus' state cult, there is the *Manjusai wečere metere qooli bitxe* (*Man-chou chi-shen chi-t'ien tien-li*)[20] covering the sacrifices of the ruling Ayisin Gioro clan, and there are similar works for the cults of other Manchu clans. The folk tale *Nišan saman-i bitxe* should also be mentioned, since it provides rare insights into the shamanist culture of the early Manchus.[21]

Over the course of the Ch'ing dynasty, the importance of Manchu gradually declined. Bilingual publications, with few exceptions, were first written in Chinese and then translated into Manchu, and almost all Manchu source material, even from the earliest period, was carried over in one form or another into Chinese. For historians of the middle and late Ch'ing, Manchu records can be useful, but they are not necessary. For students of the early Ch'ing, however, especially those studying the first half of the seventeenth century, Manchu is essential. Fortunately, it is an easy language, and for anyone who reads Chinese, as little as a year of study can unlock the vast store of Manchu sources.[22]

BIBLIOGRAPHY

Fuchs, Walter, *Beiträge zur mandjurischen Bibliographie und Literatur*, Tokyo, 1936.

——, 'Neue Beiträge zur mandjurischen Bibliographie und Literatur', *Monumenta Serica* VII (1942), pp. 1-37.

——, *Chinesische und mandjurische Handschriften und seltene Drucke: Nebst einer Standortliste der sonstigen Mandjurica*, Verzeichnis der orientalischen Handschriften in Deutschland, vol. 12, part 1, Wiesbaden, 1966.

[19] See, *inter alia*, O. Franke and B. Laufer, *Epigraphische Denkmäler aus China, Erster Teil: Lamaistische Kloster-Inschriften aus Peking, Jehol und Si-ngan*, 2 parts (Berlin, 1914). The earliest Manchu inscriptions are not included in the above. See Fuchs, *Beiträge zur mandjurischen Bibliographie und Literatur*, p. 128.

[20] See the French translation by Ch. de Harlez, 'La religion des Tartares orientaux: Mandchous et Mongols, comparée à la religion des anciens Chinois, d'après les textes indigènes, avec le rituel tartare de l'empereur K'ien long', *Mémoires couronnés et autres mémoires*, vol. 40 (Académie royale de Belgique, Brussels, 1887), pp. 1-216 + 8 plates (translation pp. 61-172).

[21] See M.P. Volkova, ed. and tr., *Nishan' samani bitkhe (Predanie o nishanskoi shamanke)*, Pamiatniki literatury narodov vostoka, Teksty, Malaia seriia, vol. 7 (Moscow, 1961).

[22] See Erich Hauer, 'Why the Sinologue Should Study Manchu', *Journal of the North-China Branch of the Royal Asiatic Society* LXI (1930), pp. 156-64.

Fuchs, Walter, 'Die mandjurische Literatur', in B. Spuler, ed., *Handbuch der Orientalistik*, Part 1, vol. 5, fasc. 3: Tungusologie, Leiden/Köln, 1968, pp. 1-7.

Gimm, Martin, 'Zu den mandjurischen Sammlungen der Sowjetunion, I: Nachträge zum Handschriftenkatalog von M.P. Volkova', *T'oung Pao* LIV (1968), pp. 288-309.

Ikegami Jirō, 'Yōroppa ni aru Manshūgo bunken ni tsuite', *Tōyō gakuhō* XLV, 3 (December 1962), pp. 105-21, and supplement to the same in *Tōyō gakuhō* XLVII, 3 (December 1964), pp. 144-6.

Kanda Nobuo, 'Present State of Preservation of Manchu Literature', *Memoirs of the Research Department of the Toyo Bunko* XXVI (1968), pp. 63-95.

Kuo-li Feng-t'ien t'u-shu kuan tien-pan shu-mu, Mukden, [1934].

Li Teh Ch'i, ed. Yu Dawchyuan, *Union Catalogue of Manchu Books in the National Library of Peiping and the Library of the Palace Museum*, Peiping, 1933.

Mambun shoseki shū, Tenri toshokan, Zempon shashin shū, no. 6, Tenri, 1955.

Misig, L., *Ulayan Bayatur qota-daki Ulus-un nom-un sang-un Manju nom-un kömügen-dür bayiy-a Manju nom-un yarčay*, Studia Mongolica Instituti Linguae et Litterarum Comiteti Scientiarum et Educationis Altae Reipublicae Populi Mongoli [*sic*], vol. 1, fasc. 29, Ulan Bator, 1959.

Poppe, Nicholas, Hurvitz, Leon, and Okada Hidehiro, *Catalogue of the Manchu-Mongol Section of the Toyo Bunko*, Tokyo and Seattle, 1964.

T'ao Hsiang, comp., *Ku-kung tien-pen shu-k'u hsien-ts'un mu*, 3 vols., Peiping, 1933, especially vol. 3.

Volkova, Maiia Petrovna, *Opisanie man'chzhurskikh rukopisei Instituta narodov Azii* [*A Description of Manchu Manuscripts in the Institute of Asian Peoples*], Moscow, 1965.

Watanabe Kuntarō, comp., *Manshūgo tosho mokuroku*, Ajiya kenkyū, vol. 3, Osaka, 1925; revised 1932.

史 XVI: Arabic Sources

D. D. LESLIE

Long before the rise of the Mongols, when Marco Polo and other European travellers ventured as far as China and recorded their observations, Arab and other Persian speakers were voyaging to China. Some of the reports can only be treated as travellers' yarns (forerunners of the *Arabian Nights*), but others are completely convincing. These are essential for any study of Chinese trade and relations with India, western Asia, and Europe, during the T'ang and Sung.

Reports of embassies and other contacts between Persia and China are found for the seventh century and earlier, in both Chinese and Persian sources. Persian navigators are known to have reached China in the seventh or eighth century. Chinese sources mention the sacking of Canton by Po-ssu (Persian) and Ta-shih (Arab) sailors in 758. For a time thereafter Canton was avoided, but it was reopened in 792. In the Huang Ch'ao rebellion of 878 a large number of foreigners were slaughtered (in Khānfū in particular), and thereafter commerce again slackened. But from the eighth century on, a steady trickle of information on China was spreading westwards to the Arab countries. Arab knowledge was mostly derived from the sea traffic, Persian partly from overland commerce.

Our extant sources, which start about 850, are of two kinds: travellers' reports and tales, and geographical descriptions.[1] The latter are of course based on the former, and repeat the same information, but they occasionally give facts not found in any extant eye-witness account, and cannot be overlooked. Of the travellers' reports, by far the most valuable and reliable are the two descriptions in the book edited by Abu-Zaid. The first account, *'Aḥbār al-Sīn wa l-Hind*, based on a voyage by an unknown traveller, attributed to a merchant Sulaiman, is dated 851. It is less 'marvellous' than all later accounts, and the most convincing of all. The second half, by Abu-Zaid somewhat before 916, includes information from another traveller Ibn-Wahab, who claims to have spoken to the Chinese Emperor in Khumdān (Ch'ang-an). Other travellers of importance were Abu-Dulaf in the tenth century and Ibn-Battūtah in the fourteenth. Less significant is the account

[1] I am excluding inscriptions in Arabic found in mosques in Ch'üan-chou, K'ai-feng, Hang-chou, and elsewhere.

attributed to Buzurg, full of marvels and with the nuggets of truth difficult to extract.

Perhaps the first Arab writer to give a serious description of China was Ibn-Khurdādhbih, ninth century. His work describes in detail the routes, both by sea and overland, of various merchants, including Jews travelling from Europe to China. Among the cities on the way to China and the Far East are Aden, Oman, Basra, Siraf, and Ray. Ya'qūbi was another ninth-century Arab who wrote an original geographical description. These two works are not based on the voyage of 'Sulaiman'. The next important work, by Ibn-al-Faqīh, *c.* 902, is less original.

In 943, Mas'ūdī produced his vast *Murūj al-Dhahab* (*Les Prairies d'Or*). Though based on Abu-Zaid, this includes valuable material on China, and sums up the Arab knowledge of the time. Of the many later geographers, we should mention Ibn-Hauqal, Yāqūt, Idrīsī, and Abu'lfida; the last-named sum up the knowledge of the twelfth and fourteenth centuries. The anonymous Persian work *Hudūd al-'Ālam* of *c.* 982-3 is more systematic, but based largely on the earlier Arab accounts. It adds a little about the western regions of China. Korea is identified, and possibly Japan.

All the Arab travellers recount marvels and unbelievable facts. The routes described are mostly dubious, and only three or four accounts can be taken as authentic. Even the voyage of Ibn-Battūtah in the fourteenth century has been queried.[2] We are faced continually with the problem that the geographical knowledge of these voyagers was poor. The identification of towns mentioned is also by no means certain.

'Sulaiman' arrived at Khānfū (almost the only town he mentions, though Abu-Zaid also mentions Khumdān), but Ibn-Battūtah arrived first at Zaitun, going thence to Sīn-kalān, and to Khansa. Ibn-Khurdādhbih mentions the ports of Lūqīn, Khānfū, Jānfū and Qāntū, identified as Hanoi (Lung-pien), Canton (Kuang-fu), Ch'üan-chou (Ch'üan-fu), and Yang-chou (Chiang-tu).[3] Later writers mention other cities and ports. Rashīd al-Dīn (1304) refers to Fūjū (Fu-chou) and Zaitun (Ch'üan-chou), and also Namghin (K'ai-feng). Abu'lfida writes of Khansa, formerly Khānqū (southeast of Zaitun, with a lake), and Zaitun, formerly Schindjou, as the two ports of China. He also mentions Yandjou and Khandjou, presumably Yang-chou and Canton. Shanghai is also noted. It is worth pointing out that, in 1277, offices for foreign traders were established in Shanghai, Kan-p'u, Ch'üan-chou, and Ning-po, and in 1293, also in Hang-chou, Wen-chou, and Canton.

---

[2] Similar doubts, even less justified, have been expressed concerning the journey of Marco Polo. We should note that sailors' and travellers' descriptions may be less solid than those by scholars. Nor can one argue from what has not been included.

[3] See Kuwabara Jitsuzō, 'On P'u Shou-keng', p. 2 and Tazaka Kōdō, *Chūgoku ni okeru Kaikyō no denrai to sono kōtsū*, pp. 367-8.

It is generally accepted that Khansa is Hang-chou (Marco Polo's Quinsay; Hsing-tsai), Zaitun is Ch'üan-chou (Tz'u-t'ung?), Khumdān is Ch'ang-an, Sīn-kalān is Canton. Pelliot is convinced that Khānfū must be Canton (Kuang-[chou]-fu),[4] and in this case Abu'lfida must have been wrong, for Khānqū and Khānfū (easily mixed up in Arabic writing) clearly refer to the same town. Levy has a detailed comparison of the Chinese account in the *Chiu T'ang-shu* and *Hsin T'ang-shu* of the revolt of Huang Ch'ao in 878-9 (the attack on Canton being in 879, that on Hang-chou in 878)[5] with the Arab account of the revolt of Bānshū and the sacking of Khānfū in 264 A.H. (i.e. October 877-September 878) as found in Abu-Zaid (and in Mas'ūdī). There is a possibility that Khānfū is Kan-p'u, the port of Hang-chou, mentioned by Marco Polo as Gampu. Several scholars have supported this, but the view of Pelliot and Kuwabara that the ninth century traders concentrated in Canton (Khānfū), whilst Zaitun (Ch'üan-chou) and Khansa (Hang-chou), were the main trading ports in the thirteenth century, is to be preferred.[6]

Plagiarism was of course normal, and most accounts are second-hand. Later descriptions, of the twelfth to fourteenth centuries, are still based, partly at least, on the ninth century reports, and it is difficult to decide how reliable they are for the China of their own time.

These Arab reports are of particular value for the description of the life of the Muslim communities in the coastal ports. It is interesting to read of the 'extra-territorial' appointments of Muslim leaders in Canton (Sulaiman, and also Ibn-Battūtah). We also gain some information about other minorities in China, Jews, Nestorians, and Zoroastrians. These accounts describe the Chinese officialdom and trading and monetary transactions. Religion and comparison with Muslim customs were of special interest to these visitors.

They also mention the produce of China, in particular the spices, including aloes and musk,[7] precious stones, minerals, metal coinage (see Abu-Zaid), fruits, porcelain, paper money (Ibn-Battūtah). Sulaiman and Abu-Zaid were interested in anthropological aspects, and their remarks on hygiene and sex, funeral customs, eunuchs and prostitution, may be compared to the native sources, and to similar comments by Ennin, Marco Polo, and other foreign visitors.

BIBLIOGRAPHICAL NOTES

Texts and Translations of Main Arab (and Persian) Sources, Arranged Chronologically

[4] *Notes on Marco Polo*, p. 731.
[5] But see Kuwabara Jitsuzō, 'On P'u Shou-keng', pp. 10-11.
[6] Ibid., p. 3 and Pelliot, *Notes*, pp. 730-1.
[7] See Gaston Wiet, *Ya'ḳūbī: Les Pays*, p. 235.

Ibn-Khurdādhbih, *Kitāb al-Masālik wa l-Mamālik,* ninth century (*c.* 846, re-written *c.* 886). De Goeje, *Bibliotecha Geographorum Arabicorum,* vol. 6, 1889.

'Sulaiman', *'Aḥbār al-Sīn wa l-Hind,* 851 (published by Abu-Zaid, *c.* 916). Text (of 1811 by Langlès) in J. T. Reinaud, *Relation des voyages faits par les Arabes et les Persans dans l'Inde et à la Chine,* Paris, 1845. Other translations are by Gabriel Ferrand in *Voyage du marchand arabe Sulaymân en Inde et en Chine, rédigé en 851,* Paris, 1922; Albert T'Serstevens in *Les précurseurs de Marco Polo: textes intégraux établis,* Paris, 1959; and especially J. Sauvaget in *Relation de la Chine et de l'Inde,* Paris, 1948.

Ya'qūbi, *Kitāb al-Buldān, c.* 889-90. De Goeje, *Bibliotecha,* vol. 7, 1892. Gaston Wiet, *Ya'kūbī: Les Pays,* Cairo, 1937.

Ibn-Rustah, *Kitāb al-A'lāq al-Nafīsah, c.* 903. De Goeje, *Bibliotecha,* vol. 7, 1892. Gaston Wiet, *Les atours précieux,* Cairo, 1955.

Ibn-al-Faqīh, *Mukhtasar Kitāb al-Buldān, c.* 903. De Goeje, *Bibliotecha,* vol. 5, 1885. See also Yāqūt.

Abu-Zaid Ḥasan al-Sirāfī, *Silsilat al-Tawārīkh,* towards 916. Text and translation by Reinaud, *Relation.* Those of the present century are in Ferrand, *Voyage* and T'Serstevens, *Les précurseurs.* See also a review of Ferrand by Pelliot in *T'oung Pao* XXI (1922); and Levy, *Biography of Huang Ch'ao.*

Qudāmah, *Kitāb al-Kharāj,* early tenth century. De Goeje, *Bibliotecha,* vol. 6, 1889.

Mas'ūdī, *Murūj al-Dhahab (wa Ma'ādin al-Jawhar),* 943. Text and translation by C. Barbier de Meynard and J. Pavet de Courteille in *Maçoudi: Les Prairies d'Or,* 9 vols., Paris, 1861-77. See especially vol. 1, pp. 300ff.

——, *Kitāb al-Tanbīh wa l-Ishrāf,* 955. De Goeje, *Bibliotecha,* vol. 8, 1894. Translation by Carra de Vaux in *Le livre de l'avertissement et de la revision,* Paris, 1896.

Abu-Dulaf Mis'ar, *Ajā'ib al-Buldān,* tenth century. Quoted by several, including Ibn-al-Nadīm, Yāqūt, and Qazwīnī. A. von Rohr-Sauer, *Das Abû Dulaf Bericht,* Bonn, 1939. Cf. C. de Schloezer, *De Itinere Asiatico Commentarius,* 1845, and also V. Minorsky in *Oriens* V (1952), pp. 23-7.

Attributed to Buzurg ibn-Shahriyār (of Rāmhurmuz), *Kitāb Ajā'ib al-Hind,* tenth century. Text and translation by P. A. van der Lith and L. Marcel Devic in *Livre des merveilles de l'Inde,* Leiden, 1883-6; see also J. Sauvaget in *Mémorial Sauvaget,* Damascus, 1954, vol. 1.

Al-Iṣtakhrī, *Kitāb Masālik wa l-Mamālik,* tenth century. De Goeje, *Bibliotecha,* vol. 1, 1870.

Anon. (Persian), *Hudūd al-'Ālam, c.* 982-3. Translation by V. Minorsky in *Hudūd al-'Ālam 'The Regions of the World' A Persian Geography,* London, 1937. See 'Chīnīstan'.

Ibn-Ḥauqal, *Kitāb Sūrat Al-Ard, c.* 988. De Goeje, *Bibliotecha,* vol. 2, 1873;

J.H. Kramers and G. Wiet, *Ibn Hauqal: Configuration de la terre*, 2 vols. Beirut, Paris, 1964.

Muqaddasī, *Ahsan al-Taqāsim fi Ma'rīfat al-'Aqālīm*, *c.* 985-90. De Goeje, *Bibliotecha*, vol. 3, 2nd ed., 1906. Partial translation by A. Miquel in *Ahsan at-taqāsim fi ma'rifat al-aqālīm* (*La meilleure répartition pour la connaissance des provinces*), Damascus, 1963.

Ibn-al-Nadīm, *Kitāb al-Fihrist*, eleventh century. See G. Flügel, *Kitāb al-fihrist*, Leipzig, 1871-2.

Idrīsī, *Nuzhat al-Mushtāq fi 'Khtirāq al-Afäq*, early twelfth century. Translation by S. Maqbul Ahmad in *India and the Neighbouring Territories*, Leiden, 1960; text by Ahmad in 1954.

Tāhir al-Marvazī, *Tabā'i' al-Hayawān*, *c.* 1120. Text and translation by V. Minorsky in *Sharaf Al-Zamān Tāhir Marvazī on China, the Turks and India*, London, 1942. Cf. Chou Yi-liang in *Harvard Journal of Asiatic Studies* IX (1945-7), pp. 13-23.

Yāqūt, *Kitāb Mu'jam al-Buldān*, *c.* 1200. F. Wüstenfeld, *Jacut's Geographisches Wortebuch*, 6 vols., 1866-73. Partial translation by W. Jwaideh in *The Introductory Chapters of Yāqūt's Mu'jam al-Buldān*, Leiden, 1959.

Ibn-al-Athīr, *Al-Kāmil*, twelfth century. C. J. Tornberg, *Chronikon quod Perfectissimum Inscribitur*, Leiden, 1867-74.

Rashīd al-Dīn (Persian), *Jāmi al-Tawārikh*, 1304. M. Quatremère, *Histoire des Mongols de la Perse, écrite en persan par Raschid-Eldin*, Paris, 1836. Translations by E. Blochet in *Histoire générale du monde*, Paris, 1911, and Karl Jahn in *Geschichte Gāzān-Hān's aus dem Ta'rih-i-Mubārak-i-Gāzānī des Rašid al-Dīn Fadlallāh b. 'Imād al-Daula Abūl-Hair*, London, 1940.

Abu'lfida, *Taqwīm al-Buldān*, *c.* 1321. Text and translation by Joseph Toussaint Reinaud in *Géographie d'Aboulféda*, vol. 2a, Paris, 1848, and by Stanislas Guyard in vol. 2b, 1883. Used Ibn-Sa'id, *c.* 1250. See especially 'Chine (Sîn)' in vol. 2b., pp. 122-5.

Ibn-Battūtah, *Tuhfat al-Nuzzār fi Gharā'ib al-Amsār*, 1354. Text and translation by C. Defrémery and B.R. Sanguinetti in *Voyages d'Ibn Batoutah*, 4 vols., Paris, 1953; among many other translations, see H.A.R. Gibb, *Ibn Battúta, Travels in Asia and Africa, 1325-54*, London, 1929, revised ed. London, 1962.

Some of these are of only marginal interest for China. We might add, too, Al-Bīrūnī, tenth century, Maqdisī, tenth century, Ibn Wasif, eleventh century, Ibn al-Baytār, twelfth century, Al-Qazwīnī, thirteenth century.

Secondary Sources

Alavi, S. M. Ziauddin, *Arab Geography in the Ninth and Tenth Centuries*, Aligarh, 1965.

Blachère, R. and Darmaun, H., *Extraits des principaux géographes arabes du Moyen Âge*, Paris, 1957.

De Goeje, M.J., *Bibliotecha Geographorum Arabicorum*, Leiden, 1870-92.

Encyclopaedia of Islam (first edition), articles on 'China', 'Djughrāfiyā'. The new edition is not yet complete.

Ferrand, Gabriel, *Relations de voyages et textes géographiques arabes, persans, et turks relatifs à l'Extrême-Orient du VIII au XVII siècles*, 2 vols., Paris, 1913, 1914.

Hirth, Fr. and Rockhill, W.W., *Chau Ju-kua: His Work on the Chinese and Arab Trade in the Twelfth and Thirteenth Centuries, entitled Chu-fan-chi*, St Petersburg, 1911. Useful for the Chinese ports.

Hourani, George Fadlo, *Arab Seafaring in the Indian Ocean in Ancient and Early Medieval Times*, Princeton, 1951, also in Arabic, 1958.

Huzzayin, S.A., *Arabia and the Far East: their Commercial and Cultural Relations in Graeco-Roman and Irano-Arabian Times*, Cairo, 1942.

Krachkovskii, I.IU, *Istoriia arabskoi geographicheskoi literatury*, Moscow, Leningrad, 1957.

Kuwabara Jitsuzō, 'On P'u Shou-keng', *Memoirs of the Research Department of the Toyo Bunko* II (1928), pp. 1-79, VII (1935), pp. 1-104.

Laufer, Berthold, *Sino-Iranica*, Chicago, 1919. Of interest for plants, spices, medicines, etc.

Levy, Howard, S., *Biography of Huang Ch'ao*, Berkeley and Los Angeles, 1955. See especially Appendix III 'Arab Accounts'.

Lewicki, Tadeusz, 'Les premiers commerçants arabes en Chine', *Rocznik orientalistyczny* XI (1935), pp. 172-86.

Miquel, André, *La géographie humaine du monde musulman jusqu'au milieu du 11e siècle*, Paris, La Haye, 1967.

Needham, Joseph (with Wang Ling), *Science and Civilisation in China*, vol. 1, Cambridge, 1954. See 'Conditions of Travel of Scientific Ideas and Techniques between China and Europe', esp. pp. 170ff for routes.

Pelliot, Paul, *Notes on Marco Polo*, 2 vols., Paris, 1963. See especially vol. 1, pp. 264-78; vol. 2, pp. 730-1 (Çaitun, Gampu, Sin).

Reinaud, Joseph Toussaint, *Géographie d'Aboulféda*, Paris, 1848. Part I 'Introduction générale à la géographie des Orientaux'.

Sauvaget, Jean, and Cahen, Claude, *Introduction to the History of the Muslim East: A Bibliographical Guide*, Berkeley and Los Angeles [from French], 1965. See especially pp. 37-9, 134-6.

Tazaka Kōdō, *Chūgoku ni okeru Kaikyō no denrai to sono kōtsū*, 2 vols., Tokyo, 1964.

Yule, H., and Cordier, H., *Cathay and the Way Thither*, 4 vols., London, 1913-16. See especially vol. 1, pp. 124-45.

A Note on Names

Arab and Persian names cause difficulty. A man may be mentioned under several aliases; moreover there is a plethora of romanisations. I have given the most commonly found form in European sources. For full names of people and of books, and further bibliography, see:

Brockelmann, C., *Geschichte der arabischen Literatur*, Leiden, 1943-9.

Miquel, André, *La géographie humaine du monde musulman jusqu'au milieu du 11ᵉ siècle*, Paris, La Haye, 1967, pp. XIII-L.

The Encyclopaedia of Islām (new edition), vol. 1, Leiden, London, 1960; vol. 2, 1965; vol. 3, 1965-9, etc., Abu'l-Fidā, Abū Dulaf, Al-Bīrūnī, Buzurg (b. Shahriyar), Ibn Al-Athīr, Ibn Baṭṭūṭa, Ibn al-Faḳīh, Ibn Ḥawḳal, Ibn Khurradādhbih, Ibn al-Nadīm (Abu'l-Faradj), etc.

史 XVII: Western Sources

OTTO BERKELBACH van der SPRENKEL

The range, in time, variety and scope, of the material covered by this chapter is so great that no more than a preliminary mapping will be attempted here, while detailed references will be included only by way of illustration.

The West's earliest sure knowledge of China—leaving aside the tales and legends of Antiquity[1]—begins with the accounts of European traders, travellers, and missionaries in the thirteenth and fourteenth centuries; and a line is properly drawn between these and the later continuous stream of observation, description, and explication, soon broadening to a flood, that began to flow in the sixteenth century and has continued since then without remission, to leave, in Western languages, a literary deposit the extent of which can today hardly be appreciated without the help of detailed bibliographical surveys.

The first period, which antedates the invention of printing in Europe, is dominated by the Franciscans and Marco Polo. Europe's first authentic accounts of the Mongol empire, and first reliable (if second-hand) reports of China, come from the Franciscan emissaries John of Plano Carpini (in Asia 1245-7) and William of Rubruquis (1253-5). The most influential of the Friars was Odoric of Pordenone, who left Europe *c.* 1316, was in China 1322-4, and returned to Italy in 1330. He dictated his narrative the following year, shortly before his death. The importance of his work for the spread of knowledge about Asia in Europe is attested by the large number of extant manuscripts (seventy-three, compared with only five of Friar John's *History of the Mongols*).

In a class by itself is Marco Polo's *Description of the World*. Polo left Europe for China, accompanying his father and uncle, in 1270, returning to Venice a full quarter of a century later. He was the first Westerner to know China well, travelling widely over the country in the service of its Mongol rulers. He was an interested and accurate observer, and the

---

[1] An exception should perhaps be made for the Byzantine historian Theophylactus Simocatta (sixth-seventh centuries) whose brief account of China in his *Historiae*, commonly dismissed as the work of a credulous teller of tales, has been interestingly validated by Peter A. Boodberg in 'Marginalia to the Histories of the Northern Dynasties', *Harvard Journal of Asiatic Studies* III (1938), pp. 223-43.

Description, written down to his dictation in 1298-9, achieved immediate success (119 manuscript versions in various languages are known), though his story did not always command the belief of its readers.

Excellent texts, in well annotated editions, now exist for all these works, thanks to the labours of such scholars as Avezac, Pauthier, Yule, Cordier, Rockhill, Beazley, Benedetto, Wyngaert, Moule, and Pelliot.

This first stage in the Western discovery of China ended with the break-up of the *Pax Mongolica* and the virtual closing of the Silk Road across Eurasia. The interruption was brief. By the beginning of the sixteenth century, Western enterprise, mainly Iberian, stimulated by the challenge to travel and traffic presented by Muslim control of the lucrative spice trade, had opened the sea route to the East Indies and China. The Portuguese, under Vasco da Gama, rounded Africa and reached Calicut on India's west coast in 1498; and a Portuguese ship anchored off Canton in 1516. Religious motives had, from the first, been associated with the pursuit of commercial goals, and missionaries accompanied both private and official missions into the Eastern seas. This was fortunate, as clerics were commonly better instructed, more generally curious, and more articulate than the average run of merchants. Of the three men whose eyewitness narratives were combined and elaborated in González de Mendoza's *Historia . . . del gran Reyno de la China* (Rome, 1585), the first, Galeote Pereira, was a layman—soldier as well as sailor and merchant adventurer, taken prisoner and held in south China 1549-52; the second was Gaspar da Cruz, a Portuguese Dominican, whose *Tractado* (Evora, 1569-70) made use, with other material, of Pereira's narrative; and the third was also a religious, Martín de Rada, a Spanish Augustinian, whose *Relación* is a report of his visit to Fukien in 1575. These three writings form the second part of Mendoza's *Historia* (pp. 151-264 of the original edition), and follow a first part divided into three books concerned respectively with China's geography (pp. 1-25), religious condition (pp. 26-56), and political and social order (pp. 57-150).[2]

The *Historia* is important for several reasons. In the first place, it was an immensely successful, and therefore influential, book. In the thirty years following its first appearance it was translated into Italian, French, English, Latin, German, and Dutch, and was printed altogether thirty-five times. Boxer is certainly right when he says that 'Mendoza's book had been read by the majority of well-educated Europeans at the beginning of the seventeenth century'.[3] Furthermore, Mendoza was the first to collect

---

[2] For González de Mendoza's book, see the reprint (Madrid, 1944) in the series España Misionera; and, in English, the reprint of the 1588 translation by R. Parke, edited by G.T. Staunton, and introduced by R.H. Major, in Hakluyt Society, Series I, nos. XIV-XV (London, 1853-4 and reprints). Also Cordier, *Bibliotheca Sinica*, Vol. 1, cols. 8-16; and Streit, *Bibliotheca Missionum*, vol. 4, pp. 531-43.

[3] C.R. Boxer, *South China in the Sixteenth Century*, in Hakluyt Society, Series II, no. CVI (London, 1953), p. xvii. In this volume Boxer provides translations, with exemplary annota-

together and arrange systematically in a single volume everything that was then known in the West about China. In its scope, matter, and ordering, his book stands as the first in a notable series of compilations which includes those of du Halde, the Abbé Grosier, John Francis Davis, Bazin-Pauthier, and Samuel Wells Williams (after which the 'magisterium' was no longer transmitted).

The reporting of China, which thus got off to a good start around the turn of the sixteenth-seventeenth centuries, made astonishing progress during the next two hundred years. This was due almost entirely to the Jesuits belonging to, or associated with, the China Mission—with some small but significant assistance from their religious rivals.

The task which the Jesuit missionaries set themselves—the conversion of China to Christianity—was a formidable one. It is no matter for surprise that, although impressive tactical successes were achieved in the closing years of the Ming and during the K'ang-hsi reign, its failure was total. Nevertheless, the fact that so many of the missionaries, from Ricci at the beginning to Amiot at the end, were as indefatigable in scholarship as they were devoted in religion, ensured that while they failed in their mission to interpret Christianity to the Chinese, they were brilliantly successful in interpreting China to the West. In letters, pamphlets, and folios, in travel notes, translations, and learned monographs, they sent back a flood of information to Europe on every aspect of China's past history and present condition. This immense documentation is of the greatest value for the study of Chinese society and culture. All of the descriptive material, which makes up a large proportion of the whole, is written from personal observation by educated and insatiably curious observers who had every motive for interesting their countrymen and co-religionists at home in the Middle Kingdom.

Of the great compilations for which the Jesuits were responsible, it will suffice to mention only the *Mémoires concernant . . . les Chinois*[4] and the *Lettres édifiantes et curieuses*;[5] and, from the latter, to instance as typical examples of

---

tion, of the narratives of Pereira, da Cruz, and de Rada, accompanied by an excellent bibliography (pp. 344-60) and glossaries.

[4] The full title of this great collection of articles and monographs is *Mémoires concernant l'histoire, les sciences, les arts, les moeurs, les usages, &c des Chinois*. The first volume was published at Paris in 1776, and the fifteenth in 1791. This included the first half of P. Amiot's 'Abrégé de l'histoire de la grande dynastie Tang'. Volume 16, with the rest of Amiot's work, appeared only in 1814, as did another volume (sometimes reckoned as the seventeenth of the series) containing P. Gaubil's 'Traité de la chronologie chinoise'. For the contents of the individual volumes, see Cordier, *Bibliotheca Sinica*, cols. 54-6.

[5] *Lettres édifiantes et curieuses écrites des missions étrangères par quelques missionnaires de la Compagnie de Jésus*, vols. 1 (Paris, 1702) to 34 (Paris, 1776). For the complex story of the later editions of this series see Cordier, *Bibliotheca Sinica*, vol. 2, cols. 926-52. The series was continued in the nineteenth century, first by the *Nouvelles lettres édifiantes des missions de la Chine et des Indes Orientales*, 8 vols. (Paris, 1818-23), and then by the *Association de la Propagation de la Foi, Annales . . . Collection faisant suite à toutes les éditions des Lettres édifiantes* (Lyon, 1827+). For details as to content, see Cordier, *Bibliotheca Sinica*, vol. 2, cols. 957-80 (covering

informative and accurate Jesuit reporting, the description of the island county of Ch'ung-ming in the mouth of the Yangtze by P. Jacquemin (1 September 1712), and the accounts of porcelain manufacture at Ching-te chen by P. d'Entrecolles (1 September 1712 and 25 January 1722).

Among the earlier part-historical part-descriptive works, pride of place goes naturally to Matteo Ricci's *Della entrata della Compagnia di Giesù e Christianità nella Cina*. This was published in its original form only in 1911 (*Opere storiche del P. Matteo Ricci*, I, ed. P. Tacchi-Venturi, Macerata), and, at last, with an impeccable sinological *apparatus criticus* by the late P. Pasquale M. D'Elia, in *Fonti Ricciane*, 3 vols. (Rome, 1942-9). It first saw the light in a Latin version made, with some minor additions of his own, by P. Nicolas Trigault, S.J., from Ricci's manuscript, and entitled *De Christiana Expeditione apud Sinas suscepta ab Societate Jesu* (Augsburg, 1615). Ricci's own work disappeared for 300 years, and was rediscovered (and published) only when a thorough search was made at the time of its author's tercentenary. However, the *De Christiana Expeditione*, with its numerous translations into the European vernacular languages, was the first work to challenge, and indeed supersede, Mendoza's *History*. It, and the Riccian original, remain today indispensable primary sources for the late Ming period.[6]

Other works which should also be mentioned are P. Alvarez Semedo's *Imperio de la China* (Madrid, 1642), and Gabriel de Magalhães' *Nouvelle relation* (Paris, 1688). Even the 'Rites Controversy', with its disastrous repercussions on the mission itself, was productive of 'source books' of major importance: outstanding among them are the Dominican Domingo Navarrete's *Tratados historicos, politicos, ethicos y religiosos de la monarchia de China* (Madrid, 1676)[7] and the Jesuit Louis Daniel le Comte's *Nouveaux mémoires sur l'état présent de la Chine*, 2 vols. (Paris, 1696).[8]

---

the years 1826-1903) and vol. 5, cols. 3601-12 (covering 1903-21). As the nineteenth century progresses, this series becomes less and less useful as a general source of information on China. Also to be noted are the *Annales de la Congrégation de la Mission* (Paris, 1834+).

[6] The Latin version was printed four times in the decade 1615-25, and seven other editions appeared in German, Spanish, French, Italian, and English during the same period. The book was more than just a history of the early years of the mission, as the subtitle makes clear: *In quibus Sinensis Regni Mores, Leges atqu: Instituta Nova illius Ecclesiae Difficillima Primordia Accurate & Summa Fide Describuntur*. Recently a new English translation has been made by Louis J. Gallagher, S.J.: *The China That Was* (Milwaukee, 1942) and, revised and more complete, *China in the Sixteenth Century: the Journals of Mathew Ricci 1583-1610* (New York, 1953).

[7] Navarrete's book is (to quote Denis Twitchett) 'a treasure of minor observations and details'. An excellent English edition is now available prepared by J.S. Cummins, *The Travels and Controversies of Friar Domingo Navarrete 1618-1686*, Hakluyt Society, Series II, nos. CXVIII-CXIX (Cambridge, 1962). See Streit and Dindinger, *Bibliotheca Missionum*, vol. 5, pp. 861-3.

[8] The range of this intelligent, well-observed, and still eminently readable book is illustrated by the collocated subtitles of the English editions of 1697-8: *Memoirs and Observations Topographical, Physical, Mathematical, Mechanical, Natural, Civil and Ecclesiastical, Made in a Late Journey through the Empire of China, and Published in Several Letters Particularly upon the Chinese*

A generation and more later was published the magistral work of P. Jean Baptiste du Halde, S.J., in four folio volumes of altogether some 2,500 pages: the *Description géographique, historique, chronologique, politique de l'Empire de la Chine et de la Tartarie chinoise* (Paris, 1735).[9] This extraordinarily rich compendium benefited from the fact that du Halde succeeded P. le Gobien in 1711 as editor of the *Lettres édifiantes* (he was responsible for *recueils* 9-26, the last of which appeared in 1743, the year of his death), and was able to draw heavily on the works, manuscript as well as published, of his fellow Jesuits of the mission, with whom he also maintained an unflagging correspondence. Du Halde was one of the first of the 'China scholars' who never visited China—a distinguished company, of which the late Arthur Waley may well prove the last representative.

It is unnecessary to go into further detail concerning the works of the Jesuit and other missionaries (Jesuit sources are considered in a separate chapter); but this literature, so instructive and informative in itself, also generated what may be described as a secondary body of writing—for the most important publications on China were quoted, expounded, assessed, attacked and defended in the new literary and scientific journals that began to appear in the seventeenth century, and to flourish in the eighteenth. This secondary literature is less well known than it deserves to be. One of the most useful of these journals is certainly the *Mémoires de Trévoux* (1701-67).[10] Others, all of considerable sinological interest, are the *Journal des savans* (from 1665), *Nouvelles de la République des lettres* (1684-1718), *Journal littéraire* (1713-37), *Bibliothèque française* (1723-46), *Journal étranger* (1754-62), *Année littéraire* (1754-90), and *Journal encyclopédique* (1756-93).[11]

The existence of two exceptionally well planned and executed bibliographical guides to this great sea of missionary descriptive and interpretative reporting, and to the derivative literature just referred to, greatly facilitates

---

Pottery and Varnishing; the Silk and other Manufactures; the Pearl Fishing; the History of Plants and Animals; with a Description of their Cities and Public Works; Number of People, their Language, Manners and Commerce; their Habits, Oeconomy, and Government. The Philosophy of Confucius. The State of Christianity, and many other Curious and Useful Remarks. See Streit and Dindinger, *Bibliotheca Missionum*, vol. 5, p. 933; and Sommervogel, *Bibliothèque*, vol. 2, cols. 1356-62.

[9] See Cordier, *Bibliotheca Sinica*, vol. 1, cols. 45-52; Streit-Dindinger, *Bibliotheca Missionum*, vol. 7, pp. 284-5; Sommervogel, *Bibliothèque*, vol. 4, cols. 34-8.

[10] The *Mémoires de Trévoux*, or, to use its proper title, *Mémoires pour l'histoire des sciences et des beaux-arts* (Trévoux, 1701-67) was the more or less official organ of the Jesuits in the eighteenth century. It began to appear in 1701, under the patronage of the Duc de Maine, at Trévoux, the capital of his principality of Dombes; and continued until 1767. It naturally took an interest in China, both as a theatre of Jesuit activity and achievement, and as the *locus* of controversy in the argument about the Chinese 'rites'. See C. Sommervogel S.J., *Table méthodique des Mémoires de Trévoux*, 3 vols. (Paris, 1864-5); and the recent study by A.R. Desautels S.J., *Les Mémoires de Trévoux et le mouvement des idées au XVIIIe siècle 1701-1734* (Rome, 1956). A successor volume on the period 1735-67 is awaited. A complete reprint of the *Mémoires* was published by Slatkine of Geneva in 1968-9.

[11] All of these journals are now easily accessible in libraries in Slatkine reprints.

its exploitation by the sinologist. The more inclusive of the two is the *Bibliotheca Missionum*, begun by P. Robert Streit, continued by P. Johannes Dindinger, and later by P. Johannes Rommerskirchen and P. Nikolaus Kowalsky. While this covers missionary writings relating to all parts of the world, two volumes are devoted to Asian missions (from 1245 to the end of the seventeenth century), and three more deal with China exclusively (to 1909).[12] The other work is the *Bibliothèque de la Compagnie de Jésus*, an enterprise that has grown from the brothers de Backer's seven octavos (1853-71) to Sommervogel's revised edition in nine quartos (1890-1909),[13] with further supplements (1911-30) bringing the total to twelve.

It is significant that both these bibliographies also list and describe manuscripts. The very large number mentioned underlines the need for much more effort and money to be applied to the task of editing and publishing this material, much of which is of the first importance not only for our knowledge of China but also for the early history of sinology. Similar considerations apply to the correspondence of the missionaries with the lay scholars of their day.

[12] Volumes 4, 5, 7, 12, and 13 deal, in part or in whole, with China. Chapters 1-3 of vol. 4, *Asiatische Missionsliteratur 1245-1599* (Freiburg, 1928, repr. 1964), on 'Die Mission in den Mongolenreichen', cover the thirteenth, fourteenth and fifteenth centuries respectively, with 371 items of which some relate to China; the last section of chapter 4, on the sixteenth century, items 1,918-2,052, comprises only China material. Chapter 5, vol. 5, *Asiatische Missions-literatur 1600-1699* (Freiburg, 1929, repr. 1964), items 2,030-811, is devoted to China; as are vol. 7, *Chinesische Missionsliteratur 1700-99* (Freiburg, 1931, repr. 1965), items 2,006-4,035; vol. 12, *Chinesische Missionsliteratur 1800-1884* (Freiburg, 1958), items 1-1,217; vol. 13, *Chinesische Missionsliteratur 1885-1909* (Freiburg, 1959), items 1,218-969. Indexes are provided for authors, persons, subjects, places, languages. This very fine work, which as a technical bibliographical accomplishment is almost beyond praise, thus covers both the 'Franciscan' and 'Jesuit' missionary periods, and also the nineteenth and present centuries virtually to the threshold of the Chinese Republic, and describes a little over 5,250 entries.

[13] This work began with the bibliography of Jesuit writings compiled by PP. Augustin and Aloys de Backer, 7 vols. (Liège, 1853-71). In preparing the second edition, 3 vols. folio (Liège, 1869-76), the de Backers were joined by P. Carlos Sommervogel. Only 200 sets were printed, none of them available for private purchase. The imposing third edition, for which Sommervogel was solely responsible, was completed a quarter of a century later, 9 vols. 4to. (Bruxelles, Paris, 1890-1900). Vols. 1-7 contain the bibliography proper; vol. 8 and the first part of 9, an extensive supplement. The last part of vol. 9 presents a re-casting of Sommervogel's *Dictionnaire des ouvrages anonymes et pseudonymes publiés par des religieux de la Compagnie de Jésus depuis sa fondation jusqu'à nos jours* (Paris, 1884, repr. Amsterdam, 1966), itself an indispensable tool for the student of Jesuit writings on China. Vol. 10 (Paris, 1909), due to P. Pierre Bliard, contains (in nearly 2,000 columns) extremely useful indexes, classified and alphabetic, to the first nine volumes. Vol. 11 (Paris, 1932), also by P. Bliard, is a much enlarged revision of P. Auguste Carayon's bibliography of the history of the Society of Jesus, a work originally conceived as part of the de Backers' bibliographical project, and first published in Paris in 1864. This volume, of course, contains works by non-Jesuit writers. The final volume contains 'additions et corrections' by P. Ernest Marie Rivière, first issued by him in five fascicles (Toulouse, 1911-30) and later collected together as vol. 12. An anastatic reprint (Héverlé, Louvain, 1960) of the complete 'répertoire topo-bio-biblio-graphique' greatly facilitates the work of the researcher by including in the margins references from the main text to all the supplements. On de Backer himself see the (anonymous) article: 'F. Augustine de Backer', *Dublin Review* NS XXVIII (1877, i), pp. 452-72.

This is perhaps the place to note the important stimulus which this intellectual traffic from China to Europe gave to the rise of secular sinology, especially in France, in the second half of the eighteenth century. Fréret, Fourmont, de Guignes, and Deshautesrayes are unthinkable without the mission, and the foundations of the scientific study of China were truly laid by them. However, sinology is another story; and here we are concerned only with 'sources' and not with the products arising from their use.

Although missionary writings predominate in the pre-1800 Western literature on China, mention must also be made of another more specialised, less voluminous but nonetheless extremely valuable class of writings: the narratives of those taking part in European embassies to the Chinese court. No adequate bibliographical account of these works yet exists.[14] The fullest, most informative, and best illustrated of them are perhaps Joan Nieuhof's account of the first embassy sent by the Dutch East India Company in 1655-7, Olfert Dapper's account of the second embassy of 1665(?), and A. E. van Braam's narrative of the embassy of 1794-5.[15] The first two Dutch works mentioned are an incomparable source for mid-seventeenth century China. Of equal interest for a picture of the Middle Kingdom at the turn of the eighteenth-nineteenth centuries are the accounts of the Macartney and Amherst embassies of 1793 and 1816. For the former, indeed, we have another of the great Western books on China, the admirable *Authentic Account of an Embassy from the King of Great Britain to the Emperor of China; Including Cursory Observations Made, and Information Obtained, in Travelling through that Ancient Empire, and a Small Part of Chinese Tartary*, by George Leonard Staunton. This appeared in 1797 in two substantial quartos of together 1,200 pages; accompanied by a folio atlas of 44 plates, containing maps, plans, and views. There was no question of its popularity. Two further editions were printed in 1797-8, numerous translations were made, and an abridged version was even issued in ten weekly numbers.[16] The few works

[14] A rather unsatisfactory book is Edward Godfrey Cox, *A Reference Guide to the Literature of Travel: I, The Old World*, Univ. of Washington Publications in Language and Literature, vol. 9 (Seattle, 1935, repr. 1948). The section 'Far East' (items 1,499-931), despite inaccuracies and *lacunae*, is of some use. The compiler's aim was 'to list in chronological order . . . down to and including the year 1800, all the books on foreign travels, voyages and descriptions printed in Great Britain, together with translations from foreign tongues . . . so far as they have come to my notice' (preface, p.v.). A most useful reference work is: H.R. Mill, comp., *Catalogue of the Library of the Royal Geographical Society* (London, 1895). 'Appendix I, Collections of Voyages and Travels, giving the contents of the volumes', pp. 525-612.

[15] For Nieuhof's *Gezantschap* (Amsterdam, 1665), Dapper's *Gedenkwaerdig bedryf* (Amsterdam, 1670), and van Braam's *Voyage de l'ambassade* (Philadelphia, 1797-8), see Cordier, *Bibliotheca Sinica*, vol. 3, cols. 2344-51. On the first book, see also the excellent article by C.C. Imbault-Huart, 'Le Voyage de l'ambassade hollandaise de 1656 à travers la province de Canton'. *Journal of China Branch of the Royal Asiatic Society* XXX (1895-6), pp. 1-73, a detailed commentary on the embassy's progress to the northern border of Kwangtung.

[16] For details of these editions, and of translations into French, Dutch, German, and Italian, see Cordier, *Bibliotheca Sinica*, vol. 4, cols. 2381-6.

here referred to do not of course exhaust the 'embassy' literature, to which the Russians and the Portuguese also made significant contributions.

With these books, we move into the nineteenth century—a century which, opening up a variety of new approaches to the observation and investigation of China, was to prove the most prolific of all in producing Western-language sources. The most obvious reason for this is that the nineteenth was *par excellence* the century of the traveller. Facilities available for moving oneself about the globe, still rather primitive in 1800, improved steadily throughout the period; and an astonishingly large number of people felt the need to acquaint first themselves, and then a wider public, with first-hand information about far-off countries and their inhabitants.

The nineteenth century was marked by a self-confident and increasingly prosperous middle class, from whose ranks came men, and women,[17] who combined a taste for travel with the financial means to indulge it. Not all the travellers were well-to-do eccentrics like Jules Verne's Phileas Fogg[18] though one can call to mind several among the 'China wanderers' whose principal motive appears to have been a simple zest for adventure. An example is Jules Léon Dutreuil de Rhins (1846-94), sailor and explorer, active in Africa, Siam and China, murdered by Tibetan villagers near Sining.[19] A more eccentric and only slightly less unfortunate traveller was Arnold Henry Savage Landor (1865-1924), whose book *In the Forbidden Land*, published in London in 1898, bore the subtitle: *An Account of a Journey into Tibet, Capture by Tibetan Lamas and Soldiers, Imprisonment, Torture, and Ultimate Release Brought about by Dr Wilson and the Political Peshkar Karak Sing-Pal*. Landor survived to write an eye-witness account of the march on

---

[17] Outstanding among Victorian lady travellers was Isabella Lucy Bishop (née Bird). For the whole of her long life (1831-1904) she suffered from poor health, in particular from a spinal complaint (which prompted her to take up horse-riding). She travelled in every part of the world, keenly looking about her, interesting herself in missionary and medical activities, and eventually writing up her travels. In 1892 she became the first woman to be admitted to the Royal Geographical Society. Her most important Far Eastern journey, made when she was well over sixty years of age, began in 1894, and lasted for three years, during which time she visited Japan, Korea (four times), Manchuria, and central and western China, founding three hospitals and an orphanage on the way. In China, she went up the Yangtze, travelled through Szechwan and over the border of Tibet, covering some 8,000 miles in fifteen months, much of it on horseback, and alone. See Anna M. Stoddart, *The Life of Isabella Bird—Mrs Bishop* (London, 1906).

[18] *Le tour du monde en quatre-vingt jours* was published in 1873, and celebrates both the traveller, the adventure of travelling, and the new means of locomotion. While Phileas Fogg did not actually set foot on Chinese soil (though he spent some hours, between steamers, in Hong Kong, and briefly sighted Shanghai), Verne later published a story, the scene of which was altogether laid in China: *Les tribulations d'un Chinois en Chine* (Paris, 1879). Jules Verne was the archetypal nineteenth century chronicler of travel. His fictional series, Les voyages extraordinaires, comprises more than sixty novels; and he also published *La découverte de la terre: Histoire générale des grands voyages et des grands voyageurs* (Paris, 1878-80), a history of exploration, in three quarto volumes.

[9] See the notice by F. Marouis in *Dictionnaire biographique français*, fasc. 70 (Paris, 1969).

Peking and relief of the legations[20] and, a description of his second visit to Tibet.[21]

Most travellers, however, were moved by considerations more sober than adventure. War accounted for some of them. A vast Western literature exists, most of it based on personal observation and some of it of considerable merit, on the Anglo-Chinese war of 1839-42; the Anglo-French war with China of 1856-60; the Taiping rebellion, especially after the occupation of Nanking in 1853; the Sino-French war of 1884-5; the Sino-Japanese war of 1894-5; the I-ho t'uan movement of 1900 and its aftermath; and the Russo-Japanese war of 1904-5, which brought Westerners into China, since her territory was made use of by the contestants as a battlefield. Both serving officers and civilian observers were diligent in placing on record accounts of what they had themselves seen, and often personally taken part in. Some of this literature is technical, and mainly of value to the professional soldier and military historian; the greater part, however, is of much more general interest for its depiction of places and peoples, political and social institutions, economic activities, manners and customs, and details of daily life.[22]

Of the books written about the Chinese wars of the nineteenth and early twentieth centuries, some were based on diaries; others were compiled from 'on the spot' reports sent home by war correspondents; others again derive a special quality from some unique opportunity for observation enjoyed by their author.[23] None of them is limited to purely military themes, as their subtitles often make clear. One example is Robert Swinhoe's *Narrative of the North China Campaign of 1860; Containing Personal Experiences of Chinese Character, and of the Moral and Social Condition of the Country, Together with a Description of the Interior of Pekin* (London, 1861). A notice of this book in the *Westminster Review* makes the point that the military part 'of the author's narrative is strikingly inferior to those parts of it which consist of his personal remarks on the manners and customs of the inhabitants: his accomplishments and position gave him great advantages for this kind of description . . . . His post as interpreter to the staff, under Sir Hope Grant, necessarily brought him into immediate contact with the natives . . . The narrative is substantially, though not in form, a diary of the proceedings of the allied forces.'[24] The *Westminster*'s earlier comment on Lord Jocelyn's book on the Opium

---

[20] *China and the Allies* (London, 1901).

[21] *Tibet and Nepal* (London, 1905).

[22] The following authors may be cited as representative of this class of traveller (for details of their works see the select bibliography at the end of the chapter): Lord Jocelyn, Commander J.E. Bingham, R.N., Commander W.H. Hall, R.N., George Wingrove Cooke, Robert Swinhoe, Charles de Mutrécy, J.M. Callery, Melchior Yvan, T.T. Meadows, Commander Lindesay Brine, R.N., Augustus Lindley ('Lin-le'), Maurice Loir, Jacques Harmant (pseudonym of A. Verdier), Roland Allen, Marcel Monnier (correspondent of *Le Temps*), Pierre Loti, and Georg Wegener.

[23] Lindley, for example, served in the Taiping forces from 1860 to 1864.

[24] *Westminster Review* NS XXI (1862), pp. 255-6.

War is not only characteristically pleasant in tone, but has a wider application than to this book alone: 'Although Lord Jocelyn does not tell us much, he tells us what he saw himself, and his story is very agreeably told. He is remarkably free from prejudice—discovers many good qualities in our new enemies, and so many proofs of civilisation in their agriculture, commerce, dwellings, and general comportment, that if they were but proficient in the art of destroying their fellow creatures, they might almost be placed on a level with ourselves.'[25]

The consular and diplomatic services brought many gifted Westerners to China in the nineteenth and twentieth centuries. One of the earliest official missions was the French, led by Théodose de Lagrené, sent in 1844 to negotiate a treaty 'of commerce and navigation'. De Lagrené's staff was a brilliant one. It included Dr Melchior Yvan and Joseph Callery, who were later to collaborate in writing one of the best accounts of the earliest phase of the Taiping rebellion. Another member was Natalis Rondot, a prolific writer on Western arts and art-technologies; author of a substantial work on France's textile trade with China; of notes on textile plants, the weaving loom, Chinese weights and measures, seeds of vegetables grown in the gardens at 'Fah-ti' on the Pearl River, the practice of infanticide, agricultural colonies; and also of a charming and instructive piece describing Chinese artifacts, shops, and studios, observed in the course of 'une promenade dans Canton';[26] and, finally, with I. Hedde, Ed. Renard, and A. Haussmann, of the *Étude pratique du commerce d'exportation de la Chine* (1847), a work in some respects to be compared with W. Milburn's *Oriental Commerce* (1813, revised by T. Thornton in 1825). All three of Rondot's co-authors, nominated, like himself, by the Chambers of Commerce of Reims, Mulhouse, Saint-Étienne, Lyon, and Paris, had come to China with the Lagrené mission. Renard published journal articles on fishing and fish-breeding, the industrial and agricultural uses of seaweeds, and the bamboo: compared with his colleagues, his was a meagre output. Auguste Haussmann wrote an interesting *Voyage en Chine, Cochinchine, Inde et Malaisie* (in three volumes, 1847-8), and a work of contemporary history.[27] Isidore Hedde produced a series of works of great interest for our knowledge of the Chinese economy in the 1840s and 1850s.[28] It is hard to imagine a diplomatic team—whose first objective was, after all, that of negotiating a treaty—with members as dedicated as these men were to informing themselves and others about the country to which they had been sent.

Among British consular and diplomatic officials who during the century

---

[25] *Westminster Review* XXXV (1841), p. 526, on Lord Jocelyn's *Six Months with the Chinese Expedition.*
[26] *Journal asiatique* 4e sér., XI (1848), pp. 34-62.
[27] *La Chine, résumé historique de l'insurrection et des événements qui ont eu lieu dans ce pays, depuis le commencement de la guerre de l'opium jusqu'en 1857* (Paris, 1864).
[28] Some of Hedde's works are listed in the select bibliography below.

produced valuable sources for the student of China (apart from those already mentioned in other contexts) the names of Edward Colborne Baber (1843-90) and Alexander Hosie (1853-1925) stand out. Baber, whose major travels were compressed into the years 1876 to 1880, can also be regarded as the virtual 'discoverer' of the Lolo people. His most important work is *Travels and Researches in Western China*.[29] Hosie, who entered the consular service in 1876, was sent in 1881, under the terms of the Chefoo Convention, as the first British consul to Chungking. In this post he made journeys which took him over 5,000 miles of often difficult terrain, and provided him with material for *Three Years in Western China, a Narrative of Three Journeys in Ssŭ-ch'uan, Kuei-chow, and Yün-nan*, published in London in 1890. His transfer to Niu-chuang led to the writing of *Manchuria: its People, Resources, and Recent History*, published in 1901, which C. R. Beazley characterised as a careful, reliable 'account of the inhabitants and administration, physical features and climate, agriculture, animal and mineral products, special industries and trade' of the region.[30] Hosie had already produced a report for the British Government on Formosa (1893), and now produced another, again largely concerned with economic matters, on the province of Szechwan (1904, revised and enlarged, Shanghai, 1922). His last, longest, and possibly most valuable work was the result of an assignment in 1910-11 to investigate how far the supposed suppression of opium cultivation in China by the Chinese authorities was a reality. His book was thus described by W. Churchill (the geographer): 'Hosie in the season of cultivation traversed the six provinces capable of raising the poppy, Shansi, Shensi, Kansu, Szechwan, Yunnan and Kueichou .... [He] left the familiar highways, avoided the railroads and rivers and picked an uncomfortable way ... He has furnished a considerable supply of information upon hamlets and paths which have not before been visited by so competent an observer.'[31] The list of British consular officers who have added to our knowledge and understanding of China could be extended much beyond these two names; but no catalogue is intended, and Baber and Hosie are cited simply as examples.

The roll is impressive, too, from other countries. Gustaaf Schlegel (1840-1903) went to China as a student interpreter for the Netherlands government in 1858, serving first in Canton, and later in Batavia. In 1872, he left the service, and five years later was appointed to a chair of Chinese created specially for him at Leiden. His 'source' writings belong to the earlier part of his career and include his numerous articles on Chinese law,

[29] See *Supplementary Papers*, R.G.S. London, 1886, containing 'A Journey of Exploration in Western Ssu-ch'uan'; 'A Journey to Ta-chien-lu'; 'Notes on a Route ... through Western Yunnan, from Tali-fu to T'eng-yueh', reproduced from the *Bluebook China* no. 2 (1879); and 'On the Tea-Trade with Tibet', reproduced from the *Gazette of India* (8 November 1879).
[30] *Geographical Journal* XVIII (1901), p. 166.
[31] *Geographical Review* I (1916), pp. 73-4 written about *On the Trail of the Opium Poppy*, 2 vols. (London, 1914).

the pioneering essay 'Iets over de prostitutie in China' (1866, which won the distinction of translation into French and German—but not into English), and his important study on the Hung League. These writings are all of first importance as source material: Schlegel's later works come into a different, though not less meritorious, category.[32]

Jan Jacob Maria de Groot (1854-1921) also went to China in the first instance as an interpreter for the Netherlands government; he was transferred to Java in 1878, and returned to China, still in government service, in 1886, to study language and customs in those parts of China from which the great proportion of Chinese immigrants into the Dutch East Indies were drawn. Two great works, one on the festivals of the Amoy Chinese, the other on Chinese religion, were products of this period of study in China.[33]

Among the Americans—S. Wells Williams apart—there is no doubt that William Woodville Rockhill (1854-1914) deserves pride of place. His government service in China, beginning in 1884, was briefly interrupted by work for the Smithsonian Institution: expeditions which he led to Mongolia and Tibet in 1888-9 and 1891-2 respectively. He returned to diplomacy in 1893, and played an important role both in the formulation of the 'open door' policy and in the post-Boxer negotiations. There is a not too substantial life by Paul A. Varg, *Open Door Diplomat, the Life of W. W. Rockhill* (Urbana, 1952). The Rockhill papers are in private hands, and, although Varg was able to make some use of them, they remain unpublished.

A last example is the Frenchman G. Eugène Simon (1829-96), consul in Ning-po and Fu-chou in the 1860s and 1870s, where, in sharp contrast to the attitude of most educated Frenchmen of his time (read, for instance, the writings of Maurice Jametel, Chavannes's teacher at the École des Langues Orientales), he admired what he saw, and wrote illuminatingly about it in a way more characteristic of the eighteenth century than of his own. His studies, still well worth consulting today, include 'Les petites sociétés d'argent en Chine' (1871), *La cité chinoise* (partial journal publication 1882, in book form 1885), and 'La famille Ouang-ming-tse' (1885), an essay of some seventy pages in which Simon relives some of his experiences of twenty years before, when he became friendly with a Chinese tea-grower's family in the hills behind Fu-chou. In these idyllic and charming pages he describes the daily life, farming practices, and economic situation of the Wang family, presenting them also as a model for France.

Source material describing the Chinese and their environment has come in good measure from the scientists, though often as a by-product of their primary preoccupations. As an illustration, I may cite the botanists and plant-hunters, from Robert Fortune (1812-80) and the Abbé Armand David (1826-1900) to F. Kingdon Ward (1885-1958). Fortune's *Three Years*

---

[32] See two of Schlegel's works listed in the bibliography below.
[33] Details of these two works are given in the bibliography below.

Wanderings in the Northern Provinces in China (1847) and his *Journey to the Tea Countries of China* (1852) are deservedly classics. The Lazarist A. David journeyed in Mongolia (1864-6), through central China to Szechwan and the Tibetan border (1869-70), and over most of 'China Proper' (1872-4), sending back bulletins from time to time to the Paris Société de Géographie and other learned bodies. E. D. Jones wrote of his *Journal* (mostly concerned with the third voyage, a book of over 700 pages published in Paris, 1875) that he 'chronicles, with much minuteness, the results of his daily observations, which possess a special interest for the student of natural history . . . but also . . . supply much interesting information with regard to the manners and customs as well as the geography of the Chinese empire.'[34] These two examples may suffice for the literature of information that we owe to the scientists: men often working in very different disciplines, but observing closely and reporting with precision on the Chinese scene.

In a very special class are the publications deriving from the private explorations and institutional expeditions of the later nineteenth and early twentieth centuries. Some of these are well known to sinologists—though contributions hidden in their appendices, separately issued monographs, and much of the other 'side literature' to which they have given rise, are less so.[35] These works constitute a library of source material about China, with the emphasis perhaps on the 'Inner Asian Frontiers' rather than on 'China Proper'—though the last is not neglected. They are monuments of a period of Western enterprise in China that has now—in most other respects we may say fortunately—passed away; and works of exactly this kind will never be produced again. Their great value to the student of the Chinese empire lies partly in the terrain covered by the missions, and in the studies undertaken, but also in the character of the men who led them. Sylvain Lévi's words, written of Sir Mark Aurel Stein, are assuredly true of him, but apply also to many of his colleagues: 'Les *Ruins of Desert Cathay* sont un journal de voyage, mais le journal d'un voyageur qui est explorateur, géographe, linguiste, historien, archéologue, intéressé à la vie du présent comme du passé.'[36]

The commercial motive was also an important one for travellers in China. Correspondingly significant is the extensive nineteenth-century literature concerning China's trade, domestic as well as foreign; her monetary and banking systems; her agriculture and mining; and indeed all aspects of her

---

[34] *Academy* XIV (1878), pp. 261-2.
[35] The following authors may be especially noted, but the list is in no way exhaustive: Wilhelm Filchner (1877-1957), Filippo de Filippi (1869-1938), Sven Hedin (1865-1952), Albert von le Coq (1860-1930), Vladimir Obruchev (1863-1956), Henri d'Ollone (1868-?), Nicolai Przheval'sky (1839-88), Ferdinand von Richthofen (1833-1905), Mark Aurel Stein (1862-1943), Albert Tafel (1877-1935), and Emil Trinkler (1896-1931). Some of the works of these writers are listed in the bibliography below.
[36] *Revue critique* NS LXXV (1913), pp. 1-2.

economic life. We have already referred to Rondot's *Étude pratique*, which, though wholly economic in content, was the by-product of a diplomatic mission. Also worth recalling is the fact that it was a group of Western businessmen interested in China's possible mineral resources, and in assessing possibilities of profitable capital investment, that in 1869 engaged the services of von Richthofen and met the expenses of the explorations that gave rise to his *China, Ergebnisse eigener Reisen*. As a typical, if rather superior example of the literature of the 'commercial traveller', we may cite the book by Thomas Thornville Cooper (1839-78), *Travels of a Pioneer of Commerce in Pigtail and Petticoats; or an Overland Journey from China towards India*, published in London in 1871. The author, whose journey was financially assisted by 'Members of the foreign community of Shanghai' and whose hope was to find a trade route leading from western China into north India, travelled through Hupeh to I-ch'ang, Chungking, and Ch'eng-tu, then to Ta-chien-lu and on into eastern Tibet. He was captured and briefly imprisoned at Wei-hsi, rescued, and enabled to make his way back to Shanghai. His book, which is well illustrated, is informative and shows him to have been an alert observer.

To exemplify a very different but equally significant type of production, no better work could be chosen than *La mission lyonnaise d'exploration commerciale en Chine* (Lyon, 1898), forming two quarto volumes of close on 900 pages. The mission was sent to China at the initiative of the Lyon Chamber of Commerce and its Report is described as follows by Louis Ravenau:

> L'importance du travail accompli répond à la largeur et au libéralisme du programme . . . . Il faut lire ce *récit de voyage* de près de 400 pages, sobre, précis et alerte . . . . Puis, dans la partie technique, les *Rapports régionaux* . . . sur le Yun-nan, sur Hong-Kong, sur le commerce de Canton et sur Pakhoi et la province de Kouang-Si, sur le Koui-Tcheou, sur le Se-Tchouan, sur le commerce de Han-K'eou;—les *Rapports spéciaux:* sur les Mines et la Métallurgie, sur la Soie, sur le Coton et les Cotonnades, sur les Corps gras, sur la Circulation monétaire, enfin le chapitre où M. Brennier étudie le mouvement commercial du port de Chang-hai et le commerce général de la Chine ainsi que le rôle actuel et possible de la France.[37]

It is worth noting here that the files of specialist and professional journals —examples are the *International Labour Review* (from 1921) and the *Transactions of the American Institute of Mining Engineers* (from 1871)—are rewarding sources of information about China in their respective fields; and that the information they provide is often extremely difficult to find elsewhere.

Another significant motive for travel to China was the hope to convert the Chinese to Christianity. Missionary activities played an important role, for the Catholic Mission, which had been struck an almost mortal blow by

---

[37] *Annales géographiques* VIII (1899), pp. 62-73.

the suppression of the Jesuits in 1773, revived in the next century; while the Protestant missions also entered the field with the arrival of Robert Morrison in 1807 and of Elijah C. Bridgman and David Abeel in 1830.[38] The main contribution of the Protestant missionary authors of the nineteenth century lay in general works presenting a broad picture of the country and its people, in travel narratives depicting life on highway and canal, in village and county town, and the pursuit of local arts and crafts, and also in more specialised descriptions of religious practices and festivals.[39]

The Catholic missionary literature of the nineteenth century, though vastly different from that produced in the two preceding centuries in accent, aim, and content, is still of first importance. It is hardly necessary to list names or mention individual works as the bibliographies referred to earlier (in notes 12 and 13) provide more than adequate guidance. It would be wrong, however, to pass over in silence the names of Fathers Joseph Gabet (1808-53) and Evariste Régis Huc (1813-60). Their achievement in reaching Lhasa was remarkable, and the influence of the latter's writings was widespread and continuing.[40] Special mention must also be made of the great

[38] On Morrison (1782-1834), see Mrs Morrison's *Memoirs of the Life and Labours of Robert Morrison*, 2 vols. (London, 1839); the judicious article by Karl Friedrich Neumann, 'Die Sinologen und ihre Werke I, Robert Morrison', *Zeitschrift der deutschen morgenländischen Gesellschaft* I (1847), pp. 91-128, 217-37; and Lindsay Ride, *Robert Morrison, the Scholar and the Man* (Hong Kong, 1957). Those of his writings that can properly be described as 'sources' include *A View of China* (Macao, 1817), *Notices Concerning China and the Port of Canton* (Malacca, 1823), and contributions to the *Indo-Chinese Gleaner* (Malacca, 1817-22), the *Evangelical Magazine* (for 1825), the *Canton Register* (from 1827), and the early volumes of the *Chinese Repository*. The last-named journal, 20 vols. (Canton, 1832-51), a rich treasure-house of materials on China, owed its existence to E.C. Bridgman (1801-61), who was also its first editor and a constant contributor. After the demise of the *Repository*, Bridgman was active in the formation of the China Branch of the Royal Asiatic Society, and was elected its first President. The extremely valuable *Journal of the North China Branch*, which began its life as the *Journal of the Shanghai Literary and Scientific Society* in 1858, opens with his Inaugural Address, delivered on 16 October, 1857. David Abeel (1804-46) is best known for his *Journal of a Residence in China and Neighbouring Countries from 1830-1833* (New York, 1834).

[39] Among the other principal contributors to this literature are W.H. Medhurst (1796-1857), Karl Gützlaff (1803-51), S. Wells Williams (1812-84), W.C. Milne (1815-63), Alexander Wylie (1815-87), Joseph Edkins (1823-1905), Justus Doolittle (1824-80), J.H. Gray (1828-90), J.L. Nevius (1829-93), E.J. Eitel (1838-1908), and A.H. Smith (1845-1932). For the most useful 'source' books of these authors, see the bibliography below. Most of the men listed above, and many more of their colleagues, published useful articles in missionary and other journals. A valuable preliminary guide to the authors and their works, covering the first two-thirds of the century, is A. Wylie's *Memorials of Protestant Missionaries to the Chinese: Giving a List of their Publications, and Obituary Notices of the Deceased* (Shanghai, 1867, reprinted, Taipei, 1967). Brief notes on missionaries, Catholic as well as Protestant, are included in Samuel Couling's *Encyclopaedia Sinica* (London, 1917). See also Clayton H. Chu, *American Missionaries in China; Books, Articles and Pamphlets Extracted from the Subject Catalogue of the Missionary Research Library*, 3 vols. (Cambridge, Mass., 1960).

[40] The story of the adventurous journey undertaken by the Lazarist Fathers Gabet and Huc is engagingly told in the latter's *Souvenirs d'un voyage dans la Tartarie, le Thibet et la Chine pendant les années 1844, 1845 et 1846*, 2 vols. (Paris, 1850). Also worth consulting is Huc's *L'empire chinois*, 2 vols. (Paris, 1854). For brief biographies of both men, and an exhaustive

series of monographs produced, over a period of almost half a century, by the Jesuit Fathers of the mission at Zi-ka-wei, the village near Shanghai which until the Communist revolution was their headquarters. This is the *Variétés sinologiques*, the first volume of which—P. Henri Havret's *L'île de Tsong-ming*—came from the Mission Press in 1892, while the sixty-sixth appeared in 1938.[41] A prestigious work published as part of this series, and of importance for an understanding of popular religion in China, is *Recherches sur les superstitions en Chine* by P. Henri Doré (1859-1931).[42] A final word should be added here in reference to the valuable and often pioneering work of Catholic missionaries in the fields of ethnology and social anthropology. Priests stationed in China's far western and northwestern provinces, well placed to observe, and linguistically and professionally equipped to understand what they saw and to interpret it, have made outstanding contributions to our knowledge of, especially, the autochthonous non-Han peoples.[43]

As the nineteenth century moved nearer its end, Western imperialist pressures upon China steadily increased, to culminate in the so-called 'scramble for concessions' of 1898. H.B. Morse had no hesitation in heading a chapter of his history describing that event 'The Impending Break-up of China';[44] and several of the European powers prepared themselves for this

---

bibliographical survey of Huc's writings, see Paul Pelliot, 'Le voyage de MM. Gabet et Huc à Lhassa' in *T'oung Pao* XXIV (1926), pp. 133-78. Pelliot defends the authenticity of Huc's account, but writes that 'en rédigeant ses *Souvenirs*, Huc les a largement arrangés pour le public. Il n'a rien "inventé", mais il a transposé pour plaire, et il a réussi. Les *Souvenirs* sont une oeuvre d'art qui laisse une impression d'ensemble plus vraie que le détail des faits n'y est exact.' See also *Bibliotheca Missionum*, vol. 12, pp. 230-8, for information concerning editions, translations and studies. This entry extending to eight pages of close print, is an excellent example of what the Streit-Dindinger bibliography has to offer.

[41] Not all volumes of the *Variétés sinologiques* are 'source' writings. In my judgment, about half would come into that category. Itemised lists of the series, giving authors, titles, etc., will be found in *Bibliotheca Missionum*, vol. 13, pp. 145-55, and in Cordier, *Bibliotheca Sinica*, vol. 2, cols. 857-9 and vol. 5, cols. 3469 and 3568-71 (to vol. 52 only).

[42] The 18 volumes that make up this work were published between 1911 and 1938. P. Doré's survey, though allowance must be made for the somewhat 'de haut en bas' attitude he adopts towards his subject matter, is conscientious, logically organised, and comprehensive; and the fact that Chinese characters are lavishly provided enhances its usefulness for reference purposes. The three parts of the *Recherches* are: I *Les pratiques superstitieuses* (vols. 1-5); II *Le panthéon chinois* (vols. 6-12); and III *Popularisation du Confucéisme, du Bouddhisme et du Taoisme en Chine* (vols. 13-18). The whole includes some hundreds of coloured illustrations after Chinese originals. An English translation of Parts I and II by M. Kennelly, S.J. (vols. 1-8) and F.D.J. Finn, S.J. (vols. 9 and 10) appeared from the T'usewei Mission Press between 1914 and 1933.

[43] This will be very clear to anyone who investigates the files of *Anthropos: Revue internationale d'ethnologie et de linguistique* (from 1906). The journal's coverage is world-wide, but there are articles dealing with China in almost every volume. *Anthropos* has been edited from the beginning by members of the Society of the Divine Word but its contributions come from members of many different religious orders, as well as from laymen. Note also the excellent *Ethnographische Beiträge aus der Ch'ing-hai Provinz*, published by the Catholic University of Peking in 1952.

[44] *The International Relations of the Chinese Empire*, vol. 3, *The Period of Subjection, 1894-1911*, ch. 5.

transaction by producing books descriptive of the parts of China they coveted, and hoped would fall to them when the awaited dismemberment occurred. Some of these works, despite the inauspicious circumstances attending their genesis, are among the best Western writings on their respective subjects. Examples are M. Carli, *Il Ce-kiang, studio geographico-economico* (Roma, 1899); A.R. Colquhoun, *China in Transformation* (London, 1898); E. von Hesse-Wartegg, *Schantung und Deutsch-China* (Leipzig, 1898); G. Krahmer, *Russland in Ostasien* (Leipzig, 1899); C. Madrolle, *Hainan et la côte continentale voisine* (Paris, 1900); F. von Richthofen, *Schantung und seine Eingangspforte Kiautschou* (Berlin, 1898).[45]

It will be clear from what has been written above that Western 'source' writings on China are valuable, various, and voluminous; and also that no researcher should contemplate trying to find his way through them unless accompanied by a guide. Such guides, first in the form of simple booklists, and then of bibliographies varying considerably in scope, in the type of material covered, and the amount of information provided, have been produced since the middle of the last century. Among the earliest were S. Wells Williams's 'List of Foreign Works upon China' in the *Chinese Repository* (18 [1849], pp. 402-44 and 657-61) and N.B. Dennys's 'Catalogue of Books &c. on China and Japan (Other than Philological) Published in the English Language', which appeared as Appendix C, pp. 1-26 of the work edited by Dennys, W.F. Mayers, and Ch. King, *The Treaty Ports of China and Japan* (Hong Kong, 1867). Both of these, and some others (notably Henri Cordier's *Catalogue of the Library of the North China Branch of the R.A.S.* [Shanghai, 1872]), were used by the brothers P.G. and O.F. von Möllendorff in compiling their *Manual of Chinese Bibliography, Being a List of Works and Essays Relating to China* (Shanghai, 1876). Theirs was the first real attempt at a Chinese bibliography, but its interest today is largely antiquarian. It was soon superseded by Cordier's magistral *Bibliotheca Sinica*. This was first published in 1878-85 in eight fascicles (cols.1-1408); and a supplement was added in 1893-5 (cols.1413-2243). The second edition, 'revue, corrigée et considerablement augmentée', appeared in 1904-8 in four volumes (cols.

---

[45] When Colquhoun's book appeared, a reviewer in *The Academy* LIV (1898), pp. 101-2, wrote: 'This work derives importance from the timeliness of its appearance ... For China, with its 350 million people, is about to fall into Western hands. The prizes will be enormous. Nothing in the book so arrests and possesses the reader as the visions it affords of the potentialities of wealth which China can no longer hide under her immemorial cloak of secrecy.' The comment of the German diplomat Max von Brandt on Carli's book is also worth recalling. He notes the connection between the hurried publication of the volume and the almost simultaneous Italian demand (in February 1899) for the cession of San-men Bay on the Chekiang coast for a naval base. Brandt, reviewing the book, writes: 'Nach einer historischen Einleitung ... geht der Verfasser zu einer Beschreibung der Provinz Tschekiang über, die, abgesehen von ihrer zentralen Lage, für ihn deswegen von besonderer Bedeutung ist, weil ... sie die einzige am Meer gelegene Provinz ist, welche nicht bereits von einer andern Macht als zu ihrer Interessensphäre gehörig angesehen wird' (*Petermanns Mitt.* 45 [1899], Lit.-Ber., no. 706). Italy's demand was successfully resisted (late May 1899).

1-3236); and a supplement to this appeared in 1922-4 (cols.3253-4428). Cordier's work has not so far been matched, and remains indispensable. It is almost impossible to find significant omissions in his bibliography as regards the older literature, though his coverage can occasionally be faulted for the nineteenth and twentieth centuries. Articles in serial publications are often, but by no means always, mentioned, and there are fairly frequent references to book reviews. Unfortunately the subject classification scheme chosen by Cordier has little to commend it (other than its simplicity); and the work still lacks a satisfactory author index and any kind of subject index. A continuation of Cordier's work, but listing monographs only, is Yuan T'ung-li's *China in Western Literature* (New Haven, 1958). This fine volume, worthy to stand side by side with its predecessor, is especially valuable for its author index (pp. 730-800), and for giving Chinese characters for the romanised names of Chinese authors. Also useful is *Index Sinicus, a Catalogue of Articles Relating to China in Periodicals and Other Collective Publications 1920-1955*, compiled by John Lust, with assistance from Werner Eichhorn and others (Cambridge, 1964). Entries total 19,734 (though many are repeated under different subject headings) and there is both an author index (pp. 579-639) and an 'index of subjects' (pp. 640-63). There are of course many specialised bibliographies (such as those mentioned in notes 12-14 and 39) as well as several more general bibliographies covering the broad orientalist field.[46]

The present writer is currently engaged in compiling a 'Selective Annotated Bibliography of Chinese History, Thought and Institutions', covering writings in Western languages (other than Russian) up to 1965 and including both books and journal articles. This enterprise, now in its eighth year, is well advanced toward completion. The present estimate, is that the number of entries will be about 8,000; each entry comprising bibliographical description, explanatory and evaluative comment, and (where books are concerned) reference to important reviews.

Experience gained in the preparation of this new China bibliography

[46] An example of the former is Yuan T'ung-li's *Economic and Social Development of Modern China, a Bibliographical Guide* (New Haven, 1956), in two parts, on economic (pp. 1-130) and social (pp. 1-87) development respectively. In the same category is C.O. Hucker's *China, a Critical Bibliography* (Tucson, 1962), which includes brief annotations, and uses an interesting subject classification. Among the bibliographical aids that survey a wider field and cover all branches of what used to be called 'Orientalism', the *Orientalische Bibliographie* founded by A. Müller and published in Berlin from 1887 to 1911 (with a final volume in 1926), and the *Orientalische Literatur-Zeitung* (1898-1944 and 1953+, but including material on the Far East only since 1922) are both useful. So also, are the *Rapports annuels* to be found in the *Journal asiatique*. An important collection of those given by Jules Mohl during the years (1840-67) that he was secretary of the Society was published as *Vingt-sept ans d'histoire des études orientales*, 2 vols. (Paris, 1879). The corresponding surveys which appeared from time to time in the *Zeitschrift der deutschen morgenländischen Gesellschaft*, the 'Wissenschaftlichen Jahresberichte', and especially those by R. Gosche in the 1860s and 1870s, are also of the greatest interest.

has convinced me that the Western-language sources on China are much greater in quantity than is usually supposed. An immense amount of valuable material lies hidden in journals, some obscure, others defunct, which few scholars know about and fewer open. In quality, too, the material is often much better than common opinion—especially contemporary opinion—would have us believe. One generation's bad book may well be an invaluable primary source for the scholar of the next generation but one. It is in the light of these convictions that this chapter has been written.

BIBLIOGRAPHY

The following covers only the nineteenth and early twentieth centuries, and purports to be no more than a sample of the literature.

Abeel, David, *Journal of a Residence in China and the Neighbouring Countries from 1830 to 1833*, New York, 1834.

Allen, Roland, *The Siege of the Peking Legations: A Diary, with Maps and Plans*, London, 1901.

Bingham, J.E., *Narrative of the Expedition to China, from the Commencement of the War to its Termination in 1842*, London, 1842.

Brine, Lindesay, *The Taiping Rebellion in China: A Narrative of its Rise and Progress, Based upon Original Documents and Information Obtained in China*, London, 1862.

Callery, J.M., and Yvan, Melchior, *L'insurrection en Chine depuis son origine jusqu'à la prise de Nankin*, Paris, 1853.

Cooke, George Wingrove, *China: Being 'The Times' Special Correspondence from China in the Years 1857-58*, London, 1858.

Cooper, Thomas Thornville, *Travels of a Pioneer of Commerce in Pigtail and Petticoats: or an Overland Journey from China towards India*, London, 1871.

de Filippi, Filippo, *Storia della spedizione scientifica italiana nel Himàlaia, Caracorùm e Turchestàn Cinese 1913-14*, Bologna, 1924.

de Groot, Jan Jacob Maria, *Jaarlijke Feesten en Gebruiken van de Emoy-Chineezen; een vergelijkende bijdrage tot de kennis van onze Chineesche medeburgers op Java. Met uitgebreide monographieën van godheden, die te Emoy worden vereerd*, Batavia, 1881, (French version as vols. 11-12 of the Annales du Musée Guimet, Paris, 1886).

——, *The Religious System of China, its Ancient Forms, Evolution, History and Present Aspect, Manners, Customs and Social Institutions Connected Therewith*, 6 vols., Leyden, 1892-1910.

de Mutrécy, Charles, *Journal de la campagne de Chine 1859-1860-1861*, Paris, 1861.

d'Ollone, Henri, *Les derniers barbares*, Paris, 1911; one of the several reports on the Mission d'Ollone (1906-9) in China, Tibet, and Mongolia.

Doolittle, Justus, *Social Life of the Chinese*, New York, 1865.

Edkins, Joseph, 'Letters from Peking', *The Academy, passim.*

Eitel, E.J., *Europe in China, the History of Hong Kong,* Hong Kong, 1895.

Filchner, Wilhelm, *Das Rätsel des Matschu,* Berlin, 1907.

——, *Wissenschaftliche Ergebnisse der Expedition Filchner nach China und Tibet 1903-05,* 10 vols., Berlin, 1908-13.

Fortune, Robert, *Journey to the Tea Countries of China,* London, 1852.

——, *Three Years Wanderings in the Northern Provinces in China,* London, 1847.

Gray, J.H., *China, a History of the Laws, Manners and Customs of the People,* London, 1878.

Gützlaff, Karl, *China Opened,* London, 1838.

Hall, W.H., *Narrative of the Voyages and Services of the Nemesis from 1840 to 1843, and of the Combined Military and Naval Operations in China; Comprising a Complete Account of the Colony of Hongkong, and Remarks on the Character and Habits of the Chinese,* London, 1844.

Harmant, Jacques, *La vérité sur la retraite de Lang-Son, mémoires d'un combattant,* Paris, 1892.

——, *Voyage en Chine, Cochinchine, Inde et Malaisie,* 3 vols., Paris, 1847-8.

Haussmann, Auguste, *La Chine, résumé historique de l'insurrection et des événements qui ont eu lieu dans ce pays, depuis le commencement de la guerre de l'opium jusqu'en 1857,* Paris, 1864.

Hedde, Isidore, *Description de l'agriculture et du tissage—Tsong-nong-sang-i-tsou-i-shi, Agriculture de la Chine,* Paris, 1850.

——, *Description méthodique des produits divers recueillis dans un voyage en Chine par I.H. ... et exposés par la Chambre de commerce de Saint-Étienne ... Exposition des produits de l'industrie sérigène en Chine,* Saint-Étienne, 1848.

——, *Mission commerciale en Chine. Industries des soies et soieries. Catalogue des produits de l'Inde et de la Chine rapportés par M.I. Hedde ... et composant l'exposition publique faite à Lyon,* Lyon, 1847.

Hedin, Sven, *Auf grosser Fahrt, Meine Expedition mit Schweden, Deutschen und Chinesen durch die Wüste Gobi 1927-28,* Leipzig, 1929. A popular book on the great Sino-Swedish Scientific Expedition to the northwestern provinces of China, 1927-35.

——, *Central Asia and Tibet,* 2 vols., London, 1903. A description of the Central Asian expedition of 1899-1902.

——, *Rätsel der Gobi. Die Fortsetzung der grossen Fahrt durch Innerasien in den Jahren 1928 bis 1930,* Leipzig, 1931. Another popular book on the great Sino-Swedish Scientific Expedition to the northwestern provinces of China, 1927-35.

——, *Scientific Results of a Journey in Central Asia,* 6 vols., Stockholm, 1904-7. A description of the Central Asian expedition of 1899-1902.

——, *Southern Tibet: Discoveries in Former Times Compared with my own Researches in 1906-1908,* 11 vols. in 9, Stockholm 1916-22. A description of the Central Asian expedition of 1906-8.

173

Hedin, Sven, *Through Asia*, 2 vols., London, 1898. A description of the Central Asian expedition of 1893-7.

Hosie, Alexander, *Manchuria: its People, Resources, and Recent History*, London, 1901.

——, *On the Trail of the Opium Poppy*, 2 vols., London, 1914.

——, *Three Years in Western China, a Narrative of Three Journeys in Ssŭ-ch'uan, Kuei-chow and Yün-nan*, London, 1890, reprinted 1897.

——, *Travels and Researches in Western China*, Royal Geographical Society, *Supplementary Papers*, London, 1886.

Huc, Evariste Régis, *L'empire chinois*, 2 vols., Paris, 1854.

——, *Souvenirs d'un voyage dans la Tartarie, le Thibet et la Chine pendant les années 1844, 1845 et 1846*, 2 vols., Paris, 1850.

La mission lyonnaise d'exploration commerciale en Chine, 1895-1897, Lyon, 1898.

Jocelyn, Lord, *Six Months with the Chinese Expedition, or Leaves from a Soldier's Note-Book*, London, 1841.

Landor, Arnold Henry Savage, *China and the Allies*, London, 1901.

——, *In the Forbidden Land, An Account of a Journey into Tibet, Capture by Tibetan Lamas and Soldiers, Imprisonment, Torture, and Ultimate Release Brought about by Dr Wilson and the Political Peshkar Karak Sing-Pal*, London, 1898.

——, *Tibet and Nepal*, London, 1905.

Lindley, Augustus, *Ti-ping Tien-kwoh*, London, 1866.

Loir, Maurice, *L'escadre de l'amiral Courbet, notes et souvenirs*, Paris, 1886.

Loti, Pierre, *Les derniers jours de Pékin*, Paris, 1901.

Meadows, T.T., *The Chinese and their Rebellions*, London, 1856.

Medhurst, W.H., *China: its State and Prospects*, Boston, 1838.

Milne, W.C., *Life in China*, London, 1857.

Monnier, Marcel, *Le drame chinois (juillet-août 1900)*, Paris, 1900.

Nevius, J.L., *China and the Chinese*, New York, 1869.

Obruchev, Vladimir, *Aus China, Reiseerlebnisse, Natur- und Völkerbilde*, 2 vols., Leipzig, 1896.

Przheval'sky, Nicolai, *From Kulja across the Tian-shan to Lob-nor*, London, 1879. A description of the author's expedition of 1876 (translated from Russian).

——, *Mongolia, the Tangut Country and the Solitudes of Northern Tibet*, London, 1876. An account of the author's expedition of 1870-3 (translated from Russian).

——, *Reisen in Tibet und am oberen Lauf des Gelben Flusses*, Leipzig, 1884. An account of the author's expedition of 1879-80 (translated from Russian).

Rondot, Natalis, Hedde, I., Renard, Ed., and Haussmann, A., *Étude pratique du commerce d'exportation de la Chine*, Paris, 1847.

Schlegel, Gustaaf, *The Thian Ti Hwui, the Hung-League, or Heaven-Earth-League. A Secret Society with the Chinese in China and [Netherlands] India*, Batavia, 1866.

——, *Uranographie chinoise*, La Haye, 1875.

Simon, G. Eugène, *La cité chinoise*, partial journal publication 1882, book form, Paris, 1885.

Smith, A.H., *Chinese Characteristics*, New York, 1890.

——, *Village Life in China*, New York, 1899.

Stein, Mark Aurel, *Innermost Asia*, 4 vols., Oxford, 1928.

——, *On Ancient Central Asian Tracks*, London, 1933.

——, *Ruins of Desert Cathay*, 2 vols., London, 1912.

——, *Sand-buried Ruins of Khotan*, London, 1903.

——, *Serindia*, 5 vols., Oxford, 1921.

Swinhoe, Robert, *Narrative of the North China Campaign of 1860; Containing Personal Experiences of Chinese Character, and of the Moral and Social Condition of the Country, Together with a Description of the Interior of Pekin*, London, 1861.

Tafel, Albert, *Meine Tibetreise 1905 bis 1908, Eine Studienfahrt durch das nordwestliche China und durch die Innere Mongolie in das östliche Tibet*, 2 vols., Stuttgart, 1914.

Trinkler, Emil, *Im Land der Stürme, mit Yak- und Kamelkaravanen durch Innerasien*, Leipzig, 1930.

von le Coq, Albert, *Auf Hellas Spuren in Osttürkistan*, Leipzig, 1926. A description of the author's second and third Turfan expeditions (of 1904-5 and 1905-7 respectively).

von Richthofen, Ferdinand, *China, Ergebnisse eigener Reisen*, 5 vols., Berlin, 1877-1912.

——, *Tagebücher aus China*, 2 vols., Berlin, 1907.

Wegener, Georg, *Zur Kriegszeit durch China 1900-1901*, Berlin, 1902.

Williams, S. Wells, *The Middle Kingdom*, New York, 1848; 1883.

史 XVIII: Jesuit Sources

PAUL A. RULE

While a great deal has been written about the Jesuit mission in China by missiologists and historians of Christian missions, there has been a curious neglect of Jesuit sources by general historians of China and social scientists.[1] The following remarks are not intended as an exhaustive treatment of the subject of Jesuit sources for Chinese history, but arise out of recent research by the author into Jesuit writings on Confucianism. They may, however, prove of interest to historians engaged in the study of late Ming and early Ch'ing history.

The published writings of the Jesuits of the old China mission (*c.* 1580 to the suppression of the Society of Jesus late in the eighteenth century) are well presented in the standard bibliographies, namely the de Backer-Sommervogel, *Bibliothèque de la Compagnie de Jésus*; Streit and Dindinger's *Bibliotheca Missionum*, vols. 4, 5, and 7; and Cordier's *Bibliotheca Sinica*. The arrangement of these works is nicely complementary, with de Backer-Sommervogel arranged by author, the *Bibliotheca Missionum* in strict chronological order, and the *Bibliotheca Sinica* by topic. However, and quite excusably in the circumstances, the treatment of manuscript sources is defective in all three. The *Bibliotheca Missionum* volumes on China are the most satisfactory since they take advantage of the earlier work of Cordier, the de Backers, and Sommervogel, and provide many more precise locations for particular manuscripts and for rarer printed works. Nevertheless, my own research in Rome, Paris, and London, has revealed many omissions; and also a process of cumulative error. For example, all three sources list in detail four volumes of manuscripts dealing with chronological and textual questions, clearly belonging to that bizarre system of interpretation of Chinese texts adopted by some of the French Jesuits in China which is commonly called 'figurism'. These manuscripts are attributed to Alexis Gollet, a quite marginal figure in the movement, and are accurately characterised by Louis Pfister, S.J., as 'un tissu de rêveries ... où l'exagération domine et où l'imagination se donne libre carrière'.[2] Yet a brief

[1] See Peter Duignan, 'Early Jesuit Missionaries: a Suggestion for Further Study', in *American Anthropologist* LX (1958), pp. 725-32.
[2] *Notices biographiques et bibliographiques sur les Jésuites de l'ancienne mission de Chine, 1552-1773*, vol. 1, p. 562.

176

examination of the manuscripts at the Archives of the French Province of the Society of Jesus at Chantilly proved beyond doubt that three of the four volumes (Brotier 143-5) are actually the work of Joachim Bouvet, a far more significant figure. They are in the clearly identifiable hand of Bouvet and their contents illuminated for me many otherwise obscure remarks and criticisms of Bouvet that I had found in correspondence in the Jesuit archives in Rome. They were unknown to J.C. Gatty whose bibliography of Bouvet's work in her edition of *Le Voiage de Siam du Père Bouvet* (Leiden, 1963) is the most thorough listing of Bouvet's works available.

The defects of the bibliography of Jesuit writings on China are quite understandable. The general bibliographies naturally follow printed library catalogues which are sometimes inaccurate, and more commonly inadequate. Many of the main collections of manuscript Jesuit material have no published catalogues. There is a valuable catalogue of the Chinese holdings of the Vatican Library produced by that indefatigable and meticulous scholar, Paul Pelliot, the 'Inventaire sommaire des manuscrits et imprimés chinois de la Bibliothèque Vaticane' (Sala Cons. MSS.512). But Pelliot produced this in a period of some three weeks—it is inscribed '13 Juin-6 Juillet 1922'—and it is indeed 'summary' and at times, I believe, erroneous. The more complete 'Inventorium Codicum Manu Scriptorum Borgianorum', cataloguing the manuscripts of the Borgia collections of the Vatican Library where much of the Jesuit material dealing with China is to be found, is not yet published. No published catalogue exists of the 'Jap.Sin' collection of the Jesuit Archives in Rome, and an important section of the Jesuit Archives is as yet uncatalogued.[3] The important French Jesuit archives at Chantilly have been described in summary form by the archivist, Joseph Dehergne, S.J.,[4] but the bibliography of many of the leading Jesuit missionaries remains incomplete. The reasons for this are many and obvious: the variety of languages in which the documents were written, the peculiar problems presented by oriental languages, the dispersion of Jesuit libraries and archives in the late eighteenth century, the existence of many copies and translations scattered throughout Europe, the problem of original and edited versions.

I would like to express here my deepest gratitude to the librarians and archivists with whom I dealt during my brief sojourn in Europe. I found them invariably most helpful and anxious that the material in their care be more widely known. I am particularly grateful to the Jesuit archivist in Rome, Father Edmond Lamalle, S.J., and his assistant Father Fejer, S.J., to Father Joseph Dehergne, S.J., of the Maison St Louis, Chantilly, and to

[3] See a preliminary listing by the Archivist, Edmond Lamalle, S.J., 'La documentation d'histoire missionnaire dans le "Fondo Gesuitico" aux archives romaines de la Compagnie de Jésus', pp. 131-76.
[4] J. Dehergne, 'Les archives des Jésuites de Paris et l'histoire des missions aux XVIIe et XVIIIe siècles'.

the stimulating suggestions of Father Henri Bernard-Maître, S.J., who is currently engaged in the unenviable task of bringing order out of the chaos of the Foucquet papers of the Vatican Library. Owing to the efforts of these and other scholars, the works of the Jesuits are being made more readily accessible to historians of China. The definitive edition of the journals of the pioneer Jesuit missionary, Matteo Ricci, was published by the late P.M. D'Elia, S.J.,[5] to complement the earlier edition by P. Tacchi-Venturi, S.J.[6] In 1938 an edition of the *Correspondance* of Ferdinand Verbiest was published by H. Josson, S.J., and L. Willaert, S.J.[7] Part of the works of the third of the 'triumvirate' of great seventeenth century missionaries, Johann Adam Schall von Bell, was edited by Henri Bernard-Maître, S.J., and translated by Paul Bornet, S.J., in 1942.[8] Mlle Gatty's edition of Joachim Bouvet's *Voiage de Siam* has already been mentioned; and an edition of the *Correspondance* of Antoine Gaubil has recently been published by Renée Simon, with biographical and bibliographical appendices by Father Joseph Dehergne, S.J.[9] Much remains to be done, not the least important being a revision of the *vademecum* of historians of the Jesuit missions in China, Louis Pfister, S.J.'s *Notices biographiques et bibliographiques sur les Jésuites de l'ancienne mission de Chine, 1552-1773*.[10] This work is indispensable, being based on many documents in the old Jesuit headquarters of Zi-ka-wei outside Shanghai, now inaccessible to students, but unfortunately it contains many errors. While working in the Jesuit archives in Rome, I found several blatant contradictions between the dates of letters before me and dates and biographical details given by Pfister.

However, the work of cataloguing and publishing the Jesuit material on China is continuing. I would like briefly to list some of the achievements and some of the *desiderata*. The periodical *Monumenta Serica* has published and continues to publish important articles on the Jesuit mission in China. Among these I would like to call attention to the bibliographical articles on 'les adaptations chinois d'ouvrages européens' by H. Bernard-Maître in *Monumenta Serica* X (1945) and XIX (1960); Boleslaw Szczesniak's article on 'The Writings of Michael Boym' in XIV (1949-55); and Joseph Dehergne's 'Les Chrétientés de Chine de la période Ming (1581-1650)' in XVI (1957). Dehergne's study in 'missionary geography' was continued into the Ch'ing period in a series of articles in the *Archivum Historicum*

---

[5] *Fonti Ricciane*, 3 vols. (Rome, 1942-9). For a bibliography of the works of Father D'Elia, complete up to shortly before his death, see P.M. D'Elia, S.J., *Il lontano confino e la tragica morte del P. João Mourão S.J.* (Lisbon, 1963), pp. 553-81.

[6] *Opere storiche del P. Matteo Ricci*, 2 vols. (Macerata, 1911-13).

[7] *Correspondance de Ferdinand Verbiest de la Compagnie de Jésus (1623-1688)* (Brussels, 1938).

[8] *Lettres et mémoires d'Adam Schall S.J.: Relation historique* (Tientsin, 1942).

[9] *Correspondance de Pékin, 1722-1759* (Geneva, 1970).

[10] Published in 1932-4 and recently photographically reprinted.

Societatis Jesu,[11] which has also published a considerable number of important documents and commentaries on the China mission. One of the difficulties of research in this field of Chinese history is the wide variety of periodicals in which important material is published—specialist journals in Chinese studies, in mission and religious history, geographical and historical journals, publications of religious orders and various national and local history groups. The missionary journals are often particularly difficult to locate and yet some of the most valuable contributions to Chinese history are to be found in them.[12] I have been fortunate in having access to the incomplete 'Selective Annotated Bibliography of Chinese History, Thought and Institutions' of O.B. van der Sprenkel, which lists under appropriate headings and with evaluative comments, books and important articles from a wide variety of periodicals, many not previously tapped by sinologists.

Despite the efforts of many individuals and the *esprit de corps* of the Society of Jesus, there remain important gaps in the publication of Jesuit material relating to China. The revised edition of Ricci's letters, begun but not finished by Father D'Elia, needs to be completed. The letters of Adam Schall should be collected in an edition along the lines of the Josson-Willaert edition of Verbiest's correspondence and a start should be made on publishing the voluminous mission correspondence in the Jesuit archives and other collections. Recently the introductory volume to the 'Japanese' series of the *Monumenta Historica Societatis Jesu* has been published by Father J.F. Schütte, S.J.[13] It is to be hoped that the 'Chinese' series will soon begin to appear, publishing the Jesuit letters in chronological order with full apparatus and notes, as has already been done with the 'Documenta Indica' and the Mexican and South American letters.

A preliminary step to a 'Documenta Sinica' series is the location of all copies and variants of the letters from China. Father Schütte, in relation to his work on the Japanese records, has already laid the groundwork for this task, but it is a huge undertaking and only an institution such as the Jesuit Historical Institute in Rome can provide the continuity and dedication required to bring it to completion. Apart from the main collections in Rome —the Jesuit Archives, Vatican Library, Vatican Archives, Biblioteca Vittorio Emanuele, the library and archives of Propaganda Fide, and the libraries and archives of various religious orders—there are substantial holdings in collections in Paris, London, Munich, Lisbon, Madrid, and many other centres. The work of collating and publishing this material has hardly begun.

There appear to be few extant records of the old Jesuit mission still in the

---

[11] XXIV (1955); XXVIII (1959); XXX (1961); and XXXVI (1967).
[12] See a listing of 1872 Catholic mission periodicals in *Bibliotheca Missionum*, vol. 23, last section; a large number of these contain material on China.
[13] *Introductio ad Historiam Societatis Jesu in Japonia* (Rome, 1968).

Far East. But some which were once thought irrevocably lost have been rediscovered recently. The Jesuit Archives in Macao were the main repository of documents of the Japanese Province and the Chinese Vice-Province of the Society of Jesus. Most letters from China passed through Macao and copies were kept. In the mid-eighteenth century, copies of important documents were made by Father Joseph Montanha, S.J., as part of a project sponsored by the Academia Real da Historia Portuguesa, and dispatched to Lisbon. On Montanha's transfer to Siam, Brother João Alvares took over the work but his copies, it appears, were sent to the Mission Procurator in Lisbon.[14] It is these copies which make up the *Jesuitas na Asia* collection of the Ajuda library in Lisbon described by C.R. Boxer and J.M. Braga in the *Boletim eclesiastico da Diocese de Macao*,[15] and later partially catalogued by Mr Braga in the same journal.[16] Mr Braga, now at the National Library of Australia, is currently completing this catalogue and I am indebted to him for much useful advice about Portuguese and other Jesuit sources and to the National Library of Australia for access to the Braga collection of rare printed and manuscript sources.

It was thought that the original Macao archives were irrevocably lost after the suppression of the Society of Jesus in Portuguese domains, but Father Schütte's detective work in Lisbon and Madrid has now established that this is not the case. In fact, Brother Alvares succeeded in secretly transferring the archives to Manila in 1761 in the ship of a friendly captain, Don Antonio Pachecho. Here they lay in the Jesuit College of San Ildefonso till the suppression of the Jesuits in Spain in 1767. When news of this reached Manila on 18 May 1768, all Jesuit possessions were seized and an inventory of the archives was produced by the Commissary for the suppression, Don Manuel Galbón y Ventura. Using this inventory, Father Schütte has established that many of the documents in the 'Cortes' collection of the Royal Academy of History in Madrid are in fact Macao originals.[17] These, together with the *Jesuitas na Asia* collection, form a useful supplement to the material extant in Rome, as well as representing the Portuguese side of the interminable jurisdictional disputes between the 'Portuguese' and other missions.

[14] See J.F. Schütte, S.J., 'Wiederentdeckung des Makao-Archivs, wichtige Bestände des alten Fernost-Archivs der Jesuiten, heute in Madrid', *Archivum Historicum Societatis Jesu* XXX (1961), pp. 90-124; and the same author's, 'P. Joseph Montanha's "Apparatos" und die Abschrift des Fernost-Archivs S.J. in Rahmen der Initiative der Academia Real da Historia Portuguesa', *Archivum Historicum* XXXI (1962), pp. 225-63.

[15] 'Algunas Notas sobre a bibliographia de Macau', pp. 188-215.

[16] Beginning in LIII (1955), pp. 15-33, and continuing through the years 1956, 1958, 1959, and 1960.

[17] See J.F. Schütte, S.J., 'Documentos sobre el Japon conservados en la Colección "Cortes" de la Real Academia de la Historia' in *Boletim de la Real Academia de Historia* CXXXXVIII (Madrid, 1961), pp. 23-60, 149-259; and 'El "Archivo del Japon": Vicisitudes del Archivo Jesuitico del Extremo Oriente y descripción de fondo existente en la Real Academia de la Historia de Madrid', *Archivo documental español* XX (Madrid, 1964).

For the historian of China, the catalogues of printed books of Jesuit origin in the great libraries of Europe, China, and Japan, are of great interest. They testify in a striking fashion to the Jesuit role as cultural intermediaries. M. Courant's catalogue of the Chinese books in the Bibliothèque Nationale, Paris,[18] includes many works in Chinese by the Jesuits as well as rare editions of Chinese works sent to Europe by the Jesuits. The earlier 1742 catalogue of Etienne Fourmont[19] gives valuable information as to their provenance, as does Julius Klaproth's catalogue of the Chinese books in the old royal library of Berlin.[20] These collections, and the collections in various libraries in Rome, are all the more valuable given the fate of many Ming and early Ch'ing works in the Emperor Ch'ien-lung's 'literary inquisition', and the present difficulty of access to libraries on the Chinese mainland.

As for the great Jesuit libraries in China, those of Peking and Zi-ka-wei, it would seem that they have been carefully preserved by the Chinese authorities. Dr J.S. Cummins recently located many of the rare European works from the old Pei-t'ang library in the Peking Municipal Library.[21] Father Verhaeren's catalogue of the Pei-t'ang collection[22] has been recently reprinted and in itself stands as a valuable historical document. The introductory 'Aperçu historique' traces the origins of the old Pei-t'ang collection back to the 'four churches' of Peking, and the catalogue establishes the provenance of many of the items going back to the time of Ricci. However, no catalogue of the Chinese works of the Pei-t'ang library has been published, nor, to my knowledge, is there a printed catalogue of the Zi-ka-wei library. There are many tantalising references in Pfister's *Notices* and in the Jesuit *Bulletin de l'Université l'Aurore* to manuscript and printed material in the Zi-ka-wei collection. One can only hope that, in the future, the old Jesuit collections on the Chinese mainland will become more accessible.

The value of the sources I have been discussing for the historian working in the fields of mission history or church history is self-evident. Less evident, however, is their value to the general historian of China, and I find misgivings in this regard quite understandable. Historians will naturally have a healthy distrust of missionary bias and the tone of much of the 'edifying and curious' Jesuit literature of the seventeenth and eighteenth centuries would reinforce this impression. However, I am convinced that the Jesuit

---

[18] *Catalogue des livres chinois, coréens, japonais etc.*
[19] *Catalogus Librorum Bibliothecae Regiae Sinicorum*, appended to Fourmont's *Linguae Sinicae Mandaricae, Hieroglyphicae, Grammatica Duplex* (Paris, 1742).
[20] *Verzeichnis der chinesischen und mandschuischen Bücher und Handschriften der Königlichen Bibliothek zu Berlin* (Paris, 1822).
[21] 'The Present Location of the Pei-t'ang Library', pp. 482-7.
[22] *Catalogue de la Bibliothèque du Pe-T'ang* (Peking, 1949, reprinted Paris, 1969). Cf. J. Dehergne, 'La bibliothèque des Jésuites français de Pékin au premier tiers du XVIIIe siècle' in *Bulletin de l'Ecole Française d'Extrême Orient* LVI (1969), pp. 125-50.

material, especially the manuscript material, may still be of great value if it is used with care and seen in context.

The great Jesuit series of published accounts—the annual letters of the late sixteenth and early seventeenth centuries;[23] the *Lettres édifiantes et curieuses* published in thirty-four volumes in Paris from 1703 to 1776 (about a third dealing with China); the *Mémoires concernant l'histoire, les sciences, les arts, les moeurs, les usages etc., des Chinois*, 17 vols. (Paris, 1776-1814)—are well known to sinologists. Less well known, however, are the travel accounts, the pioneer translations of Confucian and classical texts, the geographical works, and the scientific treatises. The manuscript sources have been almost completely neglected.

The latter are of particular importance because, from the very beginning of the Society of Jesus, a strict distinction was made by the Jesuits between material intended for publication and private letters and reports. Polanco, the secretary to the founder of the order, St Ignatius Loyola, drew up regulations enjoining Jesuits to write regularly to Rome giving full details of their activities, but he distinguishes clearly between reports which might be circulated and published and those he called *hijuelas* which were to be reserved for the eyes of the superiors of the Society.

> In the first place, placing oneself before what has to be written, one should see what has to be set down in the main letter, *id est*, what can be shown to many, as are the things of edification, and what is to be set down in the *hijuelas*, *id est*, what is not to be shown, whether it be of edification or not, as are one's own defects or those of others, and some praiseworthy things, but which are not for the knowledge of all.[24]

This practice, which continued in the seventeenth and eighteenth centuries, meant that the frankest of Jesuit accounts of the China mission remain unpublished. This 'private' correspondence is of particular importance in the late seventeenth and early eighteenth centuries when the exigencies of the 'Chinese Rites' controversy led to an increasingly polemical position in Jesuit publications. For the sake of unity in the face of the enemy, differences of opinion amongst the Jesuits themselves were not publicly aired and reports from China were carefully edited if they were published at all. A Roman decree against further publication on the question of Rites made Jesuit censors even more cautious. However, a comparison of the originals with the published letters reveals that the extent of this editing has been somewhat exaggerated.[25] In general it consists in the omission of sections regarded as superfluous or touching on the forbidden areas of discussion,

[23] D. Lach, *Asia in the Making of Europe*, Vol. 1 (Chicago, 1965), gives details of the complex publication history of the sixteenth century letters.
[24] Quoted in J. Correia-Alfonso, *Jesuit Letters and Indian History* (Bombay, 1955), p. 4.
[25] See Virgile Pinot, *La Chine et la formation de l'esprit philosophique en France* (Paris, 1932), ch. 3, and the critique by Alexandre Brou, S.J., in *Revue de l'histoire des missions* XI (1934), pp. 187-202.

and some stylistic retouching, rather than rewriting or tampering with texts.

Nevertheless, the correspondence in the Jesuit archives in Rome is more free of the 'party line', and frequently reveals differences in the interpretation of Chinese society and ideas that are of great interest to the sinologist. The Jesuit missionaries in China were no more of one mind on scholarly matters than were their brethren in Europe, but circumstances made them less free to air their differences in public. There is also extant in collections in France much of the private correspondence of the French Jesuits in China, who show themselves freer in their communications to friends, clerical and lay, in France, than with their superiors in Rome. This is a by-product of the attempt of the French mission to maintain its independence of the old 'Portuguese'[26] mission, and to a lesser extent, of the controversies amongst the French themselves. It lends a peculiar importance to the collections in Paris and Chantilly, since most of the leading sinologists amongst the eighteenth century Jesuits belonged to the French mission.

The study of the private correspondence, memorials, and reports, is indispensable to the mission historian, but it is also of value to the student of Chinese religion and society. Reports from mission stations in the provinces giving details of local conditions often usefully complement local gazetteers. The Jesuits have preserved copies, translations, and comments on memorials absent from the notoriously deficient *Shih-lu* of K'ang-hsi. They resided in areas not visited by other Europeans till the late nineteenth century and their annual reports fill in the picture of China in the late Ming and early Ch'ing dynasties.[27] Their works in Chinese testify to their knowledge of the language, or at the very least, to their close liaison with Chinese Christian scholars. Of course they necessarily sometimes misinterpreted what they saw, but their outsider's point of view led them to record much that the class bias of Chinese records distorts and conceals.

The motivation of the Jesuits was primarily religious. Even those French Jesuits who came to China officially as 'mathématiciens du Roi', i.e. scientists sent by Louis XIV to serve as advisers to K'ang-hsi and correspondents of the French Academy of Science, clearly regarded their scientific work as secondary. It served as an introduction to the court, and, perhaps more to the point, as a means of evading the Portuguese *padroado*. But they saw themselves as missionaries first and stated this frequently in both their

---

[26] The 'Portuguese' mission was not, by any means, composed solely of Portuguese nationals, but the term was used to denote those missionaries who came to China by way of Lisbon and Macao, under licence from the Portuguese king who claimed ecclesiastical jurisdiction for Portugal over China.

[27] The historical value of these annual letters is well illustrated by the manuscript 'Historia Sinarum Imperii' compiled by Thomas Dunyn-Szpot, S.J., in the first decade of the eighteenth century from the reports and letters for the period 1641-1700 received in Rome (Jesuit Archives, Rome, Jap. Sin. 102-5, 109-111).

public and private letters. However, as the eighteenth century advanced, the Chinese reaction to the Roman decisions on Chinese Rites and other factors led to stiffer controls on their missionary activities, and they became perforce primarily sinologists. They had both time and opportunity to consult Chinese scholars, to read widely in Chinese literature, and to write. Many of their works were not published till much later[28] and many remain unpublished, but their writings are undoubtedly the foundations of European sinology. They corresponded with the pioneer European orientalists such as Nicolas Fréret and Etienne Fourmont and the great nineteenth century sinologists such as J.P. Abel-Rémusat and James Legge openly and frequently acknowledged their debt to them. The history of sinology begins with the Jesuits.

The focus of attention of the Jesuit missionary-scholars was naturally Chinese religion. Yet they also had ample opportunity and a unique vantage-point from which to study the world of Chinese officials and Chinese politics. The centre of the mission was always Peking and the Jesuits associated with the court were its backbone. The nature of this association is often misunderstood. I think it is important to understand their status in Peking if we are to assess their influence and the reliability of their reporting of court affairs. It is perhaps unfortunate that so much attention has been given to the position of a few Jesuits connected with the Astronomical Bureau to the neglect of those who held no official position. Arnold Rowbotham's *Missionary and Mandarin: The Jesuits at the Court of Peking*, the best known general work on the mission, perpetuates this view as well as many other 'legends'. Apart from the fact that the vast majority of Jesuit missionaries in China never got near the court and worked in the provinces, keeping away from the attention of Chinese officials as far as possible, the 'mandarin' label misses an important point. It seems to me that the Jesuits in Peking were valued by Emperors such as K'ang-hsi precisely because they were not mandarins, not part of the system. In his illuminating study of *Ts'ao Yin and the K'ang-hsi Emperor*, Jonathan Spence has pointed out the importance to the Manchu rulers of the 'bondservants', their personal dependents, members of the inner court. It was this sort of relationship that existed between Adam Schall von Bell and the Shun-chih Emperor, and later between K'ang-hsi and a number of Jesuits. At one period K'ang-hsi was seeing them privately for at least four hours a day. They accompanied him on his hunting expeditions and were in his presence every evening. The pretext was lessons in mathematics, astronomy, music, and philosophy, but their accounts make it clear that many other subjects

---

[28] E.g. Joseph de Mailla's *Histoire générale de la Chine* was not published until thirty years after his death; Antoine Gaubil's *Traité sur la chronologie chinoise* was published in 1814 (he died in 1759); and J.-B. Régis's translation of the *I-ching* was not published till well over a century after it was written (written 1708-23, published by Julius Mohl, 1834-9).

were discussed. I have found no evidence that the Jesuits indulged in, or that K'ang-hsi permitted, political interference, but he certainly sounded out their opinions on a wide range of matters. There is only one case in which a Jesuit became, however unwittingly, embroiled in court politics, that of João Mourão, which ended tragically with his execution; and this seems to have been due to indiscretion rather than Jesuit guile.[29] K'ang-hsi seems to have valued his Jesuits as unbiased sources of information, as 'honest brokers' and 'impartial witnesses from outer space' to use Joseph Levenson's terms.[30] It is also significant that the emperor preserved the Jesuits' scientific works for his own personal use. As Henri Bernard-Maître observes, 'the Emperor K'ang-Hsi understood the importance of European sciences but he wished to reserve them for himself and for his Manchu collaborators without benefiting his Chinese subjects whom he preferred absorbed in the sterile cult of the old classical authors'.[31] Whatever his reasons, K'ang-hsi's concern for the Jesuits went so far that when the 'Portuguese' and French missions became embroiled in a bitter contest over jurisdiction and mutual independence, he several times called the parties together in his presence and urged them to live together in peace. Clearly he valued their services, and not just as astronomers, toymakers, and musicians. Not only were they what we would call today 'foreign experts' or 'technical advisers', they were much more.

In my opinion, the sustaining hope of many of the Jesuits of 'converting' the emperor was always an illusion, and one perhaps deliberately fostered by the emperor to maintain their zeal in his service. After K'ang-hsi they were far less sanguine and their enthusiasm for the Chinese system of government which communicated itself to so many European defenders of 'enlightened despotism' somewhat soured. What influence they had at court was totally inadequate to protect their brethren in the provinces. But what was a failure in their eyes remains a fascinating and fruitful episode in Sino-Western relations, and a unique historical experiment which still has much to teach us. The 'epitaph' of the mission written by the Peking survivors of the suppression of the Society of Jesus is a moving testimony to their achievement:

In the name of Jesus:
Amen!
Long unshaken but at last overcome by so many storms
It fell.
Stand, passer-by, and
Read:
And think for a little on the inconstancy of human affairs.

Here lie the French missionaries, who, while they lived, belonged to that most famous Society which in all places taught and promoted the

[29] See P.M. D'Elia, S.J., *Il lontano confino*.
[30] *Confucian China and Its Modern Fate, the Problem of Intellectual Continuity* (London, 1958), p. 158.
[31] 'Les adaptations chinois d'ouvrages européens', p. 364.

pure worship of the true God; which, in imitation, as close as human frailty allows, of Jesus whose name they bore, cultivated virtue in the midst of toil and trouble, helped their neighbour, and became all things to all men, to gain all; and through the two centuries or more in which they flourished, gave to the church its martyrs and confessors.

I, Joseph-Marie Amiot, and the remaining French missionaries of that Society, while we maintain still the worship of God, here in Peking, under the auspices and protection of the Tartaro-Chinese monarchy, won by our sciences and arts; while our French church still sheds light in the imperial palace amidst the temples of so many false gods; and, alas, secretly wishing our days to come to an end; have placed this monument of brotherly love in the funereal gloom.

Go on your way, passer-by, congratulate the dead, grieve with the living, pray for all, wonder and be silent.

In the year of Christ MDCCLXXIV,
the 14th day of October;
the 10th day of the 9th month
of the 39th year of Ch'ien-lung.[32]

'Wonder and be silent.' Wonder, perhaps, but I hope we do not allow them to be silent. The voices of those old Jesuits, as preserved in their writings, still have much to tell us about China, and perhaps ourselves.

SELECTED BIBLIOGRAPHY

Bernard, H., 'Les adaptations chinoises d'ouvrages européens. Bibliographie chronologique depuis la venue des Portugais à Canton jusqu'à la mission française de Pékin (1514-1688)', *Monumenta Serica* X (1945), pp. 1-57; 309-88.

———, 'Les adaptations chinoises d'ouvrages européens. Bibliographie chronologique. Deuxième partie: depuis la fondation de la mission française de Pékin jusqu'à la mort de l'empereur K'ien-long, 1689-1799', *Monumenta Serica* XIX (1960), pp. 349-83.

Boxer, C.R., 'Some Sino-European Xylographic Works 1622-1718', *Journal of the Royal Asiatic Society* (1947), pp. 199-215.

Boxer, C.R., and Braga, J.M., 'Algunas notas sobre a bibliographia de Macau', *Boletim eclesiastico da Diocese de Macau* XXXVII (1939), pp. 188-215.

Braga, J.M., 'Jesuitas na Asia', *Boletim eclesiastico da Diocese de Macau* LIII-LVIII (1955-1960), *passim*.

Combaluzier, F., 'Un inventaire des Archives de la Propagande (milieu du XVIIe siècle)', *Neue Zeitschrift für Missionswissenschaft* II (1946), pp. 187-200, 274-82; III (1947), pp. 49-57, 96-105.

Cordier, H., *Bibliotheca Sinica*, rev. ed., Taipei, 1966.

---

[32] Translated from the Latin in Pfister, *Notices biographiques et bibliographiques*, vol. 2, pp. 992-3.

Cordier, H., *Essai d'une bibliographie des ouvrages publiés en Chine par les Européens au XVIIe et au XVIIIe siècles*, Paris, 1883.

Courant, Maurice, *Catalogue des livres chinois, coréens, japonais etc.*, 8 parts in 3 vols., Paris, 1900-12.

Cummins, J.S., 'The Present Location of the Pei-t'ang Library', *Monumenta Nipponica* XXII (1967), pp. 482-7.

Dehergne, J., 'Les archives des Jésuites de Paris et l'histoire des missions aux XVIIe et XVIIIe siècles', in J. Metzler, ed., *De Archivis et Bibliothecis Missionibus atque Scientiae Missionum Inservientibus*, Euntes Docete XXI, Rome, 1968.

Lamalle, E., 'La Documentation d'histoire missionaire dans le "Fondo Gesuitico" aux Archives Romaines de la Compagnie de Jésus', in J. Metzler, ed., *De Archivis et Bibliothecis Missionibus atque Scientiae Missionum Inservientibus*.

Mission Catholique des Lazaristes à Pékin, *Catalogue de la Bibliothèque du Pe-T'ang*, Peking, 1949.

Pelliot, P., 'Inventaire sommaire des manuscrits et imprimés chinois de la Bibliothèque Vaticane' (ms.).

Pfister, L., *Notices biographiques et bibliographiques sur les Jésuites de l'ancienne mission de Chine, 1522-1773*, 2 vols., Shanghai, 1932-4.

Schütte, J.F., 'El "Archivo del Japon": Vicisitudes del Archivo Jesuitico del Extremo Oriente y descripción de fondo existente en la Real Academia de la Historia de Madrid', *Archivo documental español* XX, (Madrid, 1964).

Sommervogel, C., *Bibliothèque de la Compagnie de Jésus*, 12 vols., Bruxelles-Paris, 1890-1932.

Streit, R., and Dindinger, J., *Bibliotheca Missionum*, vols. 4, 5, 7, Rome, 1928-31.

史 xix: Russian Sources

C. KIRILOFF

Relations between Russia and China go back at least to the Yüan dynasty when, for a time, Mongol rule extended over both countries. With the downfall of the Yüan, all contacts between Russia and China were interrupted for some 250 years and during this period the two countries lost virtually all knowledge about each other.

It was not until the mid-sixteenth century that Russia once again became aware of China's existence. This was brought about, in the first instance, by the determined efforts of English merchant adventurers to enlist the aid of the Muscovite government in finding a passage to China either overland through Central Asia and Siberia or via the Arctic seas.[1] Russia became alive to China's existence also as a result of her conquest of Siberia, beginning towards the end of the sixteenth century. From then on, gathering intelligence on China became an important task of the Muscovite government and its officials in Siberia. As Russian dominions beyond the Urals expanded towards the east, coming closer and closer to China, the local Siberian administrators began to accumulate an increasing volume of information about that country, much of it coming from the Mongol tribes with which the Russian government had come into close contact early in the seventeenth century.

The first official Russian attempt to establish direct contact with China was made in 1608, when the Tomsk governor, acting on instructions from Moscow, despatched a group of Cossacks on a mission to Altyn Qan and China.[2] Because of internecine strife in Mongolia, these envoys failed to

---

[1] For a survey of English attempts to reach China *via* Russia and the Arctic seas, see the 'Introduction' by G.M. Asher in *Henry Hudson the Navigator*, Hakluyt Society, Series I, No. XXVII (London, 1860); T.S. Willan, *The Early History of the Russia Company: 1553-1603* (Manchester, 1956); and *Early Voyages and Travels to Russia and Persia by Anthony Jenkinson and Other Englishmen*, Hakluyt Society, No. LXXII (London, 1886).

[2] The best account in English of contacts between Muscovite envoys and the Mongol tribes in the early seventeenth century is contained in J.F. Baddeley's outstanding work, *Russia, Mongolia, China* (London, 1919). Until its recent reprint in the Burt Franklin Research and Source Works Series (New York, n.d.) this work was a bibliographical rarity. Although written more than fifty years ago, it remains a model of scholarship, and many of the documents published in it were, until recently, the only versions available to researchers outside of Russia.

reach China, but they did bring back important intelligence about that country.[3]

The first Russian mission reached China in 1618,[4] and from that time diplomatic and trade relations between the two countries have, with occasional interruptions, been maintained until the present day.

On the Russian side, these relations have been amply documented, and Russian archives contain a great wealth of materials throwing valuable light on various aspects of the history of Ch'ing and Republican China, and, in particular, on the history of Russian-Chinese relations. Russian envoys, even those sent on unofficial missions, were given exceedingly detailed instructions before they left Russia. After returning home, they presented written reports and were, in addition, repeatedly debriefed by government officials who recorded the results in lengthy transcripts.[5]

In spite of their abundance, Russian historical documents on China have not yet been adequately explored and utilised by historians, many of whom are scarcely aware of their existence. This is largely due to the fact that up to now only a small portion of these documents has been classified and published, and an even smaller portion translated from Russian.

To give some idea of the volume of Russian historical documents on China, it can be mentioned that early this century the archives of the Russian Ministry of Foreign Affairs alone contained about 25,000 pages of such documents dealing only with the forty-year period 1689-1730. Fedor Golovin's official report on the negotiations that led to the Treaty of Nerchinsk (1689) is known to run into 2,522 pages.[6] Incidentally, this report, which is bound to contain exceedingly valuable data on the early history of Sino-Russian relations, has yet to be published.[7]

In Imperial Russia, documents relating to China were stored not only in the Ministry of Foreign Affairs, but also in the archives of such bodies as the Senate, the Holy Synod, the Department of Siberian Affairs, the Central Treasury, the Directorate of Customs, and the local provincial administrations. The Imperial Academy of Sciences, national libraries, the Imperial universities at St Petersburg, Moscow, and Kazan, and other academic bodies also served as repositories for originals and copies of such documents.

---

[3] Cf. *Materialy po istorii russko-mongol'skikh otnoshenii: 1607-1636* [*Materials on the History of Russian-Mongol Relations: 1607-1636*] (Moscow, 1959), pp. 30-1.
[4] Cf. C. Kiriloff, 'The Early Relations between Russia and China', *New Zealand Slavonic Journal* IV (1969), pp. 1-32.
[5] For examples of such documents available in translation into West European languages see the instructions given to F.I. Baikov and the transcript of his debriefing upon his return from Peking: H. Nicolet de Chollet, 'La première ambassade russe en Chine', *Bulletin de l'Université l'Aurore*, Series III, III, 4(1942), pp. 777-807, and Baddeley, *Russia, Mongolia, China*, vol. 2, pp. 135-53.
[6] Cf. Cahen, *Histoire des relations de la Russie avec la Chine sous Pierre le Grand: 1689-1720*, p. 8.
[7] This report has now appeared in the second of two volumes of documents dealing with Russian-Chinese relations in the seventeenth century. See postscript.

Some of these documents were sorted out and published in collections compiled under official sponsorship. Others were edited and published by Russian scholars in various historical journals and in book form.[8]

After the 1917 Revolution, Soviet relations with China involved various government, party, and academic bodies and organisations, with the result that the relevant documents are to be found in a number of different archives.[9]

At the present time, the main corpus of documents on the early history of Russian-Chinese relations is stored in the Central State Archives of Ancient Documents. Numerous materials from the regional Siberian archives are stored also in the Leningrad branch of the Institute of History of the Academy of Sciences of the USSR. This repository is known to contain original sources on Khabarov's expedition to the Amur and other important materials dealing with the Russian penetration of the Amur basin in the mid-seventeenth century. It also contains documents from Nerchinsk throwing light on the early contacts between the local Russian administration and Ch'ing authorities. Many valuable documents are to be found in the various branches of the Archives of the Academy of Sciences of the USSR. Other main repositories of old and contemporary Russian documents are the Archives of Russian Foreign Policy, the Archives of the Ministry of Foreign Affairs of the USSR, the Central State Archives of the October Revolution, the Central State Archives of the Soviet Army, the Central State Archives of the Soviet Navy, and the Central Party Archives of the Institute of Marxism-Leninism of the Central Committee of the Communist Party of the Soviet Union.

In addition to these archives, valuable sources for China can be found in the Oriental collections of the Institute of Oriental Studies of the Academy of Sciences of the USSR (both in Moscow and, especially, in its Leningrad branch), Lenin State Library (Moscow), Saltykov-Shchedrin State Library (Leningrad), and the state universities of Moscow, Leningrad, and Kazan.[10]

Given the abundance of Russian materials on China and their dispersal

---

[8] The best bibliography of Russian sources on China is P.E. Skachkov's standard reference work *Bibliografiia Kitaia*. Useful information can also be found in C. Morley's *Guide to Research in Russian History* (Syracuse, 1951).

[9] Soviet archives have been virtually a closed area for Western researchers ever since the October Revolution. Access to archival materials can be difficult even for Soviet historians. The situation improved somewhat after Stalin's death, but at a conference of historians held in Moscow in December 1962 many speakers voiced bitter complaints about the continuing restrictions impeding access to Soviet archives; cf. *Vsesoiuznoe soveshchanie o merakh uluchsheniia podgotovki nauchno-pedagogicheskikh kadrov po istoricheskim naukam* [*All-Union Conference on Measures for the Improvement of Training of Cadres for Research and Teaching in the Historical Sciences*] (Moscow, 1964).

[10] Information on these libraries' holdings of historical materials on China and Russian-Chinese relations can be found in *Vostokovednye fondy krupneishikh bibliotek Sovetskogo Soiuza.*

among many archives and libraries, it is impossible to present a detailed description of these documents in the space of a short chapter. All that can be done here is to mention the principal categories of Russian sources, to refer to the most important published collections of Russian historical materials on China, and to give some indication of their contents.

In a survey of early Russian sources on China special mention should be made of some historians who have made particularly valuable contributions to historiography in this field. These are G.F. Müller, N.N. Bantysh-Kamenskii, G. Cahen, and J.F. Baddeley.

Gerhard Müller, a German historian, went to Russia in 1725 and was despatched by the Imperial Academy of Sciences on a historiographic survey of Siberia. He spent ten years (1733-43) travelling all over Siberia and managed to collect an immense number of documents stored in the archives of local Siberian administrations. In accordance with the instructions received from the Academy, Müller paid special attention to gathering materials bearing on the history of Russian-Chinese relations. Upon his return from this expedition, Müller was placed in charge of the national archives in Moscow and began systematising and publishing the collected materials. However, so vast was the number of documents brought by Müller from Siberia that during his lifetime he was able to edit only a fraction of them. Many of these materials were later published by the Imperial Archaeographical Commission and by the Soviet government, but the bulk of them still awaits publication.[11]

Primary sources gathered by Müller have provided a rich fount of materials for the compilers of collections of documents on the history of relations between Russia and China. Foremost among these compilers was N.N. Bantysh-Kamenskii who succeeded Müller as the director of Moscow National Archives. In 1792, Bantysh-Kamenskii finished the compilation of his monumental collection of diplomatic documents on the relations between the Russian and Chinese empires from 1619 to 1792. However, he did not receive permission to publish this work during his lifetime and it was not printed until ninety years later, in 1882.

Although the title of Bantysh-Kamenskii's work bears the dates of 1619-1792, it actually contains no documents dealing with the period prior to F.I. Baikov's mission to Peking (1654-6). For the subsequent period, however, Bantysh-Kamenskii provides a wealth of valuable materials on the history of Russian embassies to China. Later historians of Russian-Chinese relations have drawn heavily on this collection, which has not lost its value up to the present.

A considerable number of highly interesting documents is contained in

[11] The greater part of materials gathered by Müller is stored in the Leningrad branch of the Academy of Sciences of the USSR; cf. 'Dokumenty po istorii russko-kitaiskikh otnoshenii', *Vestnik Akademii nauk SSSR* X (1959), pp. 103-4.

an appendix to G. Cahen's work on the history of Russian-Chinese relations from 1689 to 1730.¹² Cahen had the good fortune to be given free access to Moscow archives and discovered there a number of unpublished primary sources on China.

An even greater contribution to this area of historical studies was made by the English historian J.F. Baddeley, who, like Cahen before him, was also allowed to rummage through the archives of the Tsarist Ministry of Foreign Affairs and likewise came across some previously unpublished valuable documents relating to China. While acknowledging the great value of the above-mentioned works and the high standard of scholarship set by their authors, however, it should be realised that they contain only a small portion of the historical materials on China known to exist in Russian archives.

In Tsarist times, some of these materials were published in compendia. Among these the most important are those compiled under the sponsorship of the official Archaeographical Commission established by the Russian government in 1834. Among the publications of this Commission mention can be made of the following collections: *Historical Documents*,¹³ *Supplements to the Historical Documents*,¹⁴ *Documents of the Archaeographical Expedition*,¹⁵ *Documents on Law and Legal Practices in Old Russia*,¹⁶ and *Russian Historical Library*.¹⁷

Some materials on Russian relations with China are included in such earlier collections of documents as *The Complete Collection of Laws and Statutes of the Russian Empire*,¹⁸ and in *Ancient Russian Library*.¹⁹

It should be noted that, as distinct from Bantysh-Kamenskii's work, these collections were not devoted primarily to Russian-Chinese relations but covered a wide subject area. As a result, materials relating to China account for only a small proportion of the total number of documents and appear to have been selected at random. Nevertheless, some of them provide valuable information on certain facets of the history of relations between the two countries.

Shortly after coming to power, the Soviets began publishing documents which until then had been kept secret in the Tsarist archives. This was done in a highly selective manner, the primary aim of the exercise being to

---

¹² G. Cahen's *Histoire* also contains a very useful annotated bibliography of Russian manuscripts and published documents on China and Russian-Chinese relations. It should be noted that the appendix with selected documents and the bibliography are contained only in the original work in French and not in its English translation.

¹³ *Akty istoricheskie*. Vol. 4 contains documents on Russian penetration of the Amur Valley and on the early phase of Russian relations with China.

¹⁴ *Dopolneniia k aktam istoricheskim*. Materials dealing with China are contained in vols. 2, 3, 4, 5, 6, 7, and 10.

¹⁵ *Akty, sobrannye v bibliotekakh i arkhivakh Rossiiskoi Imperii Arkheograficheskoi ekspeditsieiu Imperatorskoi Akademii nauk*.

¹⁶ *Akty, otnosiashchiesia do iuridicheskogo byta drevnei Rossii*.

¹⁷ *Russkaia istoricheskaia biblioteka*.

¹⁸ *Polnoe sobranie zakonov Rossiiskoi Imperii*.

¹⁹ *Drevniaia rossiiskaia vivliofika*.

buttress the new régime's accusations against the iniquities of the Tsarist government, that government's collusion with the imperialists, and its aggressive external policy. One of the most important publications in which these documents appeared was the *Red Archives*,[20] a journal in which archival materials were printed in their original form and were accompanied by comments written by Soviet historians. Most of the documents published in this journal deal with the revolutionary movement in Russia and with the international relations of Tsarist Russia, including Russia's relations with China. There are also some intelligence reports on the internal situation in China. Among the more interesting materials for a researcher on modern Chinese history are materials on Russian Far Eastern policy, the Boxer uprising, the Sino-Japanese and Russo-Japanese wars, documents disclosing Russian moves to bribe Li Hung-chang, etc.[21]

Recently, the Soviet Ministry of Foreign Affairs embarked on a big new project to publish archival documents relating to Russia's foreign policy from the beginning of the nineteenth century up to the time of the October Revolution of 1917.[22] According to the editors, this publication will make the archival materials of the Tsarist Foreign Ministry 'widely available for scholarly research and is designed to facilitate the study of Russian foreign policy in depth and in all directions'. The entire collection will be divided into six series. The first series, consisting of seven volumes, covers the period from 1801 to 1815. The first volume in this series was published in 1960.

Although doubts have been expressed about the objectivity of its compilers in selecting documents for publication,[23] the collection will undoubtedly constitute an extremely important source of materials on Russian relations with China in the nineteenth and early twentieth centuries. The first six volumes contain more than thirty documents relating to China.[24] Most of them have been published for the first time and throw new light on such aspects of Russian-Chinese relations as the problem of Russian maritime

---

[20] *Krasnyi arkhiv.* In all, 106 volumes were published from 1922 to 1941. For those who have no knowledge of Russian, reference to this source is facilitated by the existence of an English-language summary of its contents: *A Digest of the Krasnyi Arkhiv.*

[21] For some of the materials relating to China, see *A Digest of the Krasnyi Arkhiv: Vols. 1-30*, pp. 22, 129, 201, 204, 230, 245, and 283; *A Digest of the Krasnyi Arkhiv: Vols. 31-106*, pp. 31, 67, 71, 76, and 126.

[22] *Vneshniaia politika Rossii XIX i nachala XX veka.*

[23] Compare R. Quested, 'Further Light on the Expansion of Russia in East Asia: 1792-1860', *Journal of Asian Studies* XXIX, 2 (1970), p. 342: 'The aim of the editors of the collection has obviously been to select material stressing the friendly intentions of the Russian government toward China, and to exclude anything which could show the Russians in an expansionist light, or rub salt into the sores of Sino-Soviet discord. Diplomacy, in short, has motivated the Soviet authorities to exclude from this collection some of the documents most interesting to historians: diplomacy has won out over history. It may be many years before we will be able to learn the full truth from the Russian archives.'

[24] These documents are: vol. 1, nos. 99, 157, 166, 229, 232; vol. 2, Nos. 47, 95, 142, 192, 205, 476, 480; vol. 3, Nos. 2, 65, 66, 106, 113, 194, 208, 225, 230; vol. 4, Nos. 9, 26, 153, 237; vol. 5, Nos. 58, 180, 186, 225; vol. 6, Nos. 59, 124, 125.

trade in Canton, the circumstances of Golovin's abortive mission of 1805, the relations of Russian local officials in Siberia with their Chinese counterparts, and the border problem in Sinkiang. It can only be hoped that the publishers will be more expeditious in making subsequent volumes available to readers.

Of even greater importance for scholars interested in the early relations between Russia and China has been the recent appearance of the first of two volumes of documents dealing with these relations in the seventeenth century.[25] This volume, covering the period 1608-1683, contains 214 documents. A check of the contents of this volume shows that of these 214, no fewer than 140 have been published for the first time. A further examination reveals that not more than seventeen documents included in this volume have up to now been translated and published in languages other than Russian, and its significance becomes obvious if we remember that an earlier similar collection[26] contained only one document devoted to the seventeenth century.

The new collection has been very ably edited by its compilers, N.F. Demidova and V.S. Miasnikov, and contains notes, a glossary of archaic Russian terms and, something which is often lacking in Soviet publications, indexes of personal and geographical names. It is an outstanding contribution to the study of the early history of Russian-Chinese relations. Researchers will be looking forward to the forthcoming publication of the second volume, which, according to the editors, will contain some previously unpublished materials on the diplomatic moves and negotiations that resulted in the conclusion of the Russian-Chinese Treaty of Nerchinsk.

Pervye russkie diplomaty v Kitae [*The First Russian Diplomats in China*] (Moscow, 1966) is another valuable work on the early history of Russian-Chinese relations published recently by N.F. Demidova and V.S. Miasnikov. It contains different versions of reports and transcripts of debriefing of members of the first official Russian mission to China headed by Ivan Petlin (1618) and similar materials pertaining to F.I. Baikov's mission (1654-6).

Documents on the relations between the Soviet Union and China subsequent to the October Revolution can be found in the various collections put out by the Soviet Ministry of Foreign Affairs.[27] The most important of these collections is the series entitled *Documents of Foreign Policy of the USSR*.[28]

---

[25] Demidova and Miasnikov, eds., *Russko-kitaiskie otnosheniia v XVII veke.*
[26] Skachkov and Miasnikov, comp., *Russko-kitaiskie otnosheniia: 1689-1916. Ofitsial'nye dokumenty.*
[27] One such collection is entitled *Vneshniaia politika SSSR. Sbornik dokumentov,* 6 vols. covering 1917-20 (Moscow, 1944); 1921-4 (Moscow, 1944); 1925-34 (Moscow, 1945); 1935-June 1941 (Moscow, 1946); June 1941-September 1945 (Moscow, 1947); September 1945-February 1947 (Moscow, 1947).
[28] *Dokumenty vneshnei politiki SSSR.*

The first volume appeared in 1957 and, up to the present, sixteen volumes have been published covering the period from 7 November 1917 to 31 December 1933. The documents are accompanied by explanatory notes and each volume is also provided with detailed subject indexes. Items relating directly to China constitute almost one-tenth of the total contents of the collection.[29] Although some of these documents are in the nature of declarative propaganda, no historian of international relations of modern China can afford to ignore them, especially those documents that have been made public for the first time. Other published archival materials on China can be found scattered in various Russian periodicals and books.[30]

Another category of Russian sources on China is that of first-hand accounts of Russian travellers, diplomats, and residents in China. Russian explorers of China became especially active in the second half of the nineteenth century, following the establishment of Russian dominion over Central Asia and Russia's expansion into the Amur and Ussuri valleys. Most of these explorers were interested primarily in the elucidation of geographic and climatic features of the regions of north and northwestern China adjacent to Russian territories, in cartographic surveys of unmapped areas, and in China's flora and fauna. Alongside information on these subjects, however, they have left in their works a wealth of observations on socio-economic and political conditions in nineteenth century China.

While the works on China by N.M. Przheval'skii (1839-88) and V.A. Obruchev (1863-1956) are relatively well-known in the West, historical materials on China contained in the accounts of many other Russian travellers are less familiar and deserve to be mentioned here. One of the less known Russian travellers was G.E. Grum-Grzhimailo (1860-1936) who in the years 1884-90 undertook a number of expeditions to China, Mongolia and the Amur basin. Among other works he left us an account of the situation in Sinkiang at the time of the Moslem uprising. Another noteworthy work

---

[29] Of some 6,300 documents contained in the sixteen volumes of this series published thus far, about 560 are directly connected with China. However, matters concerning China are dealt with also in documents which, in the first instance, refer to other countries in the Far East or to countries actively involved in the Far East.

[30] Reference has already been made to Skachkov's standard bibliography of Russian works on China (note 8 above), but it covers only works published up to 1957. There is no annual bibliographical survey of Russian works on China, and to keep abreast with the publication of new Russian sources one has to keep watch over prepublication notices (such as those which appear in the weekly *Novye knigi*) and the contents of such Russian periodicals as *Narody Azii i Afriki, Istoriia SSSR, Voprosy istorii, Novaia i noveishaia istoriia, Kommunist, Istoricheskii arkhiv*, etc. Previously unpublished primary sources can sometimes be found also in general collections of historical texts. Thus, a recent collection of sources on the general history of Russia in the sixteenth and seventeenth centuries contains some very interesting reports on the siege of Albazin and diplomatic contacts between Russian envoys and Peking that were sent to Moscow by F.A. Golovin, the Russian plenipotentiary in the negotiations that led to the Treaty of Nerchinsk. Cf. *Khrestomatiia po istorii SSSR XVI i XVII vv.* (Moscow, 1964), pp. 534-9.

is his description of the Amur valley, especially his ethnographic survey of the indigenous inhabitants.

M.V. Pevtsov (1843-1920) left reports about a number of expeditions to Sinkiang, Tibet, and the inner provinces of China. G.N. Potanin (1835-1920) was another Russian explorer of Mongolia, Tibet, Tuva, north China, and Manchuria. He led several expeditions to those areas in the period from 1876 to 1893 and left valuable accounts of his journeys. V.I. Roborovskii (1856-1910) took part in the Tibetan expeditions led by Przheval'skii (1879-85) and Pevtsov (1889-90) and from 1893 to 1895 headed an expedition to Sinkiang. There is an interesting account of a journey made in 1892 and 1893 from Peking to Mongolia by A.M. Pozdneev.

Some of the most spectacular and valuable discoveries by Russian explorers of China were made by P.K. Kozlov (1863-1935) who took part in several expeditions under Przheval'skii, Pevtsov, and Roborovskii and who later himself organised a number of expeditions. During one such expedition in 1907-9, Kozlov discovered in the Gobi the ancient Hsi-Hsia city of Kharakhoto. The abundant materials unearthed at this site constitute an invaluable corpus of materials on the history of the Tangut Hsi-Hsia kingdom.

Russian diplomats, members of the Russian Orthodox Mission in Peking, merchants, casual travellers, and private residents have also left eye-witness accounts of events and conditions in Ch'ing and early Republican China. Many of these accounts are contained in obscure and virtually inaccessible publications or remain buried in various archives, but some are being republished or printed for the first time by Soviet publishers.

An interesting example of such works is excerpts from the diaries of K.A. Skachkov (1821-83) who, from 1849 to 1857, resided in Peking where he was in charge of the meteorological and magnetic observatory attached to the Russian Orthodox Mission. While in Peking, Skachkov kept two diaries, one of which was devoted to political events. The editors of the recent volume of excerpts from Skachkov's diaries selected for publication those entries which directly or indirectly relate to the Taiping rebellion. These documents recreate the atmosphere that obtained in the Ch'ing capital during these tumultuous years and are a useful source for research into the history of that period.

Memoirs, reports, and biographies of Soviet advisers, diplomats, and Comintern emissaries who worked in China in the 1920s constitute yet another category of materials that is of prime significance for researchers into the history of the Chinese Revolution, the history of Sino-Soviet relations, as well as the histories of the Kuomintang and Chinese Communist Party. Until recently, there was a lamentable dearth of published Russian materials on the Soviet participation in the Chinese Revolution and the Chinese civil war in the 1920s. The reticence of Soviet publishers was due to a number of reasons: the conspiratorial nature of the Soviet involvement in China; the setback of the Chinese Communists after Chiang Kai-shek's coup, attributable, at least partly, to erroneous Soviet and Comintern advice and policies (so that, from the point of view of Soviet publishers, the less that was said about these events, the better); the fact that most Soviet advisers in China in the 1920s were liquidated during the years of Stalin's terror and were consigned to the limbo of non-persons. All this, as well as certain internal and external policy considerations, resulted in the imposition of a blanket of silence over the Soviet involvement in China in the 1920s.

With the deepening of the Sino-Soviet split in the late 1950s, a decision seems to have been taken in the Soviet Union to begin publication of materials on the Soviet and Comintern participation in the Chinese Revolution of the 1920s. As a result, a whole series of works on this subject has recently become available. While a measure of healthy scepticism in assessing their objectivity may be justified, the published documents appear to be authentic and, in spite of their frequent ideological bias, provide important data on the political and military events in China in the 1920s.[31]

Some of the recently published works in this category follow. *Memoirs of a Mission's Secretary* by M.I. Kazanin throws interesting light on the efforts of the Soviet government to establish diplomatic contacts with China and consolidate the Soviet position in the Far East by adroit manoeuvring behind the façade of the 'independent' and 'neutral' Far Eastern Republic. Another book of reminiscences by the same author, *Inside Bliukher's Headquarters*, depicts the events of the Chinese Civil War in the crucial years 1925-7. On this occasion, Kazanin served as a translator on the staff of V.K. Bliukher (alias Galen or Galin), chief Soviet military adviser to the Chinese revolutionaries. The book contains some revealing details on the involvement of Soviet personnel in the inner struggle that went on during these years between the different factions in the revolutionary camp. *The Chinese Diaries: 1925-1926* by N.I. Konchits gives a good idea about the relations between the Soviet military experts and the Chinese commanders with whom they served during field operations. The author was the principal Soviet military adviser to generals Ch'eng Ch'ien and Li Chi-sheng. Published many years after his death, his diaries are said by the editors to be presented to the reader in exactly the same form in which they were written.

Two of the most interesting sources in this category are the memoirs of A.I. Cherepanov, one of the few Soviet military advisers in China in the 1920s who survived the subsequent purges. After the Japanese attack on

---

[31] For further comment on some of the books in this category, see Dan N. Jacobs, 'Recent Russian Material on Soviet Advisers in China', *The China Quarterly* XLI (1970), pp. 103-12, and J.J. Solecki, tr., 'Blücher's "Grand Plan" of 1926', *The China Quarterly* XXXV (1968), pp. 18-39.

China in 1937, Cherepanov was once again sent to China at the head of a Soviet advisory military group to Chiang Kai-shek. In his *Memoirs of a Military Adviser in China* Cherepanov describes his activities in southern China in the years 1923-5 when he played a prominent role in the setting up of the Whampoa Military Academy. Later, he was a senior military adviser in the Northern Expedition, a role described in detail in another book: *The Northern Expedition of the National Revolutionary Army of China, 1926-1927.* Cherepanov's reminiscences span one of the most kaleidoscopic periods of Chinese modern history and contain a great number of fascinating sidelights on Soviet involvement in China's internal struggle and the tug-of-war between different factions and personalities among the revolutionaries. Cherepanov's memoirs also contain a wealth of personal data on Soviet military and political workers in China in the 1920s.

Another book of reminiscences about this period, very similar to the Cherepanov memoirs, has just been published under the title *Notes on the Chinese Revolution: 1925-1927.* In the first part of his memoirs the author, A.V. Blagodatov (alias Pierre Roland), describes his work as an adviser to the Nationalist armies in North China. The second part of his book is devoted to his activities in Canton and in the Northern Expedition. Blagodatov presents in his memoirs fascinating details about the not always easy relations between Soviet military advisers and the Chinese military commanders and provides new sidelights on the Soviet attitudes to Chiang Kai-shek after the latter's break with the Chinese Communists.

Many revealing glimpses into the activities and conduct of Soviet military and political advisers are contained also in the memoirs written by Vishniakova-Akimova: *Two Years in Insurgent China, 1925-1927.* The author was the wife of a high-ranking Soviet military adviser in China and worked as a translator first with the Soviet military advisory group attached to the armies of the 'Christian' general Feng Yü-hsiang and later in Bliukher's headquarters. In 1927, a Soviet publishing-house in Leningrad put out a book entitled *Memoirs of a Volunteer: The Civil War in China* that was said to be a Russian translation of a book written in English by one Henry A. Allen, a soldier of fortune of British origin. Exactly forty years later this book has been reprinted under its original title but this time, there being no further need for such masquerade, the Soviet publishers have restored to the author his real name—V.M. Primakov. (One of the incidental results of the recent appearance of books in this category is that it is now possible for historians to establish the real identity of many Soviet advisers who at the time of their activities in China in the 1920s were for conspiratorial reasons known under assumed names.) In China, Primakov worked first as an adviser to Feng Yü-hsiang and took direct part in the latter's campaigns against Chang Tso-lin and other warlords. In 1926, Primakov chaperoned Feng Yü-hsiang when the latter went on a visit to Moscow. Primakov's book presents interesting facets of the role of Soviet military advisers, a role which was not confined to general counselling at staff level but extended to active participation in combat.

The activities in China of V.K. Bliukher, the chief Soviet military adviser to the Chinese revolutionaries, are documented in a number of works that began to appear in Russia in the late 1950s. The most detailed account of these activities is contained in the recent (1970) book *V.K. Bliukher in China*. In addition to this account, this book also contains a number of important archival materials such as Bliukher's directives to other Soviet military advisers, his assessments of the military and political situation in China and his plans of military operations.

It is virtually impossible to separate the military side of the activities of Soviet advisers in China in the 1920s from the political aspects of their work. However, as compared with the recent publicity about the role played by the Soviet military personnel in the Chinese Revolution, the activities in China of Soviet political advisers and Comintern emissaries still remain obscure and poorly documented. A notable exception in this field has been the recent (1970) publication of a collection of articles entitled *Prominent Soviet Communists—Participants of the Chinese Revolution* describing the role played in Chinese events by Karakhan, Borodin, Bliukher, Voitinskii, Mif, and Mad'iar. While far from being sufficiently detailed and unbiased, these materials fill some of the lacunae in the history of Soviet involvement in the Chinese political scene of the 1920s.

By way of conclusion it can be said that Russian historical sources on China make up a large corpus of materials of which only a minor portion has yet been made public. Of what has been published much was selected in an unsystematic manner by people who were not specialists on China. Some collections of documents reflect the political bias of their editors and publishers. Yet in spite of these shortcomings it is impossible to achieve a thorough understanding of certain aspects of the history of Ch'ing and Republican China without consulting Russian materials. Acquaintance with Russian sources becomes imperative in any research project involving Russian-Chinese relations.

BIBLIOGRAPHY

Akty istoricheskie [Historical Documents], 5 vols., St Petersburg, 1841-4.

Akty, otnosiashchiesia do iuridicheskogo byta drevnei Rossii [Documents on Law and Legal Practices in Old Russia], 3 vols., St Petersburg, 1857-84.

Akty, sobrannye v bibliotekakh i arkhivakh Rossiiskoi Imperii Arkheograficheskoi ekspeditsieiu Imperatorskoi Akademii nauk [Documents Collected in the Libraries and Archives of the Russian Empire by the Archaeographical Expedition of the Imperial Academy of Sciences], St Petersburg, 1838.

Anert, E.E., *Puteshestvie po Man'chzhurii* [*Travels in Manchuria*], St Petersburg, 1904.

Baddeley, J.F., *Russia, Mongolia, China*, London, 1919.

Bantysh-Kamenskii, N.N., *Diplomaticheskoe sobranie del mezhdu Rossiiskim i Kitaiskim gosudarstvami s 1619 po 1792 god* [*A Collection of Diplomatic Documents on the Relations between Russia and China from 1619 to 1792*], Kazan', 1882.

Barsukov, I.P., *Graf N.N. Murav'ev-Amurskii po ego pis'mam, ofitsial'nym dokumentam, rasskazam sovremennikov i pechatnym istochnikam (materialy dlia biografii)* [*Count Murav'ev-Amurskii as Revealed by His Letters, Official Documents, Accounts of his Contemporaries and Published Sources (Materials for a Biography)*], 2 vols., Moscow, 1891.

Blagodatov, A.V., *Zapiski o kitaiskoi revoliutsii: 1925-1927 gg.* [*Notes on the Chinese Revolution: 1925-1927*], Moscow, 1970.

Cahen, G., *Histoire des relations de la Russie avec la Chine sous Pierre le Grand: 1689-1720*, Paris, 1911.

Cherepanov, A.I., *Severnyi pokhod Natsional'no-revoliutsionnoi Armii Kitaia* [*The Northern Expedition of the National Revolutionary Army of China*], Moscow, 1968.

——, *Zapiski voennogo sovetnika v Kitae* [*Memoirs of a Military Adviser in China*], Moscow, 1964.

A Digest of the Krasnyi Arkhiv: Vols. 1-30, Cleveland, 1947.

A Digest of the Krasnyi Arkhiv: Vols. 31-106, Ann Arbor, 1955.

Demidova, N.F. and Miasnikov, V.S., eds., *Russko-kitaiskie otnosheniia v XVII veke: 1608-1683* [*Russian-Chinese Relations in the Seventeenth Century 1608-1683*], 2 vols., Moscow, 1969-72.

Dokumenty vneshnei politiki SSSR [*Documents of Foreign Policy of the USSR*], Moscow, 1957- .

Dopolneniia k aktam istoricheskim [*Supplements to the Historical Documents*], 10 vols., St Petersburg, 1846-72.

Drevniaia rossiiskaia vivliofika [*Ancient Russian Library*], 20 vols. + 11 vols. of supplements, Moscow, 1788-91.

Grum-Grzhimailo, G.E., *Opisanie Amurskoi oblasti* [*A Description of the Amur Province*], St Petersburg, 1894.

——, *Opisanie puteshestviia v Zapadnyi Kitai* [*An Account of an Expedition to Western China*], Moscow, 1948.

Kafarov, N.N. (Palladii), *Dnevnik arkhimandrita Palladiia za 1858 g.* [*The Diary of Archimandrite Palladius for the Year 1858*], St Petersburg, 1912.

Kartunova, A.I., *V.K. Bliukher v Kitae: 1924-1927 gg.* [*V.K. Bliukher in China: 1924-1927*], Moscow, 1970.

Kazanin, M.I., *Vshtabe Bliukhera* [*Inside Bliukher's Headquarters*], Moscow, 1966.

——, *Zapiski sekretaria missii* [*Memoirs of a Mission's Secretary*], Moscow, 1963.

Konchits, N.I., *Kitaiskie dnevniki: 1925-1926 gg.* [*The Chinese Diaries: 1925-1926*], Moscow, 1969.

Kozlov, P.K., *Mongoliia i Amdo i mertvyi gorod Khara-khoto* [*Mongolia and Amdo and the Dead City of Khara-khoto*], Moscow, 1947.

Krasnyi Arkhiv [*Red Archives*], 106 vols., Moscow, 1922-41.

Materialy, otnosiashchiesia do prebyvaniia v Kitae N.P. Ignat'eva v 1859-1860 gg. [*Materials Relating to the Sojourn in China of N.P. Ignat'ev in the Years 1859-1860*], St Petersburg, 1895.

Nevel'skoi, G.I., *Podvigi russkikh morskikh ofitserov na Dal'nem Vostoke Rossii: 1849-1855* [*Feats of the Russian Naval Officers in Russia's Far East: 1849-1855*], St Petersburg, 1897.

Obruchev, V.A., *Ot Kiakhty do Kul'dzhi. Puteshestvie v Tsentral'nuiu Aziiu i Kitai: 1892-1894* [*From Kiakhta to Kuldja. An Expedition to Central Asia and China: 1892-1894*], Moscow, 1950.

——, *Tsentral'naia Aziia, Severnyi Kitai i Nan' Shan'* [*Central Asia, North China and Nan Shan*], 2 vols., St Petersburg, 1900-1.

Polnoe sobranie zakonov Rossiiskoi Imperii [*The Complete Collection of Laws and Statutes of the Russian Empire*], three series, St Petersburg-Petrograd, 1825-1916.

Pevtsov, M.V., *Puteshestvie v Kashgariiu i Kun'lun'* [*An Expedition to Kashgaria and Kunlun*], Moscow, 1949.

Potanin, G.N., *Ocherk puteshestviia v Sychuan' i na vostochnuiu okrainu Tibeta v 1892-1893 gg.* [*An Account of an Expedition to Szechwan and the Eastern Marches of Tibet in 1892-1893*], St Petersburg, 1899.

Pozdneev, A., *Mongoliia i Mongoly* [*Mongolia and the Mongols*], 2 vols., St Petersburg, 1893, 1898.

Primakov, V.M., *Zapiski volontera: grazhdanskaia voina v Kitae* [*Memoirs of a Volunteer: The Civil War in China*], Moscow, 1967.

Przheval'skii, N., *Mongoliia i strana Tangutov* [*Mongolia and the Land of the Tanguts*], 2 vols., St Petersburg, 1875-6.

——, *Ot Kiakhty na istoki Zheltoi reki* [*From Kiakhta to the Sources of the Yellow River*], Moscow, 1948.

Roborovskii, V.I., *Puteshestvie v Vostochnyi Tian'-Shan' i v Nan'-Shan'* [*An Expedition to Eastern Tien-Shan and Nan-Shan*], Moscow, 1949.

Russkaia istoricheskaia biblioteka [*Russian Historical Library*], 39 vols., St Petersburg-Leningrad, 1872-1927.

Skachkov, K.A., *Pekin v dni taipinskogo vosstaniia* [*Peking in the Days of the Taiping Rebellion*], Moscow, 1958.

Skachkov, P.E., *Bibliografiia Kitaia* [*Bibliography of China*], 2nd ed., Moscow, 1960.

——, and Miasnikov, V.S., comp., *Russko-kitaiskie otnosheniia: 1689-1916. Ofitsial'nye dokumenty* [*Russian-Chinese Relations: 1689-1916. Official Documents*], Moscow, 1958.

Sovetskie dobrovol'tsy o pervoi grazhdanskoi revoliutsionnoi voine v Kitae. Vospominaniia [*Soviet Volunteers on the First Civil Revolutionary War in China. Reminiscences*], Moscow, 1961.

Timkovskii, E.F., *Puteshestvie v Kitai cherez Mongoliiu v 1820 i 1821 godakh* [*A Journey to China via Mongolia in the Years 1820 and 1821*], 3 vols., St Petersburg, 1824.

Veselovskii, N.I., ed., *Materialy dlia istorii Rossiiskoi dukhovnoi missii v Pekine* [*Materials for a History of the Russian Ecclesiastic Mission in Peking*], St Petersburg, 1905.

Vidnye sovetskie kommunisty—uchastniki kitaiskoi revoliutsii [*Prominent Soviet Communists—Participants of the Chinese Revolution*], Moscow, 1970.

Vishniakova-Akimova, V.V., *Dva goda v vosstavshem Kitae: 1925-1927* [*Two Years in Insurgent China: 1925-1927*], Moscow, 1965.

Vneshniaia politika Rossii XIX i nachala XX veka [*Russia's Foreign Policy in the Nineteenth and Early Twentieth Centuries*], Moscow, 1960- .

Vneshniaia politika SSSR. Sbornik dokumentov [*Foreign Policy of the USSR. A Collection of Documents*], 6 vols., Moscow, 1944-7.

Vostokovednye fondy krupneishikh bibliotek Sovetskogo Soiuza [*Oriental Collections of the Principal Libraries of the Soviet Union*], Moscow, 1963.

Postscript

When this article was already in the page-proof stage, Soviet publishers brought out at last the long-promised second volume of documents on the history of Russian-Chinese relations in the seventeenth century (Demidova and Miasnikov, eds., *Russko-kitaiskie otnosheniia v XVII veke*). This volume contains the full text of F. A. Golovin's report to his government on the Nerchinsk Treaty negotiations. This extremely valuable historical document, published now for the first time, represents a very detailed account of the activities of the Russian embassy beginning from its appointment on 20 January 1686, and concluding with Golovin's return to Moscow on 10 January 1691. In addition to a chronicle of his mission's movements and diplomatic negotiations, the report also incorporates a variety of documents that came into Golovin's hands. The text of the report has been very meticulously edited and provided with a corpus of explanatory notes and commentaries. Its publication represents an important landmark in the study of the early stage of the history of Russian-Chinese relations.

史 xx: Some Notes on Archives on Modern China

LO HUI-MIN

It is a remarkable fact, though how remarkable is little realised, that with such a long and glorious historical tradition and so traditionally-minded a people as the Chinese, the problem of archives has not until recently gained much attention in China. Few scholars reflected upon the paucity of historical monographs based on or making any significant use of archival or manuscript sources—by Chinese tradition the printed word was the ultimate authority. Though doubts about the authenticity of individual treatises were raised from time to time, questions were rarely asked about the reliability of what had long been taken for granted and used by generations of scholars as 'primary sources': dynastic histories, the *shih-lu* or 'veritable records', the *hui-yao*, local gazetteers, various encyclopaedias, and similar compilations. The thought seldom occurred, as Ts'ai Yüan-p'ei rightly reminded us, that these 'primary sources' might in fact be much mutilated and censored material and therefore very much second-hand history: censored not only because of literary, historical, and other conventions, and for official and dynastic requirements, but also because of compilers' prejudices, ignorance, personal self-regard, caution, etc.[1] These problems arise with compilations of all kinds anywhere and at any time. What is striking, however, is that if these doubts were ever present with Chinese scholars, as surely they must have been, there should have been no attempt at inquiry into and search for the original sources from which the compilations were made, leading to an examination of the whole problem of archives.

Historical circumstances have no doubt been responsible for this neglect, as much as the Confucian views on history which were synonymous with Chinese historical tradition. There was, above all, the question of availability. Chinese archives, like others, official or private, were not created for the convenience of historians, but the Chinese, being strong believers in historical and cultural continuity, an attitude which is implicit in an expression such as *wen-chang ch'ien ku-shih*, were in fact very much preoccupied with the preservation of historical or literary works for posterity. In this endeavour,

---

[1] Ts'ai Yüan-p'ei, preface to Ming-Ch'ing shih-liao, series A, vol. 1. Liang Ch'i-ch'ao also discussed this point in *Chung-kuo li-shih yen-chiu fa* (Shanghai, 1930), Chapters 4 and 5.

printing came early to their aid. Paradoxically, this favourable factor seems to have worked to archival disadvantage. For once publication was done, it was the printed version, and not the original manuscript, that assumed the greater value, to the point where the manuscripts themselves became neglected. Throughout China's long history, there have been numerous private and public libraries famous for their collections of printed works, but we hear little of any possessing manuscript sources that might be described as archives, as distinct from collections of hand-copied books. Practically every man of note in late Ch'ing China had a collection of his papers printed, but nothing was heard of the original files of the papers themselves.[2] There have been recent discoveries of hitherto unpublished papers of some of these men, but rarely of the files of which printed versions were made. It seems that once what was deemed of historical or literary merit was skimmed and printed, the originals were allowed to be dispersed or destroyed. By Imperial order, the wooden blocks from which prints of various classics were made were regularly inspected and aired to ensure that they did not fall into decay, but no similar care was taken of archives. This attitude to archives as being of little consequence beyond serving their administrative purposes, official compilations notwithstanding, is probably best reflected in the proposal made in 1909 by Chang Chih-tung, the famous viceroy of Hukwang, then a Grand Councillor in charge of the Ministry of Education. In a memorial to the throne on solving the housing problems of the Imperial Archives, Chang Chih-tung, himself a scholar of considerable merit and known as one of the promoters of learning in the late Ch'ing period, suggested that a library, which subsequently became the Peking National Library, should be built to house books but that 'the old archives [being of] no use' should be burnt.[3]

The Establishment of Archives

Fortunately for the historiography of the Ming and Ch'ing, Chang Chih-tung was dissuaded from carrying out his suggestion, but the material transferred then to the safe keeping of the newly established Historical Museum fared badly. In an attempt to arrange it, those in charge of the Historical Museum (Li-shih po-wu kuan) assigned the sorting of it to office boys and clerks. These, according to the eye-witness account of Professor Teng Chih-ch'eng, poured and spread the manuscripts out on the ground in their yard, sorting out with long sticks the papers that appeared to the naked eye to be still in good condition and filling the rest into jute sacks.[4]

[2] For a list of the collected papers of noted statesmen of the Ch'ing period published up to 1935, see Ma Feng-shen, 'Ch'ing-tai hsing-cheng chih-tu ts'an-k'ao shu-mu', parts 1 and 2 in *Pei-ta she-hui k'e-hsüeh chi-k'an* V, 3 (1935), pp. 186-272 and V, 4 (1935), pp. 467-584.
[3] Wang Kuo-wei, *Kuan-t'ang chi-lin*, 'K'u-shu lou chi', referred to by Hsü Chung-shu in 'Nei-ko tang-an chih yu-lai chi ch'i cheng-li'.
[4] Teng Chih-ch'eng, *Ku-tung so-chi* cited by Hsü Chung-shu, 'Nei-ko tang-an'.

In 1921, to meet financial difficulties, the Historical Museum sold 8,000 of these sacks to a paper-making firm for $4,000. Fortunately for the historians for a second time, the same man who had stopped the burning of the material in the first instance accidentally came across some of what the paper-making firm had itself sold to Peking street pedlars as wrapping paper. He managed to rescue some of it once again. By the time it reached its resting place, the newly established Institute of History and Philology of the Academia Sinica, in 1928, it had passed through several hands, and not only was the amount of material greatly reduced but irreparable damage had been done to what was left.[5]

This story as told by Professor Hsü Chung-shu illustrates the circumstances under which the problem of archives became for the first time an important scholarly concern for Chinese historians. Scandals such as this were by no means isolated incidents. Professor Chu Hsi-tsu, writing about his rescue of material of the Sheng-p'ing shu, has a similar story to tell,[6] and as late as 1936, the Yü-kung hsüeh-she, the Society for Chinese Historical Geography, had to fight hard to prevent a part of 'some 3,000-4,000 catties in weight' (16 ounces to a catty) of most valuable material from the same Imperial Archives, dating from the late nineteenth and early twentieth centuries, from being sold as 'funeral money' to be burnt in honour of the dead.[7] The survival of the material in various government and private organisations, including the National Peking and Tsinghua Universities, was all accidental.[8] And all indications point to the fact that what has been rescued and salvaged represents only a fraction of the original. The fact that the material acquired by these organisations was reckoned in terms of weight and often in such rough terms as, for instance, '40,000-50,000 catties', is an indication of the infant state of Chinese archival development as late as the eve of the Sino-Japanese war.[9] A start had, however, been made, a start to which many other factors had also contributed: the introduction into China of social science and scientific methods of historical inquiry, the discovery of sites and material remains of the Shang and

---

[5] More than one-third out of 120,000 catties rescued, some 50,000, were so torn and dirty that they had to be put into jute sacks, presumably to be disposed of. Almost four-fifths of the remainder are incomplete documents, so that the complete documents amount to only some 15,000 catties or one-eighth of the rescued material. See Hsü Chung-shu, 'Chung-yang yen-chiu yüan Li-shih yü-yen yen-chiu so-ts'ang tang-an ti fen-hsi', pp. 169-222.

[6] Chu Hsi-tsu, 'Ch'ing nei-ko so-shou Ming T'ien-ch'i Ch'ung-chen tang-an Ch'ing che-pa', pp. 283-7.

[7] Chao Ch'üan-teng, 'Yü-kung hsüeh-hui tsui-chin te-tao chih ching-chi tang-an', *Yü-kung* VI, 2 (1936), pp. 65-9.

[8] For archives at Peking University, Tsinghua University and the Palace Museum see Chao Ch'üan-teng, 'Pei-ching ta-hsüeh so-ts'ang tang-an ti fen-hsi', Wu Han, 'Ch'ing-hua ta-hsüeh so-ts'ang tang-an ti fen-hsi', and Shan Shih-yüan, 'Ku-kung po-wu yüan wen-hsien kuan so-ts'ang tang-an ti fen-hsi'.

[9] See Chao Ch'üan-teng, 'Yü-kung hsüeh-hui'. Practically all the archives in the above-mentioned institutions were reckoned by weight.

Chou periods, and the deprivation of China by British and French scholars of manuscript material from the Tun-huang caves in Kansu. These developments and scandals of the type which we have related combined to give the Chinese a new awareness of their historical heritage and this became reflected in the subsequent activities of Chinese scholars in seeking out, collecting, sorting, and arranging archival materials, in publishing manuscript sources and in establishing special journals and studies devoted to archival matters.[10] This work was hindered by war and political upheaval, as a result of which both established archives and government and private collections of papers suffered losses to an extent that can only be conjectured.[11] Nevertheless a good foundation had been laid, enabling not only quick recovery but rapid development in the collection and publication of archives both in the People's Republic of China and in Taiwan since 1949.

The State of Chinese Archives

There is, so far as I am aware, no comprehensive account or listing of existing archives in the People's Republic of China.[12] Great activity and seriousness of purpose in archival work are evident, however, not only in the historical journals but also in the publication of selections from archives unearthed. It would take too long and be too tedious to catalogue all this activity here. Any list would anyway be incomplete because of the gaps in our knowledge due to the unavailability of all relevant publications. The reader should consult *Chin-tai shih tzu-liao*, the journal devoted to the historical sources of modern China, which has published some valuable discoveries of manuscript sources in practically every issue since its first appearance in 1954.[13] Probably the most striking feature of the work being done on archives in the People's Republic is the new attitude towards them. Unlike former days, when archive salvage and preservation were the concern of a small number of dedicated scholars, this has now become a nation-wide activity fully supported by the government and in which the masses, made aware for the first time of the value and significance of

[10] For a list of articles and journals dealing with archives and archival problems see *Chung-kuo shih-hsüeh lun-wen so-yin*, vol. 1, pp. 136-43; vol. 2, pp. 301-3.

[11] The loss of manuscripts is difficult to reckon, and no one has made such an attempt. Judging by the dispersal and loss of such printed work as *Nei-ko ta-k'u Han-wen huang-ts'e yin-kao* (*Yen-ching hsüeh-pao* XXXI (December 1946), pp. 228-9), the extent of single-copy archives must have been great.

[12] The one non-Chinese historian to have made any significant use of the archives in China since 1949 seems to be Jean Chesneaux. For his book *Le mouvement ouvrier chinois de 1919 à 1927* (Paris, 1962), he was given access to the archives of the former International Municipal Council and of the former French concession in Shanghai.

[13] The reader is also referred to collections of archive material published in China before 1960 and listed in Albert Feuerwerker and S. Cheng, *Chinese Communist Studies of Modern Chinese History* (Cambridge, Mass., 1961) and to other collections which have appeared since, such as Nien Tzu-min, *Li Hung-chang chih P'an Ting-hsin shu-cha* (Peking, 1960) and *Sheng Hsüan-huai wei-k'an hsin-kao* (Peking, 1960).

archives, are actually taking part.[14] Closely linked with this is the new development by which archives have ceased to be, as in former times, merely governmental sources, and central government sources at that. The archives now extend to include the widest range of subjects not covered by official sources, such as business archives and private papers.[15] A third important development is that, unlike the former days of what one might describe as 'academic feudalism', when institutions competed in their own self-interest, there is now co-ordination of activity and co-operation between institutions of different interests and regions. As a result, the different bodies have been enabled to achieve a satisfactory degree of specialised coverage.

Notable work has also been and continues to be done in Taiwan, though of a different kind. In a communication to *Ch'ing-shih wen-t'i*, Professor Kuo T'ing-i, head of the Institute of Modern History of the Academia Sinica in Taipei, gives a brief description of the main archives existing in Taiwan, to which list the interested reader is referred.[16] Professor Kuo says that 'some [military men and politicians] have given us [the Institute of Modern History] their private papers, diaries, chronological biographies, autobiographies, memoirs and photos' and that the Kuomintang Archives, the other important collection of archives for modern China in Taiwan, possesses 'private papers and photographs of first-rate importance to the study of Kuomintang history'. However, archival work in Taiwan has not been a question of the acquisition of new material so far as the period before 1949 is concerned, apart from material on local Taiwan history,[17] but primarily one of sorting, classifying, and publishing selections from the materials which the Nationalist Government was able to take with it when forced to abandon the mainland. Besides, the archives, in spite of unspecific claims of their nature and extent, are essentially of government and official sources, which is natural enough. As far as these are concerned, losses and destruction occurred in the panic and upheaval preceding the government's departure from the mainland. There is the additional consideration, however, that, whereas on the mainland archivists concerned with the pre-1949

[14] The discovery and publication of many of the archives would not have been possible without the help of the descendants of their original owners. A notable example is the papers of Liu Ch'eng-chung (1822-83) on the Nien-chün, edited and published by his great-grandson Liu Hou-tse as 'Nien-chün tzu-liao ling-shih' in *Chin-tai shih tzu-liao* VI (1958), pp. 1-38. Much other material has come to light through similar efforts.

[15] The interest in business and economic material hitherto neglected is fully evident in Yen Chung-p'ing and others, *Chung-kuo chin-tai ching-chi shih t'ung-chi tzu-liao hsüan-chi* (Peking, 1955), the publication of selections of the archives of the Imperial Chinese Maritime Customs, and other compilations.

[16] Kuo Ting-yee, 'Major Institutions, and Collections on Modern and Contemporary China', pp. 11-25.

[17] For work on the archives on the local history of Taiwan see Lin Hsiung-hsiang, 'Pen-sheng shih-nien lai ti wen-hsien kung-tso', also Feng Yung, 'Liu Ming-ch'uan fu-kao tang-an cheng-li chi-lu', *T'ai-wan wen-hsien* VII, 3-4 (December 1956), pp. 89-124.

period are dealing with someone else's past in which there is little need for discretion, those now in Taiwan who were associated with the Nationalist Government are dealing with their own past and in the process they may have personal safety as well as reputation to consider. Probably for this reason, by far the most active archival work going on in Taiwan is the publication of selections of source material, predominantly of the Ch'ing period, in the Institute of Modern History under Professor Kuo's direction.[18] The National Palace Museum has the archives of the Grand Council (Chün-chi ch'u) which the Museum was able to take with it to Taiwan, consisting of some sixty cases, which Professor Kuo describes as a 'mere fraction of the vast archives' covering mainly the period from 1736 to 1911. This material like that in most other archives in Taiwan is still largely at the stage of being sorted and catalogued,[19] though some has been published.

Foreign Archives on China

Work on foreign archival material on China similar to that which is now in progress under the auspices of the Japan Academy on 'Historical Documents Relating to Japan in Foreign Countries' is still awaited.[20] The scrappy knowledge that we possess of relevant sources in various countries shows not only their immensity but their quite astonishing richness. Exploration on this by historians of China has just begun. Broadly speaking, foreign archives can be divided into four main categories: governmental, missionary, archives of non-governmental organisations, including business firms and Chambers of Commerce, and papers of individuals. We shall deal here only with the archives of more recent Chinese history, namely the period from the late eighteenth century and particularly since the First Opium War. For this period, governmental archives, of the four main types of source material mentioned above, have been the ones to which the historians have so far turned, simply because these have been relatively the most accessible, thanks to the First World War. Even so, it was not until many years after the Second World War that scholars effectively benefited from the fifty-year rule. In 1968, the British Government led the way by reducing the closed period from fifty to thirty years, a lead which few other countries have so far followed. However the archives of most governments having dealings with China and covering the greater part of our period are now open to researchers, with the probable exception of Russia.[21]

---

[18] For a list of the publication of collected archives see Kuo Ting-yee, 'Major Institutions', pp. 24-5.
[19] Li Kwang-t'ao, 'Tang-an i-T'ai ching-kuo'.
[20] *Nihon kankei kaigai shiryō mokuroku* (Tokyo, 1963-).
[21] *Krasny archiv*. A major contribution based on the Russian archives dealing with China is the book by B.A. Romanov, *Rossiya v Manchzhurii* (Leningrad, 1928), translated by S.W. Jones and published as *Russia in Manchuria (1892-1906)* (Ann Arbor, 1952). No non-Russian

I shall not attempt here to give a list of foreign archives known to me to contain material on modern China, but rather a general idea about them. In most countries there is a central archive. But insofar as material pertaining to the study of modern China is concerned, only the British Public Record Office is a truly centralised repository. The Library of Congress has in its keeping only the papers of most, but by no means all, Presidents, Secretaries of State, Ambassadors, and some other statesmen.[22] The State Department and other United States government departments maintain their own archives. Of the relevant French government material only that of the Ministry of Finance is in the Archives Nationales; all other ministries keep their own archives. The Deutsches Zentralarchiv in Potsdam has the guardianship of archives relating to China, including those of the German Foreign Ministry.[23] A large portion of the latter, which was captured by the allies after World War II, is now kept separately.[24] The Foreign Ministries of Japan, Belgium, Holland, and Italy have their own archives, and these of course contain the most material relevant to modern China in these countries.[25]

---

historian seems to have been allowed to make use of Russian archives in any significant way, and the study of Tsarist relations with China by non-Russian scholars has chiefly been based on *Krasny archiv*, a publication of selections of archives which was stopped in 1933. For a list of these publications see L.S. Rubinchek and L.W. Eisele, *A Digest of the Krasny archiv*, 2 vols. (Ohio, 1947; Ann Arbor, 1955). An English translation of some of the material concerning China has been published in *The China Social and Political Science Review*. For details see C.D. Henry Ch'en's index to vols. 1-20 of this periodical (Peiping, 1937), p. 32.

[22] There are a few notable absences from Library of Congress archives of papers which have relevance to the study of modern China, such as those of H. Hoover, F.D. Roosevelt, and H.L. Stimson.

[23] Two historians who have made significant use of the material dealing with China at the Deutsches Zentralarchiv at Potsdam are the German historian H. Stoecker—*Deutschland und China im 19 Jahrhundert* (Berlin, 1958)—and the Russian historian A.S. Jurusalimski, whose work appeared in a German translation in 1954 under the title *Die Aussenpolitik und die Diplomatie des deutschen Imperialismus am Ende des 19 Jahrhunderts*.

[24] For the captured German Foreign Ministry material on microfilm, see *A Catalog of Files and Microfilms of the German Foreign Ministry Archives 1867-1920* issued by the American Historical Association Committee for the Study of War Documents and its continuation covering 1920-45, compiled by G.O. Kent in two volumes (Stanford, 1962, 1964).

[25] The concept of archives for historical research is very new in Japan, but signs of increasing Japanese confidence in the role of the country in the recent past on the one hand, and the efforts on the part of the archivists on the other, are omens of a more rewarding future for the historian. Insofar as the archives dealing with Japan's prominent role in China are concerned, one senses perhaps a feeling that there is much to hide, and any casual inspection of the existing open archives points to the fact that much remains indeed hidden: quite apart from the purposeful destruction and accidental losses that occurred immediately before and after the Japanese debacle in 1945.

In his article listed in the bibliography, Ariizumi gives some indication of the existing archives in Japan. Since there has been hardly a prominent Japanese of modern times who has not, at one time or another, had something to do with China, the papers of any one of them might be of interest to a student of modern China. The four open archives, however, are of particular relevance. They are Kensei shiryō shitsu (Constitution Materials Room)

It is pointless to say which particular country has the most important archival material on China, since this will naturally depend on the individual researcher's area and period of interest. But generally speaking there are few anywhere to rival the British archives. These are incomparable mines of information for the student of modern China whatever his interest happens to be. Apart from the archives in the India Office Library, British governmental material on China is, as already mentioned, mostly conveniently housed in one central archive, namely the Public Record Office. This is a unique situation and one which greatly facilitates research. The Record Office also possesses the papers of many diplomats and statesmen of interest to the student of China. For obvious reasons, by far the richest British government archives on China are those of the Foreign Office. Professor Iwao's guide to the material in the Foreign Office archives relating to China and Japan, though no more than a copy of the manuscript catalogue kept at the Public Record Office, serves to give a prospective user of these records some idea of their size, if not their quality.[26] More recently David Pong has compiled a more useful guide to the material in Chinese from the British Legation (later Embassy) in Peking covering the period 1839 to 1934.[27] As for private papers and the archives of other government departments, the reader should consult M.S. Giuseppi's guide to the contents of the Public Record Office.[28]

Though newcomers to history, the Americans are probably the most

---

of the National Diet Library, the Gaimusho (Ministry of Foreign Affairs) archives, the Bōeichō (Defence Agency) archives and the newly found Kokuritsu kōmonjokan (National Archives). All of these four are post-war creations. The Gaimusho and Bōeichō archives were open to scholars after the captured archives of the ministries of Foreign Affairs, Army, and Navy were returned to Japan. The Gaimusho archives, though much depleted, are easily accessible, but not, however, those of the Bōeichō. The Kensei shiryō shitsu of the National Diet Library has made great strides since the appointment of the first archivist in 1955. Besides the collections of original papers, it has microfilm copies of collections of papers in various public institutions and private hands in Japan. The National Archives, the building of which was completed in 1971, is scheduled to open to the public in April 1972, but the transfer of papers from some of the ministries is unlikely to be completed until 1976 or even later. It is not clear what sort of material, from which ministries, is to be deposited with the National Archives, what is to be the closed period, or what will be the dividing line between the National Archives and various existing or new archives. All these problems are at present under study by the staff of the National Archives who have been seeking out archival rules, regulations and practices of various countries. One gains a hopeful impression from those in charge that the archivists of this central institution are likely to regard themselves as the keepers of historical material for research and for public education, rather than as the suspicious guardians of state and departmental secrets. The question hinges, however, on what sort of material and how large a portion of the material the National Archives can persuade various ministries to yield to it.

[26] Seiichi Iwao, *List of the Foreign Office Records Preserved in the Public Record Office in London Relating to China and Japan* (Tokyo, 1959).

[27] David Pong, 'Correspondence between the British and the Chinese in the 19th and the 20th Centuries: Chinese Language Manuscripts from the British Legation at Peking deposited in the Public Record Office, London', *Ch'ing-shih wen-t'i* II, 4 (November 1970).

[28] M.S. Giuseppi, *Guide to the Contents of the Public Record Office* (revised London, 1963).

archive-conscious of all. Practically every institution of any public significance, universities being the most notable, prides itself on possessing an archive. There are thorough and comprehensive guides to national holdings of various classes of archival material.[29] In his guide *Americans and Chinese* Professor Liu Kwang-ching has listed all archives containing material relevant to China, including government archives,[30] and the State Department archives in the National Archives, by far the most important for the study of modern China, has its own very detailed and useful catalogues of the material in its keeping.[31]

There is, however, no convenient guide to the archives, government or private, of other countries.[32] To judge by the state of government archives in some of these countries, for instance France, Belgium, Italy, and Japan, there is no reason to expect that they will be accessible to people other than their own staff, and one finds material relating to China in some of these archives still in a disorganised state, quite different from the magnificent arrangement of the British archives.[33]

Though the government archives of the various countries have been used mainly as sources for diplomatic history, it should be stressed that they have much wider value and contain rich information on many aspects of Chinese life of a type sometimes not found in Chinese sources and therefore capable of throwing quite different and revealing light on affairs and events.

Foreign Missionary, Business, and Personal Archives

The same is true of missionary archives which contain not only information on missionary activities but also on a wide range of subjects little thought of in connection with normal missionary activities. Professor Liu's guide

---

[29] There are many such guides. Among them are P.M. Hamer, *A Guide to Archives and Manuscripts in the United States* (New Haven, 1961), and *The National Union Catalog of Manuscript Collections 1959-1961* issued by the Library of Congress (Ann Arbor, 1962).

[30] Liu Kwang-ching, *Americans and Chinese: A Historical Essay and a Bibliography* (Cambridge, Mass., 1963).

[31] There are many guides to the archives of the State Department and new issues appear from time to time to bring it up to date. From among these, students will find useful that issued by the National Archives under the general title *Preliminary Inventories: General Records of the Department of State* (Washington, 1943).

[32] There are a few books dealing with European archives, such as *A Guide to the Diplomatic Archives of Western Europe* by D.H. Thomas and L.M. Case (Philadelphia, 1959), but none of them is very useful as a research guide.

[33] For the selected microfilms of captured Japanese material there are two guides, namely C.H. Uyehara, *Checklist of Archives in the Japanese Ministry of Foreign Affairs, Tokyo, Japan, 1868-1945* (Washington, 1954) and John Young, *Checklist of Microfilm Reproductions of Selected Archives of the Japanese Army, Navy, and other Government Agencies, 1868-1914* (Washington, 1959). Without having seen the full extent of the archives, it is unfair to pass any summary judgement on these selections, but from a brief examination, it would appear that the selections were done by Japanese linguists rather than trained historians who know Japanese. Insofar as the selection of Ministry of Foreign Affairs archives is concerned it adds little to the existing compilations such as *Nihon gaikō bunsho* (Tokyo, 1936-   ).

mentioned above includes a list of missionary archives in the United States and L.R. Marchant has provided us with a guide to the archives of the British Protestant Mission in China.[34] The archives of Catholic missions in China in any European country can be traced through various other guides.[35] The Vatican archives have their own guide. Unlike government archives, access to missionary archives is by favour rather than by right and the decision in all cases lies in the hands of the archivists and keepers of the records. Because of the Canonisation Law, the Vatican imposes a hundred-year closed period on all its archives.

In comparison with government and to a lesser degree missionary archives, the archives of private organisations, including business firms, as well as the papers of individuals are few and hard to trace. The Americans are alone in having a significant number of such archives open to the public. The only important archives of any private British organisation dealing with China, apart from those of the Chambers of Commerce, are the archives dealing with the early years of Jardine, Matheson & Co. in the Cambridge University Library.[36] In the present political atmosphere there is probably little likelihood of any British firms that have played an important role in China's recent past, such as the Hongkong and Shanghai Banking Corporation, Jardine, Matheson & Co., the British-China Corporation, and the Chartered Bank of Australia, India and China, making their archives available to historians. We may note, however, that Compton Mackenzie's notable history of the last named, *Realms of Silver*, was written from its private archives.[37] None of the archives of the more important Japanese business houses and the like, which would be of interest to the student of China, is known to have been opened, and the situation with similar archives in other countries is the same. The activities of most foreign business and other organisations in China can be gleaned at present only from sources other than their own.

More American and British personal papers relating to China have been made public than those of any other country including Japan. Most of these personal papers belong to diplomats and politicians. Professor Liu's American guide, however, often unintentionally gives a misleading impression of the size and value of some of these private collections by listing the total size of such collections instead of that of the portion with direct relevance to

---

[34] L.R. Marchant, *A Guide to the Archives and Records of Protestant Christian Missions from the British Isles to China 1796-1914.*

[35] For various guides to the Catholic archives, the reader is referred to the chapter on Jesuit sources by Paul A. Rule in this volume.

[36] Basing his work chiefly on these archives, Michael Greenberg has written one of the best accounts of early Sino-British relations: *British Trade and the Opening of China, 1800-1842* (Cambridge, 1951).

[37] Compton Mackenzie: *Realms of Silver: One Hundred Years of Banking in the East* (London, 1954).

China.[38] If my inspection of some forty of these collections gives me any pretence to proffer an opinion, most of the American collections of personal papers contain rather meagre material on China.[39]

Except for papers of British statesmen concerning China in a general way, such as those of Salisbury, Curzon, and Chamberlain, the papers of individuals having any dealings with China are found in the main in the Public Record Office and the School of Oriental and African Studies.[40] Two collections of private papers dealing almost exclusively with China, though with British connections, are both found outside Britain. These are the G.E. Morrison Papers in the Mitchell Library, Sydney, Australia, and the J.O.P. Bland Papers recently acquired by the Toronto University Library, Canada.[41] By virtue of their size, continuity, detail and, above all, intimacy, the Morrison Papers are undoubtedly by far the most important single, non-governmental archives on China over the period 1895 to 1920 to be found anywhere. Indeed this collection, which includes a large number of photographs and other personal effects, is the only unexpurgated archive that I know of.

The papers of individuals of other nationalities are little known. There are, however, scholars in a number of countries who have been able to obtain access to some of these collections, usually with the owner's stipulation that the papers are for the scholar's personal use only.[42] It is hoped that they will be able to persuade the owners of these papers to donate them to some public institute for the benefit of other scholars when they themselves have finished using them, if only just to test the validity of their work.

Besides national archives there are of course international archives of relevance, such as those of the League of Nations, the International Labour Office and the like. Indeed one could go on listing possible sources, hitherto

---

[38] This otherwise useful guide is defective in this respect. The so-called 'extensive archives' often contain little on China, and the guide appears to be compiled from others rather than from personal investigation. It also contains many omissions: for example, those who had no direct dealings with China, but whose papers contain material on China. Surprisingly, the papers of Paul S. Reinsch (American Minister in China 1913-19), which are in the Municipal Library of Madison, Wisconsin, are omitted, though his published memoirs are listed.

[39] The two most substantial personal archives are probably the W. Straight Papers at Cornell University Library and the W.W. Rockhill Papers in the Houghton Library at Harvard University. Marilyn Young, making use of some of the collections of the papers in the Library of Congress, has in her *Rhetoric of Empire* produced an outstanding book on Sino-American relations.

[40] See the catalogue of the Library of the School of Oriental and African Studies. Various new additions are in *Ch'ing-shih wen-t'i*, to which the reader is referred.

[41] For the Bland Papers see the notes by J. Cranmer-Byng, 'The J.O.P. Bland Papers', *Ch'ing-shih wen-t'i* II, 3 (July 1970). The papers and other material of G.E. Morrison, amounting to 255 boxes and files are in the Mitchell Library, Sydney, N.S.W., Australia.

[42] It is fairly common everywhere for a historian to be given material which he or she alone can make use of. One of the cases which historians of modern China might be particularly interested in is that of the papers of many Belgians, to which only Madame Kurgan, working under Professor Steiger of the Université Libre à Bruxelles, has access.

unregarded, but enough has been said to make the point. The London School of Oriental and African Studies is sponsoring a program, under the direction of Miss Wainwright, for the publication of a guide to archival materials relating to China and Japan in the British Isles, similar to one done for Southeast Asia.[43] We hope not only that many more private collections of papers will surface as a result of this work but that it will eventually extend to cover archives on a global scale to the benefit of all historians of modern China.

Archives as an Historical Source

The importance of archives as historical source materials needs no stressing. That there can be no history without such materials is self-evident. But the more 'original' and 'real' the material, which is what most archival sources are, the greater the danger of mistaking the tree for the forest, taking sources for history. Archival material, of all genres of written records, is most conducive to a false sense of historical security, by deceiving one with the very qualities which make it such a valuable historical source: the qualities of contemporaneity, spontaneity, immediacy, and intimacy. All these make one too often forget or, if one remembers, too lightly consider the implications of the fact that archives are primarily and predominantly the records of the ruling classes. This has always been so, is so now, and will so remain. This fact is of the greatest significance in the context of Chinese history, be they Chinese archives or non-Chinese archives with which we are dealing, but particularly is it true with the archives of Imperial China. At a time when literacy was the privilege of the few and provided the authority to rule, the archives could not but be one-sided documents. They cannot and do not tell the case of the other side, except by accident, contradiction, and default. The nature of despotic rule throughout China's long history was not, furthermore, conducive to the conservation of sources of a hostile or critical nature, rarely even from dissenting elements within the ruling class. Thus despotic rule leads to historical despotism, but despotic rule is easier to recognise than historical despotism, and despotic rule is unacceptable while historical despotism is not. It is accepted, without its being realised, with little protest and indeed with pride. Thus the majority of Chinese historical compilations have been accepted, and the archives as the original source of them all were the historical 'Al Capone' behind all these little front-line gangsters. So far, historical doubts and criticism have often aimed at finding out whether any one of these little gangsters had any real authority from his master at the back rather than questioning the authority of the master and proceeding to criticise the system itself.

[43] M.D. Wainwright and N. Matthews, *A Guide to Western Manuscripts and Documents in the British Isles Relating to South and South-East Asia* (London, 1965).

Different political conditions have not freed the non-Chinese archives mentioned in these notes from similar qualifications. Indeed as far as those relating to China are concerned, the archives of Western powers and Japan, government or private, are not only archives of the ruling class but also those of aggressors. These archives, as we have said, are capable of shedding interesting light on multifarious aspects of Chinese life, often light not provided by the Chinese archives themselves. They do so not merely because their creators saw and recorded China from a completely different point of view and were able to pick out things which the Chinese took for granted, but also because they did so from a position of privilege not only *vis-à-vis* the Chinese people at large, but *vis-à-vis* the Chinese government and ruling class as well. This fact is so obvious that it is often forgotten or, if considered, discounted. Thus, historians who condemn the Eurocentric view and treatment of Chinese history and of the relations of various countries with China see nothing wrong in continuing their studies of these subjects solely or predominantly from non-Chinese records, paying occasional spurious footnote homage to Chinese sources. Probably the best illustration of the particular nature of foreign archival material relating to China concerns the Boxer Uprising. That event, studied in isolation, has been held up, on the basis of much 'documentary' evidence, as the greatest example of Chinese 'barbarity' and 'xenophobia'. The most recently discovered such evidence is the diary of a British missionary, Lancelot Giles, which has provided its editor, L.R. Marchant, with the occasion to develop what he describes as a 'diathesis' of 'Chinese anti-foreignism', with the Boxer Uprising as its climax.[44] No Chinese sources were consulted and the Chinese side of the story is briefly dismissed, with the result that Marchant is able to say that 'although some of the actions that were taken [by foreign powers] were shocking by any standards, there is no reason to wholeheartedly condemn the activities of the [foreign] forces' because 'what they [the foreigners] did was very much comprehended by their contemporaries' and 'was not frowned upon in those days'.[45] It is because of this, because foreign aggression and atrocities were comprehended and taken for granted by foreign contemporaries, that we find even the account of someone with a rare degree of objectivity among foreigners in China, that of Dr G.E. Morrison, is one-sided. Morrison's diaries, probably one of the most powerful indictments of China and the Chinese, have graphic details about 'the Chinese barbarity' but little to say about the atrocities of which he was a witness, committed upon the Chinese people.[46] As a result, all contemporary records, government or private,

---

[44] L.R. Marchant, *The Siege of the Peking Legations: a Diary by Lancelot Giles, Edited with Introduction: Chinese Anti-Foreignism and the Boxer Uprising* (Perth, W.A., 1970).
[45] Ibid., pp. 97-8.
[46] The diary, at present under preparation, will be published by us as a part of Morrison's China papers.

are biased, and hence the whole mass of studies around this event is a distorted version, a falsification of history.

If historians are thus to be condemned for knowingly or otherwise aiding the falsification of history by an uncritical reliance upon limited sources and for not having attempted to see the other side of the story or give it equal weight, it must be pointed out that in the case of the Boxer Uprising there is relatively little Chinese material on the actual happening. Moreover, the little there is lacks the vivid detail that makes foreign sources on that event so attractive and colourful. When the foreign powers replaced the Manchu government as the despotic rulers in Peking, no records critical of them were safe to keep. So unsafe was it that even the Manchu government itself felt it necessary to destroy those records which they thought could be used against it.[47] The most truthful testimonials to foreign atrocities and vandalism could never come to light because their authors would have fallen victim to the atrocities and vandalism in question. The danger of being accused of condoning if not actually committing the crime of 'Chinese anti-foreignism', a heinous offence in the political situation for a long period subsequently, was a continuing factor accounting for the scarcity of alternative testimony. Thus, if one were to go by the so-called 'veritable records' alone, one would never realise that the sacking of Peking and the immense suffering of the inhabitants of Peking and the peasants of north China at the hands of foreign troops ever took place.[48]

This brings us to another, the third, consideration, which may be described as the chances of survival of the archival records. Apart from what has been said about Chinese sources on the Boxer Uprising, the stories told at the beginning of these notes about the archives of the Ming and Ch'ing show how precarious and accidental a matter this is. If the fate of official archives was so uncertain, the chances of survival were slim indeed for non-official archives, particularly the papers of individuals. It has rarely been taken into account that for every document that survives there are innumerable that are lost, and for every surviving archive, countless lost ones. Just as the survival of a man need not reflect his intrinsic worth, so the survival of an archive or a document need not reflect its historical merit. The contrary is often the case. It is probably this consideration more than any other that breeds cynicism about attaining any degree of historical truth, but while it may be futile to speculate on what has been lost, too few historians are sufficiently sceptical about the records at their disposal. How many of those who announce that they have consulted 'all available material'

[47] Wu Hsiang-hsiang, 'Ku-kung ts'ang ch'üan-luan shih-liao chu-shih', *Fu Ssu-nien hsien-sheng chi-nien lun-wen chi* XXIII (December, 1951), p. 161.
[48] In this connection, the reader may be interested in an article by Fang Su-sheng, 'Ch'ing shih-lu hsiu-kai wen-t'i', *Fu-jen hsüeh-chih* VIII, 2 (December, 1938), as to the care one has to take in using the *shih-lu* as a source.

fail to consider that even so the footnote they have contributed to general historical knowledge may be erroneous, but instead imagine that they have said the last word on their subject, particularly those who have a thesis or 'diathesis' to prove?

Closely connected with this, there is yet another consideration: that with the fewest possible exceptions, all archival material has been 'processed' in various ways before the historian gets to it. It is true that if archives are not created for the convenience of historians, neither are they created specifically for the glorification or justification of their creators. It is precisely because of this that they may contain 'double-edged' material. Nevertheless, the archives of Imperial China, and to a lesser degree, the government archives of other countries, are not so much purged archives as archives of purged material—purged because of imperial and official exigencies. Because of these exigencies, Chinese government archives are not strictly speaking archives of original records but of copied documents, each carefully phrased, endeavouring to hide as much as to expound, and completely lacking in 'spontaneity'.[49] This spontaneity which is so desirable is not only a matter of vividness or interest for the historian, to be processed out later by some kind of academic value-added tax, but the best indication that can be found of the character of the truth. In this sense, the greater the spontaneity of the original material, the greater should be the humility of the historian. Archival processing does not, however, only rid them of incriminating material, but equally of what appears to the archivists as 'trivial'. Chinese archives are made up essentially of the so-called 'clear copies', not drafts, and with the exception of the more or less standard imperial postscript, rarely contain minutes or marginal notes.[50] These last are the things which often give the student an insight into the working of the official mind, and they enrich and enliven some of the non-Chinese governmental sources. Private collections, particularly papers of individuals, while more personal, vivid and free-ranging, often underwent more expurgation, which, though its nature is not always easy to fathom, is often easily recognisable. It is the historian's duty to take into account what is not there through what is there.

It is this more than anything else that makes archival materials as an historical source not only valid but important. No archive can, or is meant to provide us with a ready and complete picture; what it does is to give us some widely scattered jig-saw pieces, whose assembly requires integrity as much as skill on the part of the historian. In putting the pieces together, he is as often conscious of the shape of the missing parts as of those that are

[49] For the nature and classification of Chinese Imperial archives, see Shan Shih-k'uei, 'Ch'ing-tai chih chao kao ch'ih t'i tsou piao chien shuo-lüeh' and 'Ch'ing-tai t'i-pen chih-tu k'ao', Chang Te-tse, 'Chün-chi ch'u so-ts'ang Ch'ing-ts'e chih fen-lei'; Shan Shih-yüan, 'Ch'ing-tai tang-an shih-ming fa-fan'; Fang Su-sheng, 'Ch'ing-tai tang-an fen-lei wen-t'i', etc.; and Wang Shan-tuan, 'Yung-cheng chu-p'i tsou-che lüeh-shu'.
[50] The well known postscripts of Yung-cheng are rare exceptions.

present, so that the extant evidence leads to doubts and questions concerning it. In this process comes the humility that is so vital to historical inquiry. For this and this alone, no student of history should be allowed to pass forth from a university unless and until he has sufficiently dirtied his hands —and his nostrils—in an archive.

BIBLIOGRAPHY

The following list includes only works which discuss archives, but not those which contain the archives themselves.

Ariizumi Sadao, 'Kensei shiryō shitsu no ayumi to genjō', *Kokuritsu kokkai toshokan biburosu* XXII, 9 (1971), pp. 13-20.

Chang Feng-ch'en, 'Ch'ing-tang so-chi', *Chung-yang ta-hsüeh kuo-hsüeh t'u-shu kuan nien-k'an* II (October 1929), pp. 1-4.

Chang Kuo-jui, 'Wen-hsien kuan tang-an tsai Hu ts'un-chu chi ch'i kung-tso chih ch'ing-hsing', in Wen-hsien t'e-k'an lun-ts'ung chuan-k'an ho-chi (WHTKLT), *Lun-ts'ung*, fu-lu, pp. 59-62.

Chang Te-tse, 'Chün-chi ch'u chi ch'i tang-an', in WHTKLT, *Lun-ts'ung*, lun-shu erh, pp. 57-84.

——, 'Chün-chi ch'u so-ts'ang Ch'ing-ts'e chih fen-lei', in WHTKLT, *Chuan-k'an*, pp. 15-48.

Chao Ch'üan-teng, 'Pei-ching ta-hsüeh so-ts'ang tang-an ti fen-hsi', *Chung-kuo chin-tai ching-chi shih yen-chiu chi-k'an* II, 2 (May 1934), pp. 222-54.

Ch'en Chieh-hsien, ' "Chiu Man-chou tang" shu-lüeh', *Chiu Man-chou tang*, I (Taipei, 1969), pp. 1-56.

'Cheng-li nei-ko ta-k'u Ch'ing-tai Han-wen huang-ts'e chih ching-kuo', in WHTKLT, *T'e-k'an*, pp. 9-16.

'Cheng-li nei-ko ta-k'u Man-wen huang-ts'e chih ching-kuo', in WHTKLT, *T'e-k'an*, pp. 35-6.

'Cheng-li nei-ko ta-k'u Man-wen lao-tang chih yüan-ch'i yü chi-hua', in WHTKLT, *T'e-k'an*, pp. 29-34.

Chu Hsi-tsu, 'Cheng-li Sheng-p'ing shu tang-an chi', *Yen-ching hsüeh-pao* X (December 1931), pp. 2083-2122.

——, 'Ch'ing nei-ko so-shou Ming T'ien-ch'i Ch'ung-chen tang-an Ch'ing che-pa', *Kuo-hsüeh chi-k'an* II, 2 (December 1929), pp. 383-7.

Chung-kuo k'o-hsüeh yüan Li-shih yen-chiu so ti-san so Nan-ching shih-liao cheng-li ch'u, ed., *Li-shih tang-an ti cheng-li fang-fa*, Peking, 1957.

Chung-kuo shih-hsüeh lun-wen so-yin, Peking, 1957.

Fang Su, 'Preface' to *Nei-ko ta-k'u shu-tang chiu-mu pu*, Shanghai, 1936.

Fang Su-sheng, 'Ch'ing-tai tang-an fen-lei wen-t'i', in WHTKLT, *Lun-ts'ung*, lun-shu erh, pp. 27-48.

Hsü Chung-shu, 'Chung-yang yen-chiu yüan Li-shih yü-yen yen-chiu so so-ts'ang tang-an ti fen-hsi', *Chung-kuo chin-tai ching-chi shih yen-chiu chi-k'an* II, 2 (May 1934), pp. 169-222.

——, 'Nei-ko tang-an chih yu-lai chi ch'i cheng-li', Ming-Ch'ing shih-liao, Series A, Hong Kong, 1969.

Ku Chieh-kang, 'Yü-kung hsüeh-hui ti ching-chi tang-an', in WHTKLT, *Lun-ts'ung*, pp. 71-9.

'Kuo-li Pei-p'ing ku-kung po-wu yüan wen-hsien kuan erh-shih-ssu nien-tu kung-tso pao-kao', in WHTKLT, *Lun-ts'ung*, fu-lu, pp. 15-58.

Kuo Ting-yee, 'Major Institutions and Collections on Modern and Contemporary China', *Ch'ing-shih wen-t'i* I, 7 (November 1967), pp. 11-25.

Li Kwang-t'ao, 'Chi nei-ko ta-k'u ts'an-yü tang-an', *Ta-lu tsa-chih* XI, 4 (August 1955), pp. 5-9; XI, 5 (September 1955), pp. 22-8; XI, 6 (September 1955), pp. 22-6.

——, 'Ch'ing T'ai-tsu shih-lu yü Shen-yang chiu-tang', *Ta-lu tsa-chih* XII, 10 (May 1956), pp. 4-6.

——, 'Ming-Ch'ing tang-an', *Fu Ssu-nien hsien-sheng chi-nien lun-wen chi* (July 1951), pp. 21-5.

——, 'Nei-ko ta-k'u ts'an-yü tang-an lun-ts'ung chih san', *Chung-yang yen-chiu yüan k'an* II, 2F (December 1955), pp. 61-81, 83-142.

——, 'Tang-an i-T'ai ching-kuo', Ming-Ch'ing shih-liao, Series E, I, pp. 1a-2b.

Li Yü-shu, *Jih-pen Tung-ching yu-kuan Chung-kuo chin-tai shih tzu-liao ti shou-ts'ang chi chin-tai Chung-Jih kuan-hsi shih yen-chiu ti kai-k'uang*, Taipei, 1969.

Lin Hsiung-hsiang, 'Pen-sheng shih-nien lai ti wen-hsien kung-tso', *T'ai-wan wen-hsien* IX, 1 (March 1958), pp. 51-63.

Lo Fu-i, 'Ch'ing nei-ko ta-k'u Ming-Ch'ing chiu-tang chih li-shih chi ch'i cheng-li', *Ling-nan hsüeh-pao* IX, 1 (December 1948), pp. 125-66.

Marchant, L.R., *A Guide to the Archives and Records of Protestant Christian Missions from the British Isles to China 1796-1914*, Perth, 1966.

Pei-ching tang-an kung-tso wei-yüan hui, ed., *Tang-an kung-tso yüeh-k'an.*

Shan Shih-k'uei, 'Ch'ing-tai chih chao kao ch'ih t'i tsou piao chien shuo-lüeh', in WHTKLT, *Chuan-k'an*, pp. 1-14.

——, 'Ch'ing-tai t'i-pen chih-tu k'ao', in WHTKLT, *Lun-ts'ung*, lun-shu erh, pp. 177-89.

——, 'Nei-ko ta-k'u tsa-tang chung chih Ming-tai wu-chih hsüan-pu', in WHTKLT, *Lun-ts'ung*, lun-shu erh, pp. 191-5.

Shan Shih-yüan, 'Ch'ing-tai tang·an shih-ming fa-fan', in WHTKLT, *Lun-ts'ung*, lun-shu erh, pp. 147-54.

——, 'Ku-kung po-wu yüan wen-hsien kuan so-ts'ang tang-an ti fen-hsi', *Chung-kuo chin-tai ching-chi shih yen-chiu chi-k'an* II, 2 (May 1934), pp. 270-80.

Shen Chien-shih, 'Wen-hsien kuan cheng-li tang-an pao-kao', in WHTKLT, *T'e-k'an*, pp. 1-7.

Teng K'o, 'T'an-t'an nei-ko ta-k'u tang-an', *Wen-wu* LIX, 9 (September 1959), pp. 25-7.

Wang Mei-chuang, 'Cheng-li nei-ko ta-k'u tsa-luan tang-an chi', in WHTKLT, *Lun-ts'ung*, lun-shu erh, pp. 197-205.

Wang Shan-tuan, 'Yung-cheng chu-p'i tsou-che lüeh-shu', in WHTKLT, *Chuan-k'an*, lun-shu, pp. 63-4.

Wen-hsien t'e-k'an lun-ts'ung chuan-k'an ho-chi, Taipei, 1967. This collection is a reprint of three periodicals: *Wen-hsien t'e-k'an*, *Wen-hsien lun-ts'ung*, and *Wen-hsien chuan-k'an*.

Wu Han, 'Ch'ing-hua ta-hsüeh so-ts'ang tang-an ti fen-hsi', *Chung-kuo chin-tai ching-chi shih yen-chiu chi-k'an* II, 2 (May 1934), pp. 255-69.

史　xxi: Chinese Newspapers

JOSEF FASS

Although there is no absolute unanimity among historians as to what exactly constitutes a historical source, the press, and particularly the periodical press, is generally considered to be a most important and sometimes even unique kind of source for studying the history of modern and contemporary societies. According to a traditional classification, the press, including periodical newspapers and magazines, and non-periodical pamphlets, booklets, etc., belongs to the greatest group of written sources used by historians. Within this category, the press comprises the most significant section of narrative sources.

The main tasks of the press are, on the one hand, to inform and, on the other, to influence public opinion and sometimes the ruling elements of a society as well. The proportions of these main functions of the press vary, of course. The element of information prevails in the special press, whereas that of influencing is more important in the political press, particularly in dailies.

When using the press as a historical source, one must, therefore, be extremely critical and cautious of the frequent bias appearing in it, which for various reasons does not always reflect reality accurately. In addition, the existence and activities of censors must be taken into consideration. If possible, it is preferable to confront and to combine press sources with other available sources.

Another problem connected with the use of the press as material for historical research is the vast number of newspapers and magazines and their different qualities. The main aim of this chapter is to give a short account of the history of the press in China, and to point out several at least of the most important papers and journals which can be used as sources for the political, social, and intellectual development of modern and contemporary China.

Whilst the press and its predecessors have existed in Europe since about the sixteenth century, the first traces of what could be considered as a forerunner of the later press in China are found as early as the Han period. It was, naturally, far from a public press in the modern sense, consisting merely of official bulletins or gazettes issued in the capital, at first exclusively for the needs of the bureaucracy. These bulletins, known usually under the name *ti-pao* (i.e. metropolitan gazettes), were originally a kind of correspondence or newsletters sent to the provincial authorities by their residents in the capital.[1]

A turning-point in the evolution of the *ti-pao* was undoubtedly the foundation, in the T'ang, of the Bureau of Official Reports (Chin-tsou yüan). This office was responsible for transmitting imperial edicts to the local authorities through their 'residences' in the capital, and also for handing over, in the same way, reports and other official documents from provinces to the Court.[2] The character of the *ti-pao* changed, consequently, from the former semi-private newsletters into regular official bulletins.

Moreover, during the T'ang period there appeared the first known government gazette, the so-called *K'ai-yüan tsa-pao*, which was printed in the K'ai-yüan period (713-41) of the Emperor Hsüan-tsung. A copy of this gazette is one of the very rare extant examples of the earliest Chinese printing.[3] A further development of the traditional 'press' took place during the Sung era. At that time, *ti-pao* as well as other types of 'newspapers' had already become a comparatively good source of regular information, which was highly appreciated not only by the officials, but also by broader layers of the scholar-gentry class. Typical of the growing interest in news including social gossip was the rise of a series of various official gazettes and also of unofficial tabloid news called *hsiao-pao*.[4]

Official gazettes continued to exist and develop under subsequent dynasties up to the nineteenth century, when they were gradually replaced by a modern Chinese press modelled on Western patterns. Although the official gazettes started to be printed, from the clayblocks, soon after the invention of printing in China, hand-written copies were for a long time preferred because of the bad quality of the print. This situation did not change much even after the introduction of movable type in the gazette-printing in the sixteenth century.[5]

When examining the value of the Chinese traditional 'press' as a source for historical study, one must, first of all, point out its specific features. As mentioned above, this 'press' consisted mostly of rather meagre official bulletins or gazettes which met the needs of the then bureaucracy. Consequently the *ti-pao* as well as other later types of the Chinese traditional 'press' dealt almost exclusively with official matters, such as events at the court, imperial edicts, appointments, promotions or dismissals of officials, memorials of ministers and local dignitaries, etc. Fulfilling the task of a limited source

---

[1] See Lin Yu-tang, *A History of the Press and Public Opinion in China* (Chicago, 1936), p. 14 and Tseng Hsü-pai and others, ed., *Chung-kuo hsin-wen shih* (Taipei, 1966), p. 65.
[2] See *Hsin-wen shih*, p. 71 and Lin Yu-tang, *A History of the Press*, pp. 14-16.
[3] See Ko Kung-chen, *Chung-kuo pao-hsüeh shih* (Peking, 1955), pp. 26-8.
[4] See *Hsin-wen shih*, pp. 82-4, and Lin Yu-tang, *A History of the Press*, p. 17.
[5] Ibid., pp. 11, 12, 77.

of information for a very small section of the population, the ancient Chinese 'press', on the other hand, almost never performed the function of social and political criticism. Thus, considering the nature of the traditional 'press' with all its limitation, the fact that not many authenticated copies have been preserved, and that students of ancient China's history have at their disposal other, better preserved and more complete sources, one may conclude that the traditional Chinese 'press' is not a very important historical source.

The situation is, however, quite different, for the modern Chinese press. Although some indications of possible development towards modernisation were apparent in the framework of the traditional system of Chinese journalism even before the nineteenth century, particularly since the middle of the Ch'ing era, the genuine modern Chinese press, i.e. a more or less independent press working on a commercial basis and meeting the demands of broader masses of readers, was developed only at the beginning of the nineteenth century. At first, only monthlies were published, later there were weeklies and, finally, dailies.

The early growth of the modern Chinese press was due to the efforts and activities of certain foreign missionaries and merchants. Among prominent pioneers of the Chinese missionary press were men like Robert Morrison, Karl Gützlaff, James Legge, Walter Henry Medhurst, and, somewhat later, Charles B. Hillier, Alexander Wylie, and Timothy Richard. Some of them co-operated, from the very beginning, with Chinese associates: for instance, James Legge, with one of the first advocates of reform in China, Wang T'ao, who used to be considered as the founder of modern Chinese journalism.[6]

The history of the development of the modern Chinese press can be divided into the following major stages: (1) the beginnings (1815-95), (2) the pre-revolutionary period (1895-1911), (3) the republican period (1911-27), (4) the Nationalist or Kuomintang period (1927-49), (5) the Communist period (since 1949).

The first modern Chinese magazine was *Ch'a shih-su mei-yüeh t'ung-chi chuan*, founded by Robert Morrison in Malacca on 5 August 1815.[7] The first modern magazine actually on Chinese territory appeared somewhat later. It was called *Tung-hsi yang k'ao mei-yüeh t'ung-chi chuan*, and was established by Karl Gützlaff in Canton in 1833.[8] Soon afterwards, several other missionary magazines published in Chinese followed, both in China and abroad.

Far more important, as a historical source, than the early Chinese-written missionary press is, however, the Chinese daily press, the beginnings of which

[6] Ibid., pp. 78-9.
[7] See *Hsin-wen shih*, p. 125.
[8] Ibid., p. 133.

date back to the 1850s and 1860s. At first published by foreigners and soon afterwards also by Chinese themselves, the dailies, as well as other political periodicals, already dealt much more with current events and with the principal issues China was facing at that time. This makes the dailies from their very beginning an extremely interesting and sometimes even unique source of information helping historians to know and understand better the political, economic, social, and intellectual development of nineteenth and twentieth century China.

The first Chinese daily was *Chung-wai hsin-pao*, which owed its origin to the initiative of Wu T'ing-fang in Hong Kong in 1858 as the Chinese edition of the local English journal *Daily Press*. It ceased publication in 1919.[9] The first daily on the mainland was *Shang-hai hsin-pao*, the Chinese edition of the well-known *North China Herald*. It started first as a weekly in November 1861, and became a daily on 2 July 1872. Shortly afterwards, on 31 December 1872, *Shang-hai hsin-pao* stopped publication.

Of the ever growing number of other Chinese newspapers of that period, the most important were *Shen-pao*, *Hsin-wen pao*, and *Hua-tzu jih-pao*. *Shen-pao*, founded on 30 April 1872, was for many years the most long-standing and influential Chinese newspaper. It ceased publication in 1949. *Hsin-wen pao*, another Shanghai daily, for a long time probably the second most important Chinese newspaper, was published from 17 February 1893. Competing with *Shen-pao*, it laid particular stress upon the commercial and economic problems of the country. *Hua-tzu jih-pao* appeared in Hong Kong from 1864 to 1941.[11]

The period 1895-1911 was, in many respects, one of the most brilliant epochs in the history of modern Chinese journalism. The protracted general crisis of the country and China's rapidly worsening international position, particularly after its defeat in 1895 in the war with Japan, forced some representatives of the intellectual élite and patriotic people (mostly students) to search for a way out by propagating the modernisation of China, either by means of gradual reforms or by radical transformation of the existing system and stagnating society. Consequently, there appeared at that time in China and abroad a series of new periodicals which not only reflected the principal intellectual tendencies of the period, but some of which even contributed greatly to the ideological and organisational preparation for the coming revolution of 1911.

Among the prominent periodicals advocating the reform movement and the idea of a constitution were the *Shih-wu pao*, *Ch'ing-i pao*, and *Hsin-min ts'ung-pao*. *Shih-wu pao*, an organ of the Shanghai branch of a reform society called Ch'iang-hsüeh hui, was published in Shanghai three times a month

[9] Ibid., p. 140.
[10] Ibid., pp. 143, 145.
[11] Ibid., pp. 140, 145, 147, 153.

from July 1896 until May 1898.[12] *Ch'ing-i pao*, edited by Liang Ch'i-ch'ao (one of the most famous journalists of modern China), was issued in Yokohama three times a month from 13 December 1898 until the end of 1901.[13] *Hsin-min ts'ung-pao*, a successor of the *Ch'ing-i pao* and also edited by Liang Ch'i-ch'ao, was published as a fortnightly in Yokohama from 8 February 1902 until July 1907 and was particularly famous because of its well-known ideological controversy with the revolutionary magazine *Min-pao*.[14]

Among those advocating a republican revolution three were especially prominent, *Chung-kuo jih-pao*, *Su-pao*, and *Min-pao*. *Chung-kuo jih-pao* was the first Chinese revolutionary daily, edited by Sun Yat-sen's partisans, and was published in Hong Kong from December 1899 until 1913.[15] *Su-pao* was published in Shanghai from 1896 until June 1903. It was at first a journal advocating the reform movement, but became, for a short period of several months preceding its suspension, the organ of a revolutionary society called Ai-kuo hsüeh-she. The journal is well known because of the so-called *Su-pao* case in 1903 in which Chang Ping-lin and Tsou Jung were involved.[16] *Min-pao* was the most important Chinese revolutionary periodical before 1911 and the organ of Sun Yat-sen's T'ung-meng hui. It was published somewhat irregularly from 26 November 1905 until October 1908 as a monthly; after a break of about two years, two final numbers were issued in 1910.[17]

From the numerous other Chinese political periodicals of that period, at least the *Tung-fang tsa-chih* should be mentioned. Published in Shanghai by the Shang-wu yin-shu kuan from 1904 until 1949, it has had the longest history of existence of any modern Chinese magazine and is, at the same time, one of the most useful historical sources among the Chinese periodicals of the first half of the twentieth century.[18]

The situation of the Chinese press in the period between 1911 and 1927 corresponded with the complicated and turbulent development of the first years of the Republic of China. Soon after the Ch'ing dynasty was overthrown, a great number of new, primarily political, periodicals appeared, both in the big cities and in the provinces. This sudden increase in quantity was, however, not always accompanied by adequate progress in the quality of the journalism. According to incomplete statistical data, there were some 500 dailies in the first period of the Republic, one-fifth of which were published in Peking.[19] The increase in number of periodicals continued

[12] Ibid., p. 199.
[13] Ibid., pp. 201-3.
[14] Ibid., p. 203.
[15] Ibid., pp. 206-9.
[16] Ibid., pp. 209-11.
[17] Ibid., pp. 217-18.
[18] Ibid., p. 231.
[19] Ibid., p. 263 and Lin Yu-tang, *A History of the Press*, p. 116.

during the following years, with the exception of the period of Yüan Shih-k'ai's autocratic rule.[20]

During the period 1911-27, the following dailies were probably the most interesting or influential (some of them having been founded already before 1911, the others after the Revolution): in Peking, *Ch'en-pao* (1921); in Tientsin, *I-shih pao* (1915) and *Ta-kung pao* (1902), both rather progressive; in Shanghai, *Shen-pao* (1872) and *Hsin-wen pao* (1893), both conservative, *Shih-pao* (1905), and *Min-kuo jih-pao* (1916); and in Hong Kong, *Hua-tzu jih-pao* (1864).[21]

The May Fourth Movement of 1919 and the New Culture Movement (approximately 1916-25) stimulated the second most brilliant epoch in the history of Chinese journalism. The main role in the above mentioned movements was played by a number of new magazines of a half-literary, half-political nature. Among more than 400 such magazines promulgating new ideas, new literature written in vernacular Chinese, science, democracy, social reform, and later, at least in some cases, the Russian revolution of 1917 and Communist ideology, by far the most important and influential was *Hsin ch'ing-nien*. Founded by Ch'en Tu-hsiu in Shanghai on 15 September 1915, this monthly was published, sometimes not quite regularly, until 1 July 1922. Later, between June 1923 and December 1924, four numbers of a quarterly *Hsin ch'ing-nien* appeared, edited by Ch'ü Ch'iu-pai, and finally, between April 1925 and July 1926, an irregular magazine of the same name published five numbers.[22]

Some other important magazines of that period were: *Hsin-ch'ao*, a monthly established by a group of students of the University of Peking on 1 January 1919 (this magazine, which propagated the necessity of a literary revolution, ceased publication in March 1922); *Nu-li chou-pao*, edited by Hu Shih and published in Peking in 1922 and 1923 (this magazine advocated liberalism, democracy and Dewey's pragmatism); *Hsiang-tao chou-k'an*, founded in Shanghai on 13 September 1922 by Ch'en Tu-hsiu and others as an organ of the Chinese Communist Party (it later moved to Canton and continued publication until July 1927).[23]

For the last two periods, i.e., those of the Kuomintang and Communist rule in China, only a few remarks and the most important information is given here. In both periods, the development of the press and the character of journalism have been deeply influenced by the specific features of the

---

[20] In 1921, there existed in China 1,137 periodicals, of which 550 were dailies. In 1926 there were about 2,000 periodicals, including 628 dailies. Ibid., p. 124.

[21] See *Hsin-wen shih*, pp. 326, 355, 360.

[22] See Chow Tse-tsung, *The May Fourth Movement, Intellectual Revolution in Modern China* (Cambridge, Mass., 1960), pp. 44-5.

[23] See Chow Tse-tsung, *Research Guide to the May Fourth Movement, Intellectual Revolution in Modern China, 1915-1924* (Cambridge, Mass., 1963), pp. 43, 102, 106 and Ko Kung-chen, *Pao-hsüeh shih*, pp. 191-2.

régimes, which placed the press under strict control, and by all the stormy events that have been China's experience since 1927. Nevertheless, even under such circumstances, the press has not lost the capacity to be an important source of information for historians studying contemporary China.

In the period 1927-49, attention should be paid particularly to the dailies: *Chung-yang jih-pao*, founded in Nanking on 1 February 1929 as the central organ of the Kuomintang government; *Shen-pao*, *Hsin-wen pao*, *Shih-shih hsin-pao*, and *Min-kuo jih-pao*, all published in Shanghai; *Ch'en-pao* and *Shih-chieh jih-pao*, both published in Peking; *Ta-kung pao* and *I-shih hsin-pao*, both published in Tientsin; *Hsin min-pao* and *Min-sheng pao*, both published in Nanking; and *Chung-shan jih-pao*, published in Canton. From the newspapers of the Chinese Communist Party of that time, at least two must be mentioned, namely *Hsin-hua jih-pao*, published in Chungking during the Sino-Japanese War, and *Chieh-fang jih-pao* published in Yen-an.[24] The most outstanding magazines of that period were *Tung-fang tsa-chih* and *Hsin Chung-hua*. Further material on periodical literature in the Republican period may be found in the chapter 'Sources on Kuomintang and Republican China' elsewhere in this volume.

Since the People's Republic of China was established in 1949, the whole system and structure of the press on the Chinese mainland have changed profoundly. Most of the former dailies and magazines have disappeared, and new periodicals serving the goals of the Communist Party have been founded. It is unnecessary to deal with them here, since they are considered in detail in the chapter on the sources for the People's Republic of China. It remains only to mention at least some of the main Chinese papers outside the mainland since 1949. In Taiwan the principal ones are perhaps *Chung-yang jih-pao*, *Chung-hua jih-pao*, and *Lien-ho pao*. The main Hong Kong dailies include *Hsing-tao jih-pao* and *Kung-shang jih-pao* (both pro-Kuomintang), and *Ta-kung pao* and *Wen-hui pao* (both pro-Communist).[26]

BIBLIOGRAPHY

Sample list of Chinese newspapers (before 1949).
Ch'a shih-su mei-yüeh t'ung-chi chuan, Malacca, 1815-21, monthly.
Ch'ing-i pao, Yokohama, 1898-1901, every ten days.
Chung-kuo jih-pao, Hong Kong, 1899-1913, daily.
Chung-wai hsin-pao, Ning-po, 1854-60, fortnightly.
Chung-wai hsin-pao, Hong Kong, 1858-1919, first Chinese daily.
Chung-yang jih-pao, Nanking, later Taipei, 1929- , daily.

[24] See *Hsin-wen shih*, pp. 355-61 and Lin Yu-tang, *A History of the Press*, pp. 131, 135.
[25] See *Hsin-wen shih*, pp. 812-15.
[26] Ibid., pp. 513, 518, 521-3, 739.

Hsiang-tao chou-k'an, Shanghai, later Canton, 1922-7, weekly.
Hsin-ch'ao, Peking, 1919-22, student periodical.
Hsin-min ts'ung-pao, Yokohama, 1902-7, fortnightly.
Hua-tzu jih-pao, Hong Kong, 1864-1941, daily.
Min-pao, Tokyo, 1905-10, daily.
Nu-li chou-pao, Peking, 1922-3, weekly.
Shang-hai hsin-pao, Shanghai, 1861-72, every other day, later daily.
Shen-pao, Shanghai, 1872-1949, daily.
Shih-wu pao, Shanghai, 1896-8, three times a month.
Su-pao, Shanghai, 1896-1903, very anti-Manchu.
T'u-hua hsin-pao, Shanghai, 1880-1912, monthly.
Tung-fang tsa-chih, Shanghai, then Taiwan, 1904- , monthly, later fort-
    nightly.
Tung-hsi yang k'ao mei-yüeh t'ung-chi chuan, Canton, later Singapore, 1833-7,
    monthly. First periodical published in China itself.
Wan-kuo kung-pao, Shanghai, 1875-1904.

史 XXII: Sources on Kuomintang and Republican China

STEPHEN FITZGERALD

The period of the rise and ascendancy of the Kuomintang spans the vital half-century from the collapse of the Ch'ing dynasty to the victory of the Chinese Communist Party. While the Kuomintang and its forerunners played a major and sometimes seminal role in the process of revolutionary change and modernisation, the problems of twentieth century China that have received the greatest attention since 1949 have been those related to the disintegration of the old order and the rise of the new. In the study of Republican China, the origins and development of the cause that triumphed have tended increasingly to predominate over the study of the cause that failed.

The sources discussed in the following pages relate primarily to the Kuomintang between 1911 and 1949 and China after the establishment of the National Government in Nanking. They represent a small selection from a vast amount of material and will be familiar to those who have worked on the period. The selection is intended to outline some of the more useful general sources on the Kuomintang and Nationalist China, and to indicate some of the basic source materials available for more detailed historical research. Sources dealing exclusively with such subjects as the Hsing-Chung hui, the T'ung-meng hui, the Peking Government, warlordism, the Chinese Communist Party, and Japanese puppet governments are not included.[1] Many of the sources mentioned, however, also embrace aspects of these subjects and are useful for identifying other sources on twentieth century China before 1949.

There was certainly no dearth of source material in Republican China. The emergence of modern political parties and a modern bureaucracy, the polemics of reform and revolution, and the debates on cultural values, political programs, and philosophies, all contributed to a remarkable growth in the output of documents and publications. The sources have to be tracked down in a variety of collections around the world, and all collections are deficient in some, unfortunately often the same, areas. The circumstances in which the Chinese Nationalists moved their seat of government from one city to another and then to Taiwan did not always allow a

---

[1] Some of these are discussed in the chapters on the History of the Chinese Communist Party, Newspapers, and the Overseas Chinese.

high priority to be given to the transport of archives and libraries. The Kuomintang did, nevertheless, manage to take a surprisingly large amount of material to Taiwan and this remains potentially the richest source of archive material outside the Chinese mainland, although much that is interesting and valuable is not easily accessible to scholars at present.

The main research collections in Taiwan are those of the Institute of Modern History in Academia Sinica, Nan-kang, and the Kuomintang Archives under the control of the Compiling Committee of Historical Materials of the History of the Kuomintang. The Institute of Modern History has two particularly valuable collections of the post-1911 period: the records of the Chinese Foreign Ministry from 1911 to 1927 and of the various ministries concerned with economic affairs from 1912 to 1949. The Institute has issued a number of publications based on its collections, including a checklist of the Foreign Ministry records on Sino-Japanese relations to 1927, three volumes of historical materials on Sino-Russian relations, and a series of monographs, some of which are concerned with the early Republican period. For some years the Institute has also been conducting an oral history project.

The Kuomintang Archives contain a far greater amount of material, but their extent has yet to be fully explored. In 1968, the Institute of Modern History published an index for a selection of the Kuomintang Archives covering the period 1902-49, *Chung-kuo hsien-tai shih tzu-liao tiao-ch'a mu-lu*, which also includes part of the Institute's own collection 1901-26. Although this index runs to ten volumes and one supplement, it is understood to represent only about one-tenth of the total holdings. Beginning with newspapers, periodicals, and official gazettes, the index covers such subjects as general historical materials, Sun Yat-sen, Chiang Kai-shek and other revolutionary leaders, foreign policy, the Sino-Japanese War, and the Chinese civil war. While the index does list documents of official government agencies, it does not appear to include confidential Party archives for the latter half of the Republican period. There are, however, unpublished subject catalogues in the archives, and the Kuomintang is willing to allow scholars to consult these catalogues, which appear to be quite comprehensive, and to have access to the catalogued materials on request.

A most important series of archive materials published by the Kuomintang Archives is the *Ke-ming wen-hsien*. It includes such materials as official documents, reports, decisions, directives, and announcements, as well as letters and other communications, memoirs and transcripts of oral history. The series began in 1953 and now runs to some fifty volumes. Publication of these volumes does not follow the chronological sequence of the Revolution, but is arranged according to subject or groups of subjects, and the topics covered so far have ranged from the Hsing-Chung hui to the Northern Expedition and the Sino-Japanese War.

The Kuomintang Archives has also reprinted a number of books, compilations, and newspapers of the pre-1911 period, including publications of the T'ung-meng hui and other revolutionary parties and individuals. These are issued under the general titles *Chung-hua min-kuo shih-liao ts'ung-pien*, and *Chung-hua min-kuo shih-liao ts'ung-pien ti-erh ts'e*.

Most government organisations in Taiwan also maintain their own archives, although access depends on the type and, particularly, political sensitivity of the materials concerned, rather than on set periods of time. Scholars have been able to work in the archives of the Ministries of Defence and Justice, for example, although primarily for sources on the Chinese Communist movement. The value of ministry archives for the Republican period varies greatly from one to another, and some government bodies, such as the Overseas Chinese Affairs Commission, appear to have very little material, or at least very little which can be made available to scholars.

Outside Taiwan, some of the best collections are in the United States, in the libraries at Harvard, Yale, Cornell, and Columbia Universities, the Library of Congress, and the Hoover Library. There are also significant collections in the Fung Ping Shan Library in Hong Kong, and in various libraries in Japan, Britain, and the Soviet Union. The problems of locating and obtaining materials are slowly being overcome by the publication of library catalogues and checklists, and the reprint and microfilm facilities of a number of libraries and institutions. Of special interest in this respect is the Center for Chinese Research Materials in Washington, which locates and reproduces material from various parts of the world. It initiates its own projects and welcomes requests from individuals and institutions for the reproduction of specific items. Among the items currently available from the Center are twenty-six titles on minor political parties which emerged in China in the 1940s, forty-six on the war against Japan, twelve on higher education, the thirty-seven volumes of the *Chiao-t'ung shih*, published by the Ministry of Communications from 1930 to 1937, and a number of newspapers and periodicals.

Official records and other sources of the Republican period remaining on the Chinese mainland, although closed to foreign scholars, have been collected and preserved and may one day provide a whole new fund of information for research. Publications such as the *Chung-kuo shih-hsüeh lun-wen so-yin*, and the *Ch'üan-kuo Chung-wen ch'i-k'an lien-ho mu-lu*, indicate that holdings of serial publications exceed by far any collections elsewhere in the world. The latter, based on the resources of some fifty libraries, includes meticulous information on dates, publishers, frequency and place of publication, changes in periodical titles, and the holdings in each library. It is certainly the best work of its kind. The Institute of Historical Research in the Chinese Academy of Sciences, Peking, has been engaged, since the early 1950s, on a systematic collection of historical material, from documents and newspapers to diaries and photographs and oral and written memoirs. Some of the results of this massive project have appeared in the *Chin-tai shih tzu-liao*, a bi-monthly publication from 1954 until 1959, when it was changed into an irregular series of volumes on specific subjects. In addition, there have been separate publications of the works of Sun Yat-sen and other prominent figures such as Ts'ai Yüan-p'ei,[2] personal reminiscences, and the results of oral history projects,[3] compilations of historical material by historians such as Chang Kuo-kan and Wu Yü-chang who were active in the affairs of Republican China,[4] and reprints like the excellent edition of the *Min-pao*.[5] Many of these are available outside China, and some are discussed in the very useful annotated bibliography compiled by Albert Feuerwerker and S. Cheng, *Chinese Communist Studies of Modern Chinese History*.[6]

As the period of Kuomintang rule in China recedes into the past and the personalities begin to fade into the obscurity of a lost cause, basic biographical information becomes increasingly important, for the history of the Kuomintang was pre-eminently one of personalities, cliques, and factions. Two compilations of the 1930s which deserve mention are Fan Yin-nan, *Tang-tai Chung-kuo ming-jen lu*, and Chia I-chün, *Chung-hua min-kuo ming-jen chuan*. Detailed information on government officials was published from time to time by the Ch'üan-hsü pu (Ministry of Personnel). An interesting confidential compilation by the Chinese Communist Party prepared in 1945 is the *Kuo-min tang liu-chieh chung-wei ko p'ai-hsi ming-tan*, which gives biographical notes on the members of the Central Executive Committee and the Central Supervisory Committee of the Kuomintang. Boorman and Howard's comprehensive *Biographical Dictionary of Republican China*, although not in all respects a primary source, contains many contributions from people who had first-hand knowledge of, or personal acquaintance with, the individuals concerned, and is the most useful single compilation of biographical material.[7]

The history of the Kuomintang itself to 1949 is moderately well documented, although it is to be hoped that the Kuomintang will some day make available some of the confidential documents of its more recent past,

[2] *Sun Chung-shan hsüan-chi*, 2 vols. (Peking, 1956); *Ts'ai Yüan-p'ei hsüan-chi* (Peking, 1959).
[3] For example, *Hsin-hai shou-i hui-i lu*, edited by the Hupeh Committee of the Chinese People's Political Consultative Conference, 2 vols. (Wuhan, 1957); Ho Hsiang-ning, *Hui-i Sun Chung-shan ho Liao Chung-k'ai* (Peking, 1957).
[4] Chang Kuo-kan, *Hsin-hai ke-ming shih-liao* (Shanghai, 1958). Wu Yü-chang, *Hsin-hai ke-ming* (Peking, 1961). One of the most detailed chronicles of the Pei-yang warlords is the six-volume work by T'ao Chü-yin, *Pei-yang chün-fa t'ung-chih shih-ch'i shih-hua* (Peking, 1958).
[5] *Min-pao*, 4 vols. (Peking, 1957; Supplement, 1958).
[6] See also Albert Feuerwerker, ed., *History in Communist China* (Cambridge, Mass., 1968), for a number of illuminating essays on historical research in China.
[7] Eugene Wu, *Leaders of Twentieth Century China*, is possibly the most useful introduction to biographical sources for the period.

particularly from the early 1920s onwards. To do so while Chiang Kai-shek and certain others are still living is probably politically difficult. The Party's public debates, statements, manifestos, and directives are fairly easily identified, although for the first decade of the Republic they are scattered in a wide variety of sources. They can at least be traced and dated in the writings of Party historians and theoreticians like Tsou Lu, Feng Tzu-yu, and Tai Chi-t'ao, although the full texts are not always given, and where original documents are not elsewhere available one cannot be sure how much they have been edited.[8] The function of the Kuomintang Party historians is only marginally less political than that of the official historians of imperial or Communist China, and this function has been particularly evident since 1949.

Beginning in August 1928, the Central Executive Committee of the Kuomintang published a *Chung-yang tang-wu yüeh-k'an*, the best contemporary public source on Party work, plans, and personnel. A contemporary record of Party affairs is provided also by revolutionary or Kuomintang-sponsored newspapers. The most important of the latter in the first two decades of the Republic was the *Min-kuo jih-pao*, published in Shanghai and Canton from 1914, the spiritual successor to the T'ung-meng hui newspapers published in Shanghai before the 1911 Revolution. This was eventually superseded by the official organ which commenced publication in 1928, the *Chung-yang jih-pao*. These two publications provide a chronicle both of Kuomintang and National Government history and of daily events seen from a Kuomintang perspective.[9]

From time to time, the Kuomintang also published selections of documents and historical materials. These include, for example, *Ch'ing-tang yün-tung* (1927), *Chung-kuo Kuo-min tang nien-chien* (1934), *Chung-kuo Kuo-min tang hsüan-yen chi* (1938), *Tang-wu fa-kuei hui-pien* (1939), *Chung-kuo Kuo-min tang cheng-kang cheng-ts'e chi chung-yao hsüan-yen* (1940), *Chung-kuo Kuo-min tang wu-shih nien lai wai-chiao tou-cheng ti ch'eng-kung* (1943), *Chung-kuo Kuo-min tang fa-kuei chi-yao* (1944), and the irregular serial publication of the Central Committee for the Compilation of Materials on Party History, Tang-shih shih-liao ts'ung-k'an. These compilations, of course, are selective and are best used in conjunction with Party bulletins and other sources.

The establishment of the National Government in 1927 brought with it a proliferation of the government publications characteristic of modern bureaucracies. In addition to official yearbooks in both Chinese and English, the Central Government published a *Kuo-min cheng-fu kung-pao*, thrice-monthly from April 1927 and daily from October 1929.[10] Similar

---

[8] A selection of the works of these writers is listed in the bibliography.
[9] See also Chapter XXI.
[10] Before the establishment of the National Government in 1927, the Peking government published a *Cheng-fu kung-pao* from 1912 to 1926.

kung-pao, or official gazettes, were also issued by the Executive Yüan, the Legislative Yüan, the Judicial Yüan, and the ministries and commissions under the Executive Yüan.[11] Many of the ministries also published or sponsored for more general public consumption magazines which contain articles and commentaries as well as laws and regulations.[12] Collections and compilations were also published irregularly, such as the early *Chung-hua min-kuo kuo-min cheng-fu, fu Kuang-tung sheng cheng-fu tsu-chih* (1925), *Chung-hua min-kuo fa-kuei hui-pien* (1934), *Chung-hua min-kuo hsien-hsing fa-kuei ta-ch'üan* (1934), and *Chung-hua min-kuo fa-kuei ta-ch'üan* (1937). A serial publication is the Min-kuo fa-kuei chi-k'an, which commenced in 1929. Similar collections were issued for particular areas of government work: for example, *Kuo-min cheng-fu kung-pu ch'ü-hsiang-chen chih ti-fang tzu-chih ch'üan-shu* (1930), *Wai-chiao pu fa-kuei hui-pien* (1930 and 1937), *Chiao-yü fa-ling* (1947). Some of the ministries also published their own year-books.[13]

A comprehensive collection of treaties (from 1927 to 1961) published by the Foreign Ministry in Taipei in 1958 and revised in 1963 is the *Chung-wai t'iao-yüeh chi-pien (Treaties between the Republic of China and Foreign States 1927-1961)*. The collection includes both Chinese texts and the corresponding texts in other languages. The most detailed and reliable single collection of maps produced in the period is that published in the 1934 compilation *Chung-hua min-kuo hsin ti-t'u*.

In these official publications can be traced the policies and programs of the Kuomintang, the structure and workings of the government, its initiatives, and its responses to the internal and foreign policy problems of the time. They offer some insight into the way in which Chinese officials perceived and confronted the problems and disorders of Republican China, and to some extent also they provide a general picture of the thinking of leading politicians and some of the causes of the government's successes and failures.

By far the richest source of material, however, is contained in non-official publications, particularly the periodical press, the growth of which was quite phenomenal in the 1920s and 1930s. In the pages of the many cultural and political magazines which flourished in the period may be found the ideas of leading Nationalist politicians and bureaucrats, as well as factions within the National Government and outright opponents of the Kuomintang.

[11] *Hsing-cheng yüan kung-pao* (first published 1928), *Li-fa yüan kung-pao* (1929), *Ssu-fa yüan kung-pao* (1932). Other examples are the *Nei-cheng kung-pao* (1928), *Wai-chiao pu kung-pao* (1928), *T'ieh-tao kung-pao* (1928), *Kung-shang kung-pao* (1928), *Nung-k'uang kung-pao* (1928), *Tsui-kao fa-yüan kung-pao* (1928), *Ts'ai-cheng kung-pao* (1927), *Chiao-yü kung-pao* (1929), *Hai-chün kung-pao* (1929), *Wei-sheng kung-pao* (1929), *Chiao-t'ung kung-pao* (1929), *Ch'iao-wu wei-yüan hui kung-pao* (1932).

[12] Examples are the *Nei-cheng yen-chiu yüeh-pao*, *Wai-chiao p'ing-lun*, and *Ch'iao-wu yüeh-pao*.

[13] For example, *Chung-kuo ching-chi nien-chien*, published in 1934, 1935, 1936, *Ch'üan-kuo yin-hang nien-chien*, published in 1934, 1935, 1936; *Chung-kuo wai-chiao nien-chien*, 1934, 1935, 1936; and *Nei-cheng nien-chien*, 4 vols., published once only, in 1936.

In addition to the long-established *Tung-fang tsa-chih,* and the famous *Hsin ch'ing-nien* edited by Ch'en Tu-hsiu, leading magazines which concerned themselves with current political and social issues included *Kai-tsao, Chien-she, Hsien-tao, T'ai-p'ing yang, Hsien-tai p'ing-lun, Kuo-wen chou-pao, Shih-shih yüeh-k'an, Tu-li p'ing-lun, Fu-hsing yüeh-k'an,* and *Min-chien.*[14] One of the outstanding periodicals critical of Chiang Kai-shek in the 1930s was that edited by Hu Han-min, *San-min chu-i yüeh-k'an.*[15]

Hsüeh-pao or journals, published by such universities as Tsinghua, Yenching, Ling-nan, Nanking, and Amoy, are of interest not simply for information about youth, students, education, and research, but also because they often provide commentaries on contemporary problems, and were a vehicle for scholarly discussion by many people who were directly involved in the political, economic, and cultural life of the nation. In addition to the *hsüeh-pao,* there were many other university periodicals devoted to special areas of interest. The *Ching-chi t'ung-chi chi-k'an* and the *Cheng-chih ching-chi hsüeh-pao,* for example, were published by Nankai University in Tientsin. Chinan University in Shanghai published a number of periodicals on China's relations with Southeast Asia and the Overseas Chinese, including *Nan-yang yen-chiu* and *Nan-yang ch'ing-pao.* In Canton, Chungshan University published *Hsien-tai shih-hsüeh* and *Chiao-yü yen-chiu.*

Apart from university publications, there were dozens of other periodicals dealing with either general topics or specific subjects such as politics, economics, education, foreign affairs, law, and culture.[16] Although the periodical press was exclusively the product of the literate section of the population, it is still one of the best sources of information on Chinese society and the Chinese people, and even though many of the periodicals were short-lived they are still valuable sources.

Republican China was also the period in which modern mass circulation newspapers came into their own, and they are an indispensable source. In addition to the main dailies, there were also many smaller provincial and local newspapers, some published two or three times a week. Where they can be found, they are extremely useful for studying local conditions, but there are very few collections outside China, and in many cases such collections have only a few issues. This deficiency is compensated to a limited extent by the Chinese-language newspapers published outside China, in

---

[14] Publication details of these and other periodicals are given in some of the bibliographies, and in *Ch'üan-kuo Chung-wen ch'i-k'an lien-ho mu-lu* (Peking, 1961).

[15] This is available on microfilm from the Center for Chinese Research Materials in Washington.

[16] In addition to those which deal with government and politics, some of which are mentioned above, others include, on economics, *Ching-chi hsüeh chi-k'an, Ching-chi t'ung-chi yüeh-chih, Hsin ching-chi;* on education, *Chiao-yü tsa-chih;* foreign affairs, *Wai-chiao yüeh-pao, Wai-chiao chou-pao, Wai-chiao yen-chiu;* and on law, *Chung-hua fa-hsüeh tsa-chih, Hsien-tai fa-hsüeh yüeh-k'an.*

Hong Kong, Southeast Asia, and the United States. One of the foremost concerns of the Hong Kong and Overseas Chinese newspapers was China, and they offer a rich source of information on events in China, particularly in the south, as well as the activities of the Kuomintang among the Overseas Chinese. There are fairly extensive holdings of the Hong Kong, United States, Malayan, and Singapore Chinese newspapers in the Fung Ping Shan Library in Hong Kong, the Harvard-Yenching Library, the Library of Congress, the Hoover Library, the University of Singapore Library, and the British Museum.

Newspapers, periodicals, and official serial publications provide the most abundant source for the period, at least in quantity, and it is to the combing of such sources that the historian must inevitably resort. There are a number of useful indexes, although they can sometimes be a rather treacherous companion for newspapers. Indexes published in the 1930s include the *Ch'i-k'an so-yin* and the *Jih-pao so-yin*, both monthly publications of the Sun Yat-sen Institute for the Advancement of Culture and Education in Nanking; those which appeared in the *Jen-wen yüeh-k'an*; and the *Chung-wen tsa-chih so-yin*, compiled by T'an Cho-yüan. The *Chung-kuo shih-hsüeh lun-wen so-yin* is also a useful source.[17]

The 'Thought of Sun Yat-sen' provided, in theory at least, the main-stream of Kuomintang ideology. His famous lectures on the Three Principles of the People, delivered in 1924, were published in a volume edited by Tsou Lu in 1925, *San-min chu-i*. Another collection, dictated by Sun in 1917, which includes his ideas on foreign policy and international politics, is *Chung-kuo ts'un-wang wen-t'i*. A volume of selected works, *Sun Chung-shan hsien-sheng wen-chi*, edited by Kan Nai-kuang, was published in 1925. The most complete edition of his works published in the period is that edited by Hu Han-min, *Tsung-li ch'üan-chi*. A very detailed index to Sun's writings, *Tsung-li i-chiao so-yin*, was published in 1937.[18]

The more important writings of or about such prominent figures as Sun Yat-sen, Liao Chung-k'ai, Chiang Kai-shek, and Wang Ching-wei may be identified in the bibliographies, and their major works are available in most East Asian library collections. The National War College Library in Taiwan has some interesting items, which are listed in its *T'u-shu mu-lu, ti-i chi*. Nevertheless it is still necessary to cull the periodicals and daily press for texts and reports of many of their speeches and essays, and even more so for those of lesser personalities. There are many scholarly works which are

---

[17] Collections outside China can be traced through published library catalogues, and such works as *Chinese Periodicals in British Libraries* (The British Museum, London, 1965), and I. Hurlbert, comp., *Cornell University: Holdings of pre-1949 Chinese Mainland Periodicals* (Ithaca, New York, 1966).

[18] Editions of the writings of Sun and other leaders have also been published in Taiwan since 1949. See also the Peking edition of 1956, *Sun Chung-shan hsüan-chi*.

well worth examination, particularly those by people actually involved in the Kuomintang or the National Government. A few representative examples listed in the bibliography are the works of Li Chien-nung, Ch'ien Tuan-sheng, Chiang T'ing-fu, Ch'en Kung-lu, and Chia I-chün in the field of government and politics; Chang Chung-fu and Ch'en T'i-ch'iang in foreign affairs; Chang Chi-hsin and Chiang Shu-ko in education; Wu Ching-hsiung and Huang Kung-chüeh in law; Wu Ching-ch'ao in economics; and Sun Pen-wen in social problems.

One further source which is of great interest but which has remained largely untapped for purely historical purposes is contemporary fiction and drama. Some of the more prolific or talented writers have received attention for their ideas and their roles in Chinese cultural and political life, but the dramas, novels, and short stories contain also insights and information which cannot be found in other sources of the period, and they include some points of view much closer to those of the ordinary Chinese people than to those of the ruling Kuomintang. As with the English play and novel, moreover, the value of Chinese dramas, novels, and short stories as historical documents is far from being confined to those of literary merit.

There are many other Chinese sources, from diaries to films, which have not been noted in this survey, but to conclude without some reference to non-Chinese sources would be a serious omission. This was, after all, a period in which foreign influence and foreign intervention played a significant role in Chinese domestic and foreign affairs, and from the records of foreign governments to the first-hand reports of businessmen, journalists, scholars, and missionaries, non-Chinese sources are of great historical value. Among government archives, the British Foreign Office records are perhaps the best organised, and by 1980 these will be open for the whole Republican period.[19] However, official Japanese and United States records are equally valuable, as are also the diaries and private papers of foreign officials such as General Stilwell. Foreign eye-witness reports on the Chinese Communist movement in this period are well known but relatively few. On the Kuomintang and China under the National Government there is a whole literature based on the personal observations and experiences of foreigners in China, including descriptions of social and economic conditions, narratives of travels in the interior, reporting on meetings and interviews, battlefield accounts of the Kuomintang armies, and stories of the effects on the Chinese people of war, famine, pestilence, and political struggle. The bibliographies of Yuan Tung-li, Chao Kuo-chun, Charles Hucker, Raymond Nunn, and the original predecessors in the 1930s of the present *Annual Bibliography of Asian Studies* provide at least a starting point for a body of source material which in range and volume presents a formidable challenge.

[19] Lo Hui-min, *Foreign Office Confidential Papers Relating to China and Her Neighbouring Countries, 1840-1914* (Paris, 1969) contains a short additional list on the period 1915 to 1937.

BIBLIOGRAPHY

Bibliographies

Chao Kuo-chun, *Selected Works in English for a Topical Study of Modern China*, *1840-1952*, Cambridge, Mass., 1952.

Cheng-chih shu-pao chih-nan, Peiping, 1929.

Chung-kuo kung-ssu ching-chi yen-chiu chi-kuan chi ch'i ch'u-pan wu yao-lan, Shanghai, 1936.

Fairbank, John King, and Liu Kwang-ching, *Modern China, A Bibliographical Guide to Chinese Works 1898-1937*, Harvard-Yenching Institute Studies, Vol. I, Cambridge, Mass., 1950.

Feuerwerker, Albert, and Cheng, S., *Chinese Communist Studies of Modern Chinese History*, Cambridge, Mass., 1961.

Ho To-yüan, *Chung-wen ts'an-k'ao shu chih-nan*, Shanghai, 1936; revised ed., Shanghai, 1938.

Hu, David Y., *A Guide to Chinese Periodicals*, St Louis, 1966.

Hucker, Charles O., *China: A Critical Bibliography*, Tucson, 1962.

Jen-wen yüeh-k'an, Shanghai, 1930-7.

Mote, F.W., *Japanese-sponsored Governments in China 1937-1945: An Annotated Bibliography Compiled from Materials in the Chinese Collection of the Hoover Library*, Stanford, 1954.

Nunn, G. Raymond, *East Asia, A Bibliography of Bibliographies*, Occasional Paper No. 7, East-West Center Library, Honolulu, 1967.

Selected Chinese Books, 1933-1937, Peiping, 1940.

Teng Ssu-yü and Biggerstaff, K., *An Annotated Bibliography of Selected Chinese Reference Works*, Peiping, 1936; Harvard-Yenching Institute Studies, Vol. II, Cambridge, Mass., 1971.

T'u-shu chi-k'an, vols. 1-4, Peking, Kunming, Chungking, 1934-7, new series, vols. 1-8 (1940-8).

T'u-shu mu-lu, ti-i chi, Yang-ming shan, 1960.

Yang Chia-lo, comp., *T'u-shu nien-chien*, 2 vols., Nanking, 1933.

Yuan Tung-li, *China in Western Literature*, New Haven, Conn., 1958.

General Works

Boorman, Howard L., and Howard, Richard C., *A Biographical Dictionary of Republican China*, 4 vols., New York, 1967, 1968, 1970, 1971.

Chang Chi-hsin, *Chung-kuo chiao-yü hsing-cheng ta-kang*, Shanghai, 1934.

Chang Chung-fu, *Chung-hua min-kuo wai-chiao shih*, Peiping, 1936.

Chang Shao-wu, *Chung-kuo ke-ming lun*, Hang-chou, 1934.

Ch'en Kung-lu, *Chung-kuo chin-tai shih*, Shanghai, 1935.

Ch'en P'ei-wei and Hu Ch'ü-fei, comp., *Tsung-li i-chiao so-yin*, Shanghai, 1937.

Ch'en T'i-ch'iang, *Chung-kuo wai-chiao hsing-cheng*, Chungking, 1943.

Ch'i-k'an so-yin, Nanking, 1933-7, published monthly.

Chia I-chün, *Chung-hua min-kuo ming-jen chuan*, 2 vols., Peiping, 1932-3.

——, *Chung-hua min-kuo shih*, Peiping, 1930.
Chiang Shu-ko, *Chung-kuo chin-tai chiao-yü chih-tu*, Shanghai, 1934.
Chiang T'ing-fu (T.F. Tsiang), *Chung-kuo chin-tai shih*, Ch'ang-sha, 1939.
Ch'ien Tuan-sheng and others, *Min-kuo cheng-chih shih*, 2 vols., Ch'ang-sha, 1939.
Chin-tai shih tzu-liao, Peking, August 1954-9. In 1959 this serial publication was replaced by a series of volumes issued under the same title.
Ch'ing-tang yün-tung, ed., and pub. Ch'ing-tang yün-tung chi-chin hui, 1927.
Ch'üan-kuo Chung-wen ch'i-k'an lien-ho mu-lu 1833-1949, Peking, 1961.
Chung-hua min-kuo fa-kuei hui-pien, edited by the Legislative Yüan, Shanghai, 1934.
Chung-hua min-kuo fa-kuei ta-ch'üan, 5 vols., Shanghai, 1937.
Chung-hua min-kuo hsien-hsing fa-kuei ta-ch'üan. Shanghai, 1934.
Chung-hua min-kuo kuo-min cheng-fu, fu Kuang-tung sheng cheng-fu tsu-chih, Shanghai, 1925.
Chung-kuo hsien-tai shih tzu-liao tiao-ch'a mu-lu, 10 vols., and one supplementary vol., Nan-kang, Taiwan, 1968.
Chung-kuo Kuo-min tang cheng-kang cheng-ts'e chi chung-yao hsüan-yen, Chungking, 1940.
Chung-kuo Kuo-min tang fa-kuei chi-yao, Chungking, 1944.
Chung-kuo Kuo-min tang hsüan-yen chi, Chungking, 1938.
Chung-kuo Kuo-min tang nien-chien, n.p., 1934.
Chung-kuo Kuo-min tang wu-shih nien lai wai-chiao tou-cheng ti ch'eng-kung, Chungking, 1943.
Chung-kuo shih-hsüeh lun-wen so-yin, 2 vols., Peking, 1957.
Chung-wai t'iao-yüeh chi-pien (Treaties between the Republic of China and Foreign States (1927-1961)), edited by the Ministry of Foreign Affairs, Taipei, 1963.
Fan Yin-nan, *Tang-tai Chung-kuo ming-jen lu*, Shanghai, 1931.
Feng Tzu-yu, *Chung-hua min-kuo k'ai-kuo ch'ien ke-ming shih*, 3 vols., Chungking, 1945.
——, *Chung-kuo ke-ming yün-tung erh-shih-liu nien tsu-chih shih*, Shanghai, 1948.
——, *Ke-ming i-shih*, Shanghai, 1946.
Hu Han-min, ed., *Tsung-li ch'üan-chi*, 5 vols., and 4 collections, Shanghai, 1930.
Jih-pao so-yin, Nanking, 1934-7, published monthly.
Kan Nai-kuang, ed., *Sun Chung-shan hsien-sheng wen-chi*, Canton, 1925.
Ke-ming wen-hsien, Taipei, vol. 1, 1953, vol. 47, 1969.
Kuo-min tang liu chieh chung-wei ko p'ai-hsi ming-tan, n.p., 1945.
Li Chien-nung, *Chung-kuo chin pai-nien cheng-chih shih*, 2 vols., Shanghai, 1947.
Sun Pen-wen, *Hsien-tai Chung-kuo she-hui wen-t'i*, 4 vols., Chungking, 1943.
Sun Wen, *Chung-kuo ts'un-wang wen-t'i*, Shanghai, 1928.
——, *San-min chu-i*, Canton, 1925.

Tai Chi-t'ao, *Kuo-min ke-ming yü Chung-kuo Kuo-min tang*, n.p., 1925.

T'an Cho-yüan, comp., *Chung-wen tsa-chih so-yin*, 2 vols., Canton, 1935.

Tang-shih shih-liao ts'ung-k'an, irregular serial publication in the 1940s of the Central Committee for the Compilation of Materials on Party History of the Central Executive Committee of the Kuomintang, published by Cheng-chung shu-chü.

Tang-wu fa-kuei hui-pien, 2 vols., n.p., 1939.

Ting Wen-chiang, Weng Wen-hao, and Tseng Shih-ying, comp., *Chung-hua min-kuo hsin ti-t'u*, Shanghai, 1934.

Tsou Lu, *Chung-kuo Kuo-min tang shih-kao*, revised ed., Chungking, 1944.

——, *Chung-kuo Kuo-min tang shih-lüeh*, Chungking, 1945.

Wu Ching-ch'ao, *Chung-kuo ching-chi chien-she chih lu*, Chungking, 1943.

Wu Ching-hsiung and Huang Kung-chüeh, *Chung-kuo chih-hsien shih*, 2 vols., Shanghai, 1937.

Wu, Eugene Wen-chin, *Leaders of Twentieth Century China: An Annotated Bibliography of Selected Chinese Biographical Works in the Hoover Library*, Stanford, 1956.

史 XXIII: Sources on the History of the Chinese Communist Party[1]

CHÜN-TU HSÜEH

This chapter is primarily concerned with Chinese and English written sources on the history of the Chinese Communist Party.[2] With regard to Chinese sources, the material that has already been covered in my two-volume annotated bibliography, *The Chinese Communist Movement*, will not be mentioned here again.[3]

In 1963, Howard L. Boorman, then Director of the Research Project on Men and Politics in Modern China at Columbia University and now Professor of History and Director of the East Asian Studies Program at Vanderbilt University, remarked in a review article that:

> Mature synthesis of the history of communism in China has been hampered by inadequate sources, inadequate bibliographical controls, inadequate reference tools, and inadequate monographic work. Though extensive, the primary sources on the history of the Chinese party are in no way comparable to those which exist, for example, on the history of the Soviet party. Existing Chinese sources are scattered, and controls are only gradually emerging. The most important contributions to date are the annotated bibliographies prepared by Hsüeh Chün-tu at the Hoover Institution, which have brought large quantities of primary

[1] The author wishes to thank Mr John Ma, Curator-Librarian of the East Asian Collection of the Hoover Institution, Stanford University, for his helpful suggestions during the author's visit at Stanford in February, 1970, for the preparation of this chapter.
[2] The oral history projects such as those relevant to the subject conducted at Columbia University in the United States and by Academia Sinica in Taiwan will not be discussed. For a review of Japanese and other sources on the history of the Chinese Communist Party, see Eto Shinkichi's bibliographical essay (in Japanese) published in *Tōyō gakuhō* XLIII, 2 (September 1960), pp. 223-47.
[3] The two volumes, covering 1921-37 and 1937-49 (Stanford, 1960-62), contain a total of 1,241 annotated titles from the Chinese Collection of the Hoover Institution, Stanford University. The main division of the bibliography is chronological, with topical subdivisions for each period. For the holdings of the Chinese Collections at Columbia University and at Harvard University in 1949-50, see respectively Wilbur, ed., *Chinese Sources on the History of the Chinese Communist Movement*, 56 pp., and Fairbank and E-tu Zen Sun, *Chinese Communist Publications: An Annotated Bibliography of Material in the Chinese Library at Harvard*, 122 pp., mimeo. The Chinese materials on the Party history at these two universities have undoubtedly enormously increased since 1949-50. *The Research Activities of the South Manchurian Railway Company 1907-1945: A History and Bibliography* by John Young (New York, 1966) includes a chapter on the Chinese Communist movement, containing an annotated list of forty-seven important items, mostly of a documentary nature.

documents under critical control and should be on the bookshelf of every serious student of Chinese communism.[4]

Chinese Sources

The Hoover Institution probably had the best collection of Chinese Communist materials in the West at the time the bibliography was published. Since its publication in 1960-2, however, a number of other important works on the Party history have become available at Hoover and elsewhere. The most important one is probably the Ch'en Ch'eng (Shih Sou) Collection of captured communist materials which relate primarily to the Kiangsi Soviet Period of 1931-4.[5] This collection was microfilmed in 1963 by the Hoover Institution from the files of General Ch'en Ch'eng, who was then Vice-President of the Republic of China in Taiwan. Another collection in book form on the Kiangsi period that has come to light since the publication of my bibliography is the six-volume *Ch'ih-fei fan-tung wen-chien hui-pien* compiled by General Ch'en in 1935, and reprinted in 1960. Volume 2 of Tso-liang Hsiao, ed., *Power Relations within the Chinese Communist Movement 1930-1934* (Seattle, 1967) has reproduced those Chinese documents from the Ch'en Ch'eng Collection and from the collection of the Bureau of Investigation of the Chinese Ministry of Justice in Taiwan that deal with major events and political issues raised within the Communist Party, particularly from the angle of intraparty conflicts and party relations with Moscow.

Another collection of documents is the three-volume *Kung-fei huo-kuo shih-liao hui-pien*. Edited by the Editorial Committee for Compiling Material and Documents in Commemoration of the Fifty Years of the Founding of the Republic of China, it was published in Taipei in 1964.

On the general history of the Party, Wang Chien-min's three volume *Chung-kuo Kung-ch'an tang shih-kao*, published in Taipei in 1965, is a product of many years of work based on the numerous primary sources and original documents found in the library of the Bureau of Investigation, Chinese Ministry of Justice. The Library of the Bureau was set up in Taipei in 1950. It has an enormous collection of booklets, periodicals, newspapers, newsclippings, secret documents and pictures pertaining to the Chinese Communist movement. These materials were all obtained through the Kuomintang agents during the period of the civil war or captured by uprooting the Communist central and local organisations at one time or another. One-third of over 100,000 volumes in the library concerns Chinese Communism. A collection of this kind is unsurpassed by any library in the world.[6]

---

[4] *Journal of Asian Studies* XXIII, 1 (November 1963), p. 116.

[5] A table of contents of the Ch'en Ch'eng Collection was published by Ishikawa Tadao in a Japanese journal, *Hōgaku kenkyū* XXXV, 7 (July 1962), pp. 81-117. For a bibliographical review of the collection, see Tien-wei Wu, 'The Kiangsi Soviet Period', *Journal of Asian Studies* XXIX, 2 (February 1970), pp. 395-412.

[6] For a partial list of the holdings of the Collection of the Bureau of Investigation, See *Kindai*

Warren Kuo's *Analytical History of the Chinese Communist Party*, though published in English, may be mentioned here in the category of Chinese sources, partly because of the author's first-hand information on the subject. Another important work by a Chinese scholar published in recent years is Cheng Hsüeh-chia's *Chung-kung hsing-wang shih*. The first of the projected two volumes, published in Taipei in 1970, deals with the historical background and embryonic period of the Chinese Communist movement.

As to autobiographies, the most important memoir published in recent years is 'Wo ti hui-i' by Chang Kuo-t'ao, a founder of the Chinese Communist Party, who defected in 1938. It appeared in the *Ming Pao Monthly* (Hong Kong, March 1966 to February 1971). The first volume of its English version was published by the University of Kansas Press in 1971. Another memoir, by Chang Kuo-t'ao's wife, Yang Tzu-lieh, was serialised in the Hong Kong magazine *Chan-wang*, Nos. 158-182 (1 September 1968 to 1 September 1969). It contains interesting episodes on the leaders and their wives. A memoir by Kung Ch'u, an ex-communist army commander and author of *Wo yü hung-chün* (Hong Kong, 1954), appeared in instalments in the *Ming Pao Monthly* beginning March 1971.

Another valuable memoir is *Chiang-hsi su-ch'ü hung-chün hsi-ts'uan hui-i* by Ts'ai Hsiao-ch'ien, published by the Institute for the Study of Chinese Communist Problems (Taipei, 1970). It was originally published in a series in *Chung-kung yen-chiu*, a leading KMT journal on Communist China. The Institute for the Study of Chinese Communist Problems has also published *Chung-kung shou-yao shih-lüeh hui-pien*, edited by Li Feng-min (Taipei, 1969), and *Liu Shao-ch'i wen-t'i chuan-chi*, edited by Fang Chün-kuei (Taipei, 1970). The former consists of biographical chronologies on twenty top Chinese Communist leaders and a number of documents relating to them during the Cultural Revolution, while the latter contains materials on Liu Shao-ch'i unavailable elsewhere.

For details of numerous military campaigns against the Communists by the Nationalist Government, the ten-volume *Chiao-fei chan-shih* offers an enormous amount of information with many maps and charts. The book was edited and published by the Military History Bureau of the Ministry of National Defence of the Chinese Nationalist Government in Taipei in 1962. (A six-volume edition was published in 1967.) It should be noted, however, that only thirty-seven out of the total 1,248 pages deal with the 1937-45 period, the remainder concerning the years 1930-6. For the 1945-50 period, the four-volume *K'an-luan chien-shih* may be consulted. These works were also edited and published by the Military History Bureau of the Ministry of National Defence in 1962.

In China, a nation-wide collection of reminiscences was made late in the

Chūgoku kenkyū sentā ihō 9 (July 1967), pp. 8-20; and 10 (October 1967), pp. 8-24. The list was compiled by Tokuda Yoshiyuki.

1950s. As a result of this effort, voluminous sources of primary historical data were published. The following is one of the most important. The sixteen-volume *Hung-ch'i p'iao-p'iao* (*HCPP*), published in Peking from 1957 to 1961, is composed of articles of uneven quality. Written in most instances by unknown figures, it is, in the words of Professor Chalmers Johnson, 'a conglomerate collection of reminiscences ranging from tales of Chinese in Russia during the Bolshevik Revolution to analyses of major Chinese Communist battles quoting Commander-in-Chief Chu Teh.'[7]

Hsing-huo liao-yüan (Hong Kong, 1960) contains seventy articles of reminiscences on the Long March. Another collection of reminiscences under the same title, consisting of ten volumes, was edited by the Editorial Committee for Commemorating Thirty Years of the People's Liberation Army and published in Peking in 1958-61. This collection is devoted to the evolution of the People's Liberation Army (PLA) and the history of the civil war. The twelve-volume *Hung-se feng-pao* (Kiangsi, 1958-61) is mainly concerned with the personalities and battles of the Kiangsi period.

English Sources

With regard to English materials, most of them are secondary sources. The writings by Brandt, Fairbank, FitzGerald, Isaacs, North, Schwartz, Wilbur, and others in the 1950s are still useful.[8] However, some factual errors contained in these books should be noted and new interpretations of some crucial events may be needed as a result of data subsequently found. For example, the Chinese texts of the first two documents[9] in Conrad Brandt, Benjamin Schwartz, and John K. Fairbank, *A Documentary History of Chinese Communism* (Cambridge, Mass., 1952) have now been discovered in the Jay Calvin Huston Collection at Stanford University.[10]

Several significant works were published in the 1960s. *A Short History of Chinese Communism* by Franklin W. Houn was published in 1967. However, two-thirds of the book is concerned with the post-1949 period. A forthcoming book by James P. Harrison will focus on the history of the Party

---

[7] 'Foreword', in Robert Rinden and Roxane Witke, *The Red Flag Waves: A Guide to the Hung-ch'i p'iao-p'iao Collection*. The publication of this guide is a great help in the use of the *HCPP*.

[8] See bibliography for details.

[9] The first document, 'First Manifesto of the CCP on the Current Situation', dated 10 June 1922, was taken from a Russian translation and put into English. The second document, 'Manifesto of the Second National Congress of the CCP', July 1922, is a translation from a Japanese version.

[10] Jay C. Huston was U.S. vice-consul (1917-22) and consul (1923-32) in China. His collection includes manuscripts, pamphlets, placards, leaflets, and newspaper clippings, in Chinese, Russian, and English, dealing with cultural, political, and economic conditions in China with special reference to the influence of Soviet Russia and communist agencies thereon. It also includes secret reports and information exchanged between Moscow and the USSR representatives in China.

prior to 1949. A remarkable report of the United States War Department on the Chinese Communist movement, dated July 1945, was published in book form in 1968.[11] The report was originally prepared by the Military Intelligence Division of the United States War Department on the basis of more than 2,500 official and unofficial sources, with emphasis on the period from 1937-49.

On the early period of the Party history, a Columbia University M.A. thesis written by Ch'en Kung-po in 1924 is one of the most important works.[12] In addition, Jean Chesneaux's book on the Chinese labour movement has now appeared in English.[13] Of course, Edgar Snow's *Red Star Over China* remains a classic. The collaboration of Robert C. North and Xenia J. Eudin has produced two excellent documentary studies,[14] and a study of the United Front appeared in 1967.[15] On the subject of Soviet-Chinese Communist relations, in addition to Charles B. McLane's *Soviet Policy and the Chinese Communists 1931-1946* (New York, 1958), *The Comintern and the Chinese Communists 1928-1931* by Richard C. Thornton was published in 1969. Thornton argues that the controversial ' "Li Li-san line" was a deviation from the strategy set forth by the Comintern', and that it was the Comintern, not Mao Tse-tung, that originated and urged the application of the policy of protracted guerrilla warfare.

On the Kiangsi period, Victor A. Yakhontoff's *The Chinese Soviets* and *Fundamental Laws of the Chinese Soviet Republic*, both published in 1934, are familiar sources. In 1961, the Peking Foreign Languages Press published *The Red Kiangsi-Kwangtung Border Region* by Yang Shang-k'uei. In the West, the major increment in recent years is Tso-liang Hsiao's *Power Relations within the Chinese Communist Movement 1930-1934*. In this volume, published in 1961, Hsiao analyses the significance of the documents referred to previously in this chapter. Another study by Hsiao relating to the same period is *The Land Revolution in China 1930-1934*, published in 1968. *A Study of the Chinese Communist Movement* by Shanti Swarup deals mainly with the 1927-34 period. However, the study is not intended to trace the growth of the Chinese Soviet movement and of the Red Army. Its focus, as stated by its author, is 'limited to the growth—or failure to gain acceptance—of the major policies of the Chinese Communist Party which were eventually to enable the party to lead the Chinese revolution to victory'.

---

[11] Van Slyke, ed., *The Chinese Communist Movement*.
[12] Published as *The Chinese Communist Movement* (New York, 1960; 1966).
[13] The English title is *The Chinese Labor Movement 1919-1927*, and the translator is H.M. Wright.
[14] *Soviet Russia and the East 1920-27* and *M.N. Roy's Mission to China*. Roy, who was a Comintern agent in China in 1926-7, was the author of *Revolution and Counterrevolution* (Calcutta, 1946). It is a translation of the German edition of 1930 with two chapters added in 1939 and an epilogue in 1946.
[15] Van Slyke, *Friends and Enemies*.

In October 1934 the Chinese Communists were forced to leave Kiangsi. Between 1956-9 the Foreign Languages Press in Peking published several reminiscences on the subject in English. In 1963, it published *The Long March: Eyewitness Accounts.* The stories in this volume were selected and translated from the third volume of *Hsing-huo liao-yüan* mentioned previously. Among Western publications, Simone de Beauvoir's book has been translated by Austryn Wainhouse, *The Long March.* In the late 1930s the New China Information Committee of the CCP frequently issued bulletins and pamphlets in English. The English translation of Chu Teh's military report, *The Battle Front of the Liberated Areas,* is available. The report was presented at the Seventh National Congress of the CCP on 25 April 1945.

On the 1937-45 period, Chalmers A. Johnson's *Peasant Nationalism and Communist Power* remains one of the best works. It is based largely on the archives of the Japanese Army and the Asia Development Board, and is a study to 'establish a basis upon which contemporary Communism in China may be understood as a particularly virulent form of nationalism'. Material for the rectification campaign in Yen-an has been translated in Boyd Compton, ed., *Mao's China: Party Reform Documents, 1942-1944.* Between 1936 and 1940, and again between 1944 and 1945, a number of foreign observers visited Yen-an and other Chinese Communist areas.[16] It would be interesting to read their reports and writings with historical perspective and hindsight. On the civil war of 1945 to 1949, a French book by Lionel Max Chassin has been translated into English by Timothy Osato and Louis Celas, *The Communist Conquest of China,* published in 1965.

Mao Tse-tung's *Selected Works* are, of course, major sources on the Party history.[17] The long-awaited volume of the English edition of Chang Kuo-t'ao's autobiography *The Rise of the Chinese Communist Party, 1921-1927* was finally published in 1971. As to Mao himself, a number of works on him have been published.[18] Other significant biographical works include *Biographical Dictionary of Republican China,* edited by Howard L. Boorman, containing many well written biographical sketches of Chinese Communist leaders; and Donald W. Klein and Anne B. Clark, *Biographic Dictionary of Chinese Communism 1921-1965,* published 1970. The reminiscences of Li Tsung-jen (forthcoming book), which is an oral history project undertaken by T.K. Tong, contain valuable first-hand information on Chinese Commun-

---

[16] Among the correspondents or journalists were Edgar Snow, Agnes Smedley, Nym Wales, James Bertram, Haldore Hanson, Anna Louise Strong, Earl Leaf, Victor Kean, George Hatem, H. Dunham, and T.A. Bisson (later, Harrison Forman, Gunther Stein, and Israel Epstein).

[17] There are several English editions of Mao's four-volume *Selected Works* in Chinese. The Peking Foreign Languages Press published Vol. 4 in 1961, and Vols. 1-3 in 1965. The four-volume set published by the International Publishers of New York in 1954-6 corresponds to the first three volumes of the Chinese edition.

[18] See those of Emi Siao, Siao-yu, Jerome Ch'en, Stuart Schram, and John E. Rue. For details, see the bibliography at the end of the chapter.

ists. *Revolutionary Leaders of Modern China*, edited by Chün-tu Hsüeh and published by the Oxford University Press of New York in 1971, also contains several biographies of Chinese Communist leaders. Kai-yu Hsu's *Chou En-lai* deals with 'China's Grey Eminence'. To my knowledge there are no definitive studies on the lives of the Chinese Communist military leaders. Agnes Smedley's *The Great Road* deals with 'The Life and Times of Chu Teh', but it leaves much to be desired as a scholarly work. A RAND monograph, entitled *A Politico-Military Biography of Lin Piao, Part I, 1907-1949*, by Thomas W. Robinson (with translations by Anna Sun Ford) was published in 1971. My current research project, 'Kung Ch'u and the Red Army', is based on the general's memoirs. On Communist leadership, *Kuomintang and Chinese Communist Elites* by Robert C. North with the collaboration of Ithiel de Sola Pool remains a standard work.[19]

According to Mao Tse-tung's famous dictum, 'Political power grows out from the barrel of a gun'. One of the major tasks of the Chinese Communist army before 1949 was 'to establish revolutionary political power and setting up Party organizations'.[20] Therefore, no study of the Party history should neglect the army. An authoritative lengthy report on the history and condition of the Chinese Red Army, dated 1 September 1929, and published in issue No. 1 (15 January 1930) of the *Chung-yang chün-shih t'ung-hsün*, an official publication of the Military Department of the Central Committee of the Chinese Communist Party for inner party circulation and reference, has been translated into English by Chün-tu Hsüeh and Robert C. North and published in *Contemporary China* (Hong Kong, 1968). The first five chapters of Samuel B. Griffith, II, *The Chinese People's Liberation Army*, deal with the pre-1949 period. An excellent annotated bibliography on the subject is *The Chinese Red Army, 1927-1963* by Edward J.M. Rhoads, published in 1964.

Many speeches and writings of Liu Shao-ch'i, former vice-chairman of the Party and the leading victim of the Cultural Revolution, are available in English translation, including *On the Party* (Peking, 1950), which is a report on the revision of the Party Constitution delivered on 14 May 1945 to the Seventh National Congress of the Party. Chang Kuo-t'ao's 'Introduction' to *Collected Works of Liu Shao-ch'i* contains valuable information on Liu and the inner-party struggle of the top leadership in the 1930s.

Of the periodicals, the *Communist International* (British edition, 1919-35; and American edition, 1935-9) and the semi-official weekly of the Comintern, *International Press Correspondence* (*Imprecor*), 1922-41, are important sources. The latter was published first in Vienna and Berlin and from

---

[19] The book was originally published by the Stanford University Press in 1952. It is also available in World Revolutionary Elites, edited by Harold D. Lasswell and Daniel Lerner (Cambridge, Mass., 1966).
[20] Mao Tse-tung, 'On Correcting Mistaken Ideas in the Party' (December 1929), *Quotations from Chairman Mao Tse-tung* (Peking, 1967), p. 100.

1933-41 in London (renamed *World News and Views* in July 1938). Other learned journals that contain articles on Chinese Party history are *Asian Survey* (Berkeley), *The China Quarterly* (London), *Pacific Affairs* (New York; now Vancouver), and *Journal of Asian Studies*.

The already complex Party history has become more confused as a result of the Cultural Revolution in 1966-9. In the tempest, most of the Communist official historians became 'monsters' and their works 'poisonous weeds'. Until then *Thirty Years of the Communist Party of China* (1952) by Hu Ch'iao-mu, Vice-director of the Propaganda Department of the Central Committee of the CCP, was the official version of the Party history. He was one of the many victims of the Cultural Revolution. *A History of the Modern Chinese Revolution*, published in Peking in 1959 by Ho Kan-chih, undoubtedly has 'problems'. In my visit to China, October-November 1971, I learned at the Sun Yat-sen University in Canton that Ho Kan-chih's book was no longer used, but the volume by Hu Ch'iao-mu was being used 'critically'. While Red Guard posters have thrown some light on the pre-1949 period, accusations and counter-accusations have also begotten confusion rather than understanding. To close with a concluding remark of Professor Howard Boorman from his review article previously mentioned: 'The Communist Party of China still awaits its historian.'

BIBLIOGRAPHY

Boorman, Howard L., ed., *Biographical Dictionary of Republican China*, New York, 1967-71.

Chang Kuo-t'ao, *The Rise of the Chinese Communist Party, 1921-1927*, Kansas, 1971. Originally published, as 'Wo ti hui-i', in *Ming Pao Monthly* (March 1966-February 1971).

Chassin, Lionel Max, *The Communist Conquest of China*, tr. Timothy Osato and Louis Celas, Cambridge, Mass., 1965.

Ch'en, Jerome, *Mao and the Chinese Revolution*, London, 1965.

Ch'en Kung-po, *The Chinese Communist Movement*, ed. C. Martin Wilbur, New York, 1960; 1966.

Cheng Hsüeh-chia, *Chung-kung hsing-wang shih*, Taipei, 1970.

Chesneaux, Jean, *The Chinese Labor Movement 1919-1927*, tr. H.M. Wright, Stanford, 1968.

Chiao-fei chan-shih, 10 vols., Taipei, 1962; 6 vols., Taipei, 1967.

Chu Teh, *The Battle Front of the Liberated Areas*, 2nd ed., Peking, 1955.

Compton, Boyd, ed., *Mao's China: Party Reform Documents, 1942-1944*, Seattle, 1952.

de Beauvoir, Simone, *The Long March*, tr. Austryn Wainhouse, Cleveland, 1958.

Fairbank, John K., and Sun, E-tu Zen, *Chinese Communist Publications: An Annotated Bibliography of Material in the Chinese Library at Harvard*, Cambridge, Mass., 1949.

FitzGerald, C.P., *Revolution in China*, London, 1952; revised and published under the title *The Birth of Communist China*, London, 1964.

Griffith, Samuel B., II, *The Chinese People's Liberation Army*, New York, 1967.

Ho Kan-chih, *A History of the Modern Chinese Revolution*, Peking, 1959.

Hsiao Tso-liang, *Power Relations within the Chinese Communist Movement*, 2 vols., Seattle, 1961, 1967.

——, *The Land Revolution in China 1930-1934*, Seattle, 1968.

Hsu Kai-yu, *Chou En-lai*, New York, 1968.

Hsüeh Chün-tu, ed., *Revolutionary Leaders of Modern China*, New York, 1971.

——, *The Chinese Communist Movement 1921-1937*, Stanford, 1960.

——, *The Chinese Communist Movement 1937-1949*, Stanford, 1962.

Hu Ch'iao-mu, *Thirty Years of the Communist Party of China*, Peking, 1952.

Hung-ch'i p'iao-p'iao, 16 vols., Peking, 1957-61.

Hung-se feng-pao, 12 vols., Kiangsi, 1958-61.

Isaacs, Harold R., *The Tragedy of the Chinese Revolution*, Stanford, 1951; 1961; first published in Great Britain, 1938.

Johnson, Chalmers A., *Peasant Nationalism and Communist Power*, Stanford, 1962.

K'an-luan chien-shih, 4 vols., Taipei, 1962.

Klein, Donald W., and Clark, Anne B., *Biographic Dictionary of Chinese Communism 1921-1965*, 2 vols., Cambridge, Mass., 1970.

Kung-fei huo-kuo shih-liao hui-pien, Taipei, 1964.

Kuo, Warren, *Analytical History of the Chinese Communist Party*, 3 vols., Taipei, 1966-9.

Liu Shao-ch'i, *Collected Works of Liu Shao-ch'i*, 3 vols., Hong Kong, 1968-9.

McLane, Charles B., *Soviet Policy and the Chinese Communists 1931-1946*, New York, 1958.

Mao Tse-tung, *Selected Works*, 4 vols., Peking, 1961-5; 4 vols., New York, 1954-6.

North, Robert C., *Chinese Communism*, London, 1966.

——, *Moscow and the Chinese Communists*, Stanford, 1953; 1965.

——, with Pool, Ithiel de Sola, *Kuomintang and Chinese Communist Elites*, Stanford, 1952; Cambridge, Mass., 1966.

——, and Eudin, Xenia J., *M.N. Roy's Mission to China*, Berkeley, 1963.

——, *Soviet Russia and the East 1920-27*, Stanford, 1957.

Rhoads, Edward J.M., *The Chinese Red Army, 1927-1963*, Cambridge, Mass., 1964.

Rinden, Robert, and Witke, Roxane, *The Red Flag Waves: A Guide to the Hung-ch'i p'iao-p'iao Collection*, Berkeley, 1968.

Rue, John E., *Mao Tse-tung in Opposition 1927-1935*, Stanford, 1966.

Schram, Stuart, *Mao Tse-tung*, New York, 1966.

Schwartz, Benjamin I., *Chinese Communism and the Rise of Mao*, Cambridge, Mass., 1951; London, 1967.

Siao, Emi, *Mao Tse-tung: His Childhood and Youth*, Bombay, 1953.

Siao-yu, *Mao Tse-tung and I were Beggars*, Syracuse, 1959.

Smedley, Agnes, *The Great Road*, New York, 1956.

Snow, Edgar, *Random Notes on China*, Cambridge, Mass., 1957.

——, *Red Star over China*, New York, 1938; 1944; 1968.

Swarup, Shanti, *A Study of the Chinese Communist Movement*, Oxford, 1966.

The Long March: Eyewitness Accounts, Peking, 1963.

Thornton, Richard C., *The Comintern and the Chinese Communists 1928-1931*, Seattle, 1969.

van Slyke, Lyman P., *Friends and Enemies*, Stanford, 1967.

——, ed., *The Chinese Communist Movement*, Stanford, 1968.

Wales, Nym, *Red Dust: Autobiographies of Chinese Communists*, Stanford, 1952.

Wang Chien-min, *Chung-kuo Kung-ch'an tang shih-kao*, 3 vols., Taipei, 1965.

Wilbur, C. Martin, ed., *Chinese Sources on the History of the Chinese Communist Movement*, New York, 1950.

——, and How, Julie Lien-ying, eds., *Documents on Communism, Nationalism and the Soviet Advisers in China, 1918-1927*, New York, 1959.

Yakhontoff, Victor A., *Fundamental Laws of the Chinese Soviet Republic*, New York, 1934.

——, *The Chinese Soviets*, New York, 1934.

Yang Shang-k'uei, *The Red Kiangsi-Kwangtung Border Region*, Peking, 1961.

史 xxiv: Sources on the Chinese People's Republic

BILL BRUGGER

The speed with which the Chinese People's Republic was established came as a great shock, especially to scholars working in the China field. Nevertheless, by now, there has begun to emerge a general picture of exactly what source material is available for the study of the past twenty years. In the 1950s, when China scholars were trying to reorient themselves to a study of contemporary China, and social scientists had begun to realise that a study of contemporary China was a realistic possibility, a number of restrictions were imposed upon the export of books and research material. During this early period, however, most of the important newspapers and periodicals were brought out of China and they are now available in Western libraries.

From 1957-9 restrictions were eased considerably and a flood of material was unleashed. This was the period of the Great Leap Forward, and thousands of small ephemeral publications appeared. The student of contemporary China was swamped with material. By the time he had recovered from this new shock, China's three bad years had begun (1960-2) and restrictions on export of material were imposed in much harsher terms than hitherto. In the mid-1960s the situation began to ease once again. Tourists began to pour into China, a new batch of 'foreign experts' was recruited, and the exchange of material recommenced in earnest.[1] The Cultural Revolution, which began in 1966, although imposing severe restrictions on the export of certain proscribed works, was similar to the Great Leap Forward in that it saw the birth of literally thousands of new publications, many of which have found their way into Western libraries. (It also saw the suspension of most existing publications.)

We have, therefore, a comparatively rich store of research material for what must surely be the three most interesting periods in the history of the Chinese People's Republic—the early New Democratic Period (1949-51), the middle and late 1950s and the Cultural Revolution. The material for the early 1950s is detailed and exciting but very little work seems to

[1] Exchange agreements between some Western libraries and the Peking National Library have been maintained throughout the past twenty years although Peking has offered very little for exchange since 1966.

have been done on it, in striking contrast to that of the period 1956-8 which is very rich in statistical information and has provided material for many monographs. The volume of material released during the Great Leap Forward was enormous but is characterised by an unfortunate disregard for factual detail. It is consequently of more use to the political philosopher than the social scientist. One may construct a very rich picture of the various ideological currents of the late 1950s but it is very difficult to trace in any detail the many changes in social structure that appeared during this period. The Cultural Revolution material offers us detail of a very different kind. I know of no one who has read more than a fraction of the Red Guard material produced during the middle 1960s, but such that has been analysed has called into question not only most Western interpretations of Chinese politics during the past twenty years but also most published Chinese interpretations.

Party, Government, and Other Official Organs

Publications of Party and government may be divided into three types: daily newspapers, theoretical journals, and lower-level agitprop[2] material.

Most newspapers are produced by a branch of the Chinese Communist Party. The *Jen-min jih-pao* is the daily newspaper of the Party Central Committee, and each of the Provincial Committees had a similar newspaper (e.g. *Liao-ning jih-pao* and *Hsin Hu-nan pao*). It seems that the publication of most provincial newspapers has been continued under the new Provincial Revolutionary Committees. Similarly, many Municipality (*shih*) Party Committees had their own newspapers (e.g. *Ha-erh-pin jih-pao*), often accompanied by evening papers (e.g. *Pei-ching wan-pao*). The content of these types of newspaper varies considerably. *Jen-min jih-pao* is not a newspaper in the Western sense of the word. Its function is to make clear the authoritative Party standpoint on certain issues, and to throw open subjects for debate within clearly demarcated political lines. It is, therefore, very heavy reading. Provincial newspapers, on the other hand, are slightly more readable. They often repeat editorials of *Jen-min jih-pao* but contain articles showing the relevance of these editorials for the particular province. Evening newspapers are far more like the Western conception of a newspaper. Although moralistic in tone, many of them contain chatty news items and easily understandable news stories showing the implementation or non-implementation of policy. These latter are a rich source of research data. It should be remembered that the various articles by Wu Han and Teng T'o attacking Mao Tse-tung's Great Leap Forward strategy were originally

---

[2] I use the word 'agitprop' here rather than propaganda because in the early period a distinction was made between propaganda (*hsüan-ch'uan*) and agitation (*ku-tung*) though later this distinction disappeared.

carried in the *Pei-ching wan-pao*.[3] As far as the Party is concerned, these municipal-level newspapers are designed to contribute to the popular debate on policy not yet determined. Once policy is determined, a Party directive will be carried in a newspaper of slightly higher status. It is then the function of the lower-level newspapers to discuss concrete measures for the implementation of that policy.

The above deals with the Party press. Some newspapers in China are, however, not strictly Party publications. Although the general orientation of papers such as *Ta-kung pao*, *Kuang-ming jih-pao*, and *Wen-hui pao* is set by the Chinese Communist Party, they are designed to reflect the opinion of minority political groups (though, of course, not opposed to the Communist Party). This is not an empty formula, since during the early years of the Chinese People's Republic, *Kuang-ming jih-pao* carried many articles dealing with the activities of the 'democratic parties', and *Ta-kung pao* devoted much space to the activities of the commercial world. The significance of a non-Party press should not be underestimated. The Cultural Revolution, which in its early stages was aimed directly against the Party machinery, was launched in the non-Party paper *Wen-hui pao*, and carried on in another newspaper not directly affiliated to the civilian Party apparatus, *Chieh-fang chün pao*.[4]

This last is an example of yet another type of newspaper: that of state organs or mass organisations. For example, the newspaper of the All China Federation of Trade Unions was *Kung-jen jih-pao*, and the newspaper of the Chinese Communist Youth League (formerly the New Democratic Youth League) was *Chung-kuo ch'ing-nien pao*.[5] As might be expected from the above account of the accessibility of this material, several large Western libraries have substantial runs of local newspapers for the 1950s, virtually nothing for the early 1960s, and a lot for the Cultural Revolution. This has meant that more sound empirical research on society and economy at provincial level has been produced for the 1950s than for the early 1960s.

In addition to its official newspaper, the Central Committee of the Chinese Communist Party publishes a theoretical journal, *Hung-ch'i*,[6] and before the Cultural Revolution most provincial Party committees also published theoretical journals. That of the Party Committee of the Inner Mongolian Autonomous Region, for example, was *Shih-chien*, and that of

[3] It was mainly for this reason that *Pei-ching wan-pao* was suspended during the Cultural Revolution. It would seem that very few evening newspapers continued publication.
[4] For a time, when *Jen-min jih-pao* was in the hands of a group who are alleged to have opposed the Cultural Revolution, *Chieh-fang chün pao* took over the authoritative function of *Jen-min jih-pao*.
[5] Since the end of 1966 the All China Federation of Trade Unions and the Communist Youth League have been in abeyance, and their own organs have not been published. There has been talk of rebuilding the Youth League though no mention has been made of the All China Federation of Trade Unions.
[6] *Hung-ch'i* began publication in 1958. Before that the most authoritative central theoretical journal was *Hsüeh-hsi*, though this never had the status of *Hung-ch'i*.

the Peking Municipal Party Committee was *Ch'ien-hsien*. These journals frequently became vehicles for resisting Mao's Cultural Revolution policies. Since the Ninth Congress of the Chinese Communist Party (April 1969) attempts are being made to recreate provincial Party Committees and one might perhaps anticipate that such theoretical journals might again appear at some time in the future. At the time of writing (July 1971), however, none of these provincial publications has reappeared. Export of such items has always been prohibited and very few issues exist in Western libraries.

Similarly, government ministries, commissions, committees, and bureaus, such as the State Statistical Bureau, State Planning Commission, Ministry of Labour, Ministry of Heavy Industry, Ministry of Agriculture, Ministry of Communications, Ministry of the Textile Industry, the All China Federation of Supply and Marketing Co-operatives, and the Overseas Chinese Affairs Commission, published theoretical journals[7] as did mass organisations such as the All China Federation of Trade Unions, the Chinese Communist Youth League and the All China Women's Federation.[8]

These theoretical journals contain directives which have to be acted upon, notices and communications (like directives, only with less policy force), editorials which provide the basis for discussion of current problems, and discussions of a particular aspect of work in the organisation concerned. In the case of some ministerial journals, cadres of a certain rank were required as part of their job to submit to the journal a discussion on a theme of their own choosing for possible publication. These publications also contained readers' letters and criticism of individual units. It would seem that the ministerial organ has not been given enough weight in research on contemporary China. It contains much more specific information on the working of basic level units than the local newspaper, except probably in the field of agriculture.

Less important organisations such as the All China Federation of Literary and Art Circles, the Union of Chinese Drama Workers, the Sino-Soviet Friendship Association, the Chinese Buddhist Association all have official publications[9] and these provide some extremely interesting material.

[7] These journals were: *T'ung-chi kung-tso* and *T'ung-chi kung-tso t'ung-hsün* (both published by the State Statistical Bureau); *Chi-hua yü t'ung-chi* (sponsored jointly by the State Statistical Bureau and the State Planning Commission); *Chi-hua ching-chi* (sponsored jointly by the State Planning Commission and the State Economic Commission); *Lao-tung* (Ministry of Labour); *Chung kung-yeh t'ung-hsün* (Ministry of Heavy Industry); *Chung-kuo nung-pao* (Ministry of Agriculture); *Jen-min chiao-t'ung* (Ministry of Communications); *Chung-kuo fang-chih* (Ministry of Textile Industry); *Chung-yang ho-tso t'ung-hsün* (Ministry of Trade and All China Federation of Supply and Marketing Co-operatives); *Ch'iao-wu pao* (Overseas Chinese Affairs Commission).

[8] These journals were: *Chung-kuo kung-jen* (published by the All China Federation of Trade Unions); *Chung-kuo ch'ing-nien* (Chinese Communist Youth League); *Chung-kuo fu-nü* (All China Women's Federation).

[9] These publications were: *Jen-min wen-hsüeh* (published by the All China Federation of

In the early 1950s a considerable amount of effort went into the establishment of a nation-wide propaganda network, and local Party committees and Party fractions (*tang-tsu*) in lower-level ministerial echelons were required to prepare propaganda material for the various political movements, such as Democratic Reform, the Three and Five Anti Movements, etc., which took place at that time. The bulk of the propaganda material produced in the very early period took the form of pamphlets, though basic level propaganda journals were produced, and some may be found in Western libraries. For example, the periodical *Chih-pu sheng-huo* was produced in various forms in Tientsin, Wuhan, Yen-chi, and K'un-ming and deals with the work of the basic level Party branch and the duties of the Party cadre.

With the exception of the large number of literary and artistic publications which were produced mainly in the Great Leap Forward and which gave scope to the creative writing ability of the peasants and workers in various localities, very few local-level periodicals have found their way out of China.

Restricted Information

We have dealt so far with material available at bookshops which may be purchased by anyone, although some of it may well have been restricted for export at various times. There is, however, one further category which does not find its place in national bibliographies but which is of tremendously important research value—the internal (*nei-pu*) publications. My own observations in China in the middle 1960s before the Cultural Revolution led me to the conclusion that almost every school, college, university, factory, government department, commune, etc., published its own news sheet. The 'Red Guard newspapers' which appeared during the Cultural Revolution were often these under other names. Virtually none of these earlier house-organs has ever found its way into Western libraries; indeed very little restricted material in general has. A notable exception would be *Kung-tso t'ung-hsün*,[10] an internal People's Liberation Army publication restricted to officers of regimental level and above, which was captured by rebels in Tibet and found its way, *via* India, into the United States. This has given us some very useful information on the state of the armed forces and the country as a whole in the period of natural calamities. One could also include in this category the local news releases of the Hsinhua News Agency (*Hsin-hua she ti-fang hsin-wen kao*), which were sent down from the central Hsinhua office in Peking for the information of local newspaper

---

Literary and Art Circles); *Hsi-chü yen-chiu* (The Union of Chinese Drama Workers); *Chung-Su yu-hao* (The Sino-Soviet Friendship Association); *Hsien-tai Fo-hsüeh* (The Chinese Buddhist Association). They have all been suspended.
[10] These have been translated with commentary by J. Chester Ch'eng, *PLA, Kung-tso T'ung-hsün, The Politics of the Chinese Red Army* (Stanford, 1966).

editors. Libraries also hold material captured during Kuomintang raids, such as the Lien-chiang Documents,[11] and material taken from defecting naval vessels, such as the F 131 documents.[12] These examples are perhaps the most important, but this category could include anything down to the bulletin of the Refuse Collection Department of a minor factory.

Basic Reference Materials

In the bibliography at the end of this chapter are listed some sixty collections of documents and compendia of laws and decrees. These constitute only a fraction of such collections. Right from the time of liberation, collections of directives, decrees, and authoritative newspaper editorials were compiled as a guide to basic-level cadres; researchers would do well to consult them before commencing any survey of the press. I cannot but feel that a lot of time is wasted by researchers who plunge straight into reading runs of local newspapers without first examining the publications of the Party propaganda departments, which have done a lot of their material collection work for them. For example, it is possible to spend several months reading the *Nan-fang jih-pao* and *Ch'ang-chiang jih-pao* through 1951 to trace the course of the Democratic Reform Movement in the Central South. Such time can be shortened by consulting one of the cadre handbooks entitled *Kan-pu hsüeh-hsi tzu-liao* (No. 37) in which most of the key accounts have already been collected. It is possible to go through several years of the press for the late 1940s and early 1950s to trace wages policy but time can be saved by first consulting the *Chung-yang ts'ai-ching cheng-ts'e fa-ling hui-pien* issued by the Financial and Economic Affairs Committee of the Government Affairs Council.

Such short cuts are of course no substitute for a careful survey of the press, but considerable time may be saved by first consulting such collections, many of which are listed by Berton and Wu,[13] whose work is absolutely indispensable for all researchers on contemporary China.

Though I have strongly advocated the use of published collections of directives and newspaper editorials, a word of caution is in order with regard to materials collected outside the People's Republic. Some collections such as *Liu Shao-ch'i wen-t'i tzu-liao chuan-chi*, published by the Institute for the Study of Chinese Communist Problems in Taipei, and collections of material on the Cultural Revolution made by the Union Research Institute in Hong Kong are very useful whilst many others consist of little more than a random selection of articles of doubtful reliability from the Hong Kong press. The

---

[11] See C.S. Ch'en, ed., C.R. Ridley, tr, *Rural People's Communes in Lien-chiang* (Stanford, 1969).
[12] These have been reprinted by the Taiwan Institute of International Relations under the title *Tang chih-pu ku-kan hsüeh-hsi ts'ai-liao* with the English title cover *Study Materials for the CCP Branch Elite Cadres* (1970).
[13] Peter Berton and Eugene Wu, *Contemporary China: A Research Guide*, Hoover Institution Bibliographical Series XXXI (Stanford, 1967).

high prices which can be obtained for research and teaching aids have meant that a large number of marginally useful and grossly expensive items have appeared upon the Hong Kong and American markets, not the least among them collections of translated documents taken largely from the *Selected Works of Mao Tse-tung* and *Peking Review* without any reference whatsoever to the original.

Statistical Materials

Most statistical material has to be grubbed from periodicals. Apart from the periodical publications of the State Statistical Bureau mentioned earlier, *Wei-ta ti shih-nien*, giving statistics of the first ten years of the Chinese People's Republic, is a useful research source.[14] It should be borne in mind here that statistics during the Great Leap Forward were extremely unreliable, and since the Great Leap Forward they have been very hard to come by indeed. Most economists and statisticians work on estimates and argue amongst themselves as to which estimate is the most reliable.

Atlases

Though I am convinced that good comprehensive atlases must exist somewhere in China, I have never seen one, nor met anyone who has. The best available is the *Chung-hua jen-min kung-ho kuo fen-sheng ti-t'u*, the last edition of which was published in 1971[15] though no new edition has been seen in the West since 1965. The 1964 edition has been reprinted in Taiwan under, of course, a different title, *Kung-fei ch'ieh-chü hsia ti Chung-kuo ta-lu fen-sheng ti-t'u*.[16] I am told that the most useful and detailed maps on the People's Republic of China are held by the Central Intelligence Agency in Washington, and as such are unavailable to scholars.[17] What are available, however, are out-of-date maps produced by the United States Defence Department which are quite detailed and useful, and large-scale (down to 1:20,000) detailed maps dating from the early Min-kuo period which may be found in the Tōyō bunko and National Diet Library in Japan.

[14] *Wei-ta ti shih-nien Chung-hua jen-min kung-ho kuo ching-chi ho wen-hua chien-she ti t'ung-chi* (Peking, 1959). A translation was published by Peking Foreign Languages Press in 1960 entitled *Ten Great Years: Statistics of the Economic and Cultural Achievements of the Chinese People's Republic.*
[15] I am informed by visitors that current atlases of this type are not much more detailed than the earlier ones (though new railways etc. are marked). Such atlases were used widely during the 'long marches' which Red Guards made to Peking, Yen-an etc. in late 1966 and 1967.
[16] This is a fairly faithful copy of the People's Republic edition though in the explanatory text the characters *fei* (bandit) and *wei* (false) are ritually inserted.
[17] Repeated efforts have been made by scholars to obtain these maps though as yet without much success. The 1959 CIA atlas did, however, find its way into some American libraries. This was a reproduction on a larger scale of the 1956 edition of the *Chung-kuo fen-sheng ti-t'u* published in Shanghai and, according to rumour, bears little relation to the very detailed current CIA maps.

General Handbooks

The newspaper *Ta-kung pao* published annually, from 1950 to 1965, a yearbook called *Jen-min shou-ts'e* which dealt with the major directives of the year, foreign agreements concluded by the People's Republic, lists of Party and government personnel, and the activities of mass organisations.[18] It is an indispensable reference tool. The Taiwan counterpart of this is the *Chung-kung nien-pao* formerly known as the *Fei-ch'ing nien-pao*.[19] The Japanese counterpart is *Shin Chūgoku nenkan*.[20] There should also be mentioned here the various compilations made in 1959, the tenth anniversary of the Chinese People's Republic—such as *Hui-huang ti shih-nien* (2 vols.) and its echoes in Hong Kong and Taiwan.

Bibliographies

The Chinese national bibliography *Ch'üan-kuo hsin shu-mu*, produced by the Peking National Library, contained almost all the books generally released throughout the People's Republic, but, of course, did not include the more interesting internal publications. A very small percentage of the books listed in this national bibliography has left China, and it is a fruitless task for scholars to sit down with this in front of them and decide what books they need, though of course the bibliography is very useful in indicating the types of material published. In addition, the Peking National Library published an annual bibliography, *Ch'üan-kuo tsung shu-mu*, which was a digest of the *Hsin shu-mu*. The Shanghai Newspaper Library published *Ch'üan-kuo chu-yao pao-k'an tzu-liao so-yin*, which is an invaluable index of Chinese major periodicals. An important reference work in this connection is the catalogue of Chinese periodicals held by the Shanghai Newspaper Library, *Shang-hai shih pao-k'an t'u-shu kuan Chung-wen ch'i-k'an mu-lu*, which lists their holdings of China's major periodicals from 1881-1956. One should also include in this category newspaper indexes. These are monthly publications and exist for all the major newspapers, and plans have been made by the Center for Chinese Research Materials in Washington to collect and reprint some of them.

Foreign Policy Documents

Basic reference works here would include *Chung-hua jen-min kung-ho kuo t'iao-yüeh chi*, published by the Ministry of Foreign Affairs (13 vols., Peking, 1957-64), and *Chung-hua jen-min kung-ho kuo tui-wai kuan-hsi wen-chien chi* (10 vols., Peking, 1957-65). In this category there are also collected docu-

---

[18] There was no edition for 1954 probably because of controversy surrounding the Kao Kang case.
[19] Began publication in 1967.
[20] This yearbook published by the Chūgoku kenkyūjo was formerly known as *Chūgoku nenkan* (1955-61). *Shin Chūgoku nenkan* began publication in 1962.

ments on Sino-Japanese relations, Sino-Soviet relations, Sino-Indian relations, etc., as well as a mass of pamphlets and diplomatic notes, most of which exist in translation.

English-Language Material

Translating Chinese-language material into English is a full-time job for several thousand people. The People's Republic has published several English-language periodicals, of which the most important are *Peking Review*,[21] *China Reconstructs*,[22] and *China Pictorial*.[23] The New China News Agency (Hsinhua) release is published daily and contains a large amount of material translated from *Jen-min jih-pao*, radio broadcasts, and news agency releases. Western translation series include the following.

Summary of World Broadcasts,[24] published by the B.B.C. Monitoring Service, consists of a British selection of Chinese broadcast material monitored on Okinawa. It is the best source I know of up-to-date material on contemporary China, though its coverage is not particularly detailed.

Foreign Broadcast Information Service, Washington derives largely from the same sources as *Summary of World Broadcasts*, except that the selection is made in Washington. Its bias is a little different from that of *Summary of World Broadcasts*, dealing more with foreign affairs than domestic news. It also contains some items which did not originate in radio broadcasts, and its coverage is more intensive than *Summary of World Broadcasts*. Its circulation is at present restricted.

Survey of China Mainland Press (SCMP)[25] is published by the United States Consulate General in Hong Kong and contains translations of press articles. It is published together with a supplement which until recently had a restricted circulation; it has now been declassified. During the Cultural Revolution a lot of Red Guard material appeared in this supplement. *Selections from China Mainland Magazines (SCMM)* is also produced by the United States Consulate General, Hong Kong, and consists of translations of weekly and monthly periodical articles rather than items in the daily press. It was formerly known as *Extracts from China Mainland Magazines*. *Current Background* is another publication of the United States Consulate General, Hong Kong. It differs from *SCMP* and *SCMM* in that translated material is collected around themes.

---

[21] Commenced publication in 1958 replacing *People's China* (1950-7) (semi-monthly)—*Peking Review* did not cease publication in the Cultural Revolution.
[22] Commenced publication 1952: did not cease publication in the Cultural Revolution.
[23] Commenced publication 1951: did not cease publication during the Cultural Revolution.
[24] Available from the Monitoring Service of the British Broadcasting Corporation, Caversham Park, Reading, Berks, U.K.
[25] *SCMP* and the other U.S. Consulate General material is available from U.S. Government Clearing House for Federal Scientific and Technical Information, Springfield, Virginia 22151.

The Joint Publications Research Service (JPRS) is a Federal agency of the United States government. Its main function is to provide a translation service for other American government departments. It has translated many tens of thousands of pages of Chinese material in the past few years, and these are grouped under various headings. The amount of paper involved is colossal; most libraries consequently prefer to buy their JPRS series on microfilm. Various bibliographies (of JPRS material) have been attempted but it has been very difficult in the past to keep up with the publications of this agency, though, as one might expect, the output of JPRS translations during the Cultural Revolution was much less than previously.

Union Research Service, Hong Kong[26] is a similar publication to *Survey of China Mainland Press*. It is published by the Union Research Institute in Hong Kong. The Institute contains more translated material from local newspapers than the Consulate General material, though its scope is less wide. *China News Analysis*[27] is a weekly newsletter edited by Father La Dany in Hong Kong. It contains useful information not found elsewhere, but is fiercely anti-Communist.

Western-Language Bibliographies and Reference Works

A number of bibliographical works which include contemporary material have appeared in English, though there have been very few which deal exclusively with the People's Republic. The most useful introductory bibliographical work on contemporary China that has appeared since 1949 is *Contemporary China: A Research Guide* which has already been mentioned. Also worthy of note is a pioneer bibliography of secondary material on Chinese politics, compiled by Michel Oksenberg and others of Columbia University, New York.[28]

An annual bibliography of monographic and periodical literature in Western languages is published by the Association of Asian Studies, Ann Arbor.[29] It is anticipated that this bibliography will be computerised, and as such will surely be more comprehensive than at the moment. Work is in progress at present on a mammoth computerised bibliographical project at Stanford University, California, edited by William Skinner. Its scope includes works in a large number of languages. For a list of work in progress on contemporary China see *Modern China Studies: International Bulletin* published by the Contemporary China Institute, London.[30]

[26] Available from Union Research Institute, 9 College Road, Kowloon, Hong Kong (Box 5381).
[27] Available from Hong Kong, P.O. Box 13225.
[28] Michel Oksenberg (with Nancy Bateman and James B. Anderson), *A Bibliography of Secondary English Language Literature on Contemporary Chinese Politics* (New York, 1970).
[29] This is a supplement to the *Journal of Asian Studies*. Correspondence to 48 Lane Hall, Ann Arbor, Michigan 48104.
[30] Editor Jill Kitson, 37 Sidney Road, Twickenham, Middlesex, U.K. Subscriptions to Research Publications, 11 Nelson Road, London, S.E.10.

Biographical Data

The most comprehensive biographical file on personnel in the Chinese People's Republic has been maintained by the United States Consulate General in Hong Kong, and has been released to university libraries. This consists of 115 reels of 16mm microfilm. Each card is a reference to the activity of a certain individual on a certain occasion, or perhaps a reference to him in a periodical or newspaper article. It is potentially very useful, but its arrangement is bad and the researcher would need a considerable amount of patience to get very much value out of it. What is considerably more usable is the biographical file maintained by the Union Research Institute in Hong Kong. One or two entries are published with every edition of *Union Research Service,* and the coverage is extensive although not as wide as the Consulate General file. A number of biographical dictionaries also exist, and for the general reader these are probably more useful. Examples include (as well as Klein and Clark's and Boorman's works noted in Chün-tu Hsüeh's chapter of this volume): *Chung-kung jen-ming lu* (Taipei, 1967), English edition, *Chinese Communist Who's Who,* 2 vols. (Taipei, 1970); and *Who's Who in Communist China,* 2 vols. (Hong Kong, 1969-70).

Pamphlets

One of the richest sources of documentation on contemporary China is pamphlet literature. Insufficient use has been made of this, because comprehensive bibliographies of pamphlet literature do not exist, and there has been a tendency for traditional librarians to despise it on the grounds that pamphlets are not really scholarly works. Some of the best works on micro-societal analysis of the People's Republic of China have depended largely on pamphlet literature, which usually contained far more useful detailed descriptions of the basic-level situation than periodicals. Those libraries that did buy pamphlets bought them in a very piecemeal fashion. The result was that the pamphlet collection in each of the major libraries in the Western world is very different from the next. Some systematic attempt must be made to list the many thousand titles for the use of scholars. On the subject of industrial management alone, on a trip to five United States libraries I recently found over 100 titles. Of these one could estimate that perhaps one in five had some good research value and one in twenty appeared to be a real gem. We cannot really expect individual researchers to have the funds to visit all the major libraries in the world, and it is therefore in this field that there is the most urgent need for bibliographical work.

Material and Data

Contemporary Chinese scholarship, especially in the social sciences, has been deeply influenced by the technological revolution. From time to time emerge ambitious computer schemes which aim to convert the vast amount of material available into data which can be processed by computers. Unfortunately, funds are not yet available to undertake the establishment of computer data banks, the existence of which would indeed take a great deal of the drudgery out of research. There is some resistance to data banks on the part of traditional scholars and sometimes for very good reason. It is my personal opinion that in certain parts of the United States data collection has become a substitute for analysis. Information gathering has become an end in itself. In this, as in many fields, our technological capability has outpaced our research maturity.

The Immaturity of the Field

Social science programs dealing with contemporary China have only just been started, and the field is still in a very immature stage of development. There have been a number of conflicting tendencies which have not only restricted the field, but also restricted the availability of research material. The first of these is the conservative tendency which I mentioned before. This maintains, in its extreme form, that Sinology should have nothing at all to do with contemporary China, and that the study of contemporary China is the proper study of the journalist. The second tendency, that of the China-watcher, is dangerous in that professional China-watchers tend to apply to the Chinese situation stereotyped models of power analysis, which only partially fit the situation. When this tendency is predominant, works on theoretical problems or ideology are usually not collected on the grounds that they are insufficiently factual. The third dangerous tendency is the attempt to compartmentalise China studies under rigid disciplinary rubrics. The conventional lines of demarcation between, for example, political science, economics, sociology, and political thought, make very little sense when applied to China. An undue concentration on any one of these disciplines will produce an unbalanced material collection.

The Situation in Mid-1971

The early stages of the Cultural Revolution saw a great flood of immensely valuable material on ideology and basic level organisation. Such material was of particular value for the light it shed not only on the Cultural Revolution itself, but also the divergencies in developmental policies over the whole twenty years' history of the Chinese People's Republic. Previously un-published speeches and directives of Mao, such as those contained in *Mao Tse-tung ssu-hsiang wan-sui* and *Mao Chu-hsi wen-hsüan*, became available, as did reconstructed speeches of Liu Shao-ch'i such as those made at Tientsin in the spring of 1949. Some material dealt even with Communist Party history before 1949, though the veracity of some of the accounts has been questioned. By the end of 1968, however, there were very few so-called Red Guard publications still being published and at the time of writing very little material at all is coming out of China. The bookshops in most Chinese cities are somewhat bare, though there has been a rapid increase in the production of technical works, manuals for 'barefoot doctors', collections of editorials from national and local newspapers, and *pao-kao wen-hsüeh* in recent months. Export of all these items is forbidden and only the occasional item, such as one of the barefoot doctors' manuals, has appeared in Western libraries. We cannot say as yet whether we are going to experience a similar dearth of material to that which obtained in the years 1960-2, or whether, now that stable conditions prevail and travel to China is becoming increasingly more frequent, we will see another flood of material. Whatever happens, the last twenty years have produced a truly immense amount of basic research material, and there can be absolutely no justification at all for the claim that we just do not have enough information on how Chinese society operates. What we lack is not material, but appropriate conceptual frameworks to evaluate it and enough competent scholars to undertake this most challenging work.

BIBLIOGRAPHY

Collections of Documents
   The following list covers only a small proportion of the documentary collections available.
Cheng-fu kung-tso pao-kao, Peking, 1951.
Chiao-yü shih-nien, Peking, 1960.
Chung-hua jen-min kung-ho kuo fa-chan kuo-min ching-chi ti ti-i-ko wu-nien chi-hua, 1953-1957, Peking, 1955.
Chung-hua jen-min kung-ho kuo k'ai-kuo wen-hsien, Hong Kong, 1949.
Chung-hua jen-min kung-ho kuo Kuo-wu yüan kung-pao, Peking, 1955-
Chung-kung Wen-hua ta ke-ming tzu-liao hui-pien, Hong Kong, 1967-70. This compendium, prepared by the Contemporary China Research Institute under the general supervision of Ting Wang, so far includes 5 vols.: 1, 1967, on struggling against power holders; 2, 1969, on Teng T'o; 3, 1969, on P'eng Teh-huai; 4, 1970, on Wu Han; 5, 1970, on the Cultural Revolution in Peking. Further volumes are being prepared. The institute has also made collections of other documents on prominent figures in the Cultural Revolution: *Ch'en Po-ta wen-chi* (1949-68); *Yao Wen-yüan wen-chi* (1965-8); and *Chiang Ch'ing wen-chi* (1964-8).
Chung-kuo Kung-ch'an tang ti-pa-tz'u ch'üan-kuo tai-piao ta-hui kuan-yü fa-chan kuo-min ching-chi ti ti-erh-ko wu-nien chi-hua (1958-1962) ti chien-i, Peking, 1956.
Chung-kuo Kung-ch'an tang ti-pa-tz'u ch'üan-kuo tai-piao ta-hui wen-hsien, Peking, 1957. A collection of documents was made for the Second Session of the Eighth Congress held in 1958, though only a selection of documents (in translation) seems to have been exported.

Chung-kuo nung-yeh ho-tso hua yün-tung shih-liao, 2 vols., Peking, 1957-9.
Jen-min kung-she kuang-mang wan-chang—Kung-she ching-chi tiao-ch'a, Peking, 1960.
Jen-min kung-she wan-sui, Peking, 1960.
Jen-min kung-she wen-t'i tzu-liao, Hong Kong, 1959.
Kan-pu hsüeh-hsi tzu-liao, 59 vols., Canton, 1950-3.
Kuan-yü kuo-chi kung-ch'an chu-i tsung lu-hsien ti lun-chan, Peking, 1965.
Kung-fei Wen-hua ta ke-ming chung-yao wen-chien hui-pien, 2 vols., Taiwan, 1968 (with 1969 supplement).
Kung-pao, Peking, 1957- . The official gazette of the Standing Committee of the National People's Congress.
Kuo-min ching-chi hui-fu shih-ch'i nung-yeh sheng-ch'an ho-tso tzu-liao hui-pien, 2 vols., Peking, 1957.
Kuo-tu shih-ch'i tsung lu-hsien hsüeh-hsi ts'an-k'ao tzu-liao, 2 vols., Peking, 1954.
Liu Shao-ch'i wen-t'i tzu-liao chuan-chi, Taipei, 1970.
Mao Chu-hsi wen-hsüan, n.p., n.d. (Red Guard source).
Mao Tse-tung hsüan-chi, 4 vols., 1951, 1952, 1953, 1960. Although all of the articles in this selection of Mao Tse-tung's works antedate the establishment of the People's Republic, the importance of this work for the present time is such that it is indispensable. Some of Mao's later essays are included in *Mao Tse-tung chu-tso hsüan-tu*. *Mao Chu-hsi yü-lu*, of which a number of different editions exist, is also indispensable. Much of the material in these texts has been revised. To consult original texts, see the collection made in Japan, *Mao Tse-tung chi*, supervised by Takeuchi Minoru, Tokyo, 1970- . Not all of the ten volumes have yet been published. They will unfortunately not go beyond 1949.
Mao Tse-tung ssu-hsiang wan-sui, n.p., 1967 (Red Guard source).
Nung-tso wu ch'an-liang tiao-ch'a ching-yen hui-pien, Peking, 1960.
She-hui chu-i chiao-yü k'o-ch'eng ti yüeh-tu wen-chien hui-pien, 3 vols., 1957-8.
T'u-ti kai-ke shou-ts'e, Shanghai, 1950.
T'ung-chi kung-tso chung-yao wen-chien hui-pien, 3 vols., Peking, 1955-9.

    In addition, the following general categories of documents can be consulted: those relating to the various congresses of the All China Federation of Industry and Commerce (for details see Berton and Wu, *Contemporary China*, p. 295); those on the various national congresses of Chinese women (ibid., pp. 273-4); those relating to the various All China Youth Congresses and congresses relating to youth (ibid., pp. 270-3); documents of the various plenary sessions of the Chinese People's Political Consultative Conference and of Meetings of the National Committees of that body (ibid., pp. 256-9); various collections of documents on sessions of the National People's Congress (for a full list up to 1964 see ibid., pp. 260-3); documents of the congresses of the All China Federation of Trade Unions (ibid., p. 296); and finally, the various collections of documents on the plenary sessions of the

Seventh, Eighth and Ninth Central Committees of the Chinese Communist Party.

Compendia of Laws and Decrees

Ch'ang-k'uang ch'i-yeh shih-yung fa-kuei shou-ts'e, Peking, 1958.

Chin-jung fa-kuei hui-pien, 7 vols., Peking, 1956-62.

Chung-hua jen-min kung-ho kuo fa-kuei hui-pien, 13 vols., Peking, 1956-63. An absolutely basic collection.

Chung-hua jen-min kung-ho kuo hsien-fa hsüeh-hsi ts'an-k'ao tzu-liao, Peking, 1957.

Chung-hua jen-min kung-ho kuo min-fa tzu-liao hui-pien, Peking, 1954.

Chung-hua jen-min kung-ho kuo t'u-ti fa ts'an-k'ao tzu-liao hui-pien, Peking, 1957.

Chung-hua jen-min kung-ho kuo yu-kuan kung-an kung-tso fa-kuei hui-pien, Peking, 1958.

Chung-teng chuan-yeh chiao-yü fa-ling hui-pien, Peking, 1957.

Chung-yang jen-min cheng-fu fa-ling hui-pien, 5 vols., Peking, 1952-5. The basic law collection for the early years.

Chung-yang lao-tung fa-ling hui-pien, Peking, 1953.

Chung-yang shui-wu fa-ling hui-chi, Peking, 1952.

Chung-yang ts'ai-cheng fa-kuei hui-pien, 8 vols., Peking, 1957-60.

Chung-yang ts'ai-ching cheng-ts'e fa-ling hui-pien, 3 parts, Peking, 1950-2.

Hsüan-chü kung-tso shou-ts'e, Peking, [1953].

Hun-yin wen-t'i ts'an-k'ao tzu-liao hui-pien, Shanghai, 1950.

Kung-hui fa chi ch'i yu-kuan wen-chien, Peking, 1953.

Min-tsu cheng-ts'e wen-chien hui-pien, 3 vols., Peking, 1953, 1958, 1960. For other law and policy compendia dealing with national minorities see Berton and Wu, *Contemporary China*, pp. 244-5.

Nung-ts'un shih-yung fa-kuei shou-ts'e, Peking, 1958.

Shang-yeh shih-yung fa-kuei shou-ts'e, Peking, 1958.

Ssu-ying kung-shang yeh ti she-hui chu-i kai-tsao cheng-ts'e fa-ling hsüan-pien, Peking, 1957.

史 xxv: Sources on the Overseas Chinese

PNG POH-SENG

According to statistics provided by the Overseas Chinese Affairs Commission in Taipei there were 18,301,126 people of Chinese origin living outside China (which includes Taiwan) in 1969.[1] This figure includes the Chinese living in Hong Kong and Macao. If we exclude the approximately 3,800,000 Chinese in Hong Kong and 200,000 in Macao, the number of Overseas Chinese would be a little over 14,000,000. The ethnic Chinese who emigrated abroad were given the name *hua-ch'iao* (Overseas Chinese) because until recently they regarded themselves as Chinese citizens who had gone to sojourn in foreign countries. The term *hua-ch'iao* is gradually going out of favour among the Overseas Chinese because the bulk of them are no more sojourners in foreign lands but citizens of their countries of domicile. In time they will probably all become like the Chinese in the United States of America or Australia who regard themselves as Americans or Australians although their Chinese identity remains. Thus terms such as American Chinese, Australian Chinese, Singaporean Chinese, Malaysian Chinese, Thai Chinese, Indonesian Chinese, etc. should become more appropriate labels.

Notwithstanding their identification with their local environment, the fact of their Chinese origin is a common factor for studying their characteristics, social institutions, historical backgrounds, and problems of integration or assimilation. The history of the Overseas Chinese may therefore be regarded as an offshoot of Chinese history, but what comes hereafter, especially now that the countries in which they live have become independent nations, should ultimately become a part of their respective national histories.

As the area covered here is so vast we can do no more than make a broad survey of sources and existing published materials on the subject. First of all we shall deal briefly with sources on the Overseas Chinese as a whole and then make a bibliographical survey by regions.

General Surveys of the Overseas Chinese

There are several general histories of the Overseas Chinese. These include: Chang Hsü-kuang, *Chung-hua min-tsu fa-chan shih-kang* (Kweilin,

[1] *China Year Book 1969-1970* (Taipei), p. 394.

266

1943); Ch'en Li-t'e, *Chung-kuo hai-wai i-min shih* (Shanghai, 1946); and Narita Setsuo, *Kakyōshi* (revised ed. Tokyo, 1942).[2] The Overseas Chinese Affairs Commission of the Republic of China in Taiwan published in 1956 a general gazetteer on the overseas Chinese, *Hua-ch'iao chih tsung-chih*, which provides a compendium of factual information on the Overseas Chinese throughout the world. This was followed by surveys of separate countries. A series, Hai-wai wen-k'u, has also been published in Taipei. These are historical sketches of the Overseas Chinese in Australia, Burma, Canada, Chile, Hawaii, Indonesia, Laos, Malaya, Mexico, Singapore, and elsewhere. The volumes on Chile and Mexico are especially useful since little is known about the Chinese communities in these two countries.[3] Lee Tung-hai (David T.H. Lee) has a detailed compilation *Chia-na-ta hua-ch'iao shih* (Taipei, 1967). Then there are of course some general works in Western languages which we need not enumerate here.[4]

Primary Source Materials

An important source for the modern history of the Overseas Chinese is the Chinese newspapers published in most of the countries where Chinese communities exist. There is also relevant material from the official Chinese side in the Kuomintang archives and the Ministry of Foreign Affairs records in Taiwan. In addition there were semi-governmental periodicals published in China from time to time during the pre-World War II period, as well as reports made by the respective governments where the Chinese lived. The last is especially significant in the countries of Southeast Asia, particularly Malaya and Singapore.

As both Peking and Taipei are interested in the Chinese overseas they each maintain a special department on Overseas Chinese affairs which collects information and compiles reports on current developments, some of which are published. The Peking government has its monthly *Ch'iao-wu pao* published since 1956, while the Taipei government has its monthly bulletin *Ch'iao-wu yüeh-pao* published since 1952. Taipei has also published the *Ch'iao-sheng t'ung-hsün* since 1958.[5]

For research into existing Chinese social and other institutions within Chinese communities the obvious primary sources are the constitutions, annual and other publications of the respective societies themselves. These are most numerous in Southeast Asia.[6]

---

[2] Uchida Naosaku, *The Overseas Chinese, A Bibliographical Essay Based on the Resources of the Hoover Institution*, p. 6.

[3] T'ang Ch'eng-chin, *Chih-li hua-ch'iao shih-hua* (Taipei, 1954). Yü Shou-chih, *Mo-hsi-ko hua-ch'iao shih-hua* (Taipei, 1954).

[4] See Uchida Naosaku, *The Overseas Chinese*, p. 86, and Purcell, *The Chinese in Southeast Asia*, pp. 574-7.

[5] Ibid., pp. 4-5, 73.

[6] See below.

Sources on the Overseas Chinese by Area of Residence

The Americas: there is a fair amount of published material, both official and private, on problems concerning the Chinese in the United States of America.[7] This was partly brought about by the Chinese Exclusion Act of 1882 which placed restrictions on Chinese immigration into the United States. The relatively large Chinese population in San Francisco also attracted interest because early Chinese political leaders like Sun Yat-sen visited it several times. The question of Chinese immigration to the United States of America is thus well documented in English-language works. These include William Speer, *The Oldest and the Newest Empire: China and the United States* (Hartford, Phil., 1870); Russel H. Conwell, *Why and How, Why the Chinese Emigrate, and the Means They Adopt for the Purpose of Reaching America* (Boston, 1871); Alexander McLeod, *Pigtails and Gold Dust, A Panorama of Chinese Life in Early California* (Caldwell, 1947); and George F. Seward, *Chinese Immigration in its Social and Economic Aspects* (New York, 1881). In the Chinese language there is a comprehensive study, *Mei-kuo hua-ch'iao pai-nien chi-shih* (Hong Kong, 1954) by Wu Shang-ying.[8] Perhaps the only account about the Chinese in Cuba is Sung Hsi-jen's *Ku-pa hua-ch'iao shih-hua* (Taipei, 1958).[9] We have noted earlier that there are also accounts about the Chinese in Chile and Mexico. All three are Taipei publications.[10]

Europe: the Chinese communities in Europe are relatively small compared with those of Southeast Asia or America. According to the statistics given in the *China Handbook, 1965-1966*, there were 34,648 Chinese in the whole of Europe as of June 1965. Material on Chinese in Europe is scarce. Towards the end of the nineteenth century, Chinese labourers were recruited into Russia to construct the Baikal railway and mine gold in the Amur region. On this there are I.S. Levitov's *The Yellow Race* (St Petersburg, 1900) and Wladimir K. Arsenjew's *Russen und Chinesen in Ostsibirien* (Berlin, [1926]).[11] During the First World War Chinese labourers were also recruited to Europe to work in factories and behind the front lines, particularly in France. This resulted in Chinese immigration into several European countries. There are a few scattered writings on this question. The Chinese workers in France produced a magazine, the *Hua-kung tsa-chih*, of which Stanford University has only one number.[12] Between 1943 and 1945, the Chinese in England published the *K'ang-chan chou-pao*, while just after the war ended the *Chien-kuo chou-pao* was published (1945-7).[13] The smallness

---

[7] Uchida Naosaku, *The Overseas Chinese*, pp. 9-13, 106-8.
[8] Ibid., pp. 9-13, 84.
[9] Ibid., p. 107.
[10] Ibid., pp. 83, 84.
[11] Ibid., p. 11.
[12] Ibid., p. 108.
[13] Ibid.

of the Chinese communities in Europe and the transient nature of their stay (many went merely for education) are the reasons for their insignificance.

Japan and Korea: the Chinese in Japan and Korea have attracted little outside attention because they are, in the main, a well assimilated minority. At the turn of the century, Japan was the most popular country for Chinese students seeking Western knowledge and higher education. Similarity of writing and culture made it easier for the Chinese who settled in Japan to intermarry and become assimilated. The Sino-Japanese War of 1937 to 1945 must have made the position of Chinese citizens in Japan difficult, but since then those who remained are becoming more assimilated with the Japanese. Immigrants from Taiwan (once a Japanese colony) found less difficulty in settling down in Japan, since they had acquired Japanese modes of living. Of the Chinese in Korea, little is known. The following is some of the published material on the Chinese in Japan and Korea: Juan Wei-ts'un, *Liu-Jih hua-ch'iao kai-k'uang* (Nanking, 1933); Sung Yüeh-lun, *Liu-Jih hua-ch'iao hsiao-shih* (Taipei, 1953); and Uchida Naosaku, *Ryūnichi kakyō keizai bunseki* (Tokyo, 1950). A significant newspaper published in the 1940s is *Hua-kuang*. On Korea Uchida lists only one significant source: *Chōsen buraku chōsa hōkoku daiichisatsu kadenmin raiju Shinajin* published by the office of the Governor of Korea in 1924.[14]

Southeast Asia: the most comprehensive survey of the Chinese in the region is Victor Purcell's *The Chinese in Southeast Asia*, first published in 1951 but revised and reprinted in 1965. Other surveys in Western languages include R.S. Elegant's *The Dragon's Seed: Peking and the Overseas Chinese* (New York, 1959); N.A. Simoniya's *Overseas Chinese in Southeast Asia: a Russian Study* (New York, 1961); Wang Gungwu's *A Short History of the Nanyang Chinese* (Singapore, 1959);[15] and Stephen FitzGerald's *China and the Overseas Chinese: A Study of Peking's Changing Policy 1949-1970* (Cambridge, 1972). In Chinese a very useful survey is found in *Nan-yang nien-chien* (Singapore, 1951), which is a yearbook on affairs in Southeast Asia. There are a considerable number of other general works in Chinese and Japanese on the region, of which we will mention only two: Ide Kiwata, *Nanyō to kakyō* (Tokyo, 1941); Li Ch'ang-fu, *Nan-yang hua-ch'iao shih* (Shanghai, 1933).[16]

China's early relations with Southeast Asia lie outside the scope of the present survey. Suffice it to say that sources for such a study may be found in the dynastic histories, encyclopaedias, travelogues, and topographies.[17] On the Chinese in modern Southeast Asia, source materials may be classified

[14] Ibid., p. 118.
[15] See Purcell, *The Chinese*, pp. 574-7.
[16] Ibid., pp. 586-99, and Uchida Naosaku, *The Overseas Chinese*, p. 93.
[17] Paul Wheatley, 'Chinese Sources for the History of the Malay Peninsula in Ancient Times', in K.G. Tregonning, ed., *Malayan Historical Sources* (Singapore, 1962), pp. 1-9.

into sources on the history of the Chinese and sources on current social and other institutions. The National Library, Singapore, and the University of Singapore Library have substantial holdings of Chinese-language newspapers published in Singapore and Malaya, extending from 1880 to the present day.[18] These newspapers are a copious primary source on the history of the Overseas Chinese in Southeast Asia. From 1877 onwards the British colonial government maintained a special office called the Chinese Protectorate, later renamed Chinese Secretariat, to look after Chinese affairs. The annual and other reports of this office offer a good source for the life and conditions of the Chinese in Singapore and Malaya up to 1941, from the official angle. Besides these reports, source material may also be found in the files of the Straits Settlements, Federated Malay States, and Unfederated Malay States governments, as well as the Proceedings of the Legislative Councils of the first two administrative divisions. A number of miscellaneous government reports such as the *Report of the Chinese Marriage Committee* and the *Report of the Opium Commission* also contain useful material.[19] Other published materials will be dealt with by area and countries.

Burma and Thailand: according to statistics provided by Dr Victor Purcell, the ethnic Chinese in Burma and Thailand in 1960 numbered 350,000 and 2,670,000 respectively.[20] In the case of Burma this was roughly 3 per cent of the population and in Thailand 10 per cent. Clearly the Chinese are a more significant minority group in Thailand than in Burma. Their economic influence is also stronger in Thailand. Purcell's *The Chinese in Southeast Asia* (1965) and Uchida's bibliography contain lists of Chinese language materials on the Chinese in Burma.[21] There are also a number of Japanese works on the subject. For a general account in the English language we have still to rely on Purcell's book. Contemporary primary source material can only be found in the Chinese newspapers published in Rangoon. The following are known to have existed: *Yang-chiang hsin-pao* (1908-?); *Kuang-hua jih-pao* (1908-9); *Chüeh-min jih-pao* (1913-43); *Yang-kuang jih-pao* (1921-42); *Hua-ch'iao Mien-tien ch'en-pao* (1923-?); *Chung-kuo jih-pao* (1945-?); *Hsin Yang-kuang pao* (1945-?); *Chung-hua shang-pao* (1945-?); and *Ya-chou jih-pao* (1956-?).[22]

The Chinese in Thailand have been well studied by K.P. Landon, G.W. Skinner, and R.J. Coughlin, from the historical as well as sociological

---

[18] These are listed below as part of the bibliography to this chapter.
[19] See P.L. Burns, 'Introduction to English Language Sources in Federation of Malaya', in Tregonning, *Malayan Historical Sources*, pp. 20-35, and Ng Siew Yoong, 'The Singapore Chinese Protectorate, 1877 to 1900', *Journal of Southeast Asian History* II, 2 (March 1961), pp. 98-9.
[20] *The Chinese*, p. 3.
[21] Ibid., pp. 599-600, and Uchida Naosaku, *The Overseas Chinese*, p. 108.
[22] Lau Tzu-ching, 'Chronology of Newspapers in South-east Asia', *Journal of South Seas Society* XIII, 1 (June 1957), pp. 59-67.

angles.[23] Between them the authors have covered the ground fully and anyone interested in the subject should find adequate groundwork material. There are also a number of Chinese and Japanese works, though these are only available in some libraries.[24] Again for primary source material one has to rely on Chinese newspapers published in Bangkok, Thailand. Of these the earliest known to have existed was the *Han-ching jih-pao*, published in 1903. From then to the present time dozens of newspapers have been published, some lasting only for short periods, others still in existence.[25] A semi-monthly *Hua-ch'iao t'ien-ti* published in the 1950s should be a useful source; so also the *Hua-ch'iao yen-lun chi*, a collection of speeches made by the Overseas Chinese in Thailand, published in 1942.[26] The *Hua-ch'iao chih T'ai-kuo*, published in Taipei, is a gazetteer on the Overseas Chinese in Thailand and contains much factual information.[27]

Cambodia, Laos, and Vietnam: Cambodia has an ethnic Chinese population of 425,000, whose economic power in the land is considerable, although they represent only 6.5 per cent of the population.[28] Laos has 35,000 ethnic Chinese while Vietnam has 855,000. In Vietnam the Chinese population is mainly concentrated in the south. According to Purcell, South Vietnam now has about 800,000, while North Vietnam has only 55,000.[29] As in Cambodia the Chinese in Vietnam hold economic power disproportionate to their numbers. It was estimated that, before 1956, 80 per cent of the retail trade in South Vietnam was in Chinese hands while in the rural areas the middleman was usually a Chinese.[30] The Chinese in Laos are small in number and are of less significance.

Until recently little notice has been taken of the Chinese in Indochina, and literature on the subject is scarce. Two pre-war works may be mentioned: *De la condition des Chinois et de leur rôle économique en Indo-Chine* by René Dubreuil (Barsur-Seine, 1910) and 'Le statut des Chinois en Indo-Chine', unpublished thesis for the University of Paris by Chieu Nguyen Huy.[31] There is also an undated work *Les congrégations chinoises en Indochine française* by Nguyen Quoc Dinh (Paris, undated).[32] In recent years William E. Wilmott has made a special study of the Chinese in Cambodia resulting

---

[23] See Purcell, *The Chinese*, p. 578, and Maurice Freedman & William E. Willmott, 'South-east Asia, with Special Reference to the Chinese', *International Social Science Journal* XIII, 2 (1961), p. 268.
[24] Purcell, *The Chinese*, pp. 601-2.
[25] Lau Tzu-ching, 'Chronology', pp. 59-67.
[26] Uchida Naosaku, *The Overseas Chinese*, p. 133.
[27] Purcell, *The Chinese*, p. 601.
[28] William E. Willmott, *The Chinese in Cambodia* (Vancouver, 1967), p. 15.
[29] Purcell, *The Chinese*, p. 3. It should be added, however, that estimates on this figure vary greatly.
[30] Freedman and Willmott, 'South-east Asia', p. 255.
[31] Purcell, *The Chinese*, pp. 578-9.
[32] Willmott, *The Chinese*, p. 122.

in a doctoral dissertation for London University entitled 'Chinese Society in Cambodia with Special Reference to the System of Congregations in Phnom-Penh'. This research is published in *The Political Structure of the Chinese Community in Cambodia* (London, 1970). It is expected that Willmott will publish the other parts of his research in due course. Chinese-language newspapers published in Cambodia are a useful source. They include the *Mei-chiang jih-pao* and *Mien-hua jih-pao*, both published in Phnom Penh.[33] Little else in Chinese may be found on the subject.

On the Chinese in Vietnam there is Phan-van Thinh's unpublished doctoral dissertation 'Les Chinois au Vietnam', University of Paris, 1954, and various articles. The United States Joint Publications Research Office has a volume *Indochina: the Ethnic Minorities of North Vietnam* (Washington, 1958),[34] but unfortunately it has extremely little to say about the Chinese. Luong Nhi Ky has written a Ph.D. dissertation for the University of Michigan entitled 'The Chinese in Vietnam: A Study of Vietnamese-Chinese Relations with Special Attention to the Period 1862-1961'. Joel Martin Halpern has published a book, *The Role of the Chinese in Lao society* (Los Angeles, 1961), which seems to be the only study of its kind.[35] In Chinese there are Chang Wen-ho's general account, *Yüeh-nan Kao-mien Liao-kuo hua-ch'iao ching-chi* (Taipei, 1956), which covers Vietnam, Cambodia, and Laos, and Hsin Tsu-k'ang's *Liao-kuo hua-ch'iao chiao-yü* (Taipei, 1960), which deals with Chinese education in Laos. More has been written on the Chinese in Vietnam, including a few works in Japanese.[36] Among the numerous Chinese newspapers published in Vietnam are *Hsin Tung-ya pao* (1941-5) and *Wu-pao* (1946-?).[37]

Indonesia and the Philippines: although there are over 2,700,000 ethnic Chinese in Indonesia, they represent a distinct minority in the country. Proportionately they are less numerous than the Chinese in Thailand, and politically their position is more precarious. Notable studies on the subject in English are: Tan Giok-lan, *The Chinese Community in a Sundanese town; A Study in Social and Cultural Accommodation* (Ithaca, N.Y., 1961); L.E. Williams, *Overseas Chinese Nationalism: The Genesis of the Pan-Chinese Movement in Indonesia, 1900-1916* (Glencoe, Ill., 1960); D.E. Willmott, *The Chinese of Semarang: A Changing Minority in Indonesia* (Ithaca, N.Y., 1960); and, by the same author, *The National Status of the Chinese in Indonesia 1900-58* (Ithaca, N.Y., 1961). Source materials in Chinese and Japanese include *Yin-tu-ni-hsi-ya hua-ch'iao wen-t'i tzu-liao* (Peking, 1951) edited by the Hua-ch'iao wen-t'i yen-chiu hui; *Kai-shan Ho-Yin hua-ch'iao tai-yü wen-t'i* (Nanking, 1943), a

[33] Ibid., pp. 121-2.
[34] See Purcell, *The Chinese*, p. 579.
[35] Ibid.
[36] Ibid., pp. 602-3.
[37] Lau Tzu-ching 'Chronology', pp. 64-5.

report by the Chinese Ministry of Foreign Affairs on the treatment of Chinese in Indonesia: *Batabia kakyō chōsa* (Batavia, 1939), an investigation into the Chinese in Batavia; and others. Of secondary Chinese works, the following may be mentioned: Ch'en I-ling, *Yin-ni hsien-chuang yü hua-ch'iao* published in Taipei in 1954, which deals with the Chinese in present-day Indonesia; and Tai Hung-ch'i, *Yin-ni hua-ch'iao ching-chi* (Taipei, 1956) dealing with the economic position of the Chinese.[38] As expected, the Chinese in Indonesia have published many newspapers over the years. The earliest of these was the *T'e-hsüan ts'o-yao* published in Batavia (1823-6).[39] The most important of the Chinese newspapers in Indonesia is the *Sin Po*, but there are many others.

According to Purcell's estimate there were 180,000 Chinese in the Philippines in 1947 (Skinner put it at 270,000 or 1.2 per cent of the population). As in Indonesia, the Chinese in the Philippines are a distinct minority, though they accounted for an estimated 55 to 80 per cent of the country's internal trade before the war. Since then the Chinese share of the retail trade has declined, and in 1954 it was only 12 per cent.[40]

There are now a number of monographs on the Chinese in the Philippines, of which we may mention the following three: Edgar B. Wickberg, *The Chinese in Philippine Life 1850-1898* (New Haven, 1965); Jacques Amyot, *The Chinese Community of Manila: A Study of Adaptation of Chinese Familism to the Philippine Environment* (Chicago, 1960); and George Henry Weightman, *The Philippine Chinese: A Cultural History of a Marginal Trading Community* (Ithaca, 1960). In addition, various articles have appeared. There are also a fair number of Chinese and Japanese writings.[41] For primary material, however, one has to depend on the numerous Chinese newspapers. The earliest Chinese newspaper published in Manila was the *Hua-pao* (1888-9).[42] As in the case of the Overseas Chinese elsewhere, one important archival source is the Overseas Chinese Affairs Commission in Taipei, which makes surveys and keeps records of the Overseas Chinese.

Malaya, Singapore, and Borneo: the Chinese in Malaya, Singapore, and Borneo are unique on account of their numbers. In Singapore they are an ethnic majority representing over 76 per cent; in Malaya they represent 37 per cent; in Sarawak 32 per cent; and Sabah 25 per cent. Over the entire region (excluding Brunei) the Chinese represent a majority group of 42.2 per cent.[43] It should be noted that in countries like Singapore and Malaya the ethnic Chinese are not a *minority*. In Malaya it is therefore a question of political partnership, and upon how well the partnership holds up will

---

[38] Purcell, *The Chinese*, pp. 507-8.
[39] Lau Tzu-ching, 'Chronology', pp. 59-67.
[40] Freedman and Willmott, 'South-east Asia', p. 257.
[41] Purcell, *The Chinese*, p. 609-10.
[42] Lau Tzu-ching, 'Chronology', pp. 60-7.
[43] Png Poh-seng, 'The Chinese in Singapore and Malaysia', *Asia Magazine* (7 May 1967).

depend the harmonious relations of the virtually tri-racial Malaysian society of Malays, Chinese, and Indians. In Singapore it is essentially a question of the accommodating spirit of the numerically superior ethnic Chinese in a quadri-racial society of Chinese, Indians, Malays, and Eurasians.

Victor Purcell has pioneered the study of the Chinese in Malaysia, which in his book included Singapore.[44] Sociological studies of the Chinese in Singapore have been made by Maurice Freedman and a few others.[45] As indicated earlier on, there are available source materials in government reports, files, and vernacular newspapers. In the field of Chinese social institutions, the Chinese in Singapore, Malaya, and the Bornean territories offer a rich source. Clan and district associations, business guilds, and other Chinese-organised societies abound. Even including Hong Kong, Singapore and Malaya perhaps offer sociologists the best repository of this type of traditional Chinese institution. Of course with the passage of time the functions and purposes of these societies have changed; nevertheless it is for scholars to observe such changes and to offer reasons for them. Material for such studies is found in the constitutions and annuals of individual societies,[46] as well as in their records. For historical studies, the collection of Chinese newspapers available in Singapore, Malaya, Sarawak, and Sabah contains volumes of material.[47] The *Lat pau* (1887-1932), published in Singapore, runs into 144 reels of microfilm, and offers scholars a wealth of information on Chinese activities in Singapore during the years covered. The earliest known Chinese newspaper published in this region, however, was the *T'ien-hsia hsin-wen* (1828-9), published in Malacca.[48]

Surprisingly, there is no study in depth in the Chinese language, although there are many small books and factual accounts. For biographies of the Chinese in Singapore in the nineteenth century, the most valuable contemporary work is still Song Ong Siang, *One Hundred Years' History of the Chinese in Singapore* (London, 1923) which has recently been reprinted. In Chinese there is Shen Wei-tse, ed., *Hsin-chia-p'o hua-ch'iao ming-jen chuan* (Singapore, 1950). Biographies of the Chinese in Malaya are collected in Hsü Yü-chiao, *Nan-yang ssu-chou fu hua-ch'iao shang-yeh chiao-t'ung lu* (Ipoh, 1928). The only proper study of the Chinese in Borneo is T'ien Ju-k'ang's *The Chinese in Sarawak, a Study of Social Structure* (London, 1953).[49] Deserving mention is Wilfred Blythe's study *The Impact of Chinese Secret Societies in Malaya* (London, 1969). A collection of translated articles on the Chinese

---

[44] *The Chinese in Malaya* (London, 1948).
[45] Maurice Freedman, *Chinese Family and Marriage in Singapore* (London, 1957), and other books and articles. Other sociological writings come from Marjorie Topley, Barrington Kaye, William H. Newell, Stephen Yeh and J.A. Elliott.
[46] There is a small collection in the University of Singapore Library.
[47] See Lau Tzu-ching, 'Chronology', pp. 59-64, and bibliography below.
[48] Ibid., p. 59.
[49] Purcell, *The Chinese*, pp. 582, 604-6.

in Southeast Asia has been published in the *Tung-nan-ya yen-chiu hsüeh-pao* (Singapore) II, 1 (October 1971).

Miscellaneous countries: other areas in which there are small numbers of Chinese include Australia, New Zealand, India, Ceylon, and various parts of Africa. Because of the smallness of the Chinese communities in these countries their influence is minimal. In the series Hua-ch'iao ching-chi ts'ung-shu, published in Taiwan, economic surveys were made of the Chinese in a number of countries. Among these are volumes on the Chinese in Africa, Australia, India, and Ceylon: Hsiao Tz'u-yin, *Fei-chou hua-ch'iao ching-chi* (Taipei, 1956); Liu Ta-jen, *Ao-chou hua-ch'iao ching-chi* (Taipei, 1958); and Yü Hsü-hsien, *Yin-tu Hsi-lan hua-ch'iao ching-chi* (Taipei, 1956). In addition there is a small volume by Ch'en Chih-fu entitled *Ao-chou chi lü-Ao hua-ch'iao* (Shanghai, 1947).[50]

The Chinese in Australia published several newspapers in the early decades of this century. These were the *Tung Wah News*, *Tung Wah Times*, and *Chinese Times*, which are available in the Mitchell Library, Sydney. At the Australian National University a dissertation on the Chinese in Sydney and Melbourne during the first two decades of this century has been written.[51] Finally, the following Western-language publications on the Chinese minorities may be noted: S. Gluckstein, *Black, White or Yellow? The South African Labour Problem, The Case for and against the Introduction of Chinese Coolies* (London, 1904); Ng Bickleen Fong, *The Chinese in New Zealand, A Study in Assimilation* (Hong Kong, 1959); Enoch George Payne, *Die Einführung der Chinesenarbeit in Südafrika* (Bonn, 1909); Guy Scholefield, *Asiatic Immigration in New Zealand; its History and Legislation* (Honolulu, 1927).[52]

BIBLIOGRAPHY

The following are (or contain) the few noteworthy bibliographies on the Overseas Chinese:

Hua-ch'iao wen-t'i tzu-liao so-yin, edited by the Chung-kuo ch'iao-cheng hsüeh-hui, Taipei, 1956 and 1957.

Index to Chinese Periodical Literature on Southeast Asia 1905-1966 (Nan-yang yen-chiu Chung-wen ch'i-k'an tzu-liao so-yin), edited by the Institute of Southeast Asia, Singapore, 1968.

Nevadomsky, Joseph-John, and Li, Alice, *The Chinese in Southeast Asia. A Selected and Annotated Bibliography of Publications in Western Languages 1960-1970*, Occasional Paper No. 6, Center for South and Southeast Asian Studies, University of California, Berkeley, 1970.

[50] Uchida Naosaku, *The Overseas Chinese*, pp. 77-9.
[51] C.F. Yong, 'The Chinese in New South Wales and Victoria, 1901-1921, with Special Reference to Sydney and Melbourne', unpublished doctoral dissertation, Department of History, School of General Studies, Australian National University, 1967.
[52] See Uchida Naosaku, *The Overseas Chinese*, pp. 70, 134.

Oey Giok Po, *Survey of Chinese Language Materials on Southeast Asia in the Hoover Institute and Library*, Ithaca, 1953.

Purcell, Victor, *The Chinese in Southeast Asia*, second ed., London, 1965.

Uchida Naosaku, *The Overseas Chinese, A Bibliographical Essay Based on the Resources of the Hoover Institution*, Stanford, 1960.

Holdings of Chinese Newspapers in Singapore Libraries

Title	Holdings	Holdings on microfilm Year	Reels	Location
Chin nam poh	1913-20			USL
China Press	1951-7	1951-7	14	NLS
Chong shing jit pao	1907-10, 1949-51	1907-10, 1949-51	16	USL
Chunan Morning Post	1930			NLS
Hwa chiao jit pau	1945-6			NLS
Jit shin pau	1899-1901	1899-1900	2	USL
Kin kwok Daily News	1951-7	1951-7	9	NLS
Kok min jit poh	1914-19			USL
Kwong wah jit poh	1927-41, 1951-62	1937, 1951-7	14	USL
Lat pau	1887-1932	1887-1932	144	USL
Lien pang Daily News	1952-5	1952-5	6	NLS
Min-kuo jih-pao	1930-4			NLS
Nam kew poo	1911-14			NLS
Nan yang si pau	1927-30			NLS
Nanfang Evening Post	1950-1, 1955-63			USL
Nanyang siang pau	1923-41, 1945-52, 1955-	1923-41, 1945-52	119	NLS
Penang sin pao	1895-1941			USL
Shonam jit pau	1942			USL
Sin chew jit poh	1929-52, 1955-	1929-41, 1945-53	187	USL
Sin chung jit poh	1935-40			NLS
Sin kok min jit poh	1919-40	1919-40	104	USL
Sin pin jih pao	1951-7, 1960	1951-7 & continuing	63+	NLS
Sing pao	1890-8			USL
Southern Press	1923-5			NLS
Sun poo	1909-10	1909-10	4	USL

Thien nan shin pao	1898-1905			USL
Union Times	1908-46	1908-31 & continuing	99+	USL

Abbreviations:
USL   University of Singapore Library
NLS   National Library, Singapore

史 xxvi: Lexicology as a Primary Source Material for the History of Modern China

JEAN CHESNEAUX[1]

Modern linguistics are apt to appear disconcertingly esoteric. Nevertheless, historians should be pleased with the attempts being made by
some linguists to study language, not just as a closed phenomenon, but as
the reflection of a given historical and social reality. There is a definite need
for the study of syntax, speech, and historical context to form an auxiliary
branch of history, on a par with bibliography and epigraphy; suffice it to
mention here the enormous difference that exists between Leninist language
and Stalinist language (phrasal structure, metaphors, linking of sentences,
etc.), a difference expressive of all that separates the Leninist and Stalinist
versions of Marxism. However, I wish in this chapter to discuss not just
lexicology, a more specialised field of study, but the instances where the
interrelationship between linguistics and history is particularly striking.
The history of modern China, as I would like to show by a few typical
examples, is in some ways the history of key-words, 'master words' as Rudyard
Kipling calls them, which mark out every important crisis and every
significant social group.

Historians who wish to use lexicology as source material for the history
of modern China must first try to define the following linguistic phenomena, the analysis of which will be useful in their researches.

Creation of new terms: this may be a matter of the invention of a term
ex nihilo, as, for example, the term *ke-ming hua* ('revolutionise') used to
express the belief that the revolutionary process must touch people at the
depth of their beings, not merely change the political structure of a society.
In other cases, a term which already exists in everyday speech is given a
special political meaning. Thus *fan-shen* literally 'to turn over', takes on the
sense of undergoing a deep personal transformation through carrying out
the revolutionary struggle. *Ta yüeh-chin* (the Great Leap Forward), is
another example. These terms, utterly banal and innocuous in the 1930s,
have come to stand for the whole communist dynamic, on the one hand the
period of the return to agrarian radicalism (1946-8) and on the other, of
the break with the Soviet model of socialism (1958-60).

[1] Translated by Alyce Mackerras from a French original.

278

Shifts of meaning: as T.A. Hsia has shown, during the period of the communes and the Great Leap Forward, a large number of military terms were deliberately transferred to the sphere of economic production.[2] A fighter (*chan-shih*) becomes a worker in the field of production, and the battle front (*chan-hsien*) becomes an area where it is vital to concentrate the efforts of the masses.

Borrowings: it is fairly well established that the first Chinese terms used to denote socialism (*she-hui chu-i*), communism (*kung-ch'an chu-i*), and trade unions (*tsu-ho*), were borrowed from Japanese. Concepts of modern socialism were introduced into China by young radical intellectuals studying in Japan during the early years of the twentieth century. These modern-style intellectuals also looked to the West. The words they used to try and introduce their fellow countrymen to science (*sai-yin-ssu*) and to democracy (*te-mo-k'e-la-hsi*), were completely meaningless to the average Chinese of the second decade of the century. But this scarcely worried these Western-oriented modernists; on the contrary, they believed it necessary to stress the fact that help had to come from outside: the two gentlemen, Mr Sai and Mr Te were called in from a long way off to the bedside of the 'sick man of Asia'.

Substitution of terms: historians before 1949, seeing everything as they did from the point of view of the interests of the gentry, normally used the name *Nien-fei*, i.e. 'the Nien bandits', when referring to the great rebellion of 1850-60. Since liberation, the name *Nien-chün* ('the Nien army') has been used on the mainland; it is a question of a reversal of the political perspective on the peasant movements of the pre-industrial epoch.

Rejection of words: the Rebel Governments which were set up under the direction of the Communists in south China between 1928 and 1934, readily took the name 'Chinese Soviets' (*Su-wei-ai*), as an indication that, although their experiment was a new one, the October Revolution continued to supply the undisputed terms of reference. Since 1949, this term has disappeared completely from the historical literature of People's China; instead, the emphasis is placed on the uniqueness of the Chinese experience.

Distinctions of meaning between related terms: it is surely no accident that the two terms *kung* 公 , and *kung* 共 , both of which contain the idea of public ownership, occupy different places in communist terminology. The first is associated with the idea of an archaic utopia (*T'ien-hsia wei-kung*, a world where everything is held in common, says the *Book of Rites*). It is this *kung* 公 which has been used not only for the People's Communes of 1958, but also for the Paris Commune of 1871. The other *kung* 共 , in contrast, is associated with scientific communism, the Communist Party, and the public administration of the companies surrendered by the national capital-

[2] T.A. Hsia, *Metaphor, Myth, Ritual and the People's Communes*, Studies in Chinese Communist Terminology, No. 7 (Berkeley, 1961).

ists in 1956. In the same way, it would be interesting to undertake a detailed linguistic-political study of the various names which have been used for the rebel areas under the control of the communist armed forces after 1927, and relate them to the shifting of the centre of gravity to the countryside. These guerrilla bases were called by a whole series of different names:

> *Ko-chü ti-ch'ü* (annexed regions, cut off from the rest of the country). This term, a purely descriptive one, corresponds to the period (around 1930) when the strategy of the communist bases was not yet founded on a coherent ideological analysis but only in response to pragmatic needs.
>
> *Hung-se ti-ch'ü* (red areas). This name emphasises the revolutionary character of the rebel zones, as does the term *ke-ming ch'ü* (revolutionary areas).
>
> *Pien-ch'ü* (border regions), a geo-political concept which stresses the characteristic location of these areas, on the borders of two or more adjoining provinces.
>
> *Chieh-fang ch'ü* (liberated areas), a term which indicates that the revolutionary situation has developed to the point where a transfer of state power is imminent.

In all the above examples, whatever the linguistic phenomenon under consideration (borrowing, invention, shift of meaning, etc.), we are dealing with significant terms. They serve a double function, subjective and objective. On the subjective level, they express the common feelings, the complicity, the *connivance* (a word proposed very judiciously by the French school of political lexicology), which exist among people who belong to the same social group or the same political movement, or who are living through the same crisis in history. The meanings of these terms might be perfectly clear from the point of view of abstract linguistics, but they hold a special significance for those who have shared a common experience with which these terms are associated. From an objective point of view, these terms are also signs, or signals. They crystallise and sum up the most significant problems of a particular social group or of a particular moment in time. They are the manifestations, the landmarks, by which we can determine the character and the direction of a given historical situation.

These remarks are valid for any society and any situation—a study of the terminology of the Black Panthers would undoubtedly be the best way to reach an understanding of their movement. In China, however, the role of words as indexes of situations seems to be especially important. It is the old Confucian concept of *cheng-ming* which some Western scholars often translate as 'the rectification of names', although the verb *cheng* contains no idea of correcting a wrong but means simply appropriateness, a deep correspondence between words and their object.

Significant words can, in the first place, help to delineate the social and ideological profile of a given group (social class, political organisation, or association). In this way, the language of Chinese secret societies, their slogans, the titles of their officers, their passwords, and their slang, form an excellent introduction to the study of these clandestine groups. For the purposes of a recent collective work,[3] a list has been compiled of several hundred such words. These reflect both the dissenting and rebellious characters of the secret societies in their relationships with established society and, at the same time, their tendency to reconstruct within their own underground circles alternative rigid social structures, expressed in such phrases as *ta ta-yu* (to go on a voyage, to attack a village); *wei-wu yao-tzu* (place of military terror and of debauchery, i.e., the yamen, the seat of the administration); *lao ta-ko* (eldest brother, name of the leaders of the Ko-lao hui); *hung-kun* (red staff, a rank in the Triad).

A study of the vocabulary of the industrial proletariat during the early stage of the worker movement (1920-5) is equally stimulating.[4] One sees how the worker movement and the conditions of the workers contained, at the same time, elements of both the very primitive and the very modern. *Pao-kung* is contract labour, the semi-slavery which made the worker completely dependent on the labour contractor, free wage-earners existing only in name. *Ta-ch'ang* means the early protests against the inhumanity of the factories, a Chinese version of Luddite machine-breaking. But the workers had already experienced industrial trade unions based on large-scale enterprises (*ch'an-yeh kung-hui*) and not just crafts. They acknowledged the authority of the Strike Committee (*pa-kung wei-yüan hui*) in the event of stoppages of work; they celebrated May Day (*Wu-i chieh*). In the same way, the life and history of the Communist Party could easily be summarised by a list of significant terms: the alliance of 1924 with the Kuomintang (*Kuo-kung ho-tso*) and the rectification of 1942 (*cheng-feng*), internationalism and armed struggle, etc.

The study of lexicology can also help one grasp the outline and the atmosphere of a political event or of a national crisis. The May Fourth Movement, for example, possesses its own distinctive vocabulary: *chiu-kuo* (save the nation), *Wai cheng kuo-ch'üan, Nei ch'u kuo-tsei* (externally, struggle for sovereignty; internally, throw out the traitors).[5] One could equally well, as L. Bianco has done in his study of the kidnapping of Chiang Kai-shek in Sian in 1936,[6] summarise the key themes of Chinese political sensibilities

---

[3] Cf. appendix No. III ('Terminologie des sociétés secrètes') of the collective work *Mouvements populaires et sociétés secrètes en Chine aux XIXᵉ et XXᵉ siècles* (Paris, 1970), pp. 457-71.
[4] Cf. my study, 'Quelques termes relatifs à la vie ouvrière chinoise vers 1920', in *Mélanges de sinologie offerts à Monsieur Paul Demiéville* (Paris, 1966), vol. 1, pp. 17-25.
[5] Chow Tse-tsung, *The May Fourth Movement* (Cambridge, Mass., 1960), pp. 20-3. It is a pity that such a rich study as this does not include a systematic inventory of the political lexicology of the 'May Fourth'; cf. the wish I have expressed at the conclusion of this chapter.
[6] L. Bianco, 'L'enlèvement de Tchiang Kai-chek à Sian en 1936', unpublished thesis, University of Paris, 1968.

on the eve of the Japanese invasion by compiling a list of the main terms and slogans of 'frontism' (the movement for a united front in China against Japan)—*Han-chien* (traitors to China); *ta-hui Tung-pei* (fighting our way back to the northeast); *kung-t'ung ti-jen* (the common enemy); *chiu-kuo chen-hsien* (front for national salvation), etc.

Through the study of lexicology, one may also discover, in a significant term, the expression of a political analysis or a decision of policy. The earliest treatises on Western science published in Chinese by Jesuits such as Schall and Verbiest used the term *hsi-fa* (Western) to describe Jesuit learning; the Jesuits deliberately stressed that the superiority of this learning was due to its Western provenance so that later they could draw on this in their arguments for the superiority of the religion of these same Westerners. But K'ang-hsi refused to fall into the trap; he ordered that the works translated by the Jesuits be called simply *hsin-fa*, modern: it was the new ideas they contained and not their region of origin, which in his eyes justified their introduction into China.[7]

Equally revealing are the terms around which, towards 1880, were crystallised the most basic of political debates, that as to the strategy of the Peking government toward the West. One school of thought wanted a policy of conciliation, even to the extent of borrowing from the West certain of its methods and 'administering China in a Western manner' (*yang-wu*); the other claimed to constitute a 'pure school' (*ch'ing-liu*), opposed to any form of compromise with the West and also to the corruption of certain elements at Court.[8] The contrast between these two terms reveals the clash between the two policies.

One of the most recent examples of policy-making reflected in the appropriate choice of words can be seen in the tripartite discussions of the spring of 1967 over the supplying of arms to North Vietnam. The People's Republic of China, then in the middle of the Cultural Revolution, refused to let the arms through because they were 'revisionist'. An agreement was finally reached, on the intervention of the Vietnamese, by which the arms were allowed transit through China: it was decided that their destination (Vietnam, whose anti-imperialist struggle China was supporting) was more important than their origin. So the cases of arms were daubed with big characters reading 'Vietnamese arms' as soon as they crossed the Soviet border; after that it was perfectly in order for China to allow them transit.

Through the study of vocabulary, one also gains a vivid impression of the feelings of the Chinese people concerning particular problems or situa-

---

[7] J. Needham and J. Chesneaux, 'Les sciences en Extrême-Orient du XVIe au XVIIIe siècle', in R. Taton, *Histoire générale des sciences*, vol. 1, p. 724.

[8] Cf. L.E. Eastman, *Throne and Mandarins, China's Search of a Policy during the Sino-French Controversy, 1880-1885* (Cambridge, Mass., 1967).

tions. Paul A. Cohen,[9] for example, has shown that the hostility felt by both the *literati* and the ordinary people toward the Christian missionaries since the time of the Opium Wars was expressed by traditional terms which date back to well before the introduction of Christianity to China: *i-tuan*, *tso-tao*, *hsieh*—all three carry the connotation of an ideology whose religious practice deviates from the way traditionally approved by the sages and the classics. The term *hsieh* was the strongest of the three: 'in some contexts [it] had additional overtones of a supernatural, uncanny power which gains ascendancy over the individual and leads him astray; in other contexts, it plainly refers to the gamut of excesses and irregularities in the sexual sphere'.[10] These terms are in contrast to *cheng-tao*, the 'straight (right) path'. The hostility toward the missionaries thus had social and psychosocial roots which went much deeper than the 'xenophobia' which the missionaries generally gave as the explanation for the hostility they encountered.

It is likewise interesting to note that People's China, so radically different from traditional China in so many essential features, continues nevertheless the classical Chinese practice of using numbered formulas to sum up a political analysis or to declare a watchword. The commune movement, for example,[11] is very rich in these quantified formulas. Examples are *wu-yeh* (the five occupations), which describes the economic polyvalence of the communes, agriculture, forestry, animal husbandry, side-occupations, and fisheries; *san-hua* (the three -isations) and *ssu-hua* (the four -isations), the militarisation of organisation, the materialisation of action and the collectivisation of daily life, to which is added a fourth point, the democratisation of administration; or *ssu ku-ting* (the four fixed things), a regular and fixed labour force, a fixed number of draught animals, a fixed number of agricultural tools, and a fixed amount of cultivated land. These numbered formulas were clearly chosen by the cadres in order to make the greatest possible impression on the peasants, by using a familiar method which dated back to very ancient times.

The study of lexicology can likewise contribute to another fundamental discussion among historians of modern China, that concerning the dialectic of tradition and innovation, of continuity and discontinuity. A study of the vocabulary of Chinese trade unions provides a good example. A trade union, *kung-hui* 工會 is also called *kung-hui* 公會, using a different character for *kung* to recall the communal tradition of the guilds, *kung-so* 公所; thus not all links are broken between the methods of organisation of workers in pre-industrial and in industrialised society. Trade unions, especially during the

[9] P.A. Cohen, *China and Christianity, the Missionary Movement and the Growth of Chinese Antiforeignism, 1860-1870* (Cambridge, Mass., 1963), p. 5.
[10] Ibid.
[11] T.S. Hsia, *The Commune in Retreat as Evidenced in Terminology and Semantics*, Studies in Chinese Communist Terminology, No. 11 (Berkeley, 1964).

early period, around 1920, were quite happy to adopt the name *chü-lo-pu*, the simple Chinese formulation of the Western word 'club' by consonantal dissociation; this term was as unfamiliar to the workers as the term *te-mo-k'e-la-hsi* was to the intellectuals. It reflects a deliberate rupture, a conscious affirmation that the methods of organisation of the proletariat are breaking with ancient Chinese tradition; this conscious innovation was particularly clear in the trade unions directed by the communist intellectuals.[12] The same dialectic of continuity and discontinuity is expressed in the term *huang-se kung-hui* (yellow unions), those tied to a patron or to the government. The term *huang* (yellow) is clearly borrowed from Western trade union language and is particularly inappropriate for China (yellow is the colour of the Imperial Majesty; moreover it is the word commonly used to describe the Chinese race). The use of this term once again bears witness to the extraneousness which characterises the Chinese worker movement in its early phase. It looked for its model of development in the practical experience and the stock of terminology of the more advanced industrial countries. The first organisers of trade unions were people who had already been in contact with these foreign countries, that is, the intellectuals; they merely grafted onto the social structure of the Chinese proletariat foreign terms and practices, such as *chü-lo-pu* or *huang-se kung-hui*. But the break is not really complete. The proletariat, of its own accord, endeavours to reintroduce these new concepts within a cultural framework with which it is familiar; a blackleg union is thus called *kung-tse kung-hui*, a union led by those who steal [the labour of others], a formula understandable to every Chinese.

The study of the exchange-houses of Shanghai around 1910, for which we are indebted to M.C. Bergère,[13] reveals the same conjunction of continuity and discontinuity. These banks, *ch'ien-chuang*, were run on traditional lines. They operated a system of credit (*hsin-yung wang-lai*); they relied mainly on guarantors (*pao-jen*); when they entered into partnerships it was by a 'gentleman's agreement' (*ho-huo*); if they experienced crises, they were local and circumstantial, as unaccountable as the sport of the elements (*feng-ch'ao*, wind and tide). However, these Shanghai banks of around 1910 were set up in a great modern port dominated by international high finance, particularly British. They were beset by the temptation to indulge in such speculation (*t'ou-chi*) as the share (*ku*) 'boom' of 1910 in which many of them were ruined; they did business with public companies (*kung-ssu*), and with modern-style banks (*yin-hang*); they followed very closely the rate of the Mexican dollar (*yang-ch'ien*). This dualism in terminology reflects the fact that, while these banks still belonged to a very archaic economic structure, they were at the same time fitted into a modern economic circuit.

[12] J. Chesneaux, *Le mouvement ouvrier chinois* (Paris, 1962), p. 273.
[13] M.C. Bergère, *Une crise financière à Shanghai à la fin de l'Ancien Régime* (Paris, 1964).

One final example should suffice to demonstrate this principle of the conjunction between innovation and tradition as seen in terminology: that of the metaphors used in the people's communes.[14] The movement to set up people's communes is completely new, as is its terminology (cf. slogans like *san-hua* and *ssu-hua* quoted above, militarisation, materialisation, collectivisation, democratisation). At the same time it is rooted in popular Chinese tradition. A term borrowed from the guerrillas of the Yen-an period is used for the small, subsidiary jobs which can be done in members' spare time and require only a small number of workers (*hsiao-hsing yün-tung chan*, 'mobile warfare on a small scale'). The struggle against natural calamities and natural obstacles, an essential element in the philosophy of the Great Leap Forward, is called *tui-t'ien hsüan-chan* (to declare war on Heaven). To make people aware of the interdependence between general economic strategy and local initiative, a basic principle of Chinese chess is invoked: *ch'üan-kuo i p'an-ch'i* (the whole country forms one chess-board). A joint meeting between cadres and people from among the masses with useful ideas is called a *Chu-ko Liang hui* (a meeting of people as wise as Chu-ko Liang).

The use of lexicology and terminology as an auxiliary branch of history is, then, profoundly stimulating and rewarding. It is to be wished that researchers and students made more systematic use of them. Every monograph published on an event or problem in the history of modern China should include at the end an annotated glossary of terms (at present authors do not even always give a simple list of the Chinese terms they have encountered). A historian who has been handling the material relevant to a particular problem over several months is in the best position to compile such a glossary—he knows how often the terms recur, their emotional overtones, their implied meanings, their value in obtaining peoples' 'connivance'. Furthermore, in the field of teaching, systematic lists of most significant terms should be rated a teaching aid of high priority, on a par with maps, chronologies, bibliographies, annotated texts, and texts with commentaries. One could even conceive of a general history of modern China in which each chapter consisted of a series of significant words and phrases together with appropriate commentary. I have given above several examples: with regard to secret societies, the worker movement, the May Fourth movement, the crisis of 1936 and the people's communes.

Language is definitely much too serious a proposition to be left to the linguists. Let us leave these gentlemen to bog themselves down in their ambitious projects and the mechanical compilation of their card-indexes. It is no good waiting around indefinitely for their Chinese-French dictionary, the preparation of which was so solemnly announced twelve years ago and

[14] T.A. Hsia, *Metaphor, Myth, Ritual.*

which may never see the light of day. 'Do it yourself', people are saying more and more frequently. This applies as much to learning as to politics or everyday technology. The analysis of lexicology, as an integral part of a given historical phenomenon, must become increasingly part and parcel of historical research and the teaching of history—and not only, to be sure, in the field of modern China.

Glossary-Index*

---

* Compiled by Colin Mackerras. Where characters are missing from Chinese and Japanese personal names, they are the authors of books or articles in a Western language in which the characters are not indicated. This glossary-index includes all authors mentioned in the book and all Chinese and Japanese works and periodicals, but only a few of the Western-language works, mostly the early ones. Note that in the alphabetic arrangement vowels with umlauts are considered as separate from those without and to follow them. So, for instance, *Yü-hai* will come later than Yung-cheng. Except for the few unhyphenated compounds, Chinese terms and names are arranged according to syllables, not combinations. So *hu-k'ou* would come before *hua-ch'iao*, *hu* preceding *hua*; but Hupeh would be later than *Hung-ch'i*, and Shansi than *Shang-shu*.

Case, L.M., 211

càtalogues, 75, 85, 123, 124; archives, 208, 210, 211, 230; Buddhist texts, 123; Chinese books in European libraries, 181; libraries, 44, 177, 181, 213, 231, 236, 258; manuscripts, 177, 180; Pei-t'ang collection, 181, 187; Taoist works, 104, 105, 106, 108–10, 112, 116, 119, 123; Tun-huang manuscripts, 128; Western sources, 181

Catholics, 167, 168, 169, 179, 212, see also Christianity, Jesuits, missionaries

cavalry, 31

Celas, Louis, 246, 248

cemeteries, 10, 11, 91, 93

censorship, 76, 181, 182–3, 197, 203, 214–15, 217, 221, 227

Center for Chinese Research Materials, 231, 235, 258

Central Asia, 36, 120, 166, 173, 174, 188, 195, 201

Central Intelligence Agency, 257

Central State Archives of Ancient Documents, 190

ceramics, 10

Ceylon, 275

Ch'a shih-su mei-yüeh t'ung-chi chuan 察世俗每月統計傳, 223, 227

Ch'ai Sang 柴桑, 82

Chalfant, F.H., 19

Chamberlain, N., 213

Chambers of Commerce, 163, 167, 208, 212

Chan Hok-lam, 63

Chan-hou Ching-Tsin hsin-huo chia-ku chi 戰後京津新獲甲骨集, 19

Chan-hou nan-pei so-chien chia-ku lu 戰後南北所見甲骨錄, 20

Chan-hou Ning-Hu hsin-huo chia-ku chi 戰後寧滬新獲甲骨集, 20

'*Chan-hou Yin-hsü ch'u-t'u ti hsin ta-kuei ch'i-pan*' 戰後殷墟出土的新大龜七版, 20

chan-hsien 戰線, 279

Chan-kuo ts'e 戰國策, 24, 27–8, 33, 34, 35

chan-shih 戰士, 279

Chan-wang 展望, 243

ch'an-yeh kung-hui 產業工會, 281

Chandra, Lokesh, 132, 134, 135, 139

Ch'ang-an 長安, 111, 121, 125, 127, 147, 148, 149

Chang Chi-hsin 張季信, 237, 238

Ch'ang-chiang jih-pao 長江日報, 256

Chang Chih-tung 張之洞, 204

Chang-chou (Fukien) 漳州, 114

Chang-chou fu-chih 漳州府志, 113

Ch'ang-ch'un chen-jen hsi-yu chi 長春眞人西遊記, 117

Ch'ang-ch'un chen-jen hsi-yu chi ti ti-li hsüeh p'ing-chu 長春眞人西遊記 的地理學評註, 117

Chang Chung-fu 張忠紱, 237, 238

Hsin-hai ke-ming shih-liao 辛亥革命史料, 232
Hsin-hai shou-i hui-i lu 辛亥首義回憶錄, 232
Hsin-hsü 新序, 33
Hsin Hu-nan pao 新湖南報, 252
Hsin-hua jih-pao 新華日報, 227
Hsin-hua she ti-fang hsin-wen kao 新華社地方新聞稿, 255
'Hsin-huo chih Tun-huang Han-chien' 新獲之敦煌漢簡, 41
Hsin-huo pu-tz'u hsieh-pen 新獲卜辭寫本, 21
Hsin min-pao 新民報, 227
Hsin-min ts'ung-pao 新民叢報, 224-5, 228
Hsin T'ang-shu 新唐書, 43, 53, 54, 55-7, 58, 62, 100, 132, 134, 149
Hsin Tsu-k'ang 辛祖康, 272
Hsin Tung-ya pao 新東亞報, 272
Hsin-wen pao 新聞報, 224, 226, 227
Hsin Wu-tai shih 新五代史, 51, 53, 54, 57-8, 62
Hsin-yang 信陽, 36
Hsin Yang-kuang pao 新仰光報, 270
hsin-yung wang-lai 信用往來, 284
Hsin Yüan-shih 新元史, 55, 78, 101
hsing 刑, 65, 68
Hsing-an hui-lan 刑案滙覽, 101
Hsing-cheng yüan kung-pao 行政院公報, 234
Hsing-Chung hui 興中會, 229, 230
hsing-fa 刑法, 67
'Hsing-fa chih' 刑法志, 100-1
Hsing-huo liao-yüan 星火燎原, 244, 246
hsing-shu 刑書, 99
Hsing-tao jih-pao 星島日報, 227
Hsing-tsai 行在, 149, see also Hang-chou
Hsinhua News Agency, 255, 259
Hsiu-chen pien-nan 修眞辨難, 110
Hsiu-chen shih-shu 修眞十書, 106
hsü 序, 57, 58, 59, 61, 62, 74, 90
Hsu Cho-yun 許倬雲, 33
Hsü Chung-shu 徐中舒, 204, 205, 218-19
Hsü Han-shu 續漢書, 43, 45
Hsü Hao 徐浩, 63
Hsü-hsien chen-lu 徐仙眞錄, 105
Hsu Kai-yu, 247, 249
Hsü Shih-ch'ang 徐世昌, 104, 106
Hsü Tao-tsang 續道藏, 104, 107, 110, 116
Hsü T'ung-chih 續通志, 69

Designed by Arthur Stokes.

Text set in Monotype Baskerville by The Griffin Press, Adelaide, South Australia, and printed by offset lithography by Kingsport Press, Inc., Kingsport, Tennessee, on Warren's University Text, an acid-free paper of extraordinary longevity, which has been watermarked with the University of South Carolina Press emblem. Binding by Kingsport Press, Inc.